OSPF
Complete
Implementation

OSPF
Complete
Implementation

John T. Moy

Addison-Wesley

Boston • San Francisco • New York • Toronto • Montreal
London • Munich • Paris • Madrid
Capetown • Sydney • Tokyo • Singapore • Mexico City

The publisher offers discounts on this book when ordered in quantity for special sales. For more information, please contact:

Pearson Education Corporate Sales Division
One Lake Street
Upper Saddle River, NJ 07458
(800) 382-3419
corpsales@pearsontechgroup.com

Visit us on the Web at www.awl.com/cseng/

Library of Congress Cataloging-in-Publication Data

Moy, John T.
      OSPF complete implementation / John T. Moy.
            p.   cm.
      Includes bibliographical references and index.
      ISBN 0-201-30966-1 (alk. paper)
      1. Internet (Computer network) 2. Routers (Computer networks) 3. Computer network protocols. 4. Computer network architectures. I. Title.
      TK5105.875.I57 M693 2000
      004.6'6--dc21   00-042981

ISBN 0-201-30966-1
Text printed on recycled paper.
1 2 3 4 5 6 7 8 9 10–CRW–04 03 02 01 00
First printing, September 2000

Contents

List of Tables

List of Figures

Preface

This book is the companion to *OSPF: Anatomy of an Internet Routing Protocol*. In keeping with the Internet tradition of valuing "rough consensus and working code," this book provides a complete OSPF implementation to go with the previous description of the OSPF protocol. The implementation is written in C++ and has been designed for portability. Two sample ports are included: (1) an OSPF routing daemon, called `ospfd`, for the Linux operating system and (2) an OSPF routing simulator, `ospf_sim`, that can be run under Linux or Windows.

The text of this book provides design documentation for the implementation, a porting guide, and user manuals for the two sample ports. The data flow and major data structures are explained, using code fragments when necessary. The complete implementation is contained in an attached CD-ROM.

Examination of an OSPF implementation allows us to explore all the nooks and crannies of the protocol. Methods to optimize an OSPF implementation are also explained. Exercises are included for readers interested in gaining experience with modifying a fairly large, real-time distributed software system.

One thing that I have learned through many years of writing networking software is that there is always more than one way of doing anything. In no way should the reader assume that this book presents the only right way to implement OSPF functionality. However, the reader should learn from this book new techniques of implementing networking software and some fine points of the OSPF routing protocol.

Audience

Like *OSPF: Anatomy of an Internet Routing Protocol*, this book is for people interested in the practical aspects of Internet routing: students of data communications, TCP/IP network administrators, protocol designers, developers of routing protocol software, and other professionals involved in the design, development, and management of TCP/IP networks. Through the exercises included in the book, software engineers can also gain experience with modifying and enhancing a fairly large and complicated real-time software system.

Because the book contains a working OSPF implementation that can be used to turn a Linux workstation into a router or as an OSPF network simulator, the book will also be of interest to nonprogrammers involved in administering, designing, and monitoring OSPF networks.

This book assumes a basic knowledge of OSPF, which can be obtained either by reading the companion book, *OSPF: Anatomy of an Internet Routing Protocol*, or from the OSPF protocol specifications themselves.

Organization of This Book

This book can be read in several ways. Those people interested only in using the `ospfd` implementation or the OSPF simulator can restrict their attention to Chapters 1, 2, 13, 14, and 15. Those people interested mainly in porting the OSPF software to other environments can concentrate on Chapter 4 and the two sample ports described in Chapters 14 and 15.

The rest of the book—in Chapters 3 and 5–12—describes an implementation of OSPF and some of its extensions in great detail. For these chapters, familiarity with the basics of the C++ programming language is assumed. Each of these chapters discusses an OSPF function, such as flooding LSAs. The chapters begin with any required elucidations of the OSPF specifications and descriptions of any novel efficiency provisions provided by the implementation and then illustrate the function through examination of code samples. The network diagram on the flyleaf, a reproduction of Figure 6.6 in *OSPF: Anatomy of an Internet Routing Protocol*, is used throughout the text in examples. Exercises at the end of each chapter are used to reinforce ideas presented and to allow readers to add features to the implementation. Answers to the exercises are not provided; however, answers to those exercises marked as bug fixes can be found in the source code on **http://www.ospf.org/software/ospfd**.

Chapter 1, Functional Specifications, describes those OSPF features and extensions that are implemented by the enclosed software and those that are not. An overview of the two sample ports—the `ospfd` routing daemon for Linux and an OSPF routing simulator named `ospf_sim`—are also given.

Chapter 2, Installation Instructions, explains how to install the OSPF routing daemon `ospfd` under Linux and the OSPF routing simulator `ospf_sim` under Linux and Windows.

Chapter 3, Software Architecture, details the software architecture of the implementation, including inputs, outputs, and the data flow through the implementation. A brief description of the major data structures and their interrelationships is provided. This chapter also explains the source file organization of the CD-ROM.

Chapter 4, Porting Guide, shows how to port the OSPF software to various environments. The layer of software between the OSPF implementation and the operating system is explained. Special porting considerations, such as how to handle various types of CPU chips, are also covered.

Chapter 5, Building Blocks, describes various utility functions that the OSPF software uses. These utility functions are provided with the software and include AVL and Patricia trees and priority queues. The implementation of timers, logging messages, and the IP routing table are also explained.

Chapter 6, The Link-State Database, describes the organization of the implementation's OSPF link-state database. Various operations on the link-state database, including the aging of LSAs, are also covered.

Chapter 7, Originating LSAs, explains how the implementation originates LSAs, including the building of each particular OSPF LSA type. This chapter also discusses rate-limiting LSA originations, refreshing LSAs, and flushing LSAs from the link-state database.

Chapter 8, Neighbor Maintenance, describes the process of discovering and maintaining OSPF neighbor relationships. This chapter also covers the initial synchronization of link-state databases between neighbors and the handling of interface state changes.

Chapter 9, Flooding, details the continuing synchronization of OSPF link-state databases through the reliable-flooding algorithm.

Chapter 10, OSPF Hierarchy, begins with a discussion of the restrictions on configuration of OSPF area boundaries. The method for distributing routing information across area boundaries and the importation of external routes into an OSPF routing domain are also explained.

Chapter 11, Routing Calculations, describes the basic OSPF routing calculations, which yield IP routing table entries. Also included in this discussion are the various events that trigger the routing table calculation, and link-state database manipulations to enable the routing calculations to run faster. Calculation of intra-area, inter-area, and external routes are covered.

Chapter 12, MOSPF Implementation, describes an implementation of the Multicast Extensions to OSPF, or MOSPF. Topics covered include the interactions between MOSPF and IGMP, the generation of group-membership-LSAs, and the MOSPF routing calculation.

Chapter 13, Configuration and Monitoring, explains how the OSPF implementation is configured. The complete list of configuration parameters is explained, together with any consequences when a given parameter is changed dynamically. The mechanism for processing configuration requests is described, as well as the graceful-exit procedure used when shutting down the OSPF software.

Chapter 14, A Routing Daemon for Linux, describes the first sample port of the OSPF software: an OSPF routing daemon called `ospfd` for the Linux operating system. This daemon is an analog for the standard `routed` RIP routing daemon provided with most UNIX-based operating systems; `ospfd` would be used by those people wanting to run OSPF instead of RIP. The method for configuring, monitoring, and debugging `ospfd` is also provided.

Chapter 15, An OSPF Simulator, describes another port of the OSPF implementation: an OSPF routing simulator called `ospf_sim` running under Linux and Windows. The method to configure and run the simulation, which is a window-based Tk/Tcl application, is given.

A number of appendices have also been provided. Manual pages for the programs contained in the OSPF software distribution are included in Appendix A. The logging messages produced by the OSPF software are explained in Appendix B. A list of projects for people interested in extending the OSPF software appears in Appendix C. The last appendix, Appendix D, reproduces the GNU General Public license covering the implementation.

Following the appendices is an extensive bibliography arranged and numbered in alphabetical order. Within the text, the citation [75], for example, refers to item 75 in the bibliography.

Bug Fixes

The OSPF software provided is labeled Release 0.1. Although I have tried to test as many functions as possible, doubtless many bugs are in the software. Bug reports can be sent to `ospfd-bugs@ospf.org`. Bug fixes for problems will be posted on `http://www.ospf.org/software/ospfd`, although possibly not in a very timely fashion.

Source Code Copyright

The GNU GENERAL PUBLIC LICENSE, Version 2, June 1991, provided in its entirety in Appendix D, covers the OSPF implementation in this book.

Acknowledgments

I would like to thank the technical reviewers who improved this book through their thoughtful and timely reviews: Robert Minnear, Patrick W. Murphy, Matthew G. Naugle, Mark J. S. Paton, and John W. Stewart, III.

I would also like to acknowledge the help of my editors at Addison Wesley over the long life of this project: Karen Gettman, Mary Harrington, Sarah Weaver, and Karen Wernholm. Thanks also to Tim Kinch for redrawing all the figures.

Thanks also to the volunteers who tested the early and very buggy versions of the OSPF software: Fredi Ammann, Edoardo Calia, and the University of New Hampshire's InterOperability Lab's Kimo Johnson, Ray LaRocca, William Lenharth, and Danut Maftei. In particular, without the thorough and creative testing performed by Kimo, this project could never have been completed.

And special thanks to my wife, Sonya Keene, for the book's design and for her extreme patience through the years that this book was being written.

J.M.
May 2000

1

Functional Specifications

This introductory chapter lists the various features provided by the enclosed OSPF (Open Shortest Path First) implementation. The two sample ports of the implementation, an OSPF routing daemon for Linux and an OSPF routing simulator, are also briefly described.

1.1   Feature Set

The OSPF source code in this book is a complete implementation of the OSPFv2 specification, RFC 2328 [75]. All OSPF interface types—namely, broadcast, point-to-point (both numbered and unnumbered), NBMA (nonbroadcast multiaccess), Point-to-MultiPoint interfaces, and virtual links—are supported. OSPF areas are also completely supported, including stub areas, configurable aggregation at area borders, and virtual links. Under configuration control, any number of external routes can be imported in AS-external-LSAs. (AS is short for Autonomous System; LSA, for link-state advertisement). When multiple equal-cost paths exist to a destination, these paths are discovered and an attempt is made to install them into the system's IP (Internet Protocol) routing table (see Section 11.3). Metrics for nonzero TOS (Type of Service) values found in LSAs are correctly parsed, but the metric values are ignored.

All the configuration parameters mentioned in Appendix C of RFC 2328 and all the writable MIB (management information base) variables in the OSPF MIB [5] pertaining to RFC 2328 functionality are configurable. The one exception is the configurable parameter `RFC1583Compatibility`, which is always set to `false` (see Section 11.5).

All configuration parameters are *dynamically* configurable. That is, configuration changes take effect immediately and cause the least disruption possible. For example, it is possible to change the OSPF Area ID of an interface; when doing so, however, the interface's state is toggled so that neighbor adjacencies over the interface will reform. See Chapter 13, Configuration and Monitoring, for a complete description of the behavior of the implementation under the various configuration changes.

A graceful shutdown procedure has been implemented. When directed to exit, the OSPF implementation will first flush all its self-originated LSAs and then terminate all its neighbor relationships. This process reduces link-state database size in the other OSPF routers and reduces reroute time. See Section 13.10 for details.

Unique Link State IDs are assigned to AS-external-LSAs, even when multiple prefixes are imported having the same address but different prefix lengths—as is possible under CIDR (classless interdomain routing) addressing. However, the algorithm used for Link State ID assignment is different from the one given in Appendix E of RFC 2328 (see Section 10.3.2).

The OSPF implementation can also be used by a host computer—one that wishes to use OSPF to build its routing tables but does not wish to forward packets as an IP router does. This is commonly called *host wiretapping*; when using the common `routed` routing daemon, which implements RIP (Routing Information Protocol), wiretapping is achieved by receiving but not sending RIP packets. When wire-tapping in the OSPF equivalent, the host collects but does not contribute to the OSPF link-state database. See Section 13.12 for details.

1.1.1 Optimizations

The implementation contains a number of optimizations to decrease both the amount of OSPF control traffic and CPU (central processing unit) consumption. As is usually the case, these optimizations have a cost: increased memory usage. However, in the trade-off of speed for memory, we have tried to compromise so as not to be too profligate with memory resources.

A sample of the optimizations included follows.

- OSPF neighbor conversations achieve bidirectional status quickly rather than waiting for periodic Hello packets (see Section 8.2).

- A ceiling is put on the number of concurrent Database Exchanges, in order to conserve memory resources and to smooth out CPU demands (see Section 8.3).

- Flooding of LSAs builds a single Link State Update packet to be sent out multiple interfaces, avoiding building and checksumming updates for all but the first interface (see Section 9.3).

- Retransmission of LSAs uses a procedure similar to TCP's (Transmission Control Protocol) slow-start, to match the LSA retransmission rate to the neighbor's rate of absorbing new LSAs (see Section 9.5).

- The origination of AS-external-LSAs is rate-limited (see Section 10.3.2).

- The OSPF routing calculations have been optimized by preparsing LSAs, thereby avoiding database lookups, bidirectional link checks, and so on during the routing calculations (see Section 11.4).

Many of the optimizations are tunable through setting various configuration parameters, as described in Chapter 13, Configuration and Monitoring.

1.1.2   Implemented OSPF Extensions

Besides a full implementation of the base OSPFv2 specification, the following optional OSPF extensions are implemented:

- *MOSPF.* The complete MOSPF (Multicast Extensions to OSPF) protocol [66] is implemented, including calculation of multicast routing entries, interaction with IGMPv2 (Internet Group Membership Protocol Version 2), origination of group-membership-LSAs and inter-area multicasting. Hooks for interaction with other multicast routing protocols, such as DVMRP (Distance Vector Multicast Routing Protocol), are also included (see Section 12.6). The router part of an IGMPv2 implementation—namely, the sending of Host Membership Queries and the reception of Host Membership Reports—is also included (see Section 12.2).

- *Demand-circuit extensions.* An implementation of the demand-circuit extensions to OSPF [64], an efficient way of running OSPF over dial-up and low-speed links, is provided. Additionally, under configuration control, AS-external-LSAs can be originated with the DoNotAge bit set, removing the necessity to refresh those LSA types (see Section 13.1).

- *OSPF Database Overflow.* The method of limiting OSPF database size, specified in RFC 1765 [68], is implemented. A ceiling on the number of nondefault AS-external-LSAs can be configured, together with a time interval to exit the database overflow state (see Section 10.3.4).

1.1.3   Exercises and Projects

In order to give you more experience with the OSPF implementation, a list of exercises is provided at the end of each chapter. These exercises require small code modifications, all of which should be verifiable by using the included OSPF routing simulator. The routing simulator runs under Linux or Windows. For Linux, all necessary development tools for recompiling the simulator are included in the standard Linux distribution. For Windows, we have used the Cygwin tools, which are a port of the GNU development tools and utilities to Windows. A copy of these tools has been included on the CD-ROM; updates for the tools can be found at **www.cygnus.com/cygwin**.

A list of more involved development projects is given in Appendix C. These code enhancements are more involved than the exercises. For example, implementation of a MIB interface and OSPF for IPv6 are listed as development projects.

1.2   Implementation Mechanics

The OSPF implementation has been written almost entirely in C++, using the GNU development tools (the C++ compiler **g++** and GNU **make**). These development tools come standard with Linux distributions and have been ported to Windows by the Cygwin project (**www.cygnus.com/cygwin**). The GNU tools are not only free, but also the finest development tools that I know of. I also make frequent use of the GNU debugger **gdb**.

The only parts of the OSPF implementation not written in C++ are

- In the Linux **ospfd** port, the configuration routines, which are written in Tcl (tool command language). Here, execution time is not an issue, and Tcl significantly reduced development time.

- The user interface—both the parsing of commands in the configuration file and the graphical user interface—used in the OSPF simulator. These are written in Tk/Tcl to speed development.

- The MD5 software we use is the "RSA Data Security Inc. MD5 Message Digest Algorithm" supplied in [91]. This software is compiled in C.

C++ was chosen for the rest of the implementation originally because I found the class organization of C++ easier to document. I have also made use of C++ class inheritance. The reputation that C++ has garnered in some corners as being inappropriate for real-time embedded applications, which is typically the environment of routing protocol software, is ill deserved. However, it does pay to keep in mind that usually every C++ **new** or **delete** is a memory allocation or free, which is expensive on many systems. I have avoided the use of C++ constructs that may not be implemented by less recent compilers, such as templates. Also, I have avoided the use of C++ streams, as stream support is, as of this writing, not very portable.

I do not claim to be an expert C++ programmer. This book is for people who want to learn how to implement routing protocols and not for people who want to learn C++ programming, for which many excellent texts exists—this text not among them. In particular, C++ purists will, I am sure, bristle at the general lack of distinction between public and private data, the sparse use of C++'s `const` construct, and many other C++ faux pas made in the implementation.

1.3 An OSPF Routing Daemon: `ospfd`

A port of the OSPF software to Linux is included. This port produces the `ospfd` program, a routing daemon similar in concept to the `routed` daemon supplied with most UNIX-like systems. The `ospfd` program turns a Linux workstation into an OSPF router. Like most routing daemons, `ospfd` is meant to be started in the Linux network initialization script.

Installation instructions for the `ospfd` program can be found in Section 2.1. Usage information can be found in the `ospfd` man page included in Appendix A. Detailed usage information, and a discussion of the implementation of the `ospfd` routing daemon can be found in Chapter 14, A Routing Daemon for Linux.

The `ospfd` configuration data is placed in the file `/etc/ospfd.conf`. This file is encoded in human-readable ASCII and can be written with any text editor. The exact syntax of the file is described both in the manual page and in Section 14.1. The routing daemon can be reconfigured dynamically by editing the configuration file to reflect the new configuration and then sending the `ospfd` process a SIGUSR1 signal: `kill -s USR1` *pid*, where *pid* is the Linux process ID of the `ospfd` program. Side effects of dynamic reconfiguration are discussed in Chapter 13, Configuration and Monitoring.

Fatal errors and errors encountered in the Linux system interface are logged by using the Linux `syslog` facility. The OSPF software also has a detailed internal logging facility, which is discussed in Chapter 5, Building Blocks, and in Section 14.5. These logging messages are written to the file `/var/log/ospfd.log`; the required severity of messages before they are written to the file is configurable. A description of each logging message, including its logging level, can be found in Appendix B. Two monitoring programs—a command line interpreter called `ospfd_mon` and an HTML-based monitor called `ospfd_browser`—are also supplied. They are capable of dumping OSPF statistics, such as the link-state database, neighbor status, and so on, in real time. Their man pages can be found in Appendix A.

The `ospfd` routing daemon can be configured to run in *host mode*. When configured to run as a host, routing table entries will be calculated by the OSPF protocol software, but `ospfd` will not originate LSAs, and therefore other OSPF routers will not try to forward traffic through the Linux workstation. This is the OSPF equivalent of `routed`'s listen-only mode. See Section 13.12 for details.

Some standard features of OSPF, such as unnumbered point-to-point interfaces, are not available in `ospfd`, due to limitations in the standard Berkeley socket interface used by Linux. See Section 1.5 for the complete list of limitations.

When MOSPF is enabled, ospfd also turns the Linux workstation into a multicast router running MOSPF as its multicast routing protocol. An ospfd running MOSPF provides analogous services to the mrouted routing daemon, substituting MOSPF for mrouted's DVMRP. In fact, in this mode, ospfd reuses the kernel interfaces that were originally developed for mrouted.

1.4   An OSPF Routing Simulator

The OSPF code has also been ported to an OSPF simulator (ospf_sim) that runs under either Linux or Windows. The simulator serves multiple functions. It allows you to test the OSPF code and any modifications that you make to it, in a large network without having access to a large number of real routers. The simulator allows you to test network configurations, especially OSPF area designs, for their validity and robustness. Finally, the simulator can be used as a teaching aid to see how the OSPF protocol operates in a nontrivial network.

Installation instructions for the ospf_sim program can be found in Section 2.2. Usage information can be found in the ospf_sim man page included in Appendix A. Detailed usage information and a discussion of the implementation of the OSPF simulator can be found in Chapter 15, An OSPF Simulator.

The simulator has a graphical user interface (GUI) implemented in Tk/Tcl, which displays a map of the OSPF network that you are simulating. Colors on the map indicate the state of database synchronization between simulated routers, along with an indication of simulated time down to the tenth of a second. From the GUI, you can modify the map, adding/deleting routers, network segments, interfaces, virtual links, area aggregates, and so on. Between simulation runs, the configuration is stored in an ASCII file consisting of Tk/Tcl commands. This file can be modified in a text editor to produce large network configurations more quickly than through the GUI.

Logging messages from the simulated routers are written to standard output, with simulated time and OSPF Router ID of the logging router prepended. The same ospfd_mon program used to monitor the Linux ospfd routing daemon can also be used to collect OSPF statistics from the simulated routers.

1.5   Caveats

As Release 0.1, the OSPF software and its two ports contain bugs, many of which have already been found, particularly by the expert testers at the University of New Hampshire's Interoperability Lab [105]. But surely quite a few bugs still exist. As the GNU General Public License (Appendix D), which covers the software, states, this free software carries no warranty. In particular, people wishing to use the **ospfd** routing daemon provided may wish to test the software in the OSPF simulator, using their exact network configuration, before deploying.

Bug fixes and enhancements to the OSPF software will be posted at **http:// www.ospf.org/software/ospfd**. Bug reports can be submitted to **ospfd-bugs @ospf.org**. When submitting a bug report, as much of the following data as is available should be included:

- The version of OSPF software that you are using.

- The platform, such as Linux or Windows, and operating system version that you are running it on.

- A concise description of the problem.

- The **ospfd** routing daemon or simulator configuration file.

- A diagram of the OSPF network where the problem occurs. If the problem occurs in the simulator, this diagram is not necessary, as the network is completely described by the configuration file.

- The logging messages produced by the OSPF software before/during the failure. Also, any information that the OSPF software wrote to **syslog**.

- Packet traces that you have collected with a network analyzer before/during the problem occurrence. These should be in human-readable ASCII. Example network analyzers include **tcpdump** and commercial devices, such as the Network General Sniffer.

- If the OSPF software is crashing, you may be able to debug the problem by using the GNU debugger **gdb**. If you would like us to try to analyze the crash instead, you would need to send (1) the core dump produced, (2) the executable image, and (3) your OSPF sources. This information might be quite large, so please compress them with **gzip** before sending. On Windows, you would send a stack backtrace instead of a core dump. Even if the software is not crashing, it can be useful to examine a core dump, which you can always produce with the command **kill -s SEGV** *pid*, where *pid* is the process ID of the **ospfd** routing daemon; when debugging a simulated OSPF router, the **gdb** program can be attached to the running process (see Section 15.4).

- Any software patch that you have developed or any workaround that you have discovered.

2

Installation Instructions

This chapter explains how to install the two sample ports of the OSPF software: a routing protocol daemon, `ospfd`, that turns a Linux workstation into an OSPF router, and `ospf_sim`, an OSPF simulator that runs on either Linux or Windows.

2.1 Installation of `ospfd` (Linux Only)

The `ospfd` program was developed under Red Hat 5.2 (Linux 2.0.36), using the GNU C and C++ development tools (`gcc`, `g++`, and `make`) and the Tcl scripting language. The installation of `ospfd` on Linux takes place in the following steps.

Step 1: Install the necessary Linux packages. All the following packages come with the Red Hat Linux 5.2 distribution. Updates for the GNU tools can be found on `www.gnu.org`. Updates for Tcl can be found on `www.ajubasolutions.com`. The versions of the tools that I have been using are in parentheses.

- `gcc`: The GNU C compiler (version 2.7.2.3)

- `egcs-c++`: C++ support added to the GNU compiler, resulting in `g++` (version 1.0.3a)

- `glibc`: The standard set of C libraries (version 2.0.7)

- `glibc-devel`: The standard set of header files for programs using the standard C libraries (version 2.0.7)

- `libstdc++-devel`: The libraries and header files needed for C++ development (version 2.8.0)

- `make`: The program used to automate the compilation and linking of a program (version 3.76.1)

- **Tcl**: A powerful yet easy-to-use scripting language (version 8.0.3)

Step 2: Copy the `ospfd` sources from the CD-ROM onto your Linux system. You can put the sources anywhere on your Linux system; the following example uses a sub-directory of `/usr/local/src`. After copying the `ospfd.tar.gz` file from the CD-ROM, you extract the sources by using the `gunzip` and `tar` programs. This produces a top-level directory called `ospfd` with two subdirectories: `src`, the generic `ospfd` sources; and `linux`, the Linux-specific `ospfd` sources.

1. `cd /usr/local/src`

2. `cp /mnt/cdrom/ospfd.tar.gz .`

3. `gunzip -c ospfd.tar.gz | tar xf -`

Step 3: Make and install the `ospfd` binary. After changing into the directory of Linux-specific sources, use the `make` program, producing an executable file called `ospfd`. The `ospfd` binary and the Tcl helper file `ospfd.tcl`, which defines the syntax of the `ospfd` configuration commands, will be moved into the system directory `/usr/sbin`. In addition, a monitoring program for `ospfd`, called `ospfd_mon`, is installed in `/usr/sbin`, and the CGI application `ospfd_browser`, which allows you to monitor `ospfd` through a Web browser, is installed in `/home/httpd/cgi-bin`. See Appendix A for usage instructions for `ospfd_mon` and `ospfd_browser`.

4. `cd ospfd/linux`

5. `make install`

Step 4: Create the `ospfd` configuration file. The configuration file is named `/etc/ospf.conf` and is created by using a text editor, such as `emacs`. The syntax of the configuration file is explained in Section 14.1.

Step 5: Run the `ospfd` program. The program should be executed in the background. You may choose to automatically start `ospfd` during system initialization by adding `ospfd` to the Linux file `/etc/rc.d/rc.local`.

Note the following about the installation process.

- Most of the installation process will have to be done as root. In particular, the `ospfd` program must run as root because it opens a raw socket requiring root privileges.

- In order to run OSPF over multicast-capable network segments, such as an Ethernet, the Linux kernel must be built to include support for IP multicast.

- In order to change the directories that store the **ospfd** binaries, you must edit **ospfd/linux/Makefile**, changing **INSTALL_DIR** (for **ospfd** and **ospfd.tcl**) and **CGI_DIR** (for **ospfd_browser**) appropriately.

- If you are going to modify the **ospfd** software, you are going to want to install additional Linux software development packages. The additional packages that I used while developing **ospfd** were

  - **emacs**: A powerful text editor integrated with such other applications as **rmail** (a mail reader), the **gdb** debugger, and the **info** documentation system.

  - **rcs**: A source control system that allows you to archive previous versions of your sources, put special development on branches, automatically merge changes, and so on.

  - **gdb**: The GNU debugger, which also works inside **emacs**, allowing you to set breakpoints and to step through your source code.

  - **ElectricFence**: A debugging tool to find problems with allocating and deallocating memory. This tool just debugs calls to **malloc()** and **free()**, so to use with C++ programs, such as **ospfd**, you write global **new** and **delete** operators, which simply call **malloc()** and **free()**.

2.2　Installation of the OSPF Routing Simulator: `ospf_sim`

The OSPF simulator **ospf_sim** runs under either Linux or Windows. The following installation instructions are organized by platform. As soon as the simulator is installed, it runs the same on both platforms; instructions for running the OSPF simulator can be found in the **ospf_sim** man page (Appendix A) and Chapter 15, An OSPF Simulator.

2.2.1　Installation under Linux

The following instructions have been used to install **ospf_sim** under Red Hat 5.2 (Linux 2.0.36), using the GNU C and C++ development tools (**gcc**, **g++**, and **make**) and Tcl/Tk.

Step 1: Install the necessary Linux packages. You need all the packages used by the **ospfd** routing daemon (see Section 2.1), and the following additional package. The version of the tool that I have been using is in parentheses.

- **Tk**: A development tool enabling you to design X Windows GUIs quickly; works closely with the Tcl scripting language (version 8.0.3).

Step 2: Copy the ospf_sim sources from the CD-ROM onto your Linux system. You can put the sources anywhere on your Linux system; in the following example, we copy them into user `jqpublic`'s home directory. After copying the `ospfd.tar.gz` file from the CD-ROM, you extract the sources by using the `gunzip` and **tar** programs. This produces a top-level directory, called `ospfd`, with two subdirectories: `src`, the generic `ospfd` sources; and `ospf_sim`, the OSPF simulator sources.

1. `cd ~jqpublic`

2. `cp /mnt/cdrom/ospfd.tar.gz .`

3. `gunzip -c ospfd.tar.gz | tar xf -`

Step 3: Build the OSPF simulator. After changing into the directory of OSPF simulator sources, use the **make** program. This will produce executable files `ospf_sim` (the OSPF simulator), `ospfd_sim` (the code that each simulated router will execute), and `ospfd_mon` and `ospfd_browser`, the same monitoring programs that are used to monitor the `ospfd` routing daemon. The files `ospf_sim`, `ospfd_sim`, and `ospfd_mon` will be installed in `/usr/local/bin`, and `ospfd_browser` will be installed in `/home/httpd/cgi-bin`.

4. `cd ospfd/ospf_sim/linux`

5. `make`

Note the following about the installation process.

- To change the directories in which the binaries will be installed, edit `ospfd/ospf_sim/linux/Makefile`, changing `INSTALL_DIR` and `CGI_DIR` to the desired values. To successfully run the simulator, your choice of `INSTALL_DIR` must appear in your `PATH` environment variable.

- If you want to modify the OSPF simulator, you probably want to install additional Linux software development packages, as described earlier, in the notes for the `ospfd` installation.

2.2.2 Installation under Windows

When running under Windows, the OSPF simulator uses the Cygwin tools, which port the GNU development environment to Windows. The tools have been included on the CD-ROM, but tool updates and many more UNIX applications that have been ported to Windows using the Cygwin tools can be found at `http://sourceware.cygnus.com/cygwin`. In the following, we assume that the CD-ROM drive is `d:`.

Step 1: Install the Cygwin tools. These tools come in a self-extracting MS-DOS executable called `full.exe`. Assuming that your CD-ROM is drive `d:`, run the file `d:\x86pkgs\full.exe` from the Windows Start menu. In the following, we assume that you have installed the Cygwin tools in the standard place (`c:\cygnus\`).

Step 2: Enter the bash shell. This is done through the Windows Start menu: Start→ Programs→Cygnus Solutions→Cygwin B20. The first time you enter the bash shell, you must make a `/tmp` directory with the command `mkdir /tmp`.

Step 3: Complete installation of development environment. Inside the bash shell, we install Tk/Tcl libraries that have been compiled for Cygwin by Mumit Khan (`kahn@xraylith.wisc.edu`); we have modified them slightly to get rid of references to the MouseWheel device. Note that the bash shell uses forward slashes as directory separators, just like UNIX. You will also have to set the Windows environment variable `TCL_LIBRARY` to the value `c:\cygnus\cygwin-b20\H-i586-cygwin32\i586-cygwin32\lib\tcl8.0` to complete the installation of the Tk/Tcl libraries.

1. `cd c:/cygnus/cygwin-b20/H-i586-cygwin32/i586-cygwin32`
2. `cp d:/x86pkgs/tcltk804-cygb20_tar.gz .`
3. `gunzip -c tcltk804-cygb20_tar.gz | tar xf -`

Step 4: Copy the `ospf_sim` sources from the CD-ROM. You can put the sources anywhere on your Windows system; in this example, we copy them into the top level of the `c:` drive. After copying the `ospfd.tar.gz` file from the CD-ROM, you extract the sources by using the `gunzip` and `tar` programs. This produces a top-level directory, called `ospfd`, with two subdirectories: `src`, the generic `ospfd` sources; and `ospf_sim`, the OSPF simulator sources. All these commands are executed from the bash shell.

1. `cd /`
2. `cp d:/ospfd.tar.gz .`
3. `gunzip -c ospfd.tar.gz | tar xf -`

Step 5: Build the OSPF simulator. Installation is done within the bash shell. After changing into the `x86` subdirectory of the OSPF simulator sources, use `make`. This will produce executable files `ospf_sim` (the OSPF simulator), `ospfd_sim` (the code that each simulated router will execute), and the `ospfd_mon` and `ospfd_browser` monitoring programs. All programs will be left in the `ospfd/ospf_sim/x86` directory, except the CGI application `ospfd_browser`, which will be moved to `c:/cgi-bin`.

4. `cd /ospfd/ospf_sim/x86`
5. `make`

You will also run the OSPF simulator from the bash shell, just as you do from the Linux shell, by typing `ospf_sim config_file`, with your working directory set to `c:/ospfd/ospf_sim/x86` (see Chapter 15, An OSPF Simulator).

Step 6: Install the Apache Web Server. A version of the Apache Web Server has been included on the CD-ROM. To install this self-extracting Windows executable, run `d:\x86pkgs\apache_1_3_3.exe` from the Windows Start menu. The Apache Web Server will allow you to monitor the OSPF simulation from your Web browser; see the `ospfd_browser` man page in Appendix A. The Apache Web Server must be configured to allow CGI applications and expect them in `c:/cgi-bin`. If you have installed the

Apache Web Server in its default location, this is accomplished by editing the configuration files `srm.conf` and `access.conf` in the directory `c:\Program Files\Apache Group\Apache\conf` directory.

- File `srm.conf` should include the line

```
ScriptAlias /cgi-bin/ "C:/cgi-bin/"
```

- File `access.conf` should include the lines

```
<Directory "C:/cgi-bin">
AllowOverride None
Options None
</Directory>
```

Note the following about the installation process.

- In Windows NT, you set environment variables through Start→Settings→Control Panel. Select the System Icon, and then use its Environment tab. In Windows 95 and 98, you must edit `c:\autoexec.bat`, inserting the proper set directives.

- To get the Web server to execute the `ospfd_browser` CGI application successfully, it must be able to find the `cygwin.dll`. This requires that Windows **PATH** environment variable contain `c:\cygnus\cygwin-b20\H-i586-cygwin32\bin` (assuming standard installation of the Cygwin tools).

- The `gdb` debugger comes with the standard distribution of the Cygwin tools; see `http://sourceware.cygnus.com/cygwin/ported.html` for other programs that have been ported to the Cygwin environment, including the source control system `rcs`. The following additional software development packages have been included on the CD-ROM under `d:\x86pkgs`.

  - **NT emacs**: A version of `emacs` that runs under Windows can be found in `d:\x86pkgs\emacs-20_3_1-bin-i386_tar.gz` and can be extracted by using `gunzip` and `tar`. A pointer to this package can be found at `http://sourceware.cygnus.com/cygwin/links.html`.

  - **Tcl/Tk for Windows**: This toolset is available for Windows from `http://www.ajubasolutions.com` and has been included on the CD-ROM as the self-extracting MS-DOS executable `d:\x86pkgs\tcl805.exe`. However, this package is set up for use by programs compiled under Visual C++, not the Cygwin environment. I still find it useful for its online documentation, including widget demos with source code included, and for the `tclsh` and `wish` programs, which can be used to test your Tk/Tcl scripts.

2.3   Installing the OSPF Sources

If you don't want to use either of the two OSPF ports provided with the software but instead just want to examine the OSPF software and/or port it to other platforms, use the entire source directory on the CD-ROM, starting with the top-level **/ospfd** directory. For a detailed description of the layout of the source directory tree, see Section 3.3. Alternatively, you can copy the file **ospfd.tar.gz** from the CD-ROM and extract the source directory tree, using the command **gunzip -c ospfd.tar.gz | tar xf -**.

3

Software Architecture

We introduce the OSPF software implementation by looking at its organization. We approach the organization in two ways. First, we look at how data—OSPF protocol packets and LSAs—flow through the implementation. Then we examine the major data structures, their roles, and their interactions. This chapter ends with a description of the source file organization, so that people can navigate the sources more easily. This chapter does not discuss multicast routing; a discussion of MOSPF's data flow and data structures is provided in Chapter 12, MOSPF Implementation.

3.1   Data Flow

The data flow through the OSPF implementation is pictured in Figure 3.1. Some code must be written to port the OSPF implementation to a new platform. That part of the data flow is shaded.

In order to port the OSPF implementation to a new platform, some initialization code must be written. The main job of this initialization code is to create a system interface (`class OspfSysCalls`) so that the OSPF implementation can perform basic functions, such as send protocol packets and install routing table entries, initialize the OSPF code by creating the top-level `class OSPF`, and then read the OSPF configuration.

A main loop must also be written. The job of the main loop is to read OSPF packets received from the platform's network interfaces and to keep track of elapsed time, occasionally calling the OSPF code's timer routine so that timing functions can execute

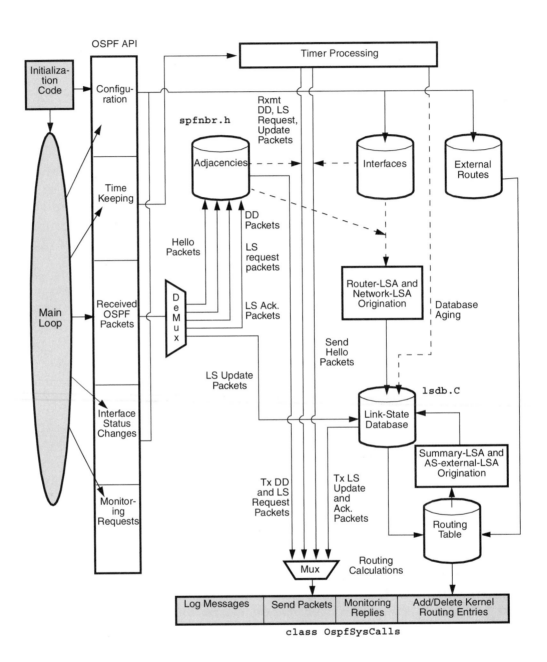

Figure 3.1 Data flow in the OSPF implementation.

properly. The main loop also receives operator input in the form of reconfiguration and monitoring requests, which it passes on to the OSPF code. Any change in an interface's operational status is also detected by the main loop and passed to the OSPF code. The main loop does not exit until the operator requests that the OSPF software be shut down.

The initialization code and the main loop communicate with the OSPF software through a well-defined API (application programming interface), which is discussed in detail in Section 4.3. Chapter 4, Porting Guide, explains in detail how to write the initialization code, main loop, and system interface in order to port the OSPF software. Two porting examples are also given in Chapters 14, A Routing Daemon for Linux and 15, An OSPF Simulator.

3.1.1   Packet Flow

When it receives an OSPF protocol packet on one of the platform's network interfaces, the main loop passes the packet to the OSPF code via a call to the API routine `OSPF::rxpkt()`. That routine demultiplexes based on OSPF packet type.

Almost all the protocol machinery in OSPF has to do with maintaining a synchronized, distributed database of LSAs. Databases are synchronized between adjacent routers. All OSPF packet types are involved in the maintenance of adjacencies. Received Hello packets cause us to create neighbor relationships (`class SpfNbr`), and the lack of Hello packets cause us to destroy the neighbor relationship. The router will become adjacent with some of its neighbors (see Section 8.3). Received Database Description and Link State Request packets progress the adjacency through a number of states in the neighbor finite state machine until synchronization of the database between the neighboring routers is ensured and it is safe to use the adjacency for forwarding. All state associated with an adjacency is contained in the `class SpfNbr` for the adjacent neighbor. The discovery and initial synchronization of adjacencies are discussed in detail in Chapter 8, Neighbor Maintenance.

After the adjacency is established with a neighboring router, database synchronization with the neighbor is maintained via the reliable-flooding procedure. Received Link State Update packets deliver new LSAs to the router, where they are installed in its link-state database. Received Link State Acknowledgment packets tell the router that an LSA has been reliably delivered to the neighbor. The implementation of reliable flooding is described in detail in Chapter 9, Flooding.

The router transmits Hello packets periodically out each interface. LS Update packets are sent when the router originates new LSAs. All other OSPF protocol packets are sent in response to received packets. For example, a received Database Description packet causes the router to send either one or more Link State Request packets or a Database Description packet in response (Section 8.3). In another example, receiving a Link State Update packet from a neighbor causes the router to send a Link State Acknowledgment packet back to the neighbor and Link State Update packets out all other interfaces (Section 9.3).

If the transmission of these packets fails—the packets are corrupted by the transmission or are dropped by either the sender or the transmitter, due to congestion—they are retransmitted, if necessary, by the OSPF timer functions (Section 3.1.3). For example, if the neighbor does not respond to a Link State Request packet, the request is retransmitted (Section 8.3), or, if a Link State Update packet does not elicit the correct Link State Acknowledgment, LSAs are packaged into another Link State Update packet for retransmission (Section 9.5).

3.1.2   LSA Flow

The collected set of LSAs that the router has in its possession is called the link-state database. The organization and the implementation of the link-state database are discussed in Chapter 6, The Link-State Database.

LSAs are installed in the database either as a result of being received in a Link State Update packet from an adjacent neighbor or when the router itself originates a new or updated LSA (Chapter 7, Originating LSAs). OSPF has several types of LSAs, as described in Section 4.2.1 of [67]. A router formats its router-LSA (Section 7.2) based on its current set of operational interfaces and adjacencies. For each of its attached network segments on which the router has become Designated Router, the router originates a network-LSA (Section 7.3). Based on the result of routing calculations, the router will originate summary-LSAs (Section 10.2.1) and AS-external-LSAs (Section 10.3.2).

For robustness reasons, each LSA in the database is continually aged, in part to ensure that each LSA the router has originated is reoriginated, or refreshed, periodically. Continual aging also ensures that LSAs originated by defunct routers are eventually removed from the database. For the implementation of database aging, see Section 6.4. For the theory behind database aging, see Section 4.2.4 of [67].

Whenever a new LSA is installed in the database, the LSA is flooded to the router's adjacent neighbors. In addition, the correct routing calculation is performed, based on the type of the new LSA, in order to update the router's routing table accordingly; see Section 11.1. The OSPF implementation maintains a local copy of the IP routing table (Chapter 5, Building Blocks). Changes to the local routing table cause matching updates to be performed on the platform's routing table, or kernel routing table, by making appropriate calls to system interface.

3.1.3   Timers

Timers are used a lot in the OSPF implementation, for varied reasons. A description of the implementation of OSPF timers can be found in Chapter 5, Building Blocks.

The most basic timer functions ensure reliable delivery of OSPF protocol packets and LSAs to neighbors. The router ensures that neighbors reliably receive its Hello packets by sending them periodically (Section 8.2). Database Description packets are retransmitted to a neighbor until acknowledged by a received Database Description packet (Section 8.3). Unanswered requests for LSAs are retransmitted in Link State Request packets. Unacknowledged LSAs are retransmitted in Link State Update packets (Section 9.5).

As mentioned earlier, LSAs are aged while they are held in the router's link-state database. This is done using a 1-second timer. See Section 6.4.

Timers are also used to rate-limit certain OSPF functions in order to bound the resource demand that OSPF places on the platform and/or network. The routing calculation is rate-limited by a 1-second timer (Section 11.2.1). The rate at which AS-external-LSAs are imported is also limited, as described in Section 10.3.2. The number of neighbors undergoing Database Exchange is rate-limited according to Section 8.3; in this case, we also use a timer to ensure that each of the limited number of Database Exchange sessions continues to make progress.

Timers are used to aggregate work into batches that can be processed more efficiently. For example, acknowledgment of LSAs is delayed in order to send fewer Link State Acknowledgment packets (Section 9.3).

In addition, timers are used for special conditions mandated by the OSPF specification. When an interface first comes up, the router must wait so that it can determine whether the attached network segment has a Designated Router (Section 8.4). At the end of a Database Exchange session, the slave side has to hang on to its last Database Description packet for some time, similar to TCP's FIN Wait state. If the router's database has overflowed, the router returns to normal operation after a timed interval (Section 10.3.4).

3.1.4   Configuration and Monitoring

The platform-specific initialization code is responsible for reading OSPF configuration and passing it to the OSPF code through the API described in Chapter 13, Configuration and Monitoring. The main loop can also pass configuration updates to the OSPF code, whereupon OSPF will dynamically reconfigure. Reconfiguration is as nondisruptive as possible. Depending on what is being reconfigured, however, some disruption in service will occur. For example, if an interface is reconfigured to no longer be an on-demand interface, it is restarted so that correct LSA instances are flooded across the link. See Chapter 13, Configuration and Monitoring, for a complete list of disruptions caused by various dynamic configuration changes.

Configuration affects the establishment of adjacencies and the contents of router-LSAs. Configuration also controls the importing of external routing information into OSPF.

The platform-specific main loop hands monitoring requests to the OSPF code by calling the API routine `OSPF::monitor()`. This interface provides access to all the information in the OSPF MIB [5]. However, standard MIB notations and protocols (SNMP, or

Simple Network Management Protocol) are not used, using instead a home-cooked packet-based query-and-response scheme, described in Section 13.13. The OSPF code replies to monitor requests by calling the platform-specific system interface routine `OspfSysCalls::monitor_response()`.

3.2   Major Data Structures

The major data structures used in the OSPF implementation and their interrelationships are shown in Figure 3.2. A single `class OSPF` is the starting point for all data structures. It contains the methods implementing the API (see Section 4.3) and the external routing information imported into OSPF, as well as pointers to the collection of OSPF areas and the complete collection of OSPF interfaces.

When the OSPF routing domain is split into pieces, called areas, it is as if a separate copy of the OSPF protocol is run in each area. Each area is represented by a `class SpfArea`. Each area contains it own link-state database. An area is defined in terms of network segments; each network segment belongs to one and only one area. An OSPF interface is assigned to the area that contains the interface's attached network segment. Each `SpfArea` class contains a list of the area's interfaces, each interface represented as a `class SpfIfc`. The operation of OSPF when multiple areas are configured is the subject of Chapter 10, OSPF Hierarchy.

Over each interface, an OSPF router tries to establish conversations with neighboring routers. Some of these conversations will develop into adjacencies, over which the link-state databases will be synchronized. Each conversation is represented in a `class SpfNbr`. In particular, each `SpfNbr` class contains the state information necessary to maintain database synchronization. Database synchronization is the subject of Chapters 8, Neighbor Maintenance, and 9, Flooding.

These structures will be examined in more detail later. A discussion of the OSPF routing table is postponed until Chapter 5, Building Blocks. The link-state database is the subject of Chapter 6, The Link-State Database. The handling of external routing information within OSPF is the subject of Sections 10.3 and 11.6.

In this implementation, the most common way to organize data structures is within an AVL tree (Chapter 5, Building Blocks). When this is done, each of the data structures inherits from `class AVLitem`, but the collected data structures show up simply as a `class AVLtree`—the implementer is expected to know from the name of the tree which kind of data structure resides in the tree and to cast accordingly. For example, in Figure 3.3, the physical interfaces are stored in `AVLtree OSPF::phyints`; to get physical interface 1, the developer would use the code snippet `PhyInt *phyp = (PhyInt *) ospf->phyints.find(1,0)`.

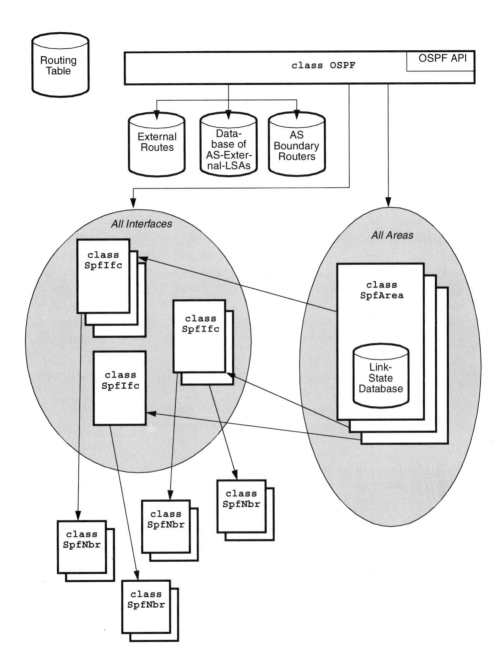

Figure 3.2 The major OSPF data structures.

3.2.1 `class OSPF`

A single `class OSPF`, pointed to by the global variable `ospf`, serves as the head of all other data structures. For example, to scan a list of all the OSPF routers, you would create a `class IfcIterator`, passing a pointer to the `OSPF` class to the constructor, like this: `iter = new IfcIterator(ospf)`. See Chapter 5, Building Blocks, for a full discussion of the iterators used by the OSPF implementation.

The `OSPF` class also contains the API, which the platform-specific code used to invoke the OSPF application. For example, to initialize the OSPF application, the platform-specific code constructs the `OSPF` class. Then, when it receives an OSPF protocol packet, the platform calls the routine `ospf->rxpkt()` so that the OSPF application will perform the required protocol processing. See Section 4.3 for a detailed discussion of the OSPF API.

The `OSPF` class contains many data items, most of which are described elsewhere in this book. However, some of the basic items contained in the `OSPF` class are listed in Figure 3.3. The `OSPF` class contains configurable parameters and hence inherits from `class ConfigItem`. The configuration process, and the precise parameters that are configurable within the `OSPF` class, are given in Chapter 13, Configuration and Monitoring.

```
                                                                          ospf.h
 48 class OSPF : public ConfigItem {
 50      const rtid_t myid;    // Our router ID
 60      // Dynamic data
 63      SpfIfc *ifcs;         // List of interfaces
 65      int n_extImports;     // # Imported AS externals
 66      AVLtree extLSAs;      // AS-external-LSAs
 67      uns32 ase_xsum;       // checksum of AS-external-LSAs
 68      AVLtree ASBRtree;     // AVL tree of ASBRs
 69      ASBRrte *ASBRs;       // Singly-linked ASBR routing table entries
 85      AVLtree phyints;      // Physical interfaces
106
107      SpfArea *areas;       // List of areas
110      int n_area;           // Number of actively attached areas
114      uns16 ospf_mtu;       // Max IP datagram for all interfaces
334 };
335
336 // Declaration of the single OSPF protocol instance
337 extern OSPF *ospf;
                                                                          ospf.h
```

Figure 3.3 Basic items in `class OSPF`.

The OSPF Router ID can be found in `OSPF::myid` and can be accessed via the method `OSPF::my_id()`. The OSPF Router ID is passed as an argument to the `class OSPF`'s constructor. In order to change the router's OSPF Router ID, you must shut down the OSPF protocol by calling the API routine `ospf->shutdown()` and then bring up the OSPF application from scratch again by constructing a new `OSPF` class, rereading the configuration data, and so on.

`OSPF::ifcs` is the list of the router's OSPF interfaces. In order to scan the list of interfaces, you use the `IfcIterator` class described in Chapter 5, Building Blocks. An interface is a connection to an IP subnet. Each interface has a maximum transmission unit (MTU): the largest packet that can be transmitted out the interface without fragmentation. The minimum of these MTUs is stored in `OSPF:: ospf_mtu`; this is the largest packet that can be flooded out all interfaces simultaneously without any fragmentation (see Section 9.6). A physical subnet can have multiple IP subnets. The connection to a physical subnet is represented as a `class PhyInt` (file `phyint.h`); the collection of physical interfaces is found in `OSPF::phyints`.

The database of AS-external-LSAs is kept within the `OSPF` class, as it is common to all regular OSPF areas. (What isn't a regular OSPF area? Stub areas and NSSAs (not-so-stubby areas); see Sections 7.2 and 7.4 of [67]). `OSPF::extLSAs` is the database of AS-external-LSAs, each represented by a `class ASextLSA` (Section 10.3.2). The sum of the LS Checksum fields of these AS-external-LSAs is stored in `OSPF::ase_xsum`; this value would by reported in the OSPF MIB variable `ospfExternLsaCksumSum`. The originators of the AS-external-LSAs are called AS boundary routers (ASBRs); the path(s) to each ASBR are stored in a `class ASBRrte` (file `rte.h`), and these classes are both added to the AVL tree `OSPF::ASBRtree` and linked into the list `OSPF::ASBRs`. Each external route that the router itself may import into OSPF is represented by a `class ExRtData`; these classes are organized into the AVL tree `OSPF::extImports`.

`OSPF::areas` is the list of areas known to the router; to scan the list of areas, you use `class AreaIterator`. An *active area* is one to which the router currently has one or more operational interfaces. The number of active areas is stored in `OSPF::n_area`. As an example, the router is an OSPF area border router if and only if `OSPF::n_area > 1`.

3.2.2 Global Variables

Most data within the OSPF implementation is referenced via the single `OSPF` class. However, the implementation uses a few global variables. These global variables are declared in file `ospf.C` and are displayed in Figure 3.4.

The starting point for almost all data kept by the OSPF implementation is `ospf`, the global variable for the aforementioned single `OSPF` class.

The current list of timer tasks is kept in the global variable `timerq`. See Chapter 5, Building Blocks, for a description of how tasks are added to and deleted from the timing queue.

A pointer to the system interface class, which is part of the platform-specific code that must be written for each port of the implementation, is kept in `sys`. Whenever it wishes to use a system interface, the OSPF implementation makes a call to one of the

```
                                                                        ospf.C
26 // Globals
27 OSPF *ospf;
28 PriQ timerq;            // Global timer queue
29 OspfSysCalls *sys;      // System call interface
30 INtbl *inrttbl; // IP routing table
31 FWDtbl *fa_tbl;         // Forwarding address table
32 INrte *default_route; // The default routing entry (0/0)
33 ConfigItem *cfglist;    // List of configurable classes
34 PatTree MPath::nhdb;    // Next hop(s) database
                                                                        ospf.C
```

Figure 3.4 Global variables used in the OSPF implementation.

methods implemented by `sys`. For example, to send an OSPF protocol packet, the OSPF implementation will call `sys->sendpkt()`. Section 4.2 describes the system interface in great detail.

The OSPF implementation keeps an internal copy of the IP routing table and then uses the system interface to copy individual routing table entries into the platform's kernel routing table. A pointer to the internal copy of the routing table is kept in `inrttbl`. Chapter 5, Building Blocks, explains how this table is organized and manipulated. A pointer to the default route within the routing table, represented by the special prefix `0/0`, is kept in `default_route` for convenience. The next hops used in routing table entries are kept in a separate database, `MPath::nhdb`, so that multiple routing table entries can point to the same next-hop entry.

A separate table, `fa_tbl`, is kept for those forwarding addresses that appear in AS-external-LSAs. This allows us to calculate the cost of each forwarding address before scanning the potentially large set of AS-external-LSAs, speeding the calculation of external routes (see Section 11.6).

All C++ classes containing configurable parameters inherit from `class ConfigItem` and are enqueued on the global list `cfglist`. This allows us to easily determine which configurable classes are no longer referenced after the configuration is reloaded; see Section 13.11.

3.2.3 `class SpfArea`

You can divide an OSPF routing domain into *areas*. The advantage in using multiple areas is that you can build a larger routing domain. The resource demands on any one router is related to the size and the number of its directly attached areas only. The implementation of area routing is explained in Chapter 10, OSPF Hierarchy. See Chapter 6 in [67] for a complete description of OSPF area routing. To scan through the entire list of the router's OSPF areas, you use the `class AreaIterator`.

Most OSPF mechanisms, such as flooding, the Dijkstra calculation, and so on, are performed on an area basis. Therefore, the data structure representing an OSPF area, **class SpfArea**, contains much of the basic OSPF protocol data. Some of the major items within the **SpfArea** class are listed in Figure 3.5.

―― spfarea.h

```
 32 class SpfArea : public ConfigItem {
 33     const aid_t a_id;      // Area ID
 36     // Link-state database
 37     AVLtree rtrLSAs;       // router-LSAs
 38     AVLtree netLSAs;       // network-LSAs
 39     AVLtree summLSAs;      // summary-LSAs
 40     AVLtree asbrLSAs;      // asbr-summary-LSAs
 41     AVLtree grpLSAs;       // group-membership-LSAs
 42     uns32 db_xsum;         // Database checksum
 49     // Dynamic parameters
 50     class SpfIfc *a_ifcs;  // List of associated interfaces
 51     int n_VLs;             // Fully adjacent VLs through this area
 52     bool a_transit;        // Transit area?
 59     AVLtree abr_tbl;       // RTRrte's for area border routers
 60
 61  public:
 62     bool a_stub;           // Options supported by area
 65     AVLtree ranges;        // Area address ranges
 69     int n_active_if;       // Number of active interfaces
 75     uns16 a_mtu;           // Max IP datagram for all interfaces
 78
 79     inline bool is_stub();
 80     inline bool is_transit();
 82     inline aid_t id();
 88     inline RTRrte *find_abr(uns32 rtrid);
 89     RTRrte *add_abr(uns32 rtrid);
104     void RemoveIfc(class SpfIfc *);
105     void IfcChange(int increment);
131 };
```

―― spfarea.h

Figure 3.5 Basic items in **class SpfArea**.

SpfArea::a_id is the area's OSPF Area ID. It is set in the class constructor and can be accessed by using **SpfArea::id()**.

The link-state database is kept within the **SpfArea** class, organized as separate binary trees for each distinct LS type: **SpfArea::rtrLSAs** for the area's router-LSAs, **SpfArea::netLSAs** for network-LSAs, **SpfArea::summLSAs** for summary-LSAs, **SpfArea::asbrLSAs** for ASBR-summary-LSAs, and **SpfArea::grpLSAs** for group-membership-LSAs (NSSAs and opaque-LSAs are not supported). The sum of all the

LSAs' LS Checksum fields is kept in `SpfArea::db_xsum`; this is the equivalent of the OSPF MIB's `ospfAreaLsaCksumSum`.

The list of the router's interfaces to the area is kept in `SpfArea::a_ifcs`. The number of operational interfaces is kept in `SpfArea::n_active_if`; we say that the area is active if and only if `SpfArea::n_active_if > 0`. An area is notified of the change in operational status of one of its interfaces by calling `SpfArea::IfcChange()`. Interfaces are deleted from an area by using `SpfArea::RemoveIfc()`.

An area is called a *transit area* if it can carry data traffic that neither originates nor terminates in the area itself. The OSPF backbone area is always a transit area. Nonzero areas carry transit traffic if and only if one or more routers have established virtual links through the area. The area's transit status is kept in `SpfArea::a_transit` and can be read by using `SpfArea::is_transit()`. If the router itself is the endpoint of virtual links using the area as a transit area, `SpfArea::n_VLs` is incremented.

At the other end of the spectrum, *stub areas* can never carry transit traffic and are limited in other ways also (see Section 7.2 of [67]). Whether an area has been configured as a stub is stored in `SpfArea::a_stub`; stub status is read by using `SpfArea::is_stub()`.

In order to process summary-LSAs during the routing calculation and determine whether the other end of a virtual link is reachable, the OSPF router keeps track of the cost to each of the area's border routers. Each area border router is represented by a `class RTRrte`. These classes are kept in the binary tree `SpfArea::abr_tbl`. To add an area border router to the table, you use `SpfArea::add_abr()`; to find an area border router, you use `SpfArea::find_abr()`.

A router can be configured to aggregate an area's prefixes before advertising the area's routing information to other areas. Each configured aggregate is represented by a `class Range`, and the set of ranges is stored in `SpfArea::ranges`.

In order to determine the maximum size packet that can be flooded out all an area's interfaces simultaneously, the smallest MTU of any of the area's interfaces is stored in `SpfArea::a_mtu`.

3.2.4 `class SpfIfc`

The various OSPF interface types are represented by distinct C++ classes, all inheriting from the base `class SpfIfc`. The resulting interface class hierarchy is shown in Figure 3.6. The classes `SpfIfc` and `DRIfc`, the latter representing those interface types that elect a Designated Router, are used only as base classes and are never instantiated on their own. Broadcast interfaces are represented by `class BroadcastIfc`, NBMA interfaces by `class NBMAIfc`, point-to-point interfaces by `class PPIfc`, virtual links by `class VLIfc` and Point-to-MultiPoint interfaces by `class P2mPIfc`.

To scan through the router's OSPF interfaces, you use the `class IfcIterator`. Depending on the constructor used, you can examine all the router's interfaces or just those attached to a specific OSPF area.

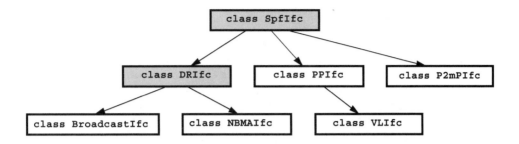

Figure 3.6 The interface class hierarchy. Classes used only as base classes are shaded.

The basic items within the **SpfIfc** class are shown in Figure 3.7. Among the many configurable items in the **SpfIfc** class—most of which are timers, which are not shown—the basic ones are

- The interface's IP address, stored in **SpfIfc::if_addr**; unnumbered interfaces have **SpfIfc:if_addr** set to 0.0.0.0.

- The address mask stored in **SpfIfc::if_mask** and read by **SpfIfc::mask()**.

- An identifier for the corresponding physical interface in **SpfIfc::if_phyint**.

- The MIB-II **IfIndex** value assigned to the interface in **SpfIfc::if_IfIndex**. This parameter is used to identify an unnumbered interface.

- The OSPF area to which the interface attaches, a pointer to which is stored in **SpfIfc::if_area** and is read with **SpfIfc::area()**.

- When OSPF cryptographic authentication is run on the interface, **SpfIfc::if_keys** holds the list of MD5 keys active for the interface, each key represented by a **class CryptK**. Packet transmission and reception functions for the interface walk through the list of keys by using **class KeyIterator**.

- The maximum size of an IP datagram that can be sent out the interface without fragmentation, stored in **SpfIfc::mtu**.

The IP address of the attached IP subnet is stored in **SpfIfc::if_net** and is read with **SpfIfc::net()**. The state of the OSPF interface, in terms of the interface state machine (described in Section 8.4), is stored in **SpfIfc::if_state**.

Each of the neighboring routers with which the router is communicating over the interface is represented by a **class SpfNbr**. These neighbor classes are chained in **SpfIfc::if_nlst**, and a count of them is in **SpfIfc::if_nnbrs**. The number of these neighbor relationships that have progressed to full adjacencies is in **SpfIfc::if_nfull**. To scan the list of neighbors, you use the **class NbrIterator**, which takes the interface as argument to its constructor.

```
                                                                    ──── spfifc.h
109 class SpfIfc : public ConfigItem {
110   protected:
111     // Configurable parameters
112     InMask if_mask;        // Interface address mask
113     uns16 mtu;             // Max IP datagram in bytes
114     int if_IfIndex;        // MIB-II IfIndex
127     SpfArea *if_area;      // Associated OSPF area
128     CryptK *if_keys;       // Cryptographic keys
130     InAddr if_net;         // Resulting network number
141     // Dynamic parameters
145     int if_state;          // Current interface state
152     // FSM action routines
153     virtual void ifa_start() = 0;
159   public:
160     // Configurable parameters
161     InAddr if_addr;        // Interface IP address
162     int if_phyint;         // The physical interface
164     class SpfNbr *if_nlst; // List of associated neighbors
165     int if_nnbrs;          // Number of neighbors
166     int if_nfull;          // Number of fully adjacent neighbors
167
168     SpfIfc(InAddr addr, int phyint); // Constructor
205     // Virtual functions
207     virtual void if_send(Pkt *, InAddr);
208     virtual void nbr_send(Pkt *, SpfNbr *);
209     virtual class SpfNbr *find_nbr(InAddr, rtid_t);
210     virtual void set_id_or_addr(SpfNbr *, rtid_t, InAddr);
211     virtual RtrLink *rl_insert(RTRhdr *, RtrLink *) = 0;
212     virtual int rl_size();
214     virtual int adjacency_wanted(class SpfNbr *np);
215     virtual int type() = 0;
216     virtual void send_hello_response(SpfNbr *np);
217     virtual bool is_virtual();
218     virtual bool is_multi_access();
219     virtual SpfArea *transit_area();
220     virtual rtid_t *vl_endpt();
221     virtual void start_hellos();
222     virtual void restart_hellos();
223     virtual void stop_hellos();
243 };
                                                                    ──── spfifc.h
```

Figure 3.7 Basic information in class SpfIfc.

C++ virtual functions are used to implement behavior that varies based on interface type. These virtual functions are listed in Figure 3.7.

- `SpfIfc::ifa_start()` is the initial interface finite state machine action routine, executed once the interface becomes operational. Interfaces that elect a Designated Router go into a waiting period in order to detect the current Designated Router and Backup Designated Router, if any. All other interfaces transition immediately to their terminal point-to-point state.

- `SpfIfc::if_send()` sends OSPF protocol packets addressed to multicast addresses. On NBMA and Point-to-MultiPoint networks, a separate copy is sent to each adjacent neighbor; on these networks, Hello packets are sent by using a separate mechanism.

- `SpfIfc::nbr_send()` sends an OSPF packet directly to a specified neighbor. On point-to-point networks, the destination address AllSPFRouters is still used. On all interface types, we make sure that the packet is sent out the correct physical interface. For virtual links, however, we let the kernel's routing table select the sending interface.

- `SpfIfc::find_nbr()` and `SpfNbr::set_id_or_addr()`. In a historical curiosity, OSPF identifies neighbors differently, depending on interface type. Neighbors are identified by OSPF Router ID on point-to-point interfaces and virtual links and by IP interface address on all other interfaces. Depending on which parameter identifies the neighbor, the other parameter is set on the basis of information in the OSPF Hellos received from the neighbor.

- `SpfIfc::rl_insert()`. The number and the format of individual link records within the router's router-LSA differs, based on the type of interface being described (Sections 12.4.1.1 through 12.4.1.4 of [75]). `SpfIfc::rl_size()` returns the maximum number of bytes that the link record(s) will occupy.

- `SpfIfc::adjacency_wanted()`. On interfaces that elect a Designated Router, adjacencies are not formed between neighboring routers unless one or both neighbors are either the Designated Router or the Backup Designated Router.

- `SpfIfc::type()` returns `IFT_PP` for point-to-point interfaces, `IFT_VL` for virtual links, `IFT_BROADCAST` for broadcast interfaces, `IFT_NBMA` for NBMA interfaces, and `IFT_P2MP` for Point-to-MultiPoint interfaces.

- `SpfIfc::send_hello_response()`. On NBMA networks, routers ineligible to become Designated Router respond to Hellos received from eligible routers with Hellos of their own.

- `SpfIfc::is_virtual()`. Identifies whether the interface is a virtual link. For virtual links, `SpfIfc::transit_area()` points to the virtual link's transit area, and `SpfIfc::vl_endpt()` points to the OSPF Router ID of the other endpoint (for use in logging only).

- `SpfIfc::is_multi_access()` identifies whether more than one neighbor can be attached to the interface. If so, each neighbor is required to have an IP address on the same subnet as the interface.

- `SpfIfc::start_hellos()`. On NBMA or Point-to-MultiPoint networks, Hellos are sent separately to each neighbor; on other interface types, a single Hello is multicast out the interface periodically. On NBMA networks, the Hello processing is further complicated, based on configured router priorities, as explained in Section 5.3.1 of [67]. `SpfIfc::restart_hellos()` restarts all Hello timers after interface or neighbor state changes, whereas `SpfIfc::stop_hellos()` stops the sending of Hellos on the given interface.

3.2.5   class SpfNbr

An OSPF router exchanges OSPF protocol information with neighboring routers—those routers with which the router shares one or more attached networks. The state of this protocol exchange is called a neighbor relationship, or just a plain *neighbor* from the router's perspective, and is represented by the `class SpfNbr`. A neighbor is attached to a specific interface; if the router shares multiple attached networks with another router, multiple protocol exchanges ensue, each represented by a separate `SpfNbr` class. You can walk the entire collection of neighbors associated with a specified interface by using the `class NbrIterator`.

Most of the fields within the `SpfNbr` class concern the state of link-state database synchronization between the neighbors, which is discussed in great detail in Chapters 8, Neighbor Maintenance, and 9, Flooding. Here, we restrict ourselves to the most basic items in the `SpfNbr` class, as shown in Figure 3.8.

- The neighbor's IP address is in `SpfNbr::n_addr`, and its OSPF ID is in `SpfNbr::n_id`. These two parameters are read by the functions `SpfNbr::addr()` and `SpfNbr::id()`, respectively. One of these parameters will identify the neighbor, depending on the associated interface's type, as implemented in `SpfIfc::find_nbr()`.

- As the `SpfNbr` class is allocated, it is assigned an index value in `SpfNbr::n_index`—the nth neighbor allocated is assigned the value n. The index is used to spread out neighbor-specific timers. For example, on nonbroadcast networks where separate Hellos are sent to each neighbor, a Hello is sent to the neighbor when the current time less `SpfNbr::n_index` is a multiple of the interface's `HelloInterval`.

- The neighbor's state in `SpfNbr::n_state`, read with `SpfNbr::state()`, indicates whether the router should become adjacent with the neighbor and if so, how far the adjacency formation process has progressed. The possible value of the neighbor's state is discussed in detail in Section 8.1.

——————————————————————————————————————— spfnbr.h

```
130 class SpfNbr {
131     InAddr n_addr;        // Its IP address
132     rtid_t n_id;          // Its Router ID
133     int n_index;          // Used to offset timers
134     // Dynamically learned parameters
135     int n_state;          // Current neighbor state
136     uns32 md5_seqno;      // Cryptographic sequence number
170 protected:
172     SpfIfc *n_ifp;        // Associated OSPF interface
174 public:
179     SpfNbr(SpfIfc *, rtid_t id, InAddr addr);
180     virtual ~SpfNbr();
181
182     inline SpfIfc *ifc();
183     inline int state();
188     inline InAddr addr();
189     inline rtid_t id();
234
235     virtual bool configured();
236     virtual bool dr_eligible();
255 };
```

——————————————————————————————————————— spfnbr.h

Figure 3.8 Basic items in `class SpfNbr`.

- When using OSPF cryptographic authentication over the associated interface, we require nondecreasing sequence numbers within the OSPF packet headers received from the neighbor, in order to protect against replay attacks. (See Section 11.7 of [67].) The last sequence number received from the neighbor is stored in `SpfNbr::md5_seqno`.

- A pointer to the interface associated with the neighbor is kept in `SpfNbr::n_ifp` and is read with `SpfNbr::ifc()`.

Neighbors are usually dynamically discovered through the transmission and reception of OSPF Hello packets (Section 8.2). However, on nonbroadcast networks, it may be necessary to configure the identity of neighboring routers (see Section 5.3.1 of [67]). When a neighbor is configured, it is represented as a `class StaticNbr`, which derives from `SpfNbr`, as shown in Figure 3.9.

The following virtual functions are defined for `class SpfNbr`.

- `SpfNbr::configured()` returns `true` for statically configured neighbors and `false` otherwise. When Hellos cease to be heard from a neighbor or the neighbor is otherwise found to be inoperative, storage associated with the neighbor is returned to the heap unless the neighbor has been statically configured.

```
                                                                    ———— spfnbr.h
307 class StaticNbr : public SpfNbr, public ConfigItem {
308     bool _dr_eligible;
309     bool active;
310 public:
311     inline StaticNbr(SpfIfc *, InAddr);
312     virtual bool configured();
313     virtual bool dr_eligible();
314     virtual void clear_config();
317 };
                                                                    ———— spfnbr.h
```

Figure 3.9 The `class StaticNbr`: statically configured neighbors.

- `SpfNbr::dr_eligible()` indicates whether the neighbor is eligible to become Designated Router or Backup Designated Router. This information is configured for static neighbors and is otherwise learned dynamically by testing whether the DR Priority in Hellos received from the neighbor is nonzero.

3.3   File Organization

The source code file organization is shown in Figure 3.10. All the generic code is located in the `ospfd/src` directory. The C++ files use a `.c` extension, with the header files using a `.h` extension. To the left of each file name is the file's size in kilobytes. Source code files written for the two ports of the OSPF software are located in separate directories, as described in Chapters 14, A Routing Daemon for Linux, and 15, An OSPF Simulator. The source code files reformatted to include line numbers, just as they appear within the figures in this book, can be found in the CD-ROM's `format` directory, with the suffixes `.Cfmt` and `.hfmt`, respectively.

3.3.1   Packet Formats, LSA Formats, Protocol Constants

Several C++ header files contain structure definitions that define the layout of OSPF protocol packets and LSAs as they appear on a network segment. Use of these structures for the transmission and the reception of protocol packets is described in Section 4.4.1. Data in these structures appears in network byte order, as opposed to machine byte order, which is used throughout the rest of the OSPF implementation; see Section 4.4.2 for details.

Architectural constants for the OSPF protocol, such as the maximum value that an LSA's Age field can attain (MaxAge), are specified in the file `arch.h`. The OSPF implementation builds the complete IP header for each protocol packet sent and assumes that IP headers are provided for each received packet; the necessary definitions for an IP

2 arch.h	2 iterator.h	3 pat.C	10 spflood.C
4 asbrlsa.C	3 lsa.C	2 pat.h	3 spfnbr.C
11 asexlsa.C	6 lsa.h	8 phyint.C	5 spfnbr.h
7 avl.C	3 lsalist.C	3 phyint.h	4 spforig.C
3 avl.h	3 lsalist.h	3 priq.C	1 spfparam.h
2 cksum.C	6 lsdb.C	2 priq.h	3 spfpkt.h
2 config.C	3 lshdr.h	4 rte.C	1 spftype.h
4 config.h	2 mcache.h	6 rte.h	8 spfutil.C
1 contrib	9 monitor.C	8 rtrlsa.C	2 spfutil.h
6 dbage.C	3 monitor.h	5 spfack.C	3 spfvl.C
2 dbage.h	10 mospf.C	8 spfarea.C	1 stack.h
1 globals.h	1 mospf.h	4 spfarea.h	6 summlsa.C
4 grplsa.C	7 nbrfsm.C	10 spfcalc.C	2 system.h
3 hostmode.C	2 nbrfsm.h	6 spfdd.C	3 timer.C
6 ifcfsm.C	4 netlsa.C	5 spfhello.C	2 timer.h
2 ifcfsm.h	9 ospf.C	12 spfifc.C	
1 igmp.h	7 ospf.h	7 spfifc.h	
1 ip.h	1 ospfinc.h	3 spflog.h	

Figure 3.10 Source code file organization.

packet header are found in **ip.h**. Packet definitions for the Internet Group Management Protocol (IGMP) can be found in **igmp.h**. The file **lshdr.h** specifies the formats of all OSPF LSAs, and OSPF protocol packet formats are given in **spfpkt.h**.

Standard type definitions used by the OSPF implementation are given in the file **spftype.h** and are shown in Figure 3.11. OSPF Router IDs are represented as type **rtid_t**. Link State IDs within LSAs are represented by type **lsid_t**. Type **aid_t** is used for OSPF Area IDs. Authentication types used by OSPF are manipulated by using **autyp_t**. The basic fields within LSAs also have type definitions: **age_t** for the LS Age field, **seq_t** for the LS Sequence field, and **xsum_t** for the LSA's Checksum field.

```
                                                            ───── spftype.h
24 typedef uns32 rtid_t;          // Router ID
25 typedef uns32 lsid_t;          // Link State ID
26 typedef uns32 aid_t;           // Area IDs
27 typedef uns32 autyp_t;         // Authentication type
28                                // Fields in link state header
29 typedef uns16 age_t;           // LS age, 16-bit unsigned
30 typedef int32 seq_t;           // LS Sequence Number, 32-bit signed
31 typedef uns16 xsum_t;          // LS Checksum, 16-bit unsigned
                                                            ───── spftype.h
```

Figure 3.11 OSPF type definitions in **spftype.h**.

3.3.2 Major Data Structures

The file `globals.h` contains the definitions of the small number of global variables used by the OSPF implementation. These variables are declared in `ospf.C`, which also has many of the routines implementing OSPF's API (see Section 4.3).

The top-level OSPF data structure, `class OSPF`, is defined in `ospf.h`. That class, pointed to by the global `ospf`, contains pointers to all the other major OSPF data structures and the routines implementing the API.

The file `ospfinc.h` contains a list of header files that are included by all the C++ files in the OSPF implementation.

Files `phyint.C` and `phyint.h` implement operations that OSPF performs on a physical interface basis rather than per IP subnet. Multiple IP subnets may be defined on a given physical network segment, as described in Section 5.1 of [67]. OSPF operates mostly per IP subnet, but certain operations, such as joining multicast groups for the purpose of sending OSPF protocol packets, must be performed per physical interface.

Operations and data that are defined per OSPF area are implemented in `spfarea.C` and `spfarea.h`. The OSPF link-state database is one example of area-specific data; see Chapter 10, OSPF Hierarchy.

Operations performed per OSPF interface, such as sending protocol packets, electing the Designated Router, and so on, are implemented in `spfifc.h` and `spfifc.C`. Per neighbor operations are defined in `spfnbr.h`. Basic neighbor operations, such as neighbor identification, are implemented in `spfnbr.C`.

Hard-coded parameters used by the OSPF implementation are defined in `spfparam.h`. One example is `MAXPATH`, the maximum number of equal-cost paths that the implementation will keep track of. These parameters can be changed, although a recompilation of the OSPF code is required to do so.

The file `spfvl.C` contains those operations that are specific to virtual links, such as setting the cost of the virtual link equal to the current distance to the virtual link's endpoint area border router. See Section 10.2.3 for details.

The system interface, an implementation of which must be supplied for each port of the software, is defined in `system.h`. See Section 4.2 for a detailed explanation of the system interface and Chapters 14, A Routing Daemon for Linux, and 15, An OSPF Simulator, for two examples of system interface implementations.

3.3.3 Link-State Database

The link-state database is contained within the `SpfArea` class defined in `spfarea.h`, but the implementation of the various database operations and the internal representation of individual LSA types (such as router-LSAs) are scattered throughout several other files. Chapters 6, The Link-State Database, and 7, Originating LSAs, examine the implementation of the link-state database in detail.

The aging of LSAs within the OSPF database is implemented in **dbage.C** and **dbage.h**; see Section 6.4.

In order to make the routing calculations run more efficiently, LSAs are represented differently internally than they appear within OSPF protocol packets, as explained in Section 11.4. The internal representation of LSAs is defined in **lsa.h**. Basic operations on the LSAs themselves, such as parsing LSA headers and building the network representation from the internal LSA representation, are implemented in **lsa.C**.

In many cases, the OSPF implementation constructs lists of LSAs for special processing, such as retransmitting the LSAs to a neighbor, flushing the LSAs from the routing domain, and so on. The methods for implementing lists of LSAs can be found in **lsalist.h** and **lsalist.C** and are explained further in Section 6.3.

Basic database operations, such as adding LSAs to the database, finding LSAs in the database, flushing LSAs from the database, and so on, can be found in **lsdb.C**. Generic routines used when originating LSAs are implemented in **spforig.C**. Routines used to originate, parse, and otherwise manipulate specific LSA types are contained in files specific to the given LSA type: **asbrlsa.C** for ASBR-summary-LSAs, **asexlsa.C** for AS-external-LSAs, **grplsa.C** for group-membership-LSAs, **netlsa.C** for network-LSAs, **rtrlsa.C** for router-LSAs, and **summlsa.C** for network-summary-LSAs (also called simply summary-LSAs).

3.3.4 Initial Database Synchronization

Most of the protocol machinery in OSPF is used to maintain a distributed synchronized database between OSPF routers. Database synchronization is actively maintained across certain pairs of neighboring routers, termed adjacencies. The state associated with an adjacency is contained in the **class SpfNbr** defined within **spfnbr.h**. The methods implementing the database synchronization are spread among a number of other files.

OSPF has an interface state machine, which has two main purposes. First, it elects special routers on broadcast and NBMA segments, called the Designated Router and the Backup Designated Router, which dictate which neighboring routers on the segment become adjacent (see Section 5.2.2 of [67]). Second, the state machine ties the state of the interface to the state of its associated adjacencies, destroying adjacencies as soon as the interface becomes inoperational. The interface state machine is implemented in **ifcfsm.C** and **ifcfsm.h** and is discussed further in Section 8.4.

OSPF also has a neighbor state machine. Its purpose is to discover and to maintain communication between neighboring routers and to perform initial database synchronization with those neighboring routers selected to form adjacencies. The neighbor state machine is implemented in **nbrfsm.C** and **nbrfsm.h** and is explained in Section 8.1. The sending and receiving of Database Description packets is part of the forming of an adjacency and is implemented in **spfdd.C**.

In OSPF, a router discovers its neighbors by receiving Hellos. Unless notified of failures earlier by the physical or the data-link networking layers, a router uses the cessation of Hellos to indicate the failure of a neighboring router. Sending and receiving Hello packets is implemented in `spfhello.C` and is discussed in Section 8.2.

3.3.5 Flooding

Once an adjacency has been formed, database synchronization is maintained through OSPF's reliable-flooding algorithm (Section 4.7.2 of [67]). During flooding, LSAs are carried between OSPF routers in Link State Update packets and are acknowledged by Link State Acknowledgment packets. The sending and receiving of Link State Update packets is implemented in `spflood.C`; sending and receiving Link State Acknowledgment packets is implemented in `spfack.C`. The implementation of flooding is discussed in detail in Chapter 9, Flooding.

3.3.6 Hierarchy

OSPF has the ability to split the routing domain into regions called areas. Combined with the ability to import external routes into the OSPF routing domain, area routing yields a multilevel routing hierarchy: intra-area, inter-area, and external routing. A detailed discussion of the software implementation of hierarchy can be found in Chapter 10, OSPF Hierarchy.

Inter-area routes are advertised in summary-LSAs, which are implemented in `summlsa.C` and are discussed in Section 10.2.1. Routers importing external routing information are called AS boundary routers (ASBRs). The locations of ASBRs are advertised across areas, using ASBR-summary-LSAs (also called type-4 summary-LSAs), which are implemented in `asbrlsa.C` and are discussed in Section 10.3.1. Section 10.3.2 discusses the importing of external routes through originating AS-external-LSAs, implemented in the file `asexlsa.C`.

3.3.7 Routing Calculations

The OSPF routing calculations, described in detail in Chapter 11, Routing Calculations, can be broken along hierarchical lines: intra-area, inter-area, and external routing calculations. The intra-area routing calculation, implemented as a Dijkstra algorithm in file `spfcalc.C`, is described in Section 11.2.1. The inter-area calculation examines summary-LSAs and is implemented in `summlsa.C` and described in Section 11.2.6. The external route calculation, described in Section 11.6, examines both ASBR-summary-LSAs and AS-external-LSAs, as implemented in `asbrlsa.C` and `asexlsa.C`, respectively. The routing table calculations performed by the implementation when it is configured to act as a host instead of as a router are implemented in file **hostmode.C**.

3.3.8 Configuration and Monitoring

Configuration of the OSPF software is performed through the **OSPF::cfgXXX()** routines in the API. Each of these routines is responsible for configuring one of the major OSPF data structures—for example, an OSPF network interface. The complete list of configuration parameters is defined in the file **config.h** and is described in detail in Chapter 13, Configuration and Monitoring. Generic routines supporting configuration—for example, the ability to reread an entire configuration file—can be found in **config.C**.

A monitoring capability is also included in the OSPF implementation, allowing you to access all the information in the standard OSPF MIB [5], although not through the standard SNMP. Instead, a get and get-next query-and-response mechanism has been defined for each of the major OSPF data structures. The format of monitoring queries and responses is given in **monitor.h**. The routines that process queries, returning the correctly formatted responses, are found in **monitor.C**.

3.3.9 Utilities

The OSPF implementation includes a number of utilities, such as sorting and searching routines. These utilities are the subject of Chapter 5, Building Blocks.

The files **avl.C** and **avl.h** implement balanced trees, also called AVL trees after their inventors. These trees are useful for general sorting and searching and are the most-used data structure in the implementation, forming the basis for the link-state database, routing tables, and so on.

OSPF uses two checksum algorithms. The standard Internet one's complement checksum is used in the IP header and for OSPF datagrams; this checksum is implemented in **spfutil.C**, along with routines to build OSPF packet headers and to print OSPF logging information. The Fletcher checksum used in LSAs is implemented in **cksum.C**.

Various iterator classes, allowing you to scan the major data structures, such as interfaces, areas, and neighbors, are implemented in **iterator.h**.

Patricia trees are implemented in files **pat.C** and **pat.h**. These binary trees are particularly good when searching on large keys, such as text strings.

The files **priq.C** and **priq.h** implement priority queues, which are data structures that are very efficient for sorting events by their arrival times. Priority queues are used to implement the sort in Dijkstra's algorithm and to implement the generic timer support within OSPF.

Routing tables are implemented in the files **rte.C** and **rte.h**. Definitions of the individual logging events can be found in **spflog.h**. The file **spfutil.h** defines the general finite state machine support used by OSPF and the packet descriptor class used by the implementation. The file **stack.h** implements a stack mechanism, allowing you to push and pop elements when, for example, performing a depth-first search of a binary tree.

The timer support used internal to the OSPF implementation can be found in **timer.C** and **timer.h**.

3.3.10 MOSPF

The Multicast Extensions to OSPF (MOSPF) enable a routing domain running OSPF to also forward IP multicast datagrams. The MOSPF protocol is described in detail in Chapter 10 of [67].

MOSPF is implemented by adding the location of multicast group members to the link-state database. This location information is advertised in new LSAs called group-membership-LSAs, which are implemented in **grplsa.C**. The MOSPF routing calculation then builds a shortest-path tree between a multicast datagram's source and the various members of the destination group. This routing calculation is implemented in the file **mospf.C**. The implementation of MOSPF's routing table entries is given by the **class MospfEntry** in file **mospf.h**.

In order to originate group-membership-LSAs, the router detects the presence of group members on its locally attached network segments, using the Internet Group Management Protocol (IGMP, [19]). An implementation of the router portion of IGMP is included in **phyint.C**, as that part of IGMP is omitted from many operating systems' kernel support.

Exercises

3.1   The major OSPF data structures are interrelated, containing pointers to one another. For example, the **SpfIfc** class representing an interface contains a list of **SpfNbr** classes representing the interface's neighbors. Draw a diagram containing the major OSPF data structures and their interrelationships.

4

Porting Guide

This chapter provides information enabling you to port the OSPF code to various enviroments. Section 4.1 gives an overview of the main porting tasks. The system interface routines that must be written are the subject of Section 4.2. They provide the OSPF application with such basic functions as packet transmission, joining and leaving multicast groups, and so on. The Application Programming Interface (API)—the entry points into the OSPF code—are described in Section 4.3. Section 4.4 examines some machine dependencies that you must keep in mind when porting the code.

4.1 Porting Overview

The additional code needed to port the OSPF application can be roughly divided into an initialization section and a main loop. The initialization section sets up an environment in which the OSPF application can work. Then the main loop receives OSPF control packets from the network and keeps track of elapsed real time, calling the OSPF timer routine when necessary.

4.1.1 Initialization

First, an `OspfSysCalls` class must be created (see Section 4.2 for the functions that must be implemented within this class), a pointer to which must be stored in the global variable **sys**. As part of the class, the method **OspfSysCalls::sys_spflog()** must be implemented. The OSPF application will use this method to log significant events, a sample of which is seen in Figure 4.1. For more information on OSPF logging messages, see Chapter 5, Building Blocks. The OSPF implementation also uses the POSIX random-number generator **rand()**, which should also be initialized at this time.

```
20:56:51 OSPF.17: Sent LsReq 10.1.0.4->10.1.0.1 Ifc 10.1.0.4
20:56:52 OSPF.16: Received Hello 10.1.0.1->224.0.0.5
20:56:53 OSPF.17: Sent Hello 10.1.0.4->224.0.0.5 Ifc 10.1.0.4
20:56:54 OSPF.17: Sent LsReq 10.1.0.4->10.1.0.1 Ifc 10.1.0.4
20:56:54 OSPF.16: Received LsUpd 10.1.0.1->10.1.0.4
20:56:54 OSPF.18: New LSA(1,10.1.0.1,10.1.0.1)
20:56:54 OSPF.17: Sent DD 10.1.0.4->10.1.0.1 Ifc 10.1.0.4
20:56:54 OSPF.16: Received LsReq 10.1.0.1->10.1.0.4
20:56:54 OSPF.17: Sent LsUpd 10.1.0.4->10.1.0.1 Ifc 10.1.0.4
20:56:54 OSPF.16: Received DD 10.1.0.1->10.1.0.4
20:56:54 OSPF.34: Nbr FSM Full<-Exchange event ExchangeDone Nbr 10.1.0.1
20:56:54 OSPF.19: Originating LSA(1,192.168.1.4,192.168.1.4)
20:56:54 OSPF.16: Received LsUpd 10.1.0.1->224.0.0.5
20:56:54 OSPF.21: Failed MinArrival LSA(1,10.1.0.1,10.1.0.1) Nbr 10.1.0.1
20:56:54 OSPF.18: New LSA(2,10.1.0.1,10.1.0.1)
20:56:54 OSPF.17: Sent LsUpd 10.1.0.4->224.0.0.5 Ifc 10.1.0.4
```

Figure 4.1 Sample of OSPF logging messages.

The OSPF configuration must now be read. After the OSPF Router ID is read, the **OSPF** class should be created, a pointer to which is stored in the global variable **ospf**. All interactions between the system and the OSPF application will be made through functions contained in the **OSPF** class (see Section 4.3). In particular, the remaining OSPF configuration is downloaded into the OSPF application through successive calls to the **ospf->cfgXXX()** methods. The configuration interface is discussed in further detail in Chapter 13, Configuration and Monitoring.

The OSPF application keeps track of time in seconds and milliseconds since program start (in other words, the creation of the **OSPF** class). This time is stored in **sys_etime**.

4.1.2   The Main Loop

The main loop continuously reads OSPF control packets received by the platform's network interfaces and calls **ospf->rxpkt()** for each packet so that it can be processed by the OSPF application. The main loop should not block forever while waiting for OSPF packets. Instead, the **ospf->timeout()** function should be called to determine the maximum number of milliseconds that you can block, waiting for receive packets. You need not have a clock with millisecond granularity, although you should have clock granular-

ity of at least one-tenth second. When your clock granularity is greater than milliseconds, you can block for the next time period greater than that indicated by
`ospf->timeout()`. After waiting to receive packets but before calling `ospf->rxpkt()`
for any packets that may have come in, the elapsed time `sys_etime` should be updated,
and the OSPF timer routine `ospf->tick()` should be called so that any pending timers
are executed.

   As a response to received packets and timer ticks, the OSPF application will send
packets, install routing table entries after running its routing calculations, and so on, by
making calls to the routines that you provide in your `OspfSysCalls` class.

   You should also allow the interrupting of the main loop for two types of requests:
(1) requests for dynamic reconfiguration, which are handled by calling the appropriate
`ospf->cfgXXX()` methods (see Chapter 13, Configuration and Monitoring); and (2)
requests for program shutdown, which are handled gracefully by calling
`ospf->shutdown()` (see Section 13.10).

4.2   System Interface

Each port must provide an implementation of the `OspfSysCalls` class, listed in Figure
4.2. The OSPF implementation calls routines in this class when the underlying hardware
and software platform is required to take an action, such as to send an OSPF control
packet, install a routing table entry, or join a multicast group on a given interface. It is
expected that the port will create a derived class of the `OspfSysCalls` class, which is
why all the routines are declared **virtual**. See the **LinuxOspfd** class in file `ospfd/`
`linux/ospfd_linux.h` for an example.

   The `OspfSysCalls` class must assign a unique integer value to each physical network interface. This integer value is referred to as the variable **phyint** throughout the
code. For example, a system with five Ethernets and two point-to-point links could
assign them the values 1–7. The `OspfSysCalls` class tells the OSPF application about
the **phyint** assignments when downloading the OSPF interface information into the
application (see Section 13.2). From then on, **phyint**s are used in both the system and
the application interfaces to indicate which interface is being operated on. The
`OspfSysCalls` class is also in charge of maintaining time, which is expressed in seconds
and milliseconds since the OSPF code was started, and which the system must store in
the variable `sys_etime`.

   The header file `machdep.h` must be created for each port (see, for example, the file
`ospfd/linux/machdep.h` for the Linux `ospfd` port). This file defines the signed and
unsigned types of length 8, 16, and 32 bits, as shown in Table 4.1. Also, you must set the
MODX constant required by the Fletcher checksum algorithm, which depends on the size
of your machine's **int** data type, as described in [53] and used in the file `ospfd/src/`
`cksum.C`. The file also describes the byte swapping that must be done for the given platform, as described in Section 4.4.2.

```
25 class OspfSysCalls {
26 public:
27     InPkt *getpkt(uns16 len);
28     void freepkt(InPkt *pkt);
29     OspfSysCalls();
30     virtual ~OspfSysCalls();
31
32     virtual void sendpkt(InPkt *pkt, int phyint, InAddr gw=0)=0;
33     virtual void sendpkt(InPkt *pkt)=0;
34     virtual bool phy_operational(int phyint)=0;
35     virtual void phy_open(int phyint)=0;
36     virtual void phy_close(int phyint)=0;
37     virtual void join(InAddr group, int phyint)=0;
38     virtual void leave(InAddr group, int phyint)=0;
39     virtual void ip_forward(bool enabled)=0;
40     virtual void set_multicast_routing(bool on)=0;
41     virtual void set_multicast_routing(int phyint, bool on)=0;
42     virtual void rtadd(InAddr, InMask, MPath *, MPath *, bool)=0;
43     virtual void rtdel(InAddr, InMask, MPath *ompp)=0;
44     virtual void add_mcache(InAddr, InAddr, MCache *)=0;
45     virtual void del_mcache(InAddr src, InAddr group)=0;
46     virtual void monitor_response(struct MonMsg *, uns16, int, int)=0;
47     virtual char *phyname(int phyint)=0;
48     virtual void sys_spflog(int msgno, char *msgbuf)=0;
49     virtual void halt(int code, char *string)=0;
50 };
```

Figure 4.2 The system entry points: `class OspfSysCalls`.

Table 4.1 Machine-Dependent Fixed-Sized Types Defined in File `machdep.h`

Type	Definition
`byte`	8-bit unsigned
`uns16`	16-bit unsigned
`uns32`	32-bit unsigned
`int8`	8-bit signed
`int16`	16-bit signed
`int32`	32-bit signed

IP packets passed to either the system or application interfaces always have the packet's contents formatted in network byte order, that is, ready to be sent out a network interface. However, individual arguments in the system or application interfaces are always in machine byte order.

All memory allocation and deallocation, other than the allocation and freeing of IP packets in `OspfSysCalls::getpkt()` and `OspfSysCalls::freepkt()`, is done through the standard C++ `new` and `delete`; no other memory allocation interface need be provided by the `OspfSysCalls` class. Default implementations of `OspfSysCalls::getpkt()` and `OspfSysCalls::freepkt()` have been provided in `ospfd/src/spfutil.C`, although you may choose to override them when porting the code.

4.2.1 Routines

This section provides detailed description of the routines that must be provided as part of the system interface. Two versions of `OspfSysCalls::sendpkt()` must be provided; they are called by the OSPF application to send OSPF control packets. OSPF passes a pointer `pkt` to the IP packet (see the `InPkt` structure in Figure 4.3), which has been completely formatted for transmission: All fields in the IP header have been set, including the IP header checksum, and the packet is already in network byte order. The packet length can be read out of the `InPkt::i_len` field. The system interface must not free `pkt` after it is sent.

---
                                                                                    ip.h

```
23 typedef uns32 InAddr;
24 typedef uns32 InMask;              // Internet address mask
25
33 /* The IP packet header
34  */
35
36 struct InPkt {
37     byte i_vhlen;          // Version and header length
38     byte i_tos;            // Type-of-service
39     uns16 i_len;           // Total length in bytes
40     uns16 i_id;            // Identification
41     uns16 i_ffo;           // Flags and fragment offset
42     byte i_ttl;            // Time to live
43     byte i_prot;           // Protocol number
44     uns16 i_chksum;        // Header checksum
45     InAddr i_src;          // Source address
46     InAddr i_dest;         // Destination address
47 };
```

---
                                                                                    ip.h

Figure 4.3 The `InPkt` structure.

`void OspfSysCalls::sendpkt(InPkt *pkt, int phyint, InAddr gw=0)`

The IP packet `pkt` is to be sent out the physical interface specified by `phyint`. The IP destination specified by the IP packet will be either a local-wire multicast address (224.0.0.1-224.0.0.255), or a unicast address belonging to one of the attached network's IP subnets.

When `gw` is nonzero, the packet should be sent directly to `gw`—which will belong to one of the attached network's IP subnets—instead of to the IP destination. This latter feature is used when sending packets addressed to a multicast address out onto a non-broadcast network. If the target system cannot support this latter function, the packet should be readdressed to `gw` and the IP header checksum recalculated before sending.

`void OspfSysCalls::sendpkt(InPkt *pkt)`

Send an IP packet, with the output interface unspecified. This is used, for example, when sending OSPF control packets over a virtual link.

`bool OspfSysCalls::phy_operational(int if_phyint)`

Returns `true` if the interface identified by `phyint` is working—capable of sending and receiving packets; otherwise, returns `false`. The OSPF application code does not periodically poll for interface status changes. Interface status changes should instead be recognized by the system's kernel, and then `OSPF::phy_up()` or `OSPF::phy_down()` should be called, as appropriate.

`void OspfSysCalls::phy_open(int phyint)`

Turn on the receiving and transmitting of OSPF protocol packets on the interface identified by `phyint`.

`void OspfSysCalls::phy_close(int phyint)`

Turn off the receiving and transmitting of OSPF protocol packets on the interface identified by `phyint`.

`void OspfSysCalls::join(InAddr group, int phyint)`

Join the multicast group `group` on interface `phyint`. Used to join the AllSPFRouters multicast group (224.0.0.5) when OSPF is first enabled on an interface and to join All-DRouters (224.0.0.6) when the router becomes Designated Router or Backup Designated Router on the interface's attached network segment.

`void OspfSysCalls::leave(InAddr group, int phyint)`

Leave the multicast group `group` on interface `phyint`.

`void OspfSysCalls::ip_forward(bool enabled)`

When `enabled` is set to `true`, the platform should forward IP unicast datagrams that are neither originated by nor addressed to the platform itself (called transit traffic);

that is, the platform should function as an IP router. If **enabled** is set to **false**, the platform should act as an IP host only and not forward transit traffic.

   void OspfSysCalls::set_multicast_routing(bool on)
   If **on** is set to **true**, enable the forwarding of IP multicast datagrams in the kernel; in other words, turn the platform into an IP multicast router. If **on** is set to **false**, multicast forwarding is disabled.

   void OspfSysCalls::set_multicast_routing(int phyint, bool on)
   Enable or disable the forwarding of multicast datagrams on the interface identified by **phyint**.

   void OspfSysCalls::rtadd(InAddr net, InMask mask, MPath *mpp,
                              MPath *ompp, bool reject)
   Add or modify the platform's (or kernel's) forwarding table entry for the IP prefix specified by **net** and **mask**. Multiple equal-cost outgoing interfaces may be specified in **mpp**; the precise algorithm for load balancing traffic among the multiple interfaces is left up to the kernel. The **MPath** class representing the collection of next hops is defined in the file **ospfd/src/rte.h** and is pictured in Figure 4.4. The **mpp->npaths** next hops are contained in the array **mpp->NHs[]**; each individual next hop is represented by an **NH** structure, with **NH::phyint** providing the outgoing interface and **NH::gw** the IP address of the next-hop IP router, if any.

——————————————————————————————————————— rte.h
```
29 struct NH {
30     SpfIfc *o_ifp;        // Outgoing interface
31     int phyint; // Physical interface
32     InAddr gw;   // New hop gateway
33 };
34
35 class MPath : public PatEntry {
36   public:
37     int npaths;
38     NH   NHs[MAXPATH];
39     static PatTree nhdb;
40     static MPath *create(int, NH *);
41     static MPath *create(SpfIfc *, InAddr);
42     static MPath *create(int, InAddr);
43     static MPath *merge(MPath *, MPath *);
44     static MPath *addgw(MPath *, InAddr);
45     bool all_in_area(class SpfArea *);
46 };
```
——————————————————————————————————————— rte.h

Figure 4.4 The **MPath** data structure.

The previous list of next hops is specified in the **ompp** argument. Next hops that appeared in **ompp** but that no longer appear in the new list of next-hops **mpp** will need to be removed from the kernel forwarding entry.

If **reject** is set to **true**, matching datagrams should be discarded instead of forwarded. This is necessary to avoid packet looping in area border routers performing route aggregation; see Section 11.2.6 for details.

void OspfSysCalls::rtdel(InAddr net, InMask mask, MPath *ompp)

Delete the IP address prefix represented by **net** and **mask** from the kernel routing table. Packets that previously best matched the prefix are now forwarded based on a less specific prefix or, if no matching prefix now exists, are discarded. The **ompp** argument provides the next hops that were previously associated with the prefix.

void OspfSysCalls::add_mcache(InAddr src, InAddr group, MCache *mcrte)

Add a multicast routing table entry to the kernel, instructing the kernel how to forward multicast datagrams having IP source address **src** and IP destination the multicast **group**. The **MCache** class, representing the contents of the multicast routing table entry, is defined in the file **ospfd/src/mcache.h** and is shown in Figure 4.5.

——— mcache.h

```
43 struct DownStr {
44     int phyint;
45     InAddr nbr_addr;
46     byte ttl;
47 };
51
52 struct MCache {
53     int n_upstream;
54     int *up_phys;
55     int n_downstream;
56     DownStr *down_str;
57     InMask mask;
63 };
```

——— mcache.h

Figure 4.5 Contents of a multicast routing table entry: **struct MCache**.

The multicast routing table entry indicates that in order for the datagram to be forwarded, it must be received on one of the **mcrte->n_upstream** physical interfaces whose **phyints** appear in the array **mcrte->up_phys**. Multiple receiving interfaces are possible when two MOSPF routers are connected via multiple point-to-point links; see Section 10.3.1 of [67] for details. When forwarded, a copy of the datagram should be sent out each one of the `mcrte->n_downstream` physical interfaces; for each downstream interface, a `struct DownStr` description appears in the array `mcrte->down_str`. If the multicast datagram's time-to-live (ttl) is greater than `DownStr::ttl`, a copy of the multicast datagram should be forwarded out the interface whose `phyint` is equal to `DownStr::phyint`. If `DownStr::nbr_addr` is set to `0`, the datagram should be forwarded as a data-link multicast; otherwise, the datagram should be forwarded as a unicast to the next-hop address `DownStr::nbr_addr`.

As an example of how multicast routing table entries are used in forwarding multicast datagrams, see the function `SimSys::mc_fwd()` in file `ospfd/ospf_sim/ospfd_sim.C`.

Negative cache entries—source and group combinations whose IP multicast datagrams should not be forwarded, are specified by setting `mcrte->n_upstream` to `0`.

void OspfSysCalls::del_mcache(Inaddr src, InAddr group)
Delete the entry for IP source `src` and destination multicast `group` from the kernel's multicast routing table. The next multicast datagram specifying `src` and `group` should invoke a call to `OSPF::mclookup(InAddr src, InAddr group)` so that a new multicast routing table entry is created.

void OspfSysCalls::monitor_response(struct MonMsg *msg, uns16 code, int len, int fd)
A response to a monitoring request received on the monitoring connection `fd` is to be returned. The response is in the buffer specified by `msg`, of length `len`, and type specified by `code`. Monitoring requests are entered through the OSPF API routine `OSPF::monitor()`. For more information on the `ospfd` monitoring interface, see Section 13.13.

char *OspfSysCalls::phyname(int phyint)
Provide a human-readable name of the interface identified by `phyint`. Used when printing log messages about a given interface.

void OspfSysCalls::sys_spflog(int msgno, char *msgbuf)
Print an `ospfd` logging message. Logging messages have a message number `msgno` and a readable text string in the buffer `msgbuf`. For a complete list of the logging messages produced by the `ospfd` implementation, see Appendix B.

void OspfSysCalls::halt(char *string)
The OSPF application has encountered a fatal error, indicated in printable form by `string`. The `string` should be stored somewhere where it can be retrieved later (for example, written to a UNIX `syslog` facility), and then the program should exit.

4.2.2 POSIX Subroutines

The OSPF implementation also makes the following POSIX calls:

- `memcmp()`. Compares two octet strings in memory, returning 0 if they are equal.

- `memcpy()`. Copies one octet string to another.

- `memset()`. Fills an octet string with a specified byte value.

- `rand()`. Returns a pseudorandom number between 0 and `RAND_MAX`. The random-number generator is initialized by a call to `srand()`, which must be supplied in each port.

- `sprintf()`. Format an ASCII string in memory, given a format specification that indicates how to convert into printable ASCII the variable number of arguments that follow.

- `strlen()`. Returns the number of bytes in a null-terminated ASCII string. The null is not included in the count.

- `strncpy()`. Copies a null-terminated ASCII string, stopping at the end of the string or after a specified number of characters, whichever comes first.

4.3   Application Programming Interface

The Application Programming Interface (API) consists of the routines that the system calls in order to invoke processing by the OSPF application. These routines are all members of the base `OSPF` class and are listed in Figure 4.6.

The API is not reentrant. The system must ensure that before a new call into the API is issued, any previous call to the API has completed.

Detailed descriptions of the individual routines in the API follow. Note that discussion of the configuration API is postponed until Chapter 13, Configuration and Monitoring.

`ospf = new OSPF(router_id)`

The constructor for the `OSPF` class should be called during initialization and serves to initialize the OSPF application and to provide a handle (the global variable `OSPF *ospf`) for further communication with the OSPF application. The OSPF Router ID `router_id` must be passed to the constructor and cannot be changed for the life of the OSPF application.

`void OSPF::rxpkt(int phyint, InPkt *pkt, int plen)`

This function is called when an OSPF protocol packet `pkt` has been received on an interface `phyint`. The OSPF application will then perform the appropriate protocol processing, possibly calling such system functions as `OspfSysCalls::sendpkt()` and

```
                                                                — ospf.h
 48 class OSPF : public ConfigItem {

264      // Entry points into the OSPF code
265      OSPF(uns32 rtid);
266      void rxpkt(int phyint, InPkt *pkt, int plen);
267      int timeout();
268      void tick();
269      void monitor(struct MonMsg *msg, byte type, int size, int conn_id);
270      void rxigmp(int phyint, InPkt *pkt, int plen);
271      MCache *mclookup(InAddr src, InAddr group);
272      void join_indication(InAddr group, int phyint);
273      void leave_indication(InAddr group, int phyint);
274      void phy_up(int phyint);
275      void phy_down(int phyint);
276      MPath *ip_lookup(InAddr dest);
277      InAddr ip_source(InAddr dest);
278      InAddr if_addr(int phyint);
279      void shutdown(int seconds);
280      void logflush();
281      inline rtid_t my_id();

334 };
335
336 // Declaration of the single OSPF protocol instance
337 extern OSPF *ospf;
                                                                — ospf.h
```

Figure 4.6 The OSPF API, contained in `class OSPF`.

`OspfSysCalls::rtadd()` in response. The complete IP header of the received packet must be included, as illustrated in Figure 4.3. The length in bytes of the received IP packet, as indicated by the physical interface adapter, is passed in `plen`.

If it is impossible to know just which interface the packet was received from, as is the case with the standard BSD (Berkeley Software Distribution) socket interface, `phyint` should be set to `-1`. In this case, the OSPF application will infer the receiving interface from the IP source address in the received datagram.

`int OSPF::timeout()`

Returns the number of milliseconds before the next OSPF timer is due to fire. If the system is going to block while waiting for received OSPF protocol packets, this call gives an upper bound to the time that the application could stay blocked. A `0` is returned if timers are waiting to fire. A `-1` is returned if no OSPF application timers are pending.

```
void OSPF::tick()
```
When `OSPF::tick()` is called, the OSPF application will process all its timers that are ready to fire. This routine should be called every time the system updates the running time stored in `sys_etime`. It is not necessary to verify that timers are ready to fire before calling this routine.

```
void OSPF::monitor(struct MonMsg *msg, byte type, int size,
                   int conn_id)
```
Called to request statistical data from the OSPF application, in order to monitor its operation. Calls are made to request global statistics, area statistics, interface statistics and so on, depending on `type` and the format of `msg` (see Chapter 13, Configuration and Monitoring). The size of the request message in bytes is specified as `size`. The monitor connection making the request is identified by `conn_id`. The requested data is returned by the OSPF application in a corresponding call to `OspfSysCalls::monitor_response()`. Requests and their responses can also be matched through the `msg->hdr.id` field.

```
void OSPF::rxigmp(int phyint, InPkt *pkt, int plen)
```
Called when an IGMP packet has been received on the interface with physical interface number `phyint`. The IP header of the IGMP packet is pointed to by `pkt`, and the number of bytes received from the network (including the IP header but excluding any data-link header that has already been stripped) is given in `plen`. As with received OSPF packets, if the receiving interface is unknown, `phyint` should be set to `-1`, telling the OSPF application to infer the receiving interface from the source address in the packet's IP header. IGMP processing performed by the OSPF application is described in Section 12.2. However, if IGMP is implemented within the system kernel, the `OSPF::rxigmp()` entry point can be ignored, and `OSPF::join_indication()` and `OSPF::leave_indication()` can instead be called directly.

```
MCache *OSPF::mclookup(InAddr src, InAddr group)
```
Request for the OSPF application to build and to install a (MOSPF) routing table entry for the source `src` and destination group `group`. The resulting multicast routing table entry is returned (see Figure 4.5) and is also installed in the system's kernel via a call to `OspfSysCalls::add_mcache()`.

```
void OSPF::join_indication(InAddr group, int phyint)
```
Indicates to the OSPF application that one or more members of the multicast group `group` are on the network segment attached to interface `phyint`. This information is commonly learned through the Internet Group Management Protocol (IGMP, [27]) and will be used when originating MOSPF group-membership-LSAs and when constructing multicast routing table entries. If `phyint` is set equal to `-1`, the group is associated with the router as a whole instead of with a specific interface (see Section 5 of [66]).

`void OSPF::leave_indication(InAddr group, int phyint)`
Indicates that there are no longer any members of `group` on the network segment attached to interface `phyint`. As with `OSPF::join()`, this information is learned from IGMP and is used by MOSPF.

`void OSPF::phy_up(int phyint)`
Indicates to the OSPF application that the physical interface `phyint` is now operational—that is, capable of receiving and transmitting network traffic.

`void OSPF::phy_down(int phyint)`
Indicates to the OSPF application that the physical interface `phyint` is no longer operational. OSPF will immediately cease advertising the interface, causing traffic to be promptly rerouted around the failure.

`MPath *OSPF::ip_lookup(InAddr dest)`
Return the current list of next hops to use for packets addressed to `dest`. The next hops in `class MPath` are described in Figure 4.4. If `0` is returned, the destination is currently unreachable.

`InAddr OSPF::ip_source(InAddr dest)`
Find the source address that would be used in packets sent to the given destination `dest`. If possible, this is the IP address assigned to (one of) the interface(s) that would be used to forward packets to the destination.

`InAddr OSPF::if_addr(int phyint)`
Return the IP address associated with a given physical interface `phyint`. If the physical interface is not known to the OSPF application, `0` is returned.

`void OSPF::shutdown(int seconds)`
Requests that the OSPF application undergo its orderly shutdown procedure. This procedure is described in Section 13.10. The length of the shutdown procedure is limited to `seconds`; if at that time, the procedure is not finished, the OSPF application will exit anyway, by calling `OspfSysCalls::halt()`.

`void OSPF::logflush()`
Accumulate the previous calls to `OSPF::log()` into a single logging message, calling `OspfSysCalls::sys_spflog()` to print the resulting logging message.

`rtid_t OSPF::my_id()`
Return the router's OSPF Router ID.

4.4   Porting Considerations

Additional porting considerations involve the representation of OSPF control packets and their individual data fields as they reside in the platform's computer memory system.

4.4.1   Packet Templates

The OSPF code uses the template, or overlay, model for accessing individual data fields within OSPF protocol packets and LSAs. C++ structures are used to describe the format of an individual packet or LSA. For example, the C++ structure **InPkt**, which represents a packet's IP header, has already been displayed (Figure 4.3).

To read or write a packet's contents as it resides in computer memory, one simply casts the address of the packet to be a pointer to the appropriate structure and then reads or writes the structure's members. An example is given in Figure 4.7, where the routine **SpfIfc::finish_pkt()** completes the formatting of the OSPF packet header (**struct SpfPkt**) and IP header before transmitting the OSPF packet onto the network.

IP packet headers, OSPF packet headers, and LSAs have been defined so that they align nicely. However, some compilers will pad structures to optimize memory access, breaking the templates. This can usually be fixed by telling the compiler explicitly to pack (that is, not to pad) the template structures, using compiler-specific directives, such as **PACKED**; see your compiler manual for details.

The structures that we use for template purposes, and therefore that may need to be packed, are those in the files **ospfd/src/lshdr.h**, **ospfd/src/ip.h**, and **ospfd/src/spfpkt.h**. In particular, they are the following structures:

- **struct InPkt**. The standard 20-byte IP packet header.

- **struct SpfPkt**. The standard 24-byte OSPF packet header. This definition is contained in the definitions for the specific OSPF packet types, such as the OSPF Hello packet.

- **struct HloPkt**. The OSPF Hello packet header, including the standard OSPF packet header.

- **struct DDPkt**. The OSPF Database Description packet header, including the standard OSPF packet header.

- **struct UpdPkt**. The OSPF Link State Update packet header, including the standard OSPF packet header.

- **struct LSRef**. One of the (possibly multiple) LSA references in the body of an OSPF Link State Request packet.

---
spfutil.C

```
153 void SpfIfc::finish_pkt(Pkt *pkt, InAddr dst)
154
155 {
156     InPkt *iphdr;
157     SpfPkt *spfpkt;
158     int size;
159
160     pkt->phyint = if_phyint;
161
162     spfpkt = pkt->spfpkt;
163     size = pkt->dptr - (byte *) spfpkt;
164     spfpkt->plen = hton16(size);
165     spfpkt->p_aid = hton32(if_area->id());
166     generate_message(pkt);
167
168     iphdr = pkt->iphdr;
169     // size may have changed in call to SpfIfc::generate_message()
170     size = pkt->dptr - (byte *) iphdr;
171     iphdr->i_len = hton16(size);
172     iphdr->i_id = 0;
173     iphdr->i_ttl = is_virtual() ? DEFAULT_TTL : 1;
174     iphdr->i_src = (if_addr != 0 ? hton32(if_addr) :
                                       hton32(ospf->my_addr()));
175     iphdr->i_dest = hton32(dst);
176     iphdr->i_chksum = 0;
177     iphdr->i_chksum = ~incksum((uns16 *) iphdr, sizeof(*iphdr));
178 }
```

---
spfutil.C

Figure 4.7 An example of packet templates: `SpfIfc::finish_pkt()`.

- **struct LShdr**. The standard 20-byte OSPF LSA header. This structure is *not* included in the templates for the specific LSA types.

- **struct RTRhdr**. The header of the OSPF router-LSA, immediately following the standard OSPF LSA header.

- **struct RtrLink**. A link description in the body of a router-LSA.

- **struct TOSmetric**. A metric description for a nonzero TOS value, in a router-LSA, summary-LSA, or ASBR-summary-LSA.

- **struct NetLShdr**. The header of the OSPF network-LSA, immediately following the standard OSPF LSA header.

- **struct SummHdr**. The header of the summary-LSA or ASBR-summary-LSA, immediately following the standard OSPF LSA header.

- **struct ASEhdr.** The header of the AS-external-LSA, immediately following the standard OSPF LSA header.

- **struct GMref.** An LSA reference in the body of a group-membership-LSA.

The template method can be used for most, but not all, computer architectures. When templates cannot be used, the parts of the OSPF code that read and write OSPF protocol packets (that is, read or write accesses to the template structures) must be replaced with other machine-dependent primitives that read and write 1-, 2-, and 4-byte quantities at given packet offsets.

4.4.2 Byte Swap

The processing of multibyte integer (signed or unsigned) quantities, such as a 4-byte integer, in OSPF packets and LSAs depends on the machine's native byte order. Computer memory is typically byte addressed. However, the representation of multiple-byte integer data types in computer memory depends on the processor architecture. We call these "machine byte orders." Two common machine byte orders are shown in Figure 4.8, depicting representations of the signed 32-bit integer 0x80000001, every OSPF LSA's initial LS Sequence Number.

The little-endian architecture puts the least-significant part of the integer data in the lowest addressed (or little-end) byte. Examples of little-endian architectures are the Intel x86 processors, including the Pentium processors. The other common machine byte order is called big-endian; processors from Motorola, such as the PowerPC, are examples of this architecture. In big-endian machines, the least-significant part of the integer data is always in the highest addressed byte.

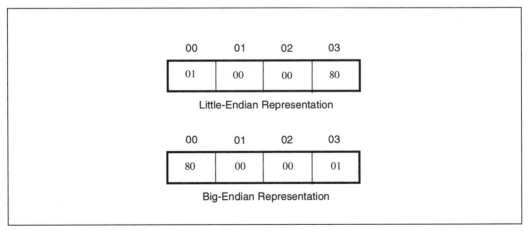

Figure 4.8 Little-endian versus big-endian architectures.

Network packets, including OSPF control packets, are always transmitted and read into computer memory in what is called network byte order, regardless of the computer architecture. Network byte order is equivalent to the big-endian representation: The least-significant part of the multiple-byte integer quantity is always in the highest addressed byte. If the machine byte order is anything but big-endian, the multiple-byte integer fields in a network packet must be converted into machine byte order before they can be further processed by a computer program. This is accomplished in the `ospfd` application code through the use of the following machine-dependent routines, which must be supplied in the file `machdep.h`:

- `uns32 ntoh32(uns32)`. Convert a 32-bit (4-byte) integer field in a packet template to host (machine) byte order.

- `uns16 ntoh16(uns16)`. Convert a 16-bit (2-byte) integer field in a packet template to host (machine) byte order.

The reverse process must be followed when writing a machine byte order integer into a 2- or 4-byte packet field for transmission onto the network. As an example, the OSPF packet size, Area ID, and source and destination addresses are converted into network byte in Figure 4.7 in preparation for transmitting the OSPF packet onto the network. The machine byte order–to–network byte order routines must also be defined in `machdep.h`.

- `uns32 hton32(uns32)`. Convert a host (machine) byte order integer into a 32-bit (4-byte) field in a packet template.

- `uns16 hton16(uns16)`. Convert a host (machine) byte order integer into a 16-bit (2-byte) field in a packet template.

A common source of bugs in many networking applications derives from the programmer's losing track of whether an integer is in machine byte order or network byte order. In the `ospfd` code, we circumvent this problem by using the following convention: Multiple-byte integers within packet and LSA templates (enumerated in Section 4.4.1) are always in network byte order, whereas all other multiple-byte integers are in machine byte order.

5

Building Blocks

In this chapter, we examine some of the basic utility classes on which the OSPF implementation is built. These classes are presented in UNIX man page format, and concentrate on the classes' functionality and programming interface. The goal is to give you enough familiarity with the classes so that when you encounter them in the source code, you will understand their use. (This chapter could be skipped on first reading and referred back to when an understanding of certain utilities becomes necessary.)

Most of these utility classes are not specific to OSPF and could be used in other applications. For example, there are several utilities for generic sorting and searching. However, each man page has a usage section that explains how the particular utility has been used in the OSPF implementation. Man pages for the OSPF applications themselves can be found in Appendix A.

NAME

class AVLitem, class AVLtree—Balanced AVL trees for generic sorting and searching on fixed-length keys

SYNOPSIS

```
#include "machdep.h"
#include "avl.h"

item = new AVLitem(uns32 index1, uns32 index2);
uns32 AVLitem::index1();
uns32 AVLitem::index2();
int AVLitem::valid();
void AVLitem::ref();
void AVLitem::deref();
bool AVLitem::not_referenced();
void AVLitem::chkref();

avltree = new AVLtree();
void AVLtree::add(AVLitem *item);
AVLitem *AVLtree::find(uns32 key1, uns32 key2=0);
AVLitem *AVLtree::previous(uns32 key1, uns32 key2=0);
void AVLtree::remove(AVLitem *item);
void AVLtree::clear();
int AVLtree::size();

iter = new AVLsearch(AVLtree *avltree);
void AVLsearch::seek(uns32 key1, uns32 key2);
void AVLsearch::seek(AVLitem *seekpoint);
AVLitem *AVLsearch::next();
```

DESCRIPTION

AVL, or balanced binary trees, are a good generic data structure for sorting and searching for items having fixed-length, relatively short keys. The routines implement AVL trees for items having two 32-bit unsigned keys: **index1** and **index2**. The **index1** key is the more significant; when the keys of two items are compared, the **index2** keys are examined only if the two items have identical **index1** keys.

To organize items into an AVL tree (**class AVLtree**), the items must inherit from the base **class AVLitem**. When items are constructed, their two AVL keys, **index1** and **index2**, must be specified. At any time, these keys can be retrieved by using

`AVLitem::index1()` and `AVLitem::index2()`. An item is then added to an AVL tree by using `AVLtree::add()`.

Knowing its keys, `AVLtree::find()` can be used to find an item in an AVL tree. Items are deleted from a tree by using `AVLtree::remove()`.

`AVLtree::clear()` removes all items from the tree. The number of items currently in an AVL tree can be determined by using `AVLtree::size()`.

The `AVLsearch` class implements a depth-first search of the AVL tree. Items are returned in increasing order of the keys `[index1, index2]`. For example, the following items would be returned in order: [1,100], [10, 10], [100, 2]. When constructing `class AVLsearch`, you specify the `AVLtree` you wish to search. The first call to `AVLsearch::next()` then gives you the tree item having the smallest key; the next call, the item having the second smallest key, and so on. A return of `0` indicates that the end of the tree has been reached. You can also skip into the tree by using `AVLsearch::seek()`, in which case the next call to `AVLsearch::next()` will yield the tree item whose key immediately follows `[key1, key2]` or immediately follows **seek-point**, depending on the variant of `AVLsearch::seek()` used.

Reference Counts

You can determine whether an item is currently on an AVL tree by using `AVLitem::valid()`; a return of **true** indicates that the item is currently on a tree. Each `AVLitem` also has a reference count field, which an application can use to track the number of times an item is referenced (that is, a pointer to the item is stored in another data structure). When an item is constructed, its reference count is set to `0`. An application can increment an item's reference count by calling `AVLitem::ref()` and can decrement the reference count by calling `AVLitem::deref()`. You can tell whether an item is no longer referenced (that is, whether an item has a reference count of `0`) by calling `AVLitem::not_referenced()`;

An AVL item can be safely freed (that is, returned to the heap via a call to **delete** `AVLitem`) when it is both no longer referenced and no longer contained on an AVL tree. This determination, including the **delete** action, is made by the `AVLitem::chkref()` method. An `AVLitem` is automatically freed when its reference count is decremented to `0` (in `AVLitem::deref()`) and it is no longer contained on an AVL tree.

USAGE

The AVL tree is the most common way of organizing data within the **ospfd** software. For example, the following items are organized as AVL trees:

- *The link-state database.* Each of the separate LSA types is organized as its own LSA tree, with `index1` set to the LSA's Link State ID and `index2` the LSA's Advertising Router. The items on the trees are superclasses of the base `class LSA`.

- *The routing table.* The routing table is a modified AVL tree, with prefix pointers added to optimize the best-match operation. Items on the routing table are superclasses of the base `class RTE`, with `index1` set to the routing table entry's network number and `index2` set to the entry's network mask.

- *An area's configured aggregates.* These are represented as instances of `class Range`, added to the AVL tree `SpfArea::ranges`; `index1` is set to the aggregate's network number, and `index2` is the aggregate's mask.

- *An area's configured host addresses.* These are represented as instances of `class HostAddr`, added to the AVL tree `SpfArea::hosts`; `index1` and `index2` indicate the prefix to advertise as a host address, in address and mask form.

- *The database of physical interfaces.* Instances of `class PhyInt` are organized into the AVL tree `OSPF::phyints`, with `index1` set to the physical interface number (`phyint`) and `index2` set to `0`.

REFERENCES

A good discussion of AVL trees can be found in Chapter 6 of [46].

NAME

class **PatEntry**, class **PatTree**—Patricia trees for sorting and searching on long variable-length keys, such as text strings

SYNOPSIS

```
#include "machdep.h"
#include "pat.h"

class PatEntry;
byte *PatEntry::key;
int PatEntry::keylen;

pattree = new PatTree;
void PatTree::add(PatEntry *item);
void PatTree::remove(PatEntry *item);
PatEntry *PatTree::find(byte *key, int keylen);
PatEntry *PatTree::find(char *key);
```

DESCRIPTION

Patricia trees are a useful data structure for sorting items with long keys, typically text strings. They are variants of radix trees, which consume less memory by allowing keys to be stored in internal nodes and leaves. Worst case, the number of comparisons, each one a bit compare, is equal to the length in bits of the key; in practice, however, the number of comparisons is usually much smaller.

To install items on a Patricia tree (class **PatTree**), the items must inherit from the base class **PatEntry**. Then **PatEntry::key** is set to point to the item's key, with **PatEntry::keylen** set equal to the key's length in bytes. **PatTree::add()** is then called to add the item to the tree. **PatTree:remove()** removes an item from the Patricia tree.

To find an item in a Patricia tree knowing only its key, **PatTree::find()** is used. The variant **PatTree::find(char *key)** can be used if you are using null-terminated ASCII strings as keys.

USAGE

The multipath database **MPath::nhdb** is organized as a Patricia tree. The items in this database are instances of **class MPath**, and the key is the array of next-hop structures (**MPath::NHs[]**) in each multipath entry. This usage is somewhat sloppy, working only because the compiler packs the next-hop structures.

The database of physical interfaces in the Linux port of **ospfd** (**LinuxOspfd::phyints**) is also a Patricia tree. Each item is represented as a **class BSDPhyInt**, and the keys are the interface names, such as **"eth0"**.

The number of items currently in a Patricia tree can be read from **PatTree::size**.

NOTES

See Chapter 17 of [98] for a good discussion of the Patricia algorithm.

NAME

class PriQElt, class PriQ—Priority queues to efficiently sort data elements, based on smallest key

SYNOPSIS

```
#include "machdep.h"
#include "priq.h"

class PriQElt;
uns32 PriQElt::cost0;
uns16 PriQElt::cost1;
byte PriQElt::tie1;
uns32 PriQElt::tie2;

queue = new PriQ();
PriQElt *PriQ::priq_gethead();
PriQElt *PriQ::priq_rmhead();
void PriQ::priq_add(PriQElt *item);
void PriQ::priq_delete(PriQElt *item);
```

DESCRIPTION

Priority queues allow you to organize a collection of elements such that the element having the smallest cost is always at the head of the queue. All operations on priority queues, such as adding an element, removing the least-cost element, or changing the cost of an existing element, are of $O(\log(n))$ expense, where n is the number of elements in the queue.

To organize a collection of data structures into a priority queue, the data structure must inherit from class PriQElt. The cost associated with the data structure can be thought of as the two-component cost [cost0, cost1], where cost0 is the most-significant part of the cost and cost1 the least significant. Given multiple items having the same cost, the data structure's tiebreakers [tie1, tie2] are examined, with the data structures having the *larger* tiebreakers being promoted toward the head of the queue. The priority queue itself is implemented as class PriQ.

The most common operations on a priority queue are to add elements and to remove the least-cost element. To add a data structure item to a priority queue, you first set the two components of the data structure's cost and their tiebreakers and then call PriQ::priq_add(). To remove the least-cost data structure from the queue, PriQ::priq_rmhead() is used. You can also access the least-cost element without removing it with `PriQ::priq_gethead()`. `PriQ::priq_delete()` removes a particular `item` from the priority queue, not necessarily the one with the least cost.

To change the cost of an item currently on the priority queue, you must remove the item from the queue, update the item's two cost components and tiebreakers, and then add the item back to the priority queue.

USAGE

The Dijkstra algorithm's candidate list is implemented by a priority queue. In this case, the data structures on the priority queue are instances of `class TNode`, the base class for router-LSAs and network-LSAs. The cost and tiebreakers for the items on the priority queue are set as `cost0`, the current path cost from the calculating node to the router-LSA or network-LSA; `cost1`, always 0; `tie1`, the LSA's LS Type; and `tie2`, the LSA's Link State ID. The setting of `tie1` ensures that all equal-cost paths are found, and the settings of `tie1` and `tie2` together implement the MOSPF tiebreaking scheme.

The timer queue is also implemented as a priority queue, this time containing superclasses of the base `class Timer`. The costs and tiebreakers in this case are set as `cost0`, the seconds part of the elapsed time until the timer is scheduled to fire; `cost1`, the milliseconds part; and the tiebreakers, unused (that is, left set to `0`).

NOTES

For a good discussion of priority queues, see Chapter 5 of [46].

NAME

class Timer, class ITimer—Single-shot and interval timers

SYNOPSIS

```
void Timer::start(int milliseconds, bool randomize=true);
void Timer::restart(int millseconds=0);
void Timer::stop();
int Timer::is_running();
virtual void Timer::action() = 0;

class ITimer : public Timer;
void ITimer::start(int milliseconds, bool randomize=true);
```

DESCRIPTION

These classes implement timer support in the OSPF implementation. To create a timer, you create a superclass of either **class Timer** (for timers that fire only once, the so-called single-shot timers) or **class ITimer** (for timers that fire periodically until they are explicitly stopped). Your class must provide an **action()** method that implements the logic that should be executed when, if ever, the timer expires. When a timer is created, it is in the stopped state.

Built on top of the base **class Timer, class ITimer** implements a separate **start()** method but otherwise inherits the methods, such as **stop()**, from the base class.

To start a timer, its **start()** method is called. The **milliseconds** argument specifies the length of the timer in milliseconds. If **randomize** is **true**, the length will be randomized. For single-shot timers, the length will then fall randomly in the interval plus or minus one-half second from the specified milliseconds. Single-shot timers specifying a length of 1 second or less are never randomized. When an interval timer is randomized, the first interval is set randomly between **0** and **milliseconds**, and successive intervals are always equal to **milliseconds** exactly. If an amount of time equal to the timer's length expires before the timer is either stopped or restarted, the timer is said to expire, and its **action()** method is called. Expired single-shot timers go into stopped state, whereas expired interval timers are always restarted unrandomized and with an interval of **milliseconds**. An attempt to start an already running timer is ignored.

You can tell whether a timer is currently running by calling **Timer::is_running()**. You can reset a running timer's interval by calling **Timer::restart()**. The timer will now fire **milliseconds** into the future, assuming no calls to **restart()** or **stop()** intervene. If **milliseconds** is set to **0**, the new interval will be taken from the argument initially provided to `start()`; in any case, the randomization directive is taken from the one specified when the timer was started. An attempt to restart a stopped timer is ignored.

A running timer is stopped by calling `Timer::stop()`. This prevents the timer's `action()` method from being called.

USAGE

The following single-shot timers are used within the `ospfd` implementation:

- `class ExitOverflowTimer`. Used to exit the database overflow state after a configured period of time.

- `class LocalOrigTimer`. Rate-limits the origination of AS-external-LSAs.

- `class WaitTimer`. Delays the Designated Router calculation on an interface until the existing Backup Designated Router (if any) is discovered.

- `class DAckTimer`. Delays the multicasting of a Link State Acknowledgment packet out an interface.

- `class InactTimer`. Firing indicates that a neighbor should be declared inoperational, due to lack of Hello packets received from the neighbor.

- `class HoldTimer`. Used to hold the final Database Description packet sent in slave mode until it seems likely that the master has received it.

- `class LsaRxmtTimer`. Firing causes the retransmission of LSAs to the neighbor, implementing the flooding algorithm's reliability scheme.

- `class ProgressTimer`. Firing indicates that the Database Exchange process with a neighbor is stuck and that we should restart it sometime in the future.

The following interval timers are used in the `ospfd` implementation:

- `class DBageTimer`. Fires every second to perform link-state database aging and other housekeeping, including running the full routing calculations when necessary.

- `class HelloTimer`. Periodically sends OSPF Hello packets out an interface.

- `class NbrHelloTimer`. Periodically sends Hellos to a neighboring OSPF router over a nonbroadcast interface.

- `class DDRxmtTimer`. Firing causes the master to retransmit the last Database Description packet it has sent.

- `class RqRxmtTimer`. Firing causes retransmission of Link State Requests to a neighbor.

IMPLEMENTATION

The timer queue is implemented as the priority queue `PriQ timerq`. It is up to the system interface to periodically call `OSPF::tick()`, which scans the timer queue, removing those timers that have expired and calling their `action()` methods.

NAME

class **AreaIterator,** class **IfcIterator,** class **NbrIterator,** class **KeyIterator**—Iterators for scanning the major OSPF data types

SYNOPSIS

```
aiter = new AreaIterator(OSPF *ospf);
SpfArea *AreaIterator::get_next();

iiter = new IfcIterator(class OSPF *ospf);
iiter = new IfcIterator(SpfArea *ap);
SpfIfc *IfcIterator::get_next();
void IfcIterator::reset();

niter = new NbrIterator(SpfIfc *ip);
SpfNbr *NbrIterator::get_next();
void NbrIterator::reset();

keyiter = new KeyIterator(SpfIfc *ip);
CryptK *KeyIterator::get_next();
```

DESCRIPTION

The iterator classes are used to scan through instances of a particular class. Each iterator has a **get_next**() method, which returns the next class instance until all instances are exhausted, in which case **0** is returned. Class instances are returned in no particular order; in particular, the iterators are not useful for MIB operations requiring lexicographic sorting. Some iterators have a **reset**() method, which restarts the class instance scanning from the beginning.

The **AreaIterator** class yields all the router's attached OSPF area data structures, each a **class SpfArea**. A pointer to the top-level **OSPF** class is given to the constructor.

The **IfcIterator** class yields either all the router's interfaces or all the router's interfaces attaching to a particular area, depending on whether the top-level **OSPF** class or a specific **SpfArea** class is given to the constructor.

The **NbrIterator** class yields all the neighbors associated with the interface **ip** given to the constructor.

The **KeyIterator** class yields all the OSPF cryptographic keys configured for the interface **ip** given to the constructor.

USAGE

Iterators are used throughout the OSPF implementation. For example, the routing calculation uses the **AreaIterator** class to run the Dijkstra algorithm over all areas simultaneously. The **IfcIterator** and **NbrIterator** classes are used by the flooding algorithm. The **KeyIterator** class is used when verifying and generating MD5 message digests on those interfaces configured for OSPF cryptographic authentication.

NOTES

If you want to search the data structures in lexicographic order, use the routines **SpfArea *OSPF::NextArea()** for areas, **SpfIfc *OSPF::next_ifc()** for (nonvirtual) interfaces, **SpfIfc *OSPF::next_vl()** for virtual links, **SpfNbr *OSPF::next_nbr()** for neighbors, and **LSA *OSPF::NextLSA()** for LSAs in the router's link-state database. These routines are used by the **ospfd** monitoring interface.

NAME

class **INtbl**, class **INrte**, class **INiterator**—The IP routing table and individual routing table entries

SYNOPSIS

```
#include "ospfinc.h"

inrttbl = new INtbl;
INrte *INtbl::add(uns32 net, uns32 mask);
INrte *INtbl::find(uns32 net, uns32 mask);
INrte *INtbl::best_match(uns32 dest);

uns32 INrte::net();
uns32 INrte::mask();
uns32 INrte::broadcast_address();
INrte *INrte::prefix();
int INrte::is_range();
int INrte::is_child(INrte *oentry);
int INrte::within_range();
void INrte::sys_install();

int RTE::valid();
byte RTE::type();
int RTE::intra_area();
int RTE::inter_area();
int RTE::intra_AS();
aid_t RTE::area();
SpfIfc *RTE::ifc();
void RTE::set_origin(LSA *V);
LSA *RTE::get_origin();
void RTE::save_state();
bool RTE::state_changed();
void RTE::set_area(aid_t);
void RTE::update(MPath *newnh);
void RTE::declare_unreachable();

iter = new INiterator(INtbl *inrttbl);
INrte *INiterator::nextrte();
```

DESCRIPTION

The IP routing table is implemented by **class INtbl**. Individual routing table entries are instances of **class INrte**, which inherits from the base **class RTE**. The IP routing table can be scanned by using the iterator **class INiterator**. The IP routing table stores and returns IP addresses, network numbers, and masks in machine byte order.

INtbl::add() adds to the IP routing table an entry whose prefix is specified by **net** and **mask**. If the entry exists in the routing table, it is simply returned. Otherwise, a new entry is allocated, and its state is set to unreachable. Routing table entries are located in the routing table using **INtbl::find()**, again specifying the prefix by net and mask. The IP routing table lookup, which would be used when forwarding data packets, is implemented in **INtbl::best_match()**. This returns the most-specific routing table entry that both matches the destination IP address **dest** and is currently reachable. If no reachable match is found, **0** is returned.

The routing table can be scanned by using the iterator **class INiterator**. The class is constructed by specifying the IP routing table **inrttbl** that is to be scanned. Successive calls to **INiterator::nextrte()** then return the individual routing table entries in the selected table, in increasing order of net and then mask. For example, the iterator would return elements in this order: 10/8, 10.1/16, 10.1/24, 10.2/16.

Routing Table Entries

Individual routing table entries are instances of **class INrte**, which is built on top of the base **class RTE**. An entry's network number and mask are returned by **INrte::net()** and **INrte::mask()**, respectively. The broadcast address used by the entry's network is returned by **INrte::broadcast_address()**.

Among the routing table entries that properly contain a particular entry, **INrte::prefix()** returns the most specific. **INrte::is_child(INrte *oentry)** returns **true** if and only if the entry is contained in **oentry**; the trivial case of **entry->is_child(entry)** does return **true**.

INrte::is_range() returns **true** if the entry's prefix has been configured to aggregate routing information for one or more attached areas. **INrte::within_range()** returns **true** if the entry is to be aggregated when advertised to other areas.

INrte::sys_install() installs the routing table entry's forwarding information into the system's kernel forwarding table.

RTE::valid() returns **true** if the entry is reachable and **false** otherwise.

RTE::type() classifies the route as one of **RT_DIRECT** (directly attached subnet), **RT_SPF** (intra-area), **RT_SPFIA** (inter-area), **RT_EXTT1** (external, type-1 metric), **RT_EXTT2** (external, type-2 metric), **RT_REJECT** (discard matching packets), **RT_STATIC** (external route imported by the router itself), and **RT_NONE** (unreachable). Unreachable entries are ignored during the routing table lookup **INtbl::best_match()**. Packets matching an entry of type **RT_REJECT** must be discarded to avoid possible packet loops caused by address aggregation. Intra-area routes, inter-area routes, and intra-AS routes (covering both intra- and inter-area) can also be detected by using **INrte::intra_area()**, **INrte::inter_area()**, and **INrte::intra_AS()**, respectively. The area with which an intra-AS route is associated is returned by **INrte::area()**.

The routing table entry's next hops can be referenced as **MPath *INrte::r_mpath**. The first of possibly multiple outgoing interfaces to use in forwarding matching packets is given by **INrte::ifc()**. Both of these will read **0** for unreachable and reject/discard entries.

The following methods are used to update the information in a routing table entry. The LSA that has caused the routing table entry to be created/updated is set with **INrte::set_origin()** and is read with **INrte::get_origin()**. The current routing/forwarding state of the entry can be saved with **INrte::save_state()**. The method **INrte::state_changed()** returns **true** if the state of the routing table has changed since the last time the state was saved. State changes may indicate that LSAs need to be (re)originated or that further routing calculations are required. **INrte::set_area()** changes the area associated with the route. **INrte::update()** sets the next hop(s) used to forward matching data packets. **INrte::declare_unreachable()** is used to set the routing table entry's state to unreachable.

USAGE

The current cost of a routing table entry is stored in **INrte::cost**. If the entry is of type "external route with type-2 metric," the external type-2 metric is stored in **INrte::t2cost**, whereas **INrte::cost** reflects the (less significant) internal cost to the route's forwarding address/advertising router.

The summary-LSAs advertising a particular prefix are chained together in that prefix's routing table entry as **INrte::summs**. To find one of these that the calculating router itself originated, **INrte::my_summary_lsa()** is used; this LSA is used to remember the Link State ID that we are currently using to advertise the prefix in summary-LSAs. To go through the summary-LSAs to see which, if any, should modify the forwarding information, the routines **INrte::run_inter_area()**, **INrte::incremental_summary()** (when modifying a single routing table entry in isolation), and **RTE::run_transit_areas()** (for the transit area adjustment required by areas with OSPF virtual links) are run.

The situation for AS-external-LSAs is similar. They are chained in **INrte::ases**, the AS-external-LSA (if any) that the router has originated for the prefix is found by **INrte::my_ase_lsa()**, and the external routing calculation for a prefix is implemented by **INrte::run_external()**.

The fact that a routing table entry has been changed during the routing table calculation can be stored in **RTE::changed**, so that it can be acted on at the completion of the calculation. This is used for certain gross changes that are not caught by the **INrte::save_state()** mechanism. **RTE::dijk_run** serves as a sort of parity check so that you can determine whether a particular entry has been touched by the full routing table calculation; if not, the entry is declared unreachable at the calculation's completion.

Data structures representing routers belonging to the calculating router's attached areas (**class RTRrte**), AS boundary routers (**class ASBRrte**), and forwarding addresses used in AS-external-LSAs (**class FWDrte**) are also built on top of the base **class RTE**. The database of forwarding addresses is implemented as **class FWDtbl**, which is built on **class INtbl**.

IMPLEMENTATION

The IP routing table is implemented as an AVL tree. Each routing table entry is indexed in the tree by its net and mask. In addition, each entry in the tree has a pointer to the immediately containing entry (less-specific match) to make the best-match calculation easy and fast.

Routing information is stored in the system kernel, using the system interface method **OspfSysCalls::rtadd()**. Routes are deleted from the kernel by using **OspfSysCalls::rtdel()**.

NOTES

Noncontiguous subnet masks are not supported. To avoid confusion, it probably would have been better to organize the routing table by prefix and length.

SEE ALSO

The man page for the multipath **class MPath**.

NAME

struct **NH**, class **MPath**—OSPF next-hop structure and the database of equal-cost paths

SYNOPSIS

```
#include "ospfinc.h"

struct NH;
class MPath;
static MPath *MPath::create(int npaths, NH *nharray);
static MPath *MPath::create(SpfIfc *ip, InAddr gw);
static MPath *MPath::create(int phyint, InAddr gw);
static MPath *MPath::merge(MPath *entry1, MPath *entry2);
static MPath *MPath::addgw(MPath *entry, InAddr gw);
bool MPath::all_in_area(class SpfArea *ap);
```

DESCRIPTION

The **NH** structure describes a routing table entry's next hop. When a routing table entry has multiple next hops, due to the equal-cost multipath logic, they are grouped into a multipath **class MPath**. These multipath classes are contained in a database so that if multiple routing table entries have the same set of next hops, they simply point to a single **MPath** class in the multipath database. Routines are provided to modify the contents of the multipath database.

The **NH** structure has the following fields: **NH::o_ifp**, the OSPF interface out which matching packets are forwarded; **NH::phyint**, the outgoing interface's physical interface number; and **NH::gw**, the IP address of the next-hop router. The **NH** structure for a directly connected network segment, which doesn't have a next-hop router, has **NH::gw** set to 0.0.0.0.

```
struct NH {
    SpfIfc *o_ifp;
    int phyint;
    InAddr gw;
};
```

Methods

MPath::create(int npaths, NH *nharray) creates a multipath entry from the first **npaths** next-hop structures in **nharray**; **MPath::create(SpfIfc *ip, InAddr gw)**

creates a multipath entry, with a single hop having outgoing interface `ip` and next-hop router `gw`; and `MPath::create(int phyint, InAddr gw)` creates a multipath entry, with a single hop specifying an outgoing physical interface of `phyint` and next-hop router `gw`. In all three cases, the multipath entry created is added to the multipath database, and a pointer to the new entry is returned. If the entry already existed in the database, a pointer to the existing entry is simply returned.

`MPath::merge(MPath *entry1, MPath *entry2)` creates a new element in the multipath database by merging the next hops found in the two existing elements `entry1` and `entry2`.

`MPath::addgw(MPath *oentry, InAddr gw)` creates a new multipath entry from the existing `oentry`. For any next hops in `oentry` that attach directly to the network segment containing the IP address `gw`, the new entry substitutes a next hop with router address `gw`. If instead `oentry` contains a next hop with router address on the same segment as the IP address `gw`, the new entry adds a next hop with router address `gw`.

The method `bool MPath::all_in_area(class SpfArea *ap)` returns `true` if all the next hops in the multipath entry belong to OSPF area `ap`.

USAGE

Multipath entries are created with `MPath::create()` during the routing table calculation (files `asbrlsa.C`, `asexlsa.C`, `spfcalc.C`, and `summlsa.C`) or when external routes are imported into OSPF (file `asexlsa.C`). `MPath::merge()` is used whenever the newly discovered path is of equal cost to the previously discovered best path(s).

`MPath::addgw()` is used when calculating the next hop for routers or forwarding addresses that are attached to one of the calculating router's local broadcast or NBMA network segments. See the routines `TNode::add_next_hop()` and `FWDrte::resolve()`, respectively.

`MPath::all_in_area()` is used to implement the split-horizon logic for summary-LSA generation; see `SpfArea::sl_cost()` in file `summlsa.C`.

The next-hop information in a multipath entry is accessed by `int MPath::npaths`, which gives the number of next hops in the entry, and `NH *MPath::NHs[]`, which allows access to the individual next hops.

NOTES

Both `struct NH` and `class MPath` are defined in `ospfd/src/rte.h`. The `MPath` database routines are implemented in `ospfd/src/rte.C`.

See Section 4.2 for a description of how physical interfaces are assigned numbers. The number of equal-cost paths in a multipath entry is limited to `MAXPATH = 4`.

NAME

struct `Pkt`—The OSPF packet descriptor

SYNOPSIS

```
#include "ospfinc.h"

pkt = new Pkt(int rcvint, InPkt *inpkt);
pkt = new Pkt;
int OSPF::ospf_getpkt(Pkt *pkt, int type, uns16 size);
void SpfIfc::finish_pkt(Pkt *pkt, InAddr dst);
bool Pkt::partial_checksum();
void OSPF::ospf_freepkt(Pkt *pkt);
```

DESCRIPTION

The `Pkt` structure describes a packet that is currently being processed by OSPF. This packet may be one that was received on an interface or one that is being built and will be later sent out an interface. The packet is kept in a memory region called the *packet buffer,* and the `Pkt` structure describes properties of this packet buffer and the IP and OSPF packet contained within.

```
struct Pkt {
    InPkt *iphdr;
    int phyint;
    bool llmult;
    bool hold;
    bool xsummed;
    SpfPkt *spfpkt;
    byte *end;
    int bsize;
    byte *dptr;
    uns16 body_xsum;

    Pkt();
    Pkt(int phy, InPkt *inpkt);
    bool partial_checksum();
};
```

The following fields describe the organization of data in the packet buffer. `Pkt::iphdr` points to the packet's IP header, `Pkt::spfpkt` the OSPF packet header, and `Pkt::end` the end of the packet buffer (which may be beyond the end of the IP and

OSPF packets). `Pkt::bsize` is the number of bytes that follow the IP header in the packet buffer; this is the maximum size of an OSPF packet that can be built in the buffer. `Pkt::dptr` is a pointer to where packet processing is currently taking place. For example, when adding LSAs to a Link State Update packet, `Pkt::dptr` points to where the next LSA should be copied into the Update packet.

A packet buffer is associated with a `Pkt` structure if and only if `Pkt::iphdr` is non-zero.

The following fields describe a received IP/OSPF packet that is contained in the packet buffer. `Pkt::phyint` indicates the physical interface that the packet was received on; it is set to `-1` if the receiving interface is unknown. `Pkt::llmult` indicates whether the packet was received as a data-link multicast/broadcast.

The following fields describe an IP/OSPF packet that will be sent out one or more of the router's interfaces. `Pkt::hold` indicates whether the packet buffer should be kept rather than freed after packet transmission. This would be the case for Database Description packets, which must be retransmitted until acknowledged. `Pkt::xsummed` indicates whether a partial OSPF packet checksum has been performed over the body of the OSPF packet; if so, this partial checksum is stored in `Pkt::body_xsum`.

Methods

The method `new Pkt(int rcvint, InPkt *inpkt)` creates a `Pkt` structure to describe an IP packet `inpkt` that has been received on physical interface `rcvint`.

`OSPF::ospf_getpkt(Pkt *pkt, int type, uns16 size)` allocates a transmit packet buffer that will be described by `pkt`; `type` indicates the OSPF packet type to be transmitted; `size`, the maximum size of the enclosing IP packet. The routine returns the size requested or `0` if the transmit buffer could not be allocated.

`SpfIfc::finish_pkt(Pkt *pkt, InAddr dst)` completes the building of an OSPF packet whose IP destination is `dst`. This completion processing includes MD5 message digest calculation (if configured for the interface) and the building of the packet's IP header.

`Pkt::partial_checksum()` calculates and stores a partial checksum of the body of the described OSPF packet. It returns `false` if no packet buffer is associated.

`OSPF::ospf_freepkt(Pkt *pkt)` frees the packet buffer associated with `pkt`, unless `pkt->hold` is `true`.

NOTES

See Section 4.2 for a description of how physical interfaces are assigned numbers.

To allocate and free the memory for the packet buffer, the respective system interface methods `OspfSysCalls::getpkt()` and `OspfSysCalls::freepkt()` are called. Default allocation consists of a `new` of a `byte` array whose size is equal to the IP packet's.

NAME

`OSPF::spflog()`, `OSPF::log()` —Print OSPF logging messages

SYNOPSIS

```
#include "ospfinc.h"
#include "spflog.h"

bool OSPF::spflog(int msgno, int level);
char *msgtext(int msgno);
void OSPF::log(int value);
void OSPF::log(char *string);
void OSPF::log(Pkt *pdesc);
void log(InPkt *iphdr);
void OSPF::log(class LShdr *lshdr);
void OSPF::log(class SpfArea *ap);
void OSPF::log(class SpfIfc *ip);
void OSPF::log(class SpfNbr *np);
void OSPF::log(InAddr *addr);
void OSPF::log(class LSA *lsap);
void OSPF::log(class INrte *rte);
void OSPF::logflush();
```

DESCRIPTION

These routines log OSPF diagnostic and tracing messages. Messages are identified by a message number `msgno`. Given a message number and a display `level` between 1 and 5, `OSPF::spflog()` attempts to log a message. The higher the display level, the more likely that the message will be displayed. `OSPF::spflog()` returns `true` if the message is being logged based on the current configuration of the logging filters. If `true` is returned, the logging message is constructed by first including a text description of the message given by `msgtext()`;

Each logging message is displayed in a single line. Additional data can be added to the logging message by using the `OSPF::log()` routines. `OSPF::log(int value)` appends the integer `value` in base 10 to the message. To append a character string to the message, `OSPF::log(char *string)` is used. `OSPF::log(Pkt *)` appends an OSPF packet's type, source, and destination to the message; `void log(InPkt *iphdr)` appends an IP packet's source and destination addresses to the message. `OSPF::log(LShdr *)` and `OSPF::log(LSA *)` append a description of an LSA to the message; LSAs are described by their LS Type, Link State ID, and Advertising Router. `OSPF::log(SpfArea *)`, `OSPF::log(SpfIfc *)`, and `OSPF::log(SpfNbr *)` append descriptions of OSPF areas, interfaces, and neighbors (respectively) to the message. `OSPF::log(InAddr *)` appends an IP address in dotted decimal notation to the message. `OSPF::log(INrte *)` appends an IP routing table entry's prefix, type, and cost to the message.

A message is deemed complete and given to the output device when either `OSPF::spflog()` is called again or `OSPF::logflush()` is invoked.

An example of the logging message produced is the following message announcing the transition of a neighbor to full adjacency:

```
Nbr FSM Full<-Exchange event ExchangeDone Nbr 10.0.0.3 Ifc Nl1
```

USAGE

Message numbers are declared in the file `ospfd/src/spflog.h`. By convention, configuration notifications start at 1, error messages at 100, and informational messages at 200.

Configurable logging filters determine whether a message identified by `msgno` will be logged at the `level` specified in `spflog()`. If `disabled_msgno[msgno]` is `true`, the message will not be logged. If `enabled_msgno[msgno]` is `true`, the message will be logged. Otherwise, the determination of whether to log a message is based solely on `level`, which must be greater than or equal to `OSPF::base_priority` for the message to be logged.

Where the messages are displayed is system-dependent. Messages are displayed by using the `OspfSysCalls::sys_spflog()` routine. The `ospfd` Linux port prints them to the file `/var/log/ospfd.log`. The OSPF routing simulator `ospf_sim` gathers together the logging messages from all the simulated routers and displays them on standard output, prefixed by simulated time and the Router ID of the simulated router producing the message.

NAME

fletcher(), incksum(), MD5Init(), MD5Update(), MD5Final()—OSI (open systems interconnection), Internet, and message digest checksum calculations

SYNOPSIS

```
#include "machdep.h"
#include "spfutil.h"
#include "contrib/md5.h"

uns16 fletcher(byte *message, int mlen, int offset);
uns16 incksum(uns16 *message, int mlen, uns16 seed=0);
extern "C" void MD5Init(MD5_CTX *context);
extern "C" void MD5Update(MD5_CTX *context, unsigned char *message,
    unsigned int mlen);
extern "C" void MD5Final(unsigned char digest[16], MD5_CTX *context);
```

DESCRIPTION

These routines checksum a block of memory that begins at **message** and is **mlen** bytes long.

The routine **fletcher()** verifies or generates the OSI checksum, (the Fletcher checksum). It is meant to be run over a message containing a 2-byte checksum field. When verifying the checksum field, **offset** is set to **0**, and **fletcher()** should return **0**. To generate the checksum field, the byte offset of the checksum field from the start of the message, starting at 1, is specified in **offset**. For example, when generating an OSPF LSA checksum, **message** points right after the LSA's Age field, and **offset** assumes a value of 15. The checksum field is then updated, and the return code can be ignored.

The routine **incksum()** verifies or generates the standard Internet checksum: the one's complement sum of all the 16-bit words in a message; (a virtual byte of 0 is appended to odd-length messages). Again, **message** is assumed to contain a 2-byte checksum field. When invoked on a properly checksummed message, **incksum()** returns **0**. To generate a correct checksum field, the message's checksum field should first be zeroed. A subsequent call to **incksum()** will then return the one's complement of the value that should be inserted into the message's checksum field.

The routines **MD5Init()**, **MD5Update()**, and **MD5Final()** calculate an MD5 digest over one or more regions of memory. Written by RSA Data Security, these routines comprise the RSA Data Security, Inc., MD5 Message-Digest Algorithm, where **context** points to the working data used by the algorithm, initialized by a call to **MD5Init()**.

Successive calls to **MD5Update**() are then made, specifying each of the memory regions to checksum in turn. Processing regions in a different order produces a different checksum. A call to **MD5Final**() then returns the checksum, or message digest, in the 16-byte array **digest**.

USAGE

OSPF packets are checksummed by using the standard one's complement Internet checksum. Packet checksums are verified in **SpfIfc::verify**(), which verifies the MD5 digest instead if OSPF MD5 cryptographic authentication has been enabled for the interface. Conversely, the Internet checksum or MD5 digest is inserted into packets that are to be transmitted out the interface by **SpfIfc::generate_message**().

OSPF LSAs use the Fletcher checksum. An LSA's checksum is verified when it is initially received by the flooding algorithm in **SpfNbr::recv_update**() and periodically thereafter in **OSPF::checkages**() to make sure that the LSA has not been corrupted while being held in the router's link-state database. A router calculates and installs the checksum in its self-originated LSAs in the routines **OSPF::lsa_reorig**() and **OSPF::age_prematurely**().

REFERENCES

The Fletcher checksum is defined in Annex B of RFC 905 [56]. The routine **fletcher**() implements the optimized algorithm outlined in RFC 1008 [53].

Several RFCs have been written about the Internet's one's complement checksum, such as RFC 1624 [90].

The algorithm and code for the MD5 digest can be found in RFC 1321 [91].

NAME

class TcpPkt—Reading and writing packetized data over a TCP (Transmission Control Protocol) connection

SYNOPSIS

```
#include "machdep.h"
#include "tcppkt.h"

tcppkt = new TcpPkt(int fd);
delete tcppkt;
int TcpPkt::receive(void **msgpp, uns16 &type, uns16 &subtype);
int TcpPkt::rcv_suspend(void **msgpp, uns16 &type, uns16 &subtype);
void TcpPkt::queue_xpkt(void *msgp, uns16 type, uns16 subtype,
     int length);
bool TcpPkt::sendpkt();
bool TcpPkt::sendpkt_suspend(void *msgp, uns16 type, uns16 subtype,
     int length);
bool TcpPkt::xmt_pending();
```

DESCRIPTION

The **TcpPkt** class is used to send and to receive packetized data over a TCP connection. An application classifies each packet by 16-bit **type** and **subtype** fields and specifies the **length** of the packet in bytes. Blocking and nonblocking calls are then provided to read packets out of and to write packets into a TCP stream.

The file descriptor of the packetized TCP connection is provided to the **TcpPkt** constructor. Data in this TCP connection should be manipulated exclusively by the **TcpPkt** send and receive methods. Opening and closing of the TCP connection are performed outside the **TcpPkt** class. In particular, the **TcpPkt** destructor does not close the TCP connection.

TcpPkt::receive(), the nonblocking read method, collects any received bytes and tries to form a complete packet. If a complete packet has been received, the length of the packet is returned, ***msgpp** is set to point to the received packet, and the **type** and **subtype** arguments are set to reflect the received packet's classification. Zero-length packets are possible, as they still convey information from their **type** and **subtype**, which are not included in the returned length. Therefore, the type value of **0** is reserved, and you can tell whether you have received a full packet by whether **type** is nonzero. The received packet resides in storage local to the **TcpPkt** class and must be completely processed and/or copied before the next call to either (blocking or nonblocking) read method. The next call to a read method may overwrite or free the previously received packet.

    `TcpPkt::rcv_suspend()` is similar, except that it blocks until an entire packet is read.

    `TcpPkt::queue_pkt()` queues the packet pointed to by **msgp** for later transmission. The nonblocking `TcpPkt::sendpkt()` transmits as many queued packets as possible without blocking; transmission of partial packets is allowed. The routine `TcpPkt::xmt_pending()` returns **true** if any queued packets remain to be transmitted.

    `TcpPkt::sendpkt_suspend()` is the blocking version of the packet send routines. It blocks until the packet pointed to by **msgp** is written to the TCP connection.

RETURN VALUES

The read methods `TcpPkt::receive()` and `TcpPkt::rcv_suspend()` return a packet's length in bytes, a pointer to the packet, and its type and subtype. If a full packet has been successfully received, the type value will be nonzero. A returned length of **-1** indicates an error, which is most likely a broken TCP connection, although possibly a mismatch in packet header versions (see IMPLEMENTATION).

    The send methods `TcpPkt::sendpkt()` and `TcpPkt::sendpkt_suspend()` return **true** if they succeed and **false** if they encounter any errors in writing to the TCP connection.

IMPLEMENTATION

Each packet in the TCP stream is constrained to have the 8-byte header pictured below. The **version** field is used to indicate changes in header format; it is currently set to **1**. The **type** and **subtype** fields can be used by the application to classify packets. The **length** field in the header indicates the size of the packet, including the 8-byte header. Note, however, that the **length** field passed in and out of the application interface covers only the application data.

```
struct TcpPktHdr {
    uns16 version;
    uns16 type;
    uns16 subtype;
    uns16 length;
};
```

USAGE

The monitoring connections between the **ospfd_mon**/**ospfd_browser** applications and **ospfd** are implemented as packetized TCP connections. In this case, the packet type fields are the monitoring commands defined in **ospfd/src/monitor.h**, which also gives the packet application body format specification in **struct MonMsg**.

The control connections between the simulation control application **ospf_sim** and the individual simulated routers running **ospfd_sim** are packetized TCP connections whose packet types and formats are defined in **ospfd/ospf_sim/sim.h**.

NOTES

The two ends of the TCP connection must agree on the meanings of the packet type and subtypes and on the format of the packet's application content. The type value of **0** must not be used, as it indicates an incomplete packet in the nonblocking **TcpPkt::receive()**.

To ensure that the nonblocking calls do not block, the socket must be put into non-blocking mode, or **select()** must be used to ensure that the socket has bytes available to read or to write.

6

The Link-State Database

The link-state database is central to OSPF. The database provides the raw data used by the routing calculations, and most of the protocol machinery in OSPF is dedicated to maintaining database synchronization among routers. In this chapter, we examine the implementation of the OSPF link-state database, including how the individual LSAs are stored internally, database operations, and the aging of the link-state database.

6.1 Link-State Database Fundamentals

Individual LSAs in the database are represented as C++ classes. Each separate LSA type is represented by a different C++ class. Router-LSAs are stored as `class rtrLSA`, network-LSAs as `class netLSA`, summary-LSAs as `class summLSA`, ASBR-summary-LSAs as `class asbrLSA`, AS-external-LSAs as `class ASextLSA`, and group-membership-LSAs as `class grpLSA`. All these classes inherit from the base `class LSA`, as shown in Figure 6.1.

Intermediate classes are used to capture the role of the LSA type in the routing calculation (see Chapter 11, Routing Calculations). For example, `class TNode` is used for the LSAs that play the role of transit vertices in the Dijkstra or SPF (Shortest Path First) calculation, and `class rteLSA` is used for those LSAs that serve as stub links on the network graph.

The base `class LSA` is shown in Figure 6.2. LSAs are arranged in AVL trees, one for each LSA type, and so each LSA inherits from `class AVLitem`. The two keys used to

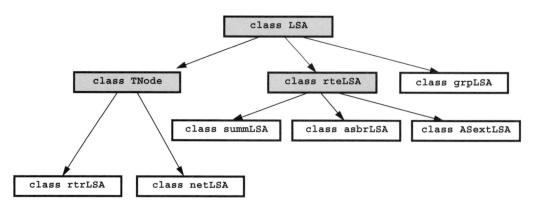

Figure 6.1 The LSA class hierarchy. Classes used only as base classes are shaded.

store the LSA within the AVL tree are the LSA's Link State ID and Advertising Router. The 20-byte header of each LSA is always stored in the **LSA** class, as shown in Table 6.1; the method that reads the header fields out of a received LSA and stores them in the **LSA** class is **LSA::hdr_parse()**. However, the body is not always stored verbatim but is instead sometimes recast into a format more amenable to the routing table calculation.

Table 6.1 Access to the Standard LSA Header Fields in the **class LSA**. **LSA::lsa_rcvage** represents LS Age when the LSA was received, not the LSA's current age.

Description	Storage	Access Method
LS Age	**LSA::lsa_rcvage***	**LSA::lsa_age()**
LS Options	**LSA::lsa_opts**	
LS Type	**LSA::lsa_type**	**LSA::ls_type()**
Link State ID	**AVLitem::_index1**	**LSA::ls_id()**
Advertising Router	**AVLitem::_index2**	**LSA::adv_rtr()**
LS Sequence Number	**LSA::lsa_seqno**	**LSA::ls_seqno()**
LS Checksum	**LSA::lsa_xsum**	
LS Length	**LSA::lsa_length**	**LSA::ls_length()**

A description of the other fields in the **LSA** class follows, except for those fields related to LSA aging; they are discussed in Section 6.4.

- When unexpected problems are encountered in preparsing an LSA for the routing calculation, indicated in **LSA::exception**, the entire body of the LSA is stored in **LSA::lsa_body**, just as it was received from the network.

```
                                                              ───────── lsa.h
34 class LSA : public AVLitem {
35 protected:
37     age_t lsa_rcvage;     // LS age when received
38     byte lsa_opts;        // LS Options
39     const byte lsa_type;       // Type of LSA
40     seq_t lsa_seqno;      // LS Sequence number
41     xsum_t lsa_xsum;      // LS checksum (fletcher)
42     uns16 lsa_length;     // Length of LSA, in bytes
44     byte *lsa_body;       // LSA body
45     class SpfArea *lsa_ap; // Containing area
49     uns16 lsa_rxmt;       // #Retransmission lists
50     uns16 in_agebin:1,    // In an age bin?
51         deferring:1,      // Awaiting deferred origination
52         changed:1,        // Changed since last flood
53         exception:1,      // Must store complete body
54         rollover:1,       // LS sequence being rolled over
55         e_bit:1,          // Type-2 external metric
56         parsed:1,         // Parsed for easy calculation?
57         sent_reply:1,     // Sent reply for older LSA received
58         checkage:1,       // Queued for xsum verification
59         min_failed:1;     // MinArrival failed
64
65     void hdr_parse(LShdr *hdr);
66     virtual void parse(LShdr *);
67     virtual void unparse();
68     virtual void process_donotage(bool parse);
69     virtual void build(LShdr *);
70     virtual void delete_actions();
72 public:
73     RTE *source;          // Routing table entry of orig. rtr
74
75     LSA(class SpfArea *, LShdr *, int blen = 0);
76     virtual ~LSA();
83     inline class SpfArea *area();
89     int cmp_instance(LShdr *hdr);
90     int cmp_contents(LShdr *hdr);
93     int refresh(seq_t);
94     void flood(class SpfNbr *from, LShdr *hdr);
96     virtual void reoriginate(int) {}
97     virtual RTE *rtentry();
110 };
                                                              ───────── lsa.h
```

Figure 6.2 Internal representation of an LSA: `class LSA`. Fields pertaining to LSA aging have
been omitted for later discussion.

- **LSA::lsa_ap** indicates the OSPF area that the LSA belongs to. That area is set to 0 for AS-external-LSAs. The area setting can be read with **LSA::area()**.

- **LSA::lsa_rxmt** is the number of neighbor retransmission lists that the LSA currently belongs to. When flushing an LSA, the LSA cannot be freed from the database until this field has become 0 (see Section 6.4.3).

- **LSA::deferring** indicates that an update of this LSA is pending until 5 seconds have elapsed from the last update (Section 6.4). **LSA::rollover** indicates that the LSA is currently undergoing sequence number rollover; we are waiting for the LSA with the maximum LS Sequence Number to be flushed before we begin again with 0x80000001 (Section 7.7). **LSA::checkage** indicates that it is time to verify the LSA's checksum and that the checksum operation has been delayed to spread out CPU load (Section 6.4.2).

- **LSA::changed** indicates whether the contents of the LSA have changed, compared to the previous instance that was installed in the database. Only changed LSAs are flooded across demand circuits (see Section 9.3).

- The external metric type for AS-external-LSAs is indicated in **LSA::e_bit**. When set, the AS-external-LSA contains a type-2 external metric.

- **LSA::parsed** indicates whether an LSA has been preparsed for use in the routing calculation. If we have parsed an LSA, we need to unparse it when removing the LSA from the database.

- When set, **LSA::sent_reply** tells us that within the last second we have responded to a received old instance of the LSA, and so we should not reply to any further old instances received (Section 9.2).

- **LSA::source** is the routing table entry for the LSA's originating router. For LSA's with area scope, this is a **class RTRrte** representing the intra-area path to the originating router. For AS-external-LSAs, this is a **class ASBRrte**, representing the best path to the originating ASBR according to the tiebreakers in Section 16.4.1 of [75].

LSA::cmp_instance(LShdr *hdr) is used to determine whether the newly received **hdr** is more recent (return code 1), the same instance (return code 0), or less recent than the LSA in the database. **LSA::cmp_contents()** is used to determine whether the contents of a newly received LSA differ from the database copy. **LSA::flood()** performs the flooding of an LSA that has just been added to the router's link-state database. These routines are described further in Chapter 9, Flooding.

LSA::refresh() reoriginates an LSA, possibly with a specified LS Sequence Number, as described in Section 7.6.

6.1.1   Virtual Functions

A number of methods within the **class LSA** vary their behavior, based on the LSA's type.

- **void LSA::parse()**. Preparse an LSA when it is added to the link-state database, to facilitate processing by the routing calculation. See Section 6.2.2 for details.

- **void LSA::unparse()**. Undo the preprocessing when removing an LSA from the database, so that the LSA will no longer be used by the routing calculation (Section 6.2.4).

- **void LSA::process_donotage()**. Called when adding or deleting an LSA from the database, in order to keep track of the number of LSAs with the DC bit clear in their Options field. All LSAs must have their DC bit set before DoNotAge LSAs can be flooded into the area. ASBR-summary-LSAs must be handled separately for indication-LSA processing; see Section 10.3.4.

- **void LSA::build()**. From the database copy, rebuild the network format of the LSA so that it can be flooded to the router's neighbors (Section 6.2.6).

- **void LSA::delete_actions()**. Type-specific actions required when an LSA is deleted from the database. For example, when a network-LSA is deleted, any remaining network-LSA with the same Link State ID must be reparsed to take the place of the deleted network-LSA in the routing calculation.

- **void LSA::reoriginate(int forced)**. Reoriginate the LSA with contents reflecting the new local router state. If **forced** is **true**, reoriginate even if the contents of the LSA have not changed. See Chapter 7, Originating LSAs.

- **RTE *LSA::rtentry()**. The routing table entry of the LSA's advertised destination, if any. For summary-LSAs and AS-external-LSAs, points to an IP routing table entry. For ASBR-summary-LSAs, points to a **class ASBRrte**.

- **bool TNode::is_wild_card()**. Used by the MOSPF routing calculation to determine whether the transit node is a wildcard multicast receiver (Section 12.4).

6.1.2   Database Organization

As mentioned earlier, the link-state database has a separate AVL tree for each type of LSA. The LSAs having area scope are contained in the area's **class SpfArea**, as shown in Figure 6.3, with **SpfArea::rtrLSAs** storing the router-LSAs; **SpfArea::netLSAs**, the network-LSAs; `SpfArea::summLSAs`, the summary-LSAs; `SpfArea::asbrLSAs`, the ASBR-summary-LSAs; and `SpfArea::grpLSAs`, the group-membership-LSAs. The sum of all the LSAs' LS Checksum fields, the OSPF MIB variable `ospfAreaLsaCksumSum`, is stored in `SpfArea::db_xsum`. AS-external-LSAs are kept in the `OSPF` class, as described in Section 3.2.1.

—— lsa.h

```
 32 class SpfArea : public ConfigItem {
 36     // Link-state database
 37     AVLtree rtrLSAs;        // router-LSAs
 38     AVLtree netLSAs;        // network-LSAs
 39     AVLtree summLSAs;       // summary-LSAs
 40     AVLtree asbrLSAs;       // asbr-summary-LSAs
 41     AVLtree grpLSAs;        // group-membership-LSAs
 42     uns32 db_xsum;          // Database checksum
 61   public:
 98     void flush_lsdb(bool everything=false);
103     void AddTypesToList(byte lstype, LsaList *lp);
131 };
```

—— lsa.h

Figure 6.3 Storage of area-scoped LSAs.

Not every `class LSA` in the code is contained in the link-state database; for example, LSAs that we are attempting to free to the heap are no longer in the database but may still be referenced in the code. An LSA is in the database if and only if it is installed in one of the AVL trees, which can be determined by using the `LSA::valid()` method.

The basic operations of finding LSAs in the database and adding and deleting LSAs to/from the database are explained in the next section. We close this section with mention of a few more special-purpose methods that manipulate the database.

`SpfArea::flush_lsdb(bool everything)` is used to delete the router's entire link-state database for an area; this operation is performed when the router no longer has operational interfaces to the area. During the orderly shutdown procedure (Section 13.10), the router withdraws the LSAs that it itself has originated from the area's link-state database, by setting `everything` to `false`.

`OSPF::flush_self_orig(AVLtree *tree)` is used to flush (that is, set their LS Ages to MaxAge and reflood) all the self-originated LSAs in a specified AVL tree.

`SpfArea::AddTypesToList(byte lstype, LsaList *lp)` adds all an area's LSAs of type `lstype` to the list of LSAs `lp`. This function is used when constructing a neighbor's database summary list at the beginning of the Database Exchange process (Section 8.3).

6.2   Database Operations

The two main database operations—adding an LSA to the database and deleting an LSA from the database—are pictured in Figure 6.4. LSAs are added to the database when either (1) the router itself has (re)originated an LSA, based on a local change in the topology, or because it is time to refresh the LSA; or (2) a new LSA has been received in a Link State Update packet from a neighboring router. In both cases, the LSA is added to an AVL tree, based on the LSA type and its area; is preparsed for use in the routing calculation; starts aging (Section 6.4); and is flooded to the router's neighbors (Section 9.3). For a detailed description of adding an LSA to the database, see Section 6.2.2.

file lsdb.C

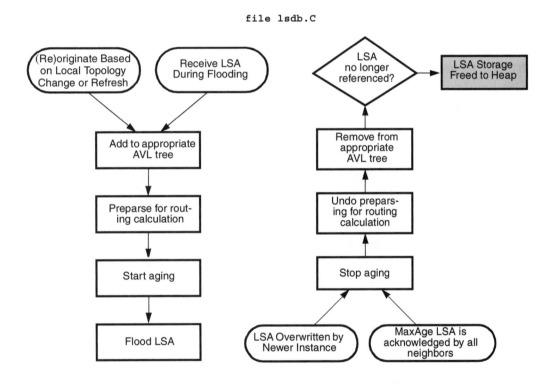

Figure 6.4 Adding and deleting LSAs to/from the link-state database. Shaded rectangle indicates operations that may be postponed.

LSAs are deleted from the database when either (1) they are overwritten by a newer instance or (2) their LS Age is equal MaxAge and, after flooding, they have been acknowledged by all adjacent neighbors. In deleting an LSA, we stop its aging, undo any preparsing that was performed for the routing calculation, remove the LSA from its

AVL tree, and, if it is no longer contained on any LSA lists, free the LSA by returning its storage to the heap. See Section 6.2.4 for details.

6.2.1 Finding LSAs in the Database

An LSA is located in the link-state database by using the function `LSA *OSPF::FindLSA` `(SpfArea *ap, byte lstype, lsid_t lsid, rtid_t rtid)`. The `ap` argument is the LSA's area, which is 0 for AS-external-LSAs. The arguments `lstype`, `lsid`, and `rtid` are the LSA's LS Type, Link State ID, and Advertising Router, respectively.

To find an LSA that the router itself has originated—that is, a self-originated LSA—`LSA *OSPF::myLSA(SpfArea *ap, byte lstype, lsid_t lsid)` is used. Sometimes, we just want to find the AVL tree to which an LSA belongs, and that is accomplished with `AVLtree *OSPF::FindLSdb(SpfArea *ap, byte lstype)`.

6.2.2 Adding an LSA to the Database: `OSPF::AddLSA()`

An LSA is added to the link-state database by using the `OSPF::AddLSA()` function (Figure 6.5).

158   Passed to the function are `ap`, the OSPF area to which the LSA belongs; `current`, the current database copy of the LSA (which may be 0); `hdr`, the new copy of the LSA (in network format) to be added to the database; and `changed`, a flag that indicates whether the contents of this new LSA are any different from the current database copy.

167-172   If there is a current database copy, it is about to be replaced, so stop its aging and remove its checksum from the sum of checksums.

174-189   If there is a current database copy and it is not currently referenced on any LSA lists (Section 6.3), we can reuse the current `LSA` class instead of allocating a new one. We simply recalculate the basic set of `LSA` class fields and start the LSA aging again. If the contents of the new LSA are no different, as would be in the common case of an LSA refresh, we add the new checksum to the sum of checksums and return. If the contents are different, we undo the preparsing of the database copy and continue with the installation in line `232`.

190-229   If we can't reuse the current database copy, we must allocate a new LSA. The correct derived class is allocated based on LS Type. The newly allocated LSA is added to the appropriate AVL tree in the class constructor, replacing the current database copy. The preparsing of the now former database copy is undone (line `226`), and we start aging the new LSA.

217-224   We set the `LSA::changed` flag to indicate whether the new LSA should be flooded over demand circuits. We should flood the new LSA over demand circuits if (1) there was no database copy, (2) the contents of the LSA have changed as indicated by the `changed` argument, or (3) we previously were flooding the database copy over demand circuits and that flood had not yet completed.

```
158 LSA *OSPF::AddLSA(SpfArea *ap, LSA *current, LShdr *hdr, bool changed)
160 {
161     LSA *lsap;
162     int blen;
163     RTE *old_rte = 0;
164     bool min_failed=false;
165
166     blen = ntoh16(hdr->ls_length) - sizeof(LShdr);
167     if (current) {
168         min_failed = current->since_received() < MinArrival;
169         old_rte = current->rtentry();
170         current->stop_aging();
171         update_lsdb_xsum(current, false);
172     }
174     if (current && current->refct == 0) {
175         // Update in place
176         if (changed)
177             UnParseLSA(current);
178         lsap = current;
179         lsap->hdr_parse(hdr);
180         lsap->start_aging();
181         lsap->changed = changed;
182         lsap->deferring = false;
183         lsap->rollover = current->rollover;
184         lsap->min_failed = min_failed;
185         if (!changed) {
186             update_lsdb_xsum(lsap, true);
187             return(lsap);
188         }
189     }
190     else {
191         switch (hdr->ls_type) {
192           case LST_RTR:
193             lsap = new rtrLSA(ap, hdr, blen);
194             break;
195           case LST_NET:
196             lsap = new netLSA(ap, hdr, blen);
197             break;
198           case LST_SUMM:
199             lsap = new summLSA(ap, hdr, blen);
200             break;
201           case LST_ASBR:
202             lsap = new asbrLSA(ap, hdr, blen);
203             break;
```

(Continued)

```
204                 case LST_ASL:
205                     lsap = new ASextLSA(hdr, blen);
206                     break;
207                 case LST_GM:
208                     lsap = new grpLSA(ap, hdr, blen);
209                     break;
210                 default:
211                     lsap = 0;
212                     sys->halt(HALT_LSTYPE, "Bad LS type");
213                     break;
214             }
215
216             // If database copy, unparse it
217             if (!current)
218                 lsap->changed = true;
219             else {
220                 lsap->changed = changed;
221                 lsap->rollover = current->rollover;
222                 lsap->min_failed = min_failed;
223                 if (current->lsa_rxmt != 0)
224                     lsap->changed |= current->changed;
225                 lsap->update_in_place(current);
226                 UnParseLSA(current);
227             }
228             lsap->start_aging();
229         }
230
231         // Parse the new body contents
232         ParseLSA(lsap, hdr);
233         update_lsdb_xsum(lsap, true);
234         // If changes, schedule new routing calculations
235         if (changed)
236             rtsched(lsap, old_rte);
237
238         return(lsap);
239 }
```

── lsdb.C

Figure 6.5 Adding LSAs to the database: `OSPF::addLSA()`.

232-233   We preparse the new LSA for the routing calculation and update the sum of LS Checksums.

235-236   If the contents of the LSA have changed, we must schedule the appropriate routing calculation by calling `OSPF::rtsched()` (Section 11.1). For summary-LSAs and AS-external-LSAs, the destination described by the LSA may also have changed when the LSA contents change, and so the old destination must also be passed to the routing calculation scheduler.

6.2.3 Preparsing LSAs

We generally don't store a received LSA in exactly the same format that it was received from the network. Instead, we convert it into an internal format that is easier to use in the routing calculation. We have been calling this conversion *preparsing* the LSA, or even just *parsing*. Section 11.4 will get into much more detail as to why this makes the routing calculations run faster. Here, we will simply examine the top-level parsing routine, `OSPF::ParseLSA()`, as shown in Figure 6.6.

```
                                                                        lsdb.C
309 void OSPF::ParseLSA(LSA *lsap, LShdr *hdr)
311 {
312     int blen;
313
314     if (lsap->parsed)
315         return;
317     blen = ntoh16(hdr->ls_length) - sizeof(LShdr);
319     if (lsap->lsa_age() != MaxAge) {
320         bool o_dna = donotage();
321         bool o_a_dna = (lsap->lsa_ap ? lsap->lsa_ap->donotage() :
                                          false);
322         lsap->exception = false;
323         lsap->parsed = true;
324         lsap->parse(hdr);
325         lsap->process_donotage(true);
326         total_lsas++;
327         if (o_dna != donotage())
328             dna_change = true;
329         if (lsap->lsa_ap && o_a_dna != lsap->lsa_ap->donotage())
330             lsap->lsa_ap->dna_change = true;
331     }
332     else
333         lsap->exception = true;
334
335     delete [] lsap->lsa_body;
336     lsap->lsa_body = 0;
338     if (lsap->exception) {
339         lsap->lsa_body = new byte[blen];
340         memcpy(lsap->lsa_body, (hdr + 1), blen);
341     }
342 }
                                                                        lsdb.C
```

Figure 6.6 Preparsing LSAs: `OSPF::ParseLSA()`.

314-315   If the LSA has already been parsed, we don't parse it again.

319-331   For all but MaxAge LSAs, we parse the LSA by calling the type-specific parse function `LSA::parse()`, an example of which is shown later. If an unexpected condition is found during type-specific processing and we cannot reproduce the network-formatted version of the LSA from the internal database representation, the `LSA::exception` flag is set. `LSA::process_donotage()` is called to keep track of the number of routers that support DoNotAge processing (Section 6.5).

332-333   We don't parse MaxAge LSAs, causing them to automatically be ignored by the routing calculation. In this case, there is no parsed internal representation, so the `LSA::exception` flag must be set.

338-341   If the exception flag has been set, we store the entire body of the LSA so that we can faithfully reproduce the network-formatted version when necessary.

As an example of the type-specific parsing of an LSA, we examine the parsing of summary-LSAs in the routine `summLSA::parse()`, shown in Figure 6.7. Recall that each summary-LSA advertises a network prefix belonging to another area.

――――――――――――――――――――――――――――――――――――― summlsa.C

```
246 void summLSA::parse(LShdr *hdr)
247
248 {
249     SummHdr *summ;
250     uns32 netno;
251     uns32 mask;
252
253     summ = (SummHdr *) (hdr + 1);
254
255     mask = ntoh32(summ->mask);
256     netno = ls_id() & mask;
257     if (!(rte = inrttbl->add(netno, mask))) {
258         exception = true;
259         return;
260     }
261     if ((ntoh32(summ->metric) & ~LSInfinity) != 0)
262         exception = true;
263     else if (lsa_length != sizeof(LShdr) + sizeof(SummHdr))
264         exception = true;
265     adv_cost = ntoh32(summ->metric) & LSInfinity;
266
267     link = rte->summs;
268     rte->summs = this;
269 }
```

――――――――――――――――――――――――――――――――――――― summlsa.C

Figure 6.7 An example of type-specific parsing: `summLSA::parse()`.

255-260   The mask for the prefix is contained in the body of the LSA. Masking the Link State
            ID with this value gives the network prefix being advertised. We store the prefix's rout-
            ing table entry in **summLSA::rte**.
261-264   We want to make sure that we can reconstruct the network-formatted version of the
            LSA (**hdr**) from just **summLSA::rte** and the advertised cost stored in **summLSA::
            adv_cost**.
267-268   All summary-LSAs for a given prefix are linked together in that prefix's routing
            table entry. When we want to recalculate the routing table entry for the prefix, we sim-
            ply have to scan the list for the LSA specifying the least cost (see Section 11.2.6).

6.2.4   Removing LSAs from the Database

We have already seen that LSAs are removed from the database when they are replaced
by newer instances. A router can also explicitly request that an LSA be deleted from the
database, by setting the LSA's LS Age field to MaxAge and then reflooding it. In this
case, the routers delete the LSA from their databases as soon as the flood has been
acknowledged by all adjacent neighbors (Section 6.4.3). In this case, the LSA is freed by
calling **OSPF::DeleteLSA()** (Figure 6.8).

── **lsdb.C**

```
403 void OSPF::DeleteLSA(LSA *lsap)
404
405 {
406     AVLtree *btree;
407
408     if (spflog(LOG_LSAFREE, 3))
409         log(lsap);
410
411     update_lsdb_xsum(lsap, false);
412     lsap->stop_aging();
413     UnParseLSA(lsap);
414     btree = FindLSdb(lsap->lsa_ap, lsap->lsa_type);
415     btree->remove((AVLitem *) lsap);
416     lsap->chkref();
417 }
```

── **lsdb.C**

Figure 6.8 Removing an LSA from the database: **OSPF::DeleteLSA()**.

411   We take the LSA's LS Checksum out of the sum of checksums.
412   The aging of the LSA is stopped.
413   We undo the parsing of the LSA, so that it will no longer be a part of the routing cal-
            culation.

414-416   We remove the LSA from its type-specific AVL tree, which will free the LSA's storage to the heap as long as the LSA is no longer referenced by any LSA lists.

An LSA is returned to the heap when it is no longer contained in the database (`LSA::valid()`) and is also no longer on any LSA lists (`LSA::refct`). For this reason, whenever an LSA is removed from the database or from an LSA list, `LSA::chkref()` is called to see whether the two conditions for freeing the LSA's storage have now been met.

6.2.5   Unparsing LSAs

When an LSA is removed from the link-state database, we undo its preparsing, also called *unparsing* the LSA. This action ensures that the LSA will no longer be used by the routing calculation and that the LSA will no longer be referenced by other OSPF data structures, allowing us to free the LSA's storage as soon as the conditions in Section 6.2.4 are met.

Unparsing LSAs is performed by the function `OSPF::UnParseLSA()`, which is pretty much the inverse of the previously described `OSPF::ParseLSA()`. The main task of `OSPF::UnParseLSA()` is to call the virtual function `LSA::unparse()`, which performs type-specific unparsing.

As an example, the unparsing of summary-LSAs is performed by `summLSA::unparse()`, as shown in Figure 6.9. This function simply removes the summary-LSA from its corresponding routing table entry, so the LSA will no longer be considered when calculating inter-area routes to the destination.

---
summlsa.C
```
274 void summLSA::unparse()
276 {
277     summLSA *ptr;
278     summLSA **prev;
279
280     if (!rte)
281         return;
282     // Unlink from list in routing table
283     for (prev = &rte->summs; (ptr = *prev);
            prev = (summLSA **)&ptr->link)
284         if (*prev == this) {
285             *prev = (summLSA *)link;
286             break;
287         }
288 }
```
summlsa.C

Figure 6.9 Unparsing summary-LSAs: `summLSA::unparse()`.

6.2.6 Building Network Copies

The format of the LSA as it is stored internally in the implementation's link-state database may be different from the format of the LSA as it was originally received from the network. As described previously, this difference results from the desire to modify the internal format to make the LSA easier to process by the routing calculations (Chapter 11, Routing Calculations).

However, it is sometimes necessary to recover the LSA's network format. Why? The reasons are numerous.

- The router may have to retransmit the LSA to one of its neighbors.

- The router needs to respond to a Link State Request packet received on one of its forming adjacencies.

- The router wants to compare the contents of the LSA with a newly originated or received instance of the LSA.

- The router wants to recalculate the LSA's checksum to verify that the LSA has not been corrupted while being held in the database.

- The router wishes to flush the LSA by setting its age to MaxAge and then reflooding, and so on.

Recovering the network format of the LSA is accomplished by calling `LShdr *OSPF::BuildLSA(LSA *lsap)`, shown in Figure 6.10.

206-210   The network format of the LSA is always built in the memory pointed to by `OSPF::build_area`. If the current size (`OSPF::build_size`) of this memory is insufficient to build the LSA in question, a new, larger build area is allocated.

213   The network format of the LSA's link-state header is built by using the copy operator `LShdr& LShdr::operator=(class LSA &lsa)`. This operation is the inverse of the previously discussed `LSA::hdr_parse()`.

214-215   If `LSA::exception` is `false`, the network format of the LSA can be recovered from the internal database format. Like parsing and unparsing, this recovery is type-specific and is accomplished by the virtual function `LSA::build()`.

216-219   If the network format can't be recovered from the internally parsed version, the network format of the body of the LSA has been stored verbatim in `LSA::lsa_body`, which is simply copied to form the network version.

As an example, Figure 6.11 shows the building of the network format of a summary-LSA from the internal `summLSA` class, implemented by `summLSA::build()`. The mask in the body of the network version is recovered from the routing table entry `summLSA::rte` (line 300), and the advertised metric is converted from the internally stored machine byte order (line 301).

```
                                                          lsa.C
200 LShdr *OSPF::BuildLSA(LSA *lsap)
202 {
203     LShdr *hdr;
204     int blen;
205
206     if (lsap->lsa_length > build_size) {
207         delete [] build_area;
208         build_size = lsap->lsa_length;
209         build_area = new byte[lsap->lsa_length];
210     }
211
212     hdr = (LShdr *) ospf->build_area;
213     *hdr = *lsap;
214     if (!lsap->exception)
215         lsap->build(hdr);
216     else {
217         blen = lsap->lsa_length - sizeof(LShdr);
218         memcpy((hdr + 1), lsap->lsa_body, blen);
219     }
220
221     return(hdr);
222 }
                                                          lsa.C
```

Figure 6.10 Recovering the network format of an LSA: `OSPF::BuildLSA()`.

```
                                                          summlsa.C
294 void summLSA::build(LShdr *hdr)
295
296 {
297     SummHdr *summ;
298
299     summ = (SummHdr *) (hdr + 1);
300     summ->mask = hton32(rte->mask());
301     summ->metric = hton32(adv_cost);
302 }
                                                          summlsa.C
```

Figure 6.11 Recovering the network format of summary-LSAs: `summLSA::build()`.

6.3 LSA Lists

The OSPF implementation uses lists of LSAs in many places, implemented by `class` `LsaList`. Lists are a way to keep track of the LSAs having a specific property, such as those that must be retransmitted to a particular neighbor until they are acknowledged.

An associated iterator, **class LsaListIterator**, is also provided, which allows you to loop through all the LSAs contained in a specific list.

```
#include "lsalist.h"

LsaList::addEntry(LSA *lsap);
void LsaList::append(LsaList *from);
void LsaList::clear();
int LsaList::count();
LSA *LsaList::FirstEntry();
int LsaList::garbage_collect();
bool LsaList::is_empty();
int LsaList::remove(LSA *lsap);

LsaListIterator::LsaListIterator(LsaList *);
LSA *LsaListIterator::get_next();
void LsaListIterator::remove_current();
LSA *LsaListIterator::search(int lstype, lsid_t id, rtid_t org);
```

6.3.1 class LsaList

LSA lists are implemented as singly linked FIFO (first in first out) lists. When an LSA is added to a list, the LSA's reference count is incremented, ensuring that the LSA's storage will not be freed until it is removed from the list.

LsaList::addEntry(LSA *lsap) adds **lsap** to the list's tail. **LsaList::append (LsaList *from)** appends the LSAs on a different list **from** to the list; the list **from** is cleared in the process. **LsaList::clear()** removes all the LSAs from the list.

LsaList::count() returns the number of LSAs currently on the list. The method **LsaList::is_empty()** tells you whether any LSAs are currently on the list. The first entry, also called the head of the list, is returned by **LsaList::FirstEntry()**.

LsaList::remove(LSA *lsap) removes the LSA **lsap** from the list. It is possible that the act of removing the LSA from the list may destroy the LSA, freeing its storage to the heap (Section 6.2.4). For that reason, care should be taken when referencing LSAs after removing them from a list. The **remove** function searches the list for all occurrences of the specified LSA.

A list may contain LSAs that are no longer part of the link-state database. Most of the time, you do not want to process these LSAs. But as long as they are contained on a list, their storage will not be freed, and they will still consume memory resources in the router. The method **LsaList::garbage_collect()** can be used to remove all such LSAs from the list.

6.3.2 `class LsaListIterator`

`LsaListIterator`s are used to traverse a list of LSAs. The constructor for the `class LsaListIterator` takes the list that you wish to traverse as its argument.

The `LsaListIterator` always points to a particular element of the list, called the *current LSA*. `LSA *LsaListIterator::get_next()` advances the current LSA to the next LSA in the list, returning the new current LSA. The very first call to `get_next()` returns the head of the list. If the whole list has been traversed, `get_next()` returns 0.

The method `void LsaListIterator::remove_current()` removes whatever LSA the iterator is currently pointing at from the list. The next call to `get_next()` will return the LSA in the list following the removed LSA. However, immediately following a call to `remove_current()`, the list's current LSA is no longer set; in particular, consecutive calls to `remove_current()` should not be performed without an intervening call to `get_next()`.

`LSA *LsaListIterator::search()` advances `current` to the next LSA that has LS Type equal to `lstype`, Link State ID equal to `id`, and Advertising Router equal to `org`. The searched-for LSA is returned or 0 if the search was unsuccessful.

6.3.3 Examples

The LSA lists used in the OSPF implementation include the following lists:

- `OSPF::MaxAge_list`. The MaxAge LSAs that are awaiting acknowledgment before they can be deleted from the link-state database.

- `OSPF::dbcheck_list`. The LSAs pending checksum verification (Section 6.4.2).

- `OSPF::replied_list`. These LSAs have been sent in Link State Update packets within the last second, as replies to less recent instances of these LSAs received during flooding. We will not make further replies for these LSAs until a full second has expired and they are removed from the list.

- The LSAs that will be retransmitted to a given neighbor unless acknowledged are implemented as three separate lists: `SpfNbr::n_pend_rxl`, `SpfNbr::n_rxlst`, and `SpfNbr::n_failed_rxl`. See the detailed example that follows and Section 9.1.

- LSA lists are used in the Database Exchange process. `SpfNbr::n_ddlst` holds the database snapshot being sent to the neighbor, `SpfNbr::n_rqlst`, the LSAs that need to be obtained from the neighbor in order to bring our link-state database up-to-date. See Section 8.3 for details.

As a detailed example of LSA list processing, we examine the routine `SpfNbr::get_next_rxmt()` (Figure 6.12). This routine returns the next LSA that should be retransmitted to the neighbor. The returned LSA belongs to one of the three LSA lists

comprising the neighbor's retransmission list; exactly which of the lists the returned
LSA belongs to is returned in the **list** argument. If none of the LSAs has been on the
neighbor's retransmission list long enough, **0** is returned, and the number of seconds
that must transpire before again examining the retransmission list is returned in the
nexttime argument.

```
                                                                  ── spfack.C
227 LSA *SpfNbr::get_next_rxmt(LsaList * &list, uns32 &nexttime)
228
229 {
230      byte interval;
231      LSA *lsap=0;
232
233      nexttime = 0;
234      interval = n_ifp->rxmt_interval();
235      do {
236          if (!nexttime && (lsap = n_rxlst.FirstEntry())) {
237              if (lsap->valid() &&
238                  lsap->since_received() < interval) {
239                  nexttime = interval - lsap->since_received();
240                  lsap = 0;
241              }
242              list = &n_rxlst;
243          }
244          else if ((lsap = n_failed_rxl.FirstEntry()))
245              list = &n_failed_rxl;
246          else
247              return(0);
248          // Verify that LSA is still valid
249          if (lsap && !lsap->valid()) {
250              list->remove(lsap);
251              rxmt_count--;
252              lsap = 0;
253          }
254      } while (lsap == 0);
255
256      return(lsap);
257 }
                                                                  ── spfack.C
```

Figure 6.12 List processing in **SpfNbr::get_next_rxmt()**.

236-243   We first look at the LSAs that have never been retransmitted to the neighbor
(**SpfNbr::n_rxlst**). LSA lists are FIFOs, so the oldest LSA is at the head of the list. If
this LSA still belongs to the link-state database and has been on the list long enough to

be retransmitted, it is returned. Otherwise, **nexttime** is set to the number of seconds that must elapse before this LSA can be retransmitted.

244-245   If no newly received LSAs are ready to retransmit, we retransmit the oldest LSA that has been retransmitted unsuccessfully before. We give previously retransmitted LSAs lowest priority because implementation errors may be keeping the neighbor from ever accepting certain LSAs, and we want to make sure that those LSAs don't get in the way of flooding all others.

249-253   The OSPF specification mandates that when an LSA is removed from the link-state database, it also be removed from all link-state retransmission lists. However, this removal can be costly, and it requires additional plumbing in an implementation. Instead, in this implementation, we simply remove defunct LSAs (**!LSA::valid()**) from retransmission lists during the normal building of retransmitted Link State Update packets. Only when a defunct LSA instance has been removed from all retransmission lists will the router return the defunct LSA instance to the heap.

6.4   Aging LSAs

All LSAs contain an LS Age field, which indicates the number of seconds that have elapsed since the LSA was originated. OSPF routers keep track of an LSA's age for robustness reasons: The age tells the routers when LSAs should be refreshed, when stale LSAs can be safely flushed from the routing domain, and so on. See Section 4.2.4 of [67] for a more detailed description of LSA aging.

The methods used to access and manipulate an LSA's aging information are as follows.

```
#include "lsa.h"
#include "dbage.h"

int LSA::do_not_age();
age_t LSA::lsa_age();
int LSA::is_aging();
age_t LSA::since_received();
void LSA::start_aging();
void LSA::stop_aging();
```

The current age of an LSA is returned by **LSA::lsa_age()**. The number of seconds the LSA has been in the database, either as a result of being received during flooding or because the router itself has originated the LSA, is given by **LSA::since_received()**.

In order to start the aging of an LSA, **LSA::start_aging()** is invoked. Aging is generally started when the LSA is added to the link-state database. To determine whether an LSA is currently aging, **LSA::is_aging()** is called. MaxAge LSAs and LSAs with the DoNotAge bit set in their LS Age field are never aged. The latter condition can

be detected by calling `LSA::do_not_age()`. The aging of an LSA must be stopped with
`LSA::stop_aging()` when removing an LSA from the link-state database.

6.4.1   Implementation

The age of each LSA in the database must be incremented by 1 each second. However,
we don't want to touch each LSA in the database every second—that would be too
expensive in terms of CPU cycles. Instead, we put all the LSAs of a given age into a single bin, as pictured in Figure 6.13. The age of an LSA is the difference between its age
bin and the bin representing LS Age 0. Every second, we simply change the bin representing LS age 0, incrementing the age of all other LSAs by comparison.

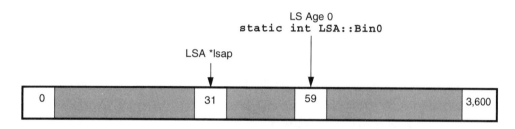

Figure 6.13 Implementation of LSA aging. All LSAs of a common age
are linked together inside a single bin.

Figure 6.14 shows the `class LSA` fields that pertain to the aging process. There are
3,601 age bins, one for every possible LS Age value between 0 and MaxAge inclusive,
implemented as the static array `LSA::AgeBins`. Each bin is a doubly linked list of LSAs,
making the process of stopping the aging of LSA (removal of an LSA from its age bin)
a fast process; the forward and backward pointers implementing this list are
`LSA::lsa_agefwd` and `LSA::lsa_agerv`, respectively. The member `LSA::in_agebin`
(Figure 6.2) indicates whether the LSA has been installed in an age bin, and if so, the age
bin is given by `LSA::lsa_agebin`. The current LS Age 0 bin is represented by the static
`LSA::Bin0`.

As an example, in Figure 6.13, the 0 age bin is currently bin 59. As a result, the age of
the LSA in bin 31 is 59–31 = 28. In 1 second, the age 0 bin will be bin 60; because the LSA
will still be in its same bin 31, its age will have incremented to 29. *Note:* The age bins in
reality form a circular space. When the 0 age bin reaches 3,600, it then wraps back to 0,
and the current age of an LSA can be thought of as the number of seconds since its age
bin was the 0 bin.

```
                                                                    lsa.h
34 class LSA : public AVLitem {
35 protected:
37     age_t lsa_rcvage;     // LS age when received
46     LSA *lsa_agefwd;      // forward link in age bins
47     LSA *lsa_agerv;       // reverse link in age bins
48     uns16 lsa_agebin;     // Age bin
62     static  LSA *AgeBins[MaxAge+1];// Aging Bins
63     static int Bin0;      // Current age 0 bin
                                                                    lsa.h
```

Figure 6.14 The `class LSA` fields pertaining to LSA aging.

The age bin containing the LSA says nothing about how long the LSA has been in the router's link-state database. For that, we need to store the LS Age field of the LSA when it was first installed in the database, which is found in `LSA::lsa_rcvage`.

In this implementation, LSAs are aged even as they are held on database summary lists (Section 8.3), link-state retransmission lists (Section 9.1), and the like. LSA lists do not contain separate copies of the LSA but instead simply reference the link-state database copy, which is always aging.

6.4.2 Actions Triggered by Database Aging

The routine `OSPF::dbage()` implements the aging of the link-state database (Figure 6.15). This routine is called once every second and performs all actions, such as LSA refresh, associated with database aging. Each of these actions is associated with one or more fixed-age bins.

153   Incrementing the LS Age 0 bin ages all LSAs in the database simultaneously.

154-155   The bins form a circular space, which wraps back to bin 0 after bin 3,600 (MaxAge).

158   We reoriginate all those LSAs that we had to defer in order to maintain a gap of `MinLSInterval` between originations. This processing, performed by `OSPF::deferred_lsas()`, simply goes through the bin representing LS Age `MinLSInterval`. All the LSAs in this bin with `LSA::deferring` set are reoriginated by calling the virtual function `LSA::reoriginate()`.

159   We verify the checksums of those LSAs whose ages are a multiple of CheckAge (15, 30, and 45 minutes) by calling `OSPF::checkages()`. This function evens out processing by enqueuing the LSAs that have these age values onto the list `OSPF::dbcheck_list`, where an equal number are verified each second.

160   We refresh our self-originated LSAs whose age has hit LSRefreshTime, by calling `OSPF::refresh_lsas()`. Those that we have originated with the DoNotAge bit set are not refreshed. LSAs are refreshed by calling the virtual function `LSA::reoriginate` (`true`), which rebuilds the LSA's contents from first principles and then increments its

```
                                                                       dbage.C
149 void OSPF::dbage()
151 {
152     // Increment age by one second
153     LSA::Bin0++;
154     if (LSA::Bin0 > MaxAge)
155         LSA::Bin0 = 0;
156
157     // Process LSAs of certain ages
158     deferred_lsas();
159     checkages();
160     refresh_lsas();
161     maxage_lsas();
162     refresh_donotages();
163
164     // Finish any flooding that was caused by age routines
165     send_updates();
166     // Check to see whether any MaxAge can be deleted
167     free_maxage_lsas();
168     // Check to see whether we need to flush DoNotAge LSAs
169     donotage_changes();
170     // If shutting down, see if we can go to next phase
171     if (shutting_down() &&
172         (--countdown <= 0 || MaxAge_list.is_empty()))
173         shutdown_continue();
175 }
                                                                       dbage.C
```

Figure 6.15 Link-state database aging: `OSPF::dbage()`.

LS Sequence Number and refloods, regardless of whether the contents of the LSA have changed (see Section 7.6).

161   Those LSAs whose ages have just reached MaxAge are reflooded by calling `OSPF::maxage_lsas()`.

162   The LSAs that we have originated with DoNotAge bit set can be refreshed on a configurable interval, as implemented in `OSPF::refresh_donotages()`.

165   If we have reoriginated deferred LSAs or refreshed LSAs or have flooded MaxAge LSAs, the call to `OSPF::send_updates()` will complete the flooding of the LSAs by sending Link State Update packets out the router's interfaces.

167   We remove MaxAge LSAs from the link-state database, if the conditions of Section 6.4.3 are met.

169   If the OSPF routing domain is no longer capable of supporting DoNotAge, we flush all LSAs with the DoNotAge bit set.

171-173   When shutting down the OSPF software, we wait until all the LSAs that we are trying to flush from the routing domain have been acknowledged, before going on to the
next stage of the shutdown process (Section 13.10).

6.4.3 Freeing LSAs

MaxAge LSAs are contained in the link-state database and in the LSA list
`OSPF::MaxAge_list` until the conditions for their removal are met in the function
`OSPF::free_maxage_lsas()` (Figure 6.16). MaxAge LSAs are not installed in any age
bin and are not aging. However, when installed in the link-state database, their
`LSA::lsa_agebin` field is set to the current LS Age 0 bin, enabling the later retrieval of
the time the MaxAge LSA was installed (`LSA::since_received()`).

── dbage.C
```
335 void OSPF::free_maxage_lsas()
337 {
338     LSA *lsap;
339     LsaListIterator iter(&MaxAge_list);
340
341     while ((lsap = iter.get_next())) {
342         if (!lsap->valid()) {
343             iter.remove_current();
344             continue;
345         }
346         if (lsap->lsa_rxmt != 0)
347             continue;
348         if (!maxage_free(lsap->ls_type()))
349             continue;
350         // OK to free. Remove from database
351         // List processing will then return
352         // to heap when appropriate
353         iter.remove_current();
354         if (lsap->rollover) {
355             lsap->rollover = false;
356             lsap->refresh(InvalidLSSeq);
357         }
358         else
359             ospf->DeleteLSA(lsap);
360     }
361 }
```
── dbage.C

Figure 6.16 Removing MaxAge LSA from the database: `OSPF::free_maxage_lsas()`.

341   All the MaxAge LSAs are on the list `OSPF::MaxAge_list`. We examine each in turn
             to see whether it can be removed from the link-state database.

342-345   The MaxAge LSA may already have been removed from the link-state database. For
             example, a newer instance of the LSA could have been received while we were still try-
             ing to remove the MaxAge LSA. In this case, we simply remove the LSA from the list of
             MaxAge LSAs. Note that the removal of the MaxAge LSA from the list may free the LSA
             to the heap (Section 6.3).

346-347   MaxAge LSAs cannot be removed from the database until they are reflooded and
             acknowledged by all the router's adjacent neighbors. `LSA::lsa_rxmt` indicates the
             number of retransmission lists that the LSA currently belongs to—that is, the number of
             adjacent neighbors that have yet to acknowledge the flood.

348-349   `OSPF::maxage_free()` checks to see whether the router is currently undergoing the
             Database Exchange process with any neighbors. If so, the MaxAge LSA cannot be
             removed from the database, for fear of disrupting the Database Exchange process (see
             Section 9.2 and Chapter 8 in [67]).

353   We are now allowed to remove the MaxAge LSA from the link-state database.

354-357   `LSA::rollover` indicates that we were trying to reoriginate the LSA, but because
             the LSA already had the maximum LS Sequence Number of MaxLSSeq, we had to flush
             the current instance of the LSA first. In this case, instead of removing the LSA from the
             database, we now reoriginate the LSA with the initial LS Sequence Number `InitLSSeq`
             by calling `LSA::refresh()` with the new LS Sequence Number as its argument.

358-359   Otherwise, we remove the LSA from the link-state database by calling `OSPF::`
             `DeleteLSA()`.

6.5   DoNotAge LSAs

The concept of LSAs that do not age (the so-called DoNotAge LSAs) was introduced by
the Demand Circuit extensions to OSPF [64]. The idea is to remove the necessity of
refreshing certain LSAs by preventing them from aging. These LSAs need to be
reflooded only when a change in LSA contents occurs.

A DoNotAge LSA has the DoNotAge bit (0x8000) set in its LS Age field. In the
`ospfd` source code, these LSAs can be detected by using the `LShdr::do_not_age()` and
`LSA::do_not_age()` methods, both of which return `true` for DoNotAge LSAs.

DoNotAge LSAs are allowed in the network only if all routers indicate that they are
capable of processing DoNotAge LSAs correctly. A router indicates its DoNotAge processing capability by setting the DC bit in the Options field of all LSAs that it originates. Throughout the following discussion, we assume that all routers are capable
of DoNotAge processing, until the final section, which discusses interoperation with
DoNotAge-incapable routers.

6.5.1 Installing in the Link-State Database

The whole point of DoNotAge LSAs is to prevent them from aging. However, the `ospfd` implementation installs them in the aging bins `LSA::AgeBins` anyway, to implement the following functions:

- The length of time that the LSA has been in the link-state database: `LSA::since_received()`

- Deferral of LSA originations so that the required interval of LSRefreshInterval is met between successive originations, as implemented by `OSPF::deferred_lsas()`

- The periodic verification of LSA checksums in `OSPF::checkages()`

DoNotAge LSAs are always inserted into the current LS Age 0 bin, regardless of their LS Age field. For DoNotAge LSAs, the function `LSA::lsa_age()`, which gives the LSA's current age, always returns the LS Age field at the time the LSA was installed into the link-state database. Those methods that look in particular age bins for the purpose of refreshing locally originated LSAs or deleting MaxAge LSAs from the database, namely, `OSPF::refresh_lsas()` and `OSPF::maxage_lsas()`, simply ignore DoNotAge LSAs.

When the ages of two LSA instances are compared, in order to see which is more recent or whether they differ semantically, the DoNotAge bit is ignored, as implemented in `LSA::cmp_instance()` and `LSA::cmp_contents()`.

6.5.2 Creation of DoNotAge LSAs

We say that a DoNotAge LSA is created when the DoNotAge bit is set in the LSA for the first time. This may occur when the LSA is originated or while an LSA is flooded throughout the routing domain.

To minimize the routing protocol traffic over demand circuits [64], the DoNotAge bit is set in LSAs flooded over those circuits, as implemented in `OSPF::build_update()`. This allows us to suppress the flooding of LSA refreshes—LSAs whose contents have not changed—over demand circuits. Setting DoNotAge will cause the routers on the other end of the circuit to hold the LSA in their databases until newer information is received, whether that be minutes or months. Three caveats should be kept in mind when discussing flooding over demand circuits.

1. If an LSA already has DoNotAge set, we always leave it set when flooding over any interface, demand circuit or not.

2. Setting an LSA's DoNotAge bit when flooding over a demand circuit does not affect the database copy, just as incrementing the LS age in flooded LSAs does not affect the database copy.

3. We do not set the DoNotAge bit when not all routers support it. The function `SpfIfc::demand_flooding()` is used to determine whether the DoNotAge bit can/should/will be set when flooding over a particular interface.

Note that the setting of DoNotAge during flooding can create the impression that routers' link-state databases are not synchronized. When two network regions are separated by one or more demand circuits, the LSA will have its DoNotAge bit clear in one region and set in the other region. In addition, the regions' LS Sequence Numbers for the LSA will diverge over time. However, the contents of the LSA will remain the same from region to region. See Section 4 of [64] for detailed examples.

We also *originate* certain LSAs with the DoNotAge bit set. The configuration parameter `CfgGen::refresh_rate` is the rate, in seconds, at which the router refreshes the AS-external-LSAs that it originates. If the refresh rate is set to a value greater than the standard 1,800 seconds, we originate AS-external-LSAs with the DoNotAge bit set (see `OSPF::lsa_reorig()`), which prevents the other routers from aging our locally originated LSAs and allows us to refresh them whenever we choose. (AS-external-LSAs were chosen because in a large link-state database, they usually comprise the majority of the LSAs. However, this refresh technique can be used with any type of LSA.) To completely disable the refresh of AS-external-LSAs, `CfgGen::refresh_rate` is set to the value `-1`.

6.5.3 Refreshing DoNotAge LSAs

When we have configured a refresh rate for AS-external-LSAs by using `CfgGen::refresh_rate`, the refresh of these LSAs is accomplished by the routine `OSPF::refresh_donotages()` (Figure 6.17). This routine is called by the main aging routine `OSPF::dbage()`, which executes every second.

310-311   We set DoNotAge in the AS-external-LSAs that we originate only if the router has been configured to lengthen the refresh interval from the default `LSRefreshTime`.

313-315   The configured refresh interval is converted to hours (`hour`) and seconds (`age`). Because the age bins span 1 hour, any locally originated DoNotAge LSAs that are due to be refreshed will be in the bin corresponding to the seconds part.

317-328   We scan that bin, looking for locally originated DoNotAge LSAs. `LSA::lsa_hour` is the number of hours that the LSA has been in the database and is maintained by `OSPF::maxage_lsas()`. If it is equal to or greater than the hours portion of the configured refresh interval, the LSA is refreshed by calling `LSA::reoriginate()` with an argument of `true`, which forces the reorigination even if the LSA's contents have not changed.

———————————————————————————————————— dbage.C

```
301 void OSPF::refresh_donotages()
302
303 {
304     uns16 age;
305     uns32 hour;
306     uns16 bin;
307     LSA *lsap;
308     LSA *next_lsa;
309
310     if (refresh_rate <= LSRefreshTime)
311         return;
312
313     hour = refresh_rate/3600;
314     age = refresh_rate%3600;
315     bin = Age2Bin(age);
316
317     for (lsap = LSA::AgeBins[bin]; lsap; lsap = next_lsa) {
318         next_lsa = lsap->lsa_agefwd;
319         if (lsap->adv_rtr() != myid)
320             continue;
321         if (!lsap->do_not_age())
322             continue;
323         if (lsap->lsa_hour >= hour) {
324             if (spflog(LOG_DNAREFR, 1))
325                 log(lsap);
326             lsap->reoriginate(true);
327         }
328     }
329 }
```

———————————————————————————————————— dbage.C

Figure 6.17 Refreshing LSAs at a configurable interval: `OSPF::refresh_donotages()`.

6.5.4 Removing from the Database

If the router that originated an LSA is no longer participating in the OSPF routing domain, we want to remove the LSA from the link-state database, or it could become full of old, useless information. However, we don't want to remove LSAs whose routers are only temporarily unreachable, or undesirable thrashing would result, deleting the LSAs only to have them originated again soon afterward.

This deletion function is usually accomplished by the LSA aging process. When the originating router disappears, its LSAs eventually reach the age of MaxAge, at which point they are flushed from the routing domain.

However, because DoNotAge LSAs are not aged, we need another scheme for removing them from the database when they are defunct. We use the following simple algorithm, implemented in `OSPF::maxage_lsas()`. When an LSA has been in the database for an exact multiple of MaxAge seconds and its originator is unreachable, we flush the LSA from the routing domain. (This is not exactly the same algorithm as specified in Section 2.3 of [64], but it is simpler and accomplishes the same objectives.)

6.5.5   Mixing with DoNotAge-Incapable Routers

We don't allow DoNotAge LSAs to be installed in the database when not all routers in the routing domain support DoNotAge. A router indicates its support of DoNotAge by setting the DC bit in the Options field of *all* its LSAs. So determining whether all routers support DoNotAge is a simple matter of keeping track of the number of LSAs that have the DC bit clear in the database.

We keep track of DoNotAge capability for each flooding scope. `OSPF::donotage()` returns **true** if all routers in attached areas, excluding stub areas, support DoNotAge. This would mean that it would be safe to set DoNotAge in AS-external-LSAs. `SpfArea::donotage()` returns **true** if all routers in the particular OSPF area support DoNotAge; this would mean that it is safe to set DoNotAge in those LSAs with area scope (for example, summary-LSAs).

Network state changes

When an LSA is being added to or deleted from the link-state database, `LSA::process_donotage()` is called to see whether the addition/deletion has affected the network's ability to process DoNotAge. For example, the first LSA installed in the database with DC bit clear turns off the network's ability to originate and to flood DoNotAge LSAs. When the network's DoNotAge capability changes, `OSPF::dna_change` (for AS-external-LSAs) or `SpfArea::dna_change` is set to **true**. This will then cause the 1-second database aging routine to take appropriate actions, calling `OSPF::donotage_changes()` (Figure 6.18).

374-390   This processing is performed when the network's ability to support DoNotAge AS-external-LSAs has changed.

377   `OSPF::dna_flushq` is the list of all DoNotAge AS-external-LSAs that we are currently trying to flush, due to lack of DoNotAge support. We flush this list, because either we now support DoNotAge AS-external-LSAs or we are going to rebuild the list from scratch.

378-385   All the regular areas must agree on the DoNotAge support. In line **382**, we originate/flush indication-LSAs as appropriate.

386-387   If the network no longer supports DoNotAge AS-external-LSAs, they must be flushed. The ones we have originated, we simply reoriginate with the DoNotAge bit off.

——— dbage.C

```
366 void OSPF::donotage_changes()
368 {
369     AreaIterator iter(this);
370     SpfArea *a;
371
372     // Reoriginate indication-LSAs?
373     // Also flush AS-external-LSAs, if necessary
374     if (dna_change) {
375         AreaIterator *oiter;
376         oiter = new AreaIterator(this);
377         dna_flushq.clear();
378         while ((a = oiter->get_next())) {
379             ASBRrte *rrte;
380             if (a->is_stub())
381                 continue;
382             // (Re)originate indication-LSAs
383             rrte = add_asbr(myid);
384             a->asbr_orig(rrte);
385         }
386         if (!donotage())
387             flush_donotage();
388         delete oiter;
389         dna_change = false;
390     }
391
392     // Now do areas whose DoNotAge capability has changed
393     while ((a = iter.get_next())) {
394         if (!a->dna_change)
395             continue;
396         a->a_dna_flushq.clear();
397         if (!a->donotage())
398             a->a_flush_donotage();
399         a->dna_change = false;
400     }
401 }
```

——— dbage.C

Figure 6.18 Processing changes in the network's DoNotAge capability:
`OSPF::donotage_changes()`.

All reorigination and flushing are rate-limited, using the same mechanism that rate-limits the original introduction of AS-external-LSAs; see Section 10.3.2.

393-400   The processing of any area whose DoNotAge capability has changed is analogous to the processing of changes in the AS-external-LSA DoNotAge capability just described.

Indication-LSAs

If any one regular (nonstub) area is incapable of processing DoNotAge, this information must be conveyed to all other regular areas. The carrier of this information is a special LSA called the indication-LSA. Indication-LSAs are ASBR-summary-LSAs listing the originating router itself and a cost of LSInfinity, guaranteeing that the LSA won't be used in any routing calculation—the only useful information is in their DC bit being clear.

The function that determines whether it is necessary to originate an indication-LSA into a given area is `SpfArea::needs_indication()`, shown in Figure 6.19. It returns `true` if an indication-LSA needs to be originated.

```
                                                                    ── asbrlsa.C
145 bool SpfArea::needs_indication()
146
147 {
148     if (a_stub)
149         return(false);
150     if (ospf->donotage())
151         return(false);
152     if (wo_donotage != 0)
153         return(false);
154     if (a_id == BACKBONE && ospf->wo_donotage == 0)
155         return(false);
156     if (dna_indications != 0) {
157         AVLsearch iter(&asbrLSAs);
158         asbrLSA *lsap;
159         if (!self_indicating)
160             return(false);
161         while ((lsap = (asbrLSA *)iter.next())) {
162             if (lsap->adv_cost != LSInfinity ||
163                 lsap->ls_id() != lsap->adv_rtr())
164                 continue;
165             if (lsap->ls_id() > ospf->my_id())
166                 return(false);
167         }
168     }
169
170     return(true);
171 }
                                                                    ── asbrlsa.C
```

Figure 6.19 Determining whether originating an indication-LSA is necessary:
`SpfArea::needs_indication()`.

148-149   Only regular areas need agree about DoNotAge capability.

150-151   If the network is capable of processing DoNotAge AS-external-LSAs, indication-LSAs should not be originated.

152-153   If `SpfArea::wo_donotage` is nonzero, LSAs other than indication-LSAs are in the area's link-state database and have their DC bit clear (this includes AS-external-LSAs with their DC bit clear). In this case, indication-LSAs are not necessary.

154-155   The propagation of indication-LSAs resembles the propagation of inter-area routing information in OSPF, using the "hub-and-spoke" distribution from nonbackbone areas to the backbone area and then down to other nonbackbone areas. As a result, you can originate indication-LSAs for the backbone area only if you have firsthand knowledge (that is, from LSAs other than indication-LSAs) of one or more nonbackbone areas' inability to process DoNotAge LSAs.

156-168   `SpfArea::dna_indications` indicates that indication-LSAs are in the area. If we have not yet originated an indication-LSA for this area (line **159**), we don't have to now. If we have originated an indication-LSA but there is also an indication-LSA from a router with a higher OSPF Router-ID (lines **162-166**), we can safely remove our indication-LSA according to the tiebreakers in Section 2.5.1.1 of [64].

Exercises

6.1   Change `OSPF::lsa_reorig()` so that the configurable refresh rate `CfgGen::refresh_rate` applies to summary-LSAs and ASBR-summary-LSAs as well as to AS-external-LSAs.

6.2   The various database aging actions, such as the refreshing of LSAs in `OSPF::refresh_lsas()`, guard against the possibility that the LSA they are currently processing will be removed from the age bin. However, if the next LSA in the age bin is removed because of the processing of the current LSA, the code will fail. (This could happen if, for example, origination of a group-membership-LSA for a nonzero area causes the origination of a backbone group-membership-LSA.) Guard against this possibility by implementing a new iterator class for age bins, which uses the `class LsaList`.

7

Originating LSAs

In this chapter, we examine how the OSPF implementation originates LSAs. These may be new LSAs or new instances of LSAs whose contents must change. But before we discuss the process of originating LSAs, we should enumerate the reasons for (re)originating an LSA.

1. A local change in router state may require that the router (re)originate one or more LSAs. For example, if one of the router's interfaces changes state (see Section 8.4), the router may need to reoriginate its router-LSA. If one of the router's neighbors changes state (Section 8.1), the router may need to (re)originate both its router-LSA and the network-LSA for the associated IP subnet. Changes in routing table entries may cause the (re)origination of summary-LSAs, and so on.

2. The router periodically reoriginates all its self-originated LSAs, for robustness. If the current instance of the LSA has been lost or corrupted or just no longer reflects the current local state, reoriginating the LSA will repair the error. See Section 7.6 for details.

3. If the router receives an LSA during flooding which updates one of its self-originated LSAs, the router must respond by reissuing the LSA with the next larger LS Sequence Number. This procedure, called "receiving self-originated LSAs," is discussed in detail in Section 7.4.

7.1   Support Routines

The steps involved in originating an LSA, beginning with the three triggers just enumerated, are shown in Figure 7.1. To begin the origination, a type-specific method is called. For example, **SpfArea::rl_orig()** is called to (re)originate the router-LSA for a given area, **SpfIfc::nl_orig()** to (re)originate the attached network segment's network-LSA, **OSPF::sl_orig()** to (re)originate summary-LSAs for all attached areas, **OSPF::asbr_orig()** to (re)originate ASBR-summary-LSAs for all attached areas, and **OSPF::ase_orig()** to (re)originate an AS-external-LSA. If instead you have a pointer to the current LSA in the database that you want to update, the virtual function **LSA::reoriginate()** can be used to start the type-specific reorigination of the LSA.

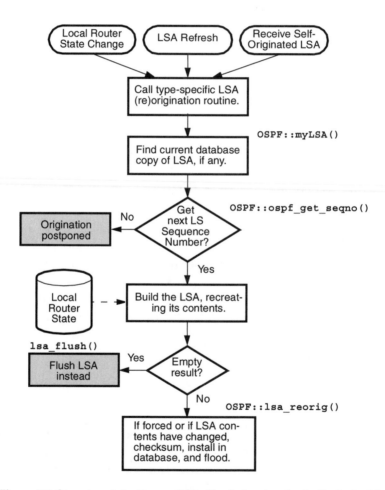

Figure 7.1 Steps in originating an LSA. Shaded rectangles indicate decisions to inhibit or postpone LSA origination.

Then you look to see whether you are updating an existing LSA, using `OSPF::myLSA()` to find the database copy, if any. The arguments to this function are the LSA's area (0 for AS-external-LSAs), its LS Type, and its Link State ID.

The LS Sequence Number to use for the next instance of the LSA is determined by calling `OSPF::ospf_get_seqno()`, shown in Figure 7.2. Besides selecting the LS Sequence Number, this function prequalifies the LSA for reorigination. If the LSA cannot be reoriginated at this moment—for example, if MinLSInterval seconds have not elapsed since the last origination of the LSA—the invalid LS Sequence Number `InvalidLSSeq` is returned. `OSPF::ospf_get_seqno()` also ensures that the scratch area where the LSA will be built (`OSPF::orig_buff`) has enough room.

── *spforig.C*

```
 78 seq_t OSPF::ospf_get_seqno(LSA *lsap, int ls_len, int forced)
 80 {
 81     if (shutting_down() || host_mode)
 82         return(InvalidLSSeq);
 83     // Allocate large LSA build buffer, if necessary
 84     if (ls_len > orig_size) {
 85         orig_size = ls_len;
 86         delete [] orig_buff;
 87         orig_buff = new byte[orig_size];
 88     }
 89
 90     if (!lsap || !lsap->valid())
 91         return(InitLSSeq);
 92     if ((!forced) &&
 93         lsap->in_agebin && lsap->since_received() < MinLSInterval) {
 94         lsap->deferring = true;
 95         if (spflog(LOG_LSADEFER, 3))
 96             log(lsap);
 97         return(InvalidLSSeq);
 98     }
 99     if (lsap->ls_seqno() == MaxLSSeq) {
100         lsap->rollover = true;
101         age_prematurely(lsap);
102         return(InvalidLSSeq);
103     }
104
105     // Normal case. Just advance old LS sequence by 1
106     return(lsap->ls_seqno() + 1);
107 }
```

── *spforig.C*

Figure 7.2 Determining the next LS Sequence Number: `OSPF::ospf_get_seqno()`.

The contents of the LSA are then created: both the LSA header and the type-specific body of the LSA. Examples can be found in Sections 7.2 and 7.3, which describe the building of router-LSA and network-LSA contents, respectively. If the body ends up being empty or if, in the case of summary-LSAs and AS-external-LSAs, the metric ends up being LSInfinity, the LSA is flushed instead of being reoriginated, by calling `lsa_flush()`.

Once the contents have been built, the reorigination process is completed by calling `OSPF::lsa_reorig()`. If the contents of the LSA have changed or if the reorigination is forced (as it would be on a periodic LSA refresh), this routine installs the new instance of the LSA in the router's link-state database and floods the LSA to the router's neighbors. `OSPF::lsa_reorig()` is shown in Figure 7.3 and is discussed in more detail later.

7.1.1 `OSPF::ospf_get_seqno()`

This routine (Figure 7.2) returns the LS Sequence Number that should be used in the next origination of the LSA. The current database copy of the LSA (`lsap`), expected length of the updated LSA in bytes (`ls_len`), and whether the LSA should be reoriginated regardless of whether its contents have changed (`forced`) are given as arguments. If the LSA should not be reoriginated at this time for any reason, the invalid LS Sequence Number `InvalidLSSeq` is returned.

81-82   If the router is in the process of shutting down or is simply acting as a host, no LSAs are originated.

84-88   The LSA will be built in the memory region `OSPF::orig_buff`, whose length in bytes is `OSPF::orig_size`. If this region is not large enough to build the new LSA instance, a new, larger memory region is allocated.

90-91   If there is no current database copy of the LSA, the LS Sequence Number is set to the initial value of `InitLSSeq`.

92-98   If the database copy was installed less than `MinLSInterval` seconds ago, we have to postpone origination of the LSA. By setting `lsap->deferring`, we ensure that `lsap->reoriginate()` will be called by the database aging routines (see Section 6.4.2) as soon as `MinLSInterval` has elapsed. The requirement for `MinLSInterval` between reoriginations is waived when the reorigination is forced, which happens when either (1) we are doing a refresh of the LSA, in which case the `MinLSInterval` test will obviously pass anyway; or (2) we are originating an LSA in response to a received self-originated LSA (Section 7.4). We also waive the `MinLSInterval` requirement when the current LSA is in the process of being flushed—that is, its age is equal to MaxAge—which is the only case when `LSA::in_agebin` will be `false`.

99-103   If the current database copy has the largest LS Sequence Number (`MaxLSSeq`), we need to wrap the LS Sequence Number in order to reoriginate the LSA. This procedure consists of flushing the database copy from the routing domain (`OSPF::age_prematurely`) and, as soon as the flush is acknowledged by all the router's neighbors, reoriginating the LSA with the initial LS Sequence Number `InitLSSeq`. Setting `LSA::rollover` informs the database aging routines to perform a reorigination as soon as the flush completes (Section 6.4.3).

106   The normal case is just incrementing the database copy's LS Sequence Number by 1 and using this as the LS Sequence Number for the new LSA instance.

7.1.2   `OSPF::lsa_reorig()`

The final step of reoriginating an LSA is the routine `OSPF::lsa_reorig()` (Figure 7.3). This routine is called when the entire LSA—its standard link-state header and type-specific body—have been formatted. The routine then determines whether a new instance of the LSA should be issued and, if so, installs the LSA in the router's link-state database and starts the flooding of the LSA to the router's neighbors.

```
───────────────────────────────────────────────── spforig.C
145 LSA *OSPF::lsa_reorig(SpfArea *ap, LSA *olsap, LShdr *hdr, int forced)
146
147 {
148     int changes;
149     LSA *lsap;
150
151     hdr->ls_age = 0;
152     if (donotage() &&
153         hdr->ls_type == LST_ASL &&
154         (refresh_rate < 0 || refresh_rate > LSRefreshTime))
155         hdr->ls_age = hton16(ntoh16(hdr->ls_age) | DoNotAge);
156     changes = (olsap ? olsap->cmp_contents(hdr) : true);
157     if (!changes && !forced && olsap->do_not_age() == hdr->do_not_age())
158         return(0);
159     // Perform origination
160     hdr->generate_cksum();
161     if (spflog(LOG_LSAORIG, 3))
162         log(hdr);
163     // Add to database and flood
164     lsap = AddLSA(ap, olsap, hdr, changes);
165     lsap->flood(0, hdr);
166     return(lsap);
167 }
───────────────────────────────────────────────── spforig.C
```

Figure 7.3 Completing the origination of an LSA: `OSPF::lsa_reorig()`.

145   The arguments to `OSPF::lsa_reorig()` are the OSPF area to which the LSA will belong (`ap`; set to 0 for AS-external-LSAs); the current database copy of the LSA, if any (`olsap`); the new instance of the LSA, formatted to be sent in OSPF Link State Update packets (`hdr`); and whether the reorigination of the LSA is required (`forced`).

151   LSAs are reoriginated with their LS Age field set to 0. The LSA age will be incremented as the LSA is flooded through the network (see Section 9.6) and as the LSA is held in each router's link-state database (Section 6.4).

152-155   This implementation can be configured to optionally originate AS-external-LSAs with the DoNotAge bit set (Section 6.5). Doing so allows us to control the refresh rate of our own AS-external-LSAs, using the configurable value `OSPF::refresh_rate` rather than the standard value of `LSRefreshTime` (30 minutes). We set the DoNotAge bit only if all routers are capable of processing the bit, as indicated by `OSPF::donotage()`.

156-158   If reorigination of the LSA is not being forced, we refuse to reoriginate the LSA if the contents of the new LSA are the same as the current database copy (see Section 9.2.1). However, if we are reoriginating the LSA with the state of the DoNotAge bit changed, as would be the case when a DoNotAge-incapable router has just been discovered, we let the origination proceed.

160   We checksum the LSA. From here on, the LSA will carry the checksum—while it is flooded and while it sits in this and other routers' databases—as proof against corruption of the LSA's contents.

164   The new instance of the LSA is added to the database (Section 6.2.2), replacing the current database copy, if it exists. In the process, if the contents of the LSA have changed (`changes`), the appropriate routing table calculation is scheduled. The internal database representation of the LSA, a `class LSA *lsap`, is returned by the database addition.

165   The reliable flooding of the LSA is begun (Section 9.3), sending the LSA out the router's interfaces in Link State Update packets and adding the LSA to neighbors' link-state retransmission lists.

166   The internal database representation of the LSA is returned to the caller, in case it needs to store type-specific information (see, for example, Section 10.3.2).

7.2   Router-LSAs

In this section, we examine the peculiarities of originating router-LSAs. Router-LSA origination uses the generic support for LSA origination described previously, with processing specific to router-LSAs being restricted to the function `SpfArea::rl_orig()`, which formats the contents of an area's router-LSA. A code fragment from this function is shown in Figure 7.4.

The usual argument to an LSA origination function, `forced`, has been given to `SpfArea::rl_orig()`, indicating whether the LSA need be originated regardless of content changes. Before the code shown in Figure 7.4, the current database copy of the router-LSA has been located (`olsap`), and a maximum possible size for the LSA (`maxlen`) has been calculated by examining all interfaces connected to the area, together with the configured host routes (Section 13.8). The maximum number of bytes that a given interface can contribute to the LSA is determined by calling `SpfIfc::rl_size()`.

```
242     maxifc = maxlen/sizeof(RtrLink);
243     if (maxifc > sz_ifmap) {
244         delete [] ifmap;
245         ifmap = new (SpfIfc *)[maxifc];
246         sz_ifmap = maxifc;
247     }
248
249     // Start with empty interface map
250     n_ifmap = 0;
251
252     // Build LSA header
253     hdr = ospf->orig_buffer();
254     hdr->ls_opts = SPO_DC;
255     if (!a_stub)
256         hdr->ls_opts |= SPO_EXT;
257     if (ospf->mospf_enabled())
258         hdr->ls_opts |= SPO_MC;
259     hdr->ls_type = LST_RTR;
260     hdr->ls_id = hton32(ospf->my_id());
261     hdr->ls_org = hton32(ospf->my_id());
262     hdr->ls_seqno = (seq_t) hton32((uns32) seqno);
263     // Router-LSA specific portion
264     rtrhdr = (RTRhdr *) (hdr+1);
265     rtrhdr->rtype = 0;
266     if (ospf->n_area > 1)
267         rtrhdr->rtype |= RTYPE_B;
268     if (ospf->n_extImports != 0)
269         rtrhdr->rtype |= RTYPE_E;
270     if (n_VLs > 0)
271         rtrhdr->rtype |= RTYPE_V;
272     if (ospf->mospf_enabled()) {
273         if (a_id != 0 && ospf->mc_abr())
274             rtrhdr->rtype |= RTYPE_W;
275         else if (ospf->inter_AS_mc)
276             rtrhdr->rtype |= RTYPE_W;
277     }
278     rtrhdr->zero = 0;
279     rtrhdr->nlinks = 0;
280
281     // Build body of router-LSA
282     rlp = (RtrLink *) (rtrhdr+1);
283     iiter.reset();
```

(Continued)

```
284        while ((ip = iiter.get_next())) {
285            if (ip->state() == IFS_DOWN)
286                continue;
287            else if (ip->state() == IFS_LOOP) {
288                rlp->link_id = hton32(ip->if_addr);
289                rlp->link_data = hton32(0xffffffffL);
290                rlp->link_type = LT_STUB;
291                rlp->n_tos = 0;
292                rlp->metric = hton16(ip->cost());
293                add_to_ifmap(ip);
294                rlp++;
295                rtrhdr->nlinks++;
296            }
297            else
298                rlp = ip->rl_insert(rtrhdr, rlp);
299        }
300
301        /* If no active interfaces to area, just flush
302         * LSA. Host addresses will get added to other areas
303         * automatically.
304         */
305        if (rtrhdr->nlinks == 0) {
306            lsa_flush(olsap);
307            return;
308        }
309
310        // Add area's host routes
311        rlp = rl_insert_hosts(this, rtrhdr, rlp);
312        // If first active area, advertise orphaned hosts
313        if (this == ospf->first_area) {
314            AreaIterator aiter(ospf);
315            SpfArea *ap;
316            while ((ap = aiter.get_next())) {
317                if (ap->n_active_if == 0)
318                    rlp = ap->rl_insert_hosts(this, rtrhdr, rlp);
319            }
320        }
```
                                                                        ───── rtrlsa.C

Figure 7.4 Formatting the router's router-LSA: `SpfArea::rl_orig()`.

Just prior to the code fragment, we have determined that the LSA can be reoriginated immediately, obtaining the new LS Sequence Number to use (`seqno`).

242-250   Based on the previously calculated maximum size for the LSA, we determine the maximum number of link descriptions (`maxifc`) that can appear in the router-LSA. We will record the OSPF interface associated with each link description in the array `SpfArea::ifmap`, for later use in the routing calculation's next-hop determination (see

Section 11.2.2). Here, we make sure that the size of the array, `SpfArea::sz_ifmap`, is large enough to handle the router-LSA that we are about to build. The number interfaces currently in the array, `SpfArea::n_ifmap`, is reset to 0 so we can begin again adding link records to the router-LSA.

253   Construction of the LSA will begin in the statically allocated buffer `OSPF::orig_buffer()`. The previous call to `OSPF::ospf_get_seqno()` has guaranteed that the buffer is large enough. We will build the LSA in network byte order, using the template method described in Section 4.4.1. `LShdr *hdr` provides the template for the standard LSA header, `RTRhdr *rtrhdr` the template for the small fixed-sized beginning of the router-LSA's body, and `RtrLink *rlp` the template for each link description appearing in the LSA body.

254-262   The standard LSA header is built. In the LSA's Options field, we always indicate that the router is capable of DoNotAge processing (line 254) and whether the router is currently running MOSPF (lines 257-258). We also set bit E in the Options field, depending on whether the LSA's area is capable of flooding AS-external-LSAs (lines 255-256), although this bit setting has no functional impact in LSAs. The Link State ID in a router-LSA is the router's OSPF Router ID (line 260).

264-279   The fixed-size part of router-LSA is built in `RTRhdr *rtrhdr`. `RTRhdr::rtype` describes additional functions that the router has taken on, on top of the base functionality of an OSPF router. `OSPF::n_area` indicates the number of areas to which the router is actively attached; if attached to more than one area, the router declares itself an area border router (line 267). If the router has one or more configured static routes (`OSPF::n_extImports`), the router declares itself an AS boundary router, even if the routes are not currently being imported in AS-external-LSAs. It doesn't hurt to declare the router an AS boundary router before the routes are imported, and this logic prevents us from having to reoriginate router-LSAs when network conditions change and we begin importing our configured static routes (see Section 10.3.2). The number of fully adjacent virtual links that the router has associated with the area is given by `SpfArea::n_VLs`; the existence of one or more of these virtual links is reflected in the router-LSA (line 271), enabling all other routers in the area to agree on the area's transit status (see Section 11.2). A MOSPF router that has been configured as an inter-area multicast forwarder declares itself as a wildcard multicast receiver to nonzero areas (lines 273-274) because these areas do not receive multicast group membership information from other areas (see Section 12.3). For an analogous reason, routers configured to forward multicast datagrams across Autonomous System (AS) boundaries declare themselves as wildcard multicast receivers (lines 275-276).

279-282   The number of link descriptions in the router-LSA, `RTRhdr::nlinks`, is initially set to 0, and we begin by installing the first link description immediately following the fixed-sized router-LSA header.

283   We're going to go through the interfaces attached to the area, in order to build the body of the LSA. However, we have already gone through the interfaces once, in order

to calculate the maximum size that the router-LSA could attain. To iterate through the set of interfaces once more, we have to reset the iterator, using **IfcIterator::reset()**.

284-299   We iterate through the interfaces attaching to the area, in order to fill out the router-LSA. If the interface is inoperational (lines **285-286**), it is not reported in the router-LSA. If the interface is in loopback (lines **287-296**), the interface's IP address is reported in the router-LSA as a stub link; in this way, the address can still be used in network diagnostics, such as **ping**. In this case, we advertise just the single address instead of the whole subnet, so as not to interfere with routing to the subnet, which may be accessible through other paths. Fully operational interfaces (lines **297-298**) are reported, varying on the interface's type (broadcast, NBMA, point-to-point, and so on), by calling the virtual function **SpfIfc::rl_insert()**. This function, specialized for point-to-point interfaces, is shown later.

305-308   If no interfaces have been added to the router-LSA, we flush the router-LSA instead of reoriginating it. This will be a no-op if there is no current copy of the router-LSA in the link-state database.

311   We add the configured host routes associated with this area to the router-LSA.

313-320   Configured host routes are typically those assigned to the router's loopback interface and are meant to be advertised regardless of the state of the router's interfaces. For that reason, if a host route has been assigned to a currently unattached area, we assign it to another attached area (**OSPF::first_area**) to maintain the host route's reachability.

323-324   We finish building the router-LSA by calculating its total length and converting the field indicating the number of advertised links, **RTRhdr::nlinks**, to network byte order so that it can be flooded onto the network.

326   If the contents of the router-LSA just built are different from the database copy or if the reorigination is being forced, **OSPF::lsa_reorig()** will install the new router-LSA in the database and start flooding the new LSA to the router's neighbors.

7.2.1   **PPIfc::rl_insert()**

The representation of an interface in the router-LSA depends on the interface's type. This behavior is captured by the virtual function **SpfIfc::rl_insert()**. The specific behavior for point-to-point interfaces is given by **PPPIfc::rl_insert()**, as shown in Figure 7.5.

107   A pointer to the header (**rtrhdr**) of the router-LSA is given as the first argument so that, as we add links to the router-LSA, we can increment the field that counts the number of links (lines **120** and **130**). The second argument (**rlp**) points to the place in the router-LSA where the next link description should be built. The routine returns a pointer to the new end of the router-LSA, where the next link description, if any, will be placed (line **132**).

112-121   If the neighbor associated with the point-to-point link is fully adjacent, a router-to-router link description is added to the router-LSA. The link description's data field con-

```
————————————————————————————————————————————— rtrlsa.C
107 RtrLink *PPIfc::rl_insert(RTRhdr *rtrhdr, RtrLink *rlp)
108
109 {
110     SpfNbr *np;
111
112     if ((np = if_nlst) && np->state() == NBS_FULL) {
113         rlp->link_id = hton32(np->id());
114         rlp->link_data = hton32(unnumbered() ? if_IfIndex : if_addr);
115         rlp->link_type = LT_PP;
116         rlp->n_tos = 0;
117         rlp->metric = hton16(if_cost);
118         if_area->add_to_ifmap(this);
119         rlp++;
120         rtrhdr->nlinks++;
121     }
122     if (state() == IFS_PP && !unnumbered() && np) {
123         rlp->link_id = hton32(np->addr());
124         rlp->link_data = hton32(0xffffffffL);
125         rlp->link_type = LT_STUB;
126         rlp->n_tos = 0;
127         rlp->metric = hton16(if_cost);
128         if_area->add_to_ifmap(this);
129         rlp++;
130         rtrhdr->nlinks++;
131     }
132     return(rlp);
133 }
————————————————————————————————————————————— rtrlsa.C
```

Figure 7.5 Add a point-to-point interface to a router-LSA: `PPIfc::rl_insert()`.

tains the IP interface address or, if the link is unnumbered, the MIB-II IfIndex value for the interface (line **114**)—for point-to-point interfaces, this field is cosmetic and not necessary for the correct functioning of the routing table's next-hop calculation. However, the interface leading to the link description must be recorded (line **118**) in order to correctly seed the next-hop calculation, as described in Section 11.2.2.

122-131   If the neighbor's IP address on a numbered link is known, it gets reported as a separate stub link. *Note:* By this logic, if our end of the link has been configured as unnumbered but the neighbor's end has been assigned an IP address, no one ends up advertising the neighbor's address (see Chapter 8 of [67]). In another option, not implemented here but allowed by the OSPF specification, a subnet could be assigned to the point-to-point link (as done by RIP) and the whole subnet advertised in a stub link.

7.2.2 `SpfIfc::rl_size()`

The virtual function `SpfIfc::rl_size()` returns the maximum number of bytes that an interface could possibly contribute to a router-LSA. As we saw earlier, a point-to-point interface could contribute two link descriptions, and so `PPIfc::rl_size()` simply returns `2*sizeof(RtrLink)`. However, things get a little more interesting for some of the other interface types. The logic for Point-to-MultiPoint interfaces is shown in Figure 7.6. A Point-to-MultiPoint interface potentially contributes one router-to-router link description for each associated neighbor and an additional link description advertising a stub route to the interface's IP address.

```
                                                              ——————— rtrlsa.C
136 int P2mPIfc::rl_size()
137
138 {
139     return((if_nnbrs+1)  *  sizeof(RtrLink));
140 }
                                                              ——————— rtrlsa.C
```

Figure 7.6 Determining the number of bytes that a Point-to-MultiPoint interface can add to a router-LSA: `P2mPIfc::rl_size()`.

7.3   Network-LSAs: `SpfIfc::nl_orig()`

As with router-LSAs, the only type-specific LSA processing involving network-LSAs is the building of the body of the network-LSA. This function is implemented in `SpfIfc::nl_orig()` (Figure 7.7).

35   The function `SpfIfc::nl_orig()` will attempt to originate a network-LSA for the network segment to which the interface attaches. As with all origination routines, the **forced** argument indicates whether the LSA should be reoriginated even if there are no changes in LSA contents.

42-45   We originate a network-LSA only if we are the network's Designated Router and one or more fully adjacent neighbors are associated with the interface. (If another router is Designated Router, our router-LSA will point to the network-LSA that that router originates. If there are no fully adjacent neighbors, the network will be reported as a stub link in our router-LSA.) If we're not supposed to originate a network-LSA, we must flush any network-LSA that we had previously originated.

47-81   We build the contents of the network-LSA. As with all LSAs, it is formatted in the static buffer allocated within the **class OSPF *ospf** (line **61**).

55-56   The maximum size that a network-LSA can attain is the sum of the fixed-length headers (LSA and network-LSA), our own OSPF Router ID, and the OSPF Router IDs of each neighbor. We don't need an exact size here, so we don't need to determine how many neighbors are fully adjacent at this point.

```
                                                           ───── netlsa.C
35 void SpfIfc::nl_orig(int forced)
37 {
38     LSA *olsap;
40     olsap = ospf->myLSA(if_area, LST_NET, if_addr);
42     if (if_state != IFS_DR)
43         lsa_flush(olsap);
44     else if (if_nfull == 0)
45         lsa_flush(olsap);
46     else {
47         LShdr *hdr;
48         NetLShdr *nethdr;
49         uns16 length;
50         seq_t seqno;
51         rtid_t *nbr_ids;
52         NbrIterator iter(this);
53         SpfNbr *np;
55         length = sizeof(NetLShdr) + (if_nfull+1)*sizeof(rtid_t);
56         length += sizeof(LShdr);
57         seqno = ospf->ospf_get_seqno(olsap, length, forced);
58         if (seqno == InvalidLSSeq)
59             return;
61         hdr = ospf->orig_buffer();
62         hdr->ls_opts = SPO_DC;
63         if (!if_area->a_stub)
64             hdr->ls_opts |= SPO_EXT;
65         if (mospf_enabled())
66             hdr->ls_opts |= SPO_MC;
67         hdr->ls_type = LST_NET;
68         hdr->ls_id = hton32(if_addr);
69         hdr->ls_org = hton32(ospf->my_id());
70         hdr->ls_seqno = hton32(seqno);
71         hdr->ls_length = hton16(length);
73         nethdr = (NetLShdr *) (hdr + 1);
74         nethdr->netmask = hton32(if_mask);
76         nbr_ids = (rtid_t *) (nethdr + 1);
77         *nbr_ids = hton32(ospf->my_id());
78         while ((np = iter.get_next()) != 0) {
79             if (np->state() == NBS_FULL)
80                 *(++nbr_ids) = hton32(np->id());
81         }
82         (void) ospf->lsa_reorig(if_area, olsap, hdr, forced);
83     }
84 }
                                                           ───── netlsa.C
```

Figure 7.7 Building the body of a network-LSA: SpfIfc::nl_orig().

57-59   If `OSPF::ospf_get_seqno()` fails to return a valid LS Sequence Number, reorigination of the network-LSA has been automatically scheduled for a later time. At that time, `SpfIfc::nl_orig()` will be reentered via a call to `netLSA::reoriginate()` (see Sections 7.5 and 7.7).

62-66   The appropriate bits are set in the network-LSA's Options field. Because we are capable of processing DoNotAge LSAs, we always set the DC bit. Setting the E bit to match the containing OSPF area's external routing capability is a courtesy that has no functional impact. The logic for setting/clearing the MC bit removes the network from the view of multicast routing whenever MOSPF is disabled on the interface attaching to the network; this is done primarily to prune excess subnets assigned to the same physical segment (see Section 14.7 of [66]).

68   The Link State ID of a network-LSA is the IP address of the Designated Router—our IP interface address, in this case. Using the IP address of the Designated Router ensures that when a router-LSA and a network-LSA point to each other—a necessity for using the link in the routing calculation—they are indicating that the originators of the two LSAs have synchronized databases (see Section 4.8 of [67]).

74   By putting the subnet mask in the body of the network-LSA, the prefix assigned to the network can be calculated by masking the network-LSA's Link State ID with the subnet mask.

77-81   The rest of the network-LSA contains the OSPF Router-IDs of the fully adjacent neighbors. The router includes itself in this list. Listing only fully adjacent neighbors means that the routing calculation will prevent packets from being forwarded between routers with unsynchronized databases, which may have incompatible ideas about the current best path to any given destination.

82   The common ending to all LSA originations, regardless of LSA type, is the function `OSPF::lsa_reorig()`, which installs the LSA in the database and starts its flooding if either the LSA's contents have changed or its reorigination is being forced.

7.4   Receiving Self-Originated LSAs

Sometimes, a router receives a new LSA from a neighbor during flooding, and the LSA's Link State ID indicates that the router itself has originated it. However, because—at least according to its LS Sequence Number—the LSA is newer than anything that the router currently has in its link-state database, how could the router have originated it? The answer must be that the router originated the LSA in a previous life—before the router's OSPF software was last restarted.

For example, in the network diagram on the flyleaf, suppose that router G has been up and running for several days. Its router-LSA now has an LS Sequence Number of 0x80000310. Then it is powered down for maintenance reasons; in the process, its Ethernet interface to 10.1.2.0/24 is removed. When router G is powered up again, it originates its router-LSA with the initial LS Sequence Number of 0x800000001 and then starts to synchronize its link-state database with its two neighbors on segment 10.1.3.0/24. Soon afterward, it receives its own router-LSA, with an LS Sequence Number of 0x80000310 and reporting the now nonexistent Ethernet interface. In order to get the rest of the OSPF routers to accept the fact that the Ethernet interface has been deleted, router G must then reoriginate its router-LSA with a higher LS Sequence Number and omit mention of the Ethernet interface. This logic is implemented in the routine `OSPF::self_originated()`. (Of course, reception of a seemingly self-originated LSA can also indicate a bigger problem: duplicate OSPF Router IDs. Such a problem must be repaired by the network operator.)

When a new LSA is received in flooding (Section 9.2), `OSPF::self_originated()` is called to determine whether this LSA is old information that the router must update. This routine is displayed in Figure 7.8.

33   The routine is called for every new LSA received during flooding: `hdr` points to the received LSA, in network format; `ap`, to the area to which the LSA belongs; and `database_copy`, to the LSA instance that has been found in the router's link-state database. The database may not contain an instance of the LSA; if it does, we are guaranteed that the instance is less recent than the newly received `hdr`.

38-40   Here, we are trying to determine whether we originated this LSA in a previous life. The LSA's Advertising Router (`LShdr::ls_org`) being equal to our OSPF Router ID is a dead giveaway. However, we must handle one other case. If another router has previously originated a network-LSA with Link State ID equal to one of our interface addresses, we must flush that LSA, or it might get in the way of the routing calculation when/if we become Designated Router on the segment and originate a network-LSA with the identical Link State ID (see Section 11.4).

47-52   At this point, we have decided that the newly received LSA should be considered to be one that we had originated. If this was a network-LSA from another router that potentially conflicts with an LSA that we might want to originate, if there is no database copy, or if we were already trying to flush the database copy, we flush the newly received LSA by calling `OSPF::age_prematurely()`. In order to flush the received LSA, it must first be added to the database. This addition is temporary, pending acknowledgment of the flush from all adjacent neighbors.

53-60   We now know that we have current data, in the form of `database_copy`, that we want the other OSPF routers to accept. So we force a reorigination of the database copy with a sequence number one larger than the one we just received. If, however, we just received the maximum LS Sequence Number, we must perform the LS Sequence Number rollover procedure (Section 7.7) before reissuing the LSA with the correct contents.

62   A return code of `true` indicates to the caller that complete processing of the received LSA has been performed and that further flooding of the received LSA should be inhibited.

```
                                                              spforig.C
33 int OSPF::self_originated(SpfArea *ap, LShdr *hdr, LSA *database_copy)
35 {
36     LSA *lsap;
37
38     if ((ntoh32(hdr->ls_org) != my_id()) &&
39         (hdr->ls_type != LST_NET || !find_ifc(ntoh32(hdr->ls_id))))
40         return(false);
41
42     // Have received update of self-originated LSA
43     if (spflog(LOG_SELFORIG, 4))
44         log(hdr);
45     // Flush if don't want to advertise
46     // Otherwise, simply bump database copy's sequence number
47     if (ntoh32(hdr->ls_org) != my_id() ||
48         (!database_copy) ||
49         database_copy->lsa_age() == MaxAge) {
50         lsap = AddLSA(ap, database_copy, hdr, true);
51         age_prematurely(lsap);
52     }
53     else if (ntoh32(hdr->ls_seqno) == (seq_t) MaxLSSeq) {
54         lsap = AddLSA(ap, database_copy, hdr, true);
55         lsap->rollover = true;
56         age_prematurely(lsap);
57         return(true);
58     }
59     else
60         database_copy->refresh(ntoh32(hdr->ls_seqno));
61
62     return(true);
63 }
                                                              spforig.C
```

Figure 7.8 Determining whether an LSA is self-originated: `OSPF::self_originated()`.

7.5   Deferred Originations

As we have seen, part of the process of selecting the next LS Sequence Number to use in reoriginating an LSA is to make sure that the minimum time between originations of any particular LSA, namely, MinLSInterval seconds, is being met. If not, `OSPF::ospf_get_seqno()` schedules a later reorigination simply by setting `LSA::deferring` in the current database copy of the LSA and by returning the invalid LS Sequence Number `InvalidLSSeq`, which tables the reorigination for the moment.

The minimum interval between originations will be met when the database copy reaches the age MinLSInterval. At that time, the database aging process (Section 6.4.2) will call the routine `OSPF::deferred_lsas()` (Figure 7.9). Going through all the LSAs with LS Age equal to `MinLSInterval` (lines **188**, **190**), this routine will find the locally originated LSA (line **194**) whose origination has been deferred. The routine then reoriginates the LSA by calling the virtual function `LSA::reoriginate()`.

---
dbage.C

```
181 void OSPF::deferred_lsas()
183 {
184     uns16 bin;
185     LSA *lsap;
186     LSA *next_lsa;
187
188     bin = Age2Bin(MinLSInterval);
190     for (lsap = LSA::AgeBins[bin]; lsap; lsap = next_lsa) {
191         next_lsa = lsap->lsa_agefwd;
192         if (!lsap->deferring)
193             continue;
194         if (lsap->adv_rtr() == myid) {
195             lsap->deferring = false;
196             lsap->reoriginate(false);
197         }
198     }
199 }
```

dbage.C

Figure 7.9 Deferred origination of LSAs: `OSPF::deferred_lsas()`.

The `LSA::reoriginate()` function then calls the function to build the contents of the LSA, install it in the database, and reflood. For example, if the LSA is a network-LSA, we want `LSA::reoriginate()` to end up calling the appropriate `SpfIfc::nl_orig()` function (Section 7.3). To see how this is done, we examine the specialized method `netLSA::reoriginate()` (Figure 7.10).

---
netlsa.C

```
100 void netLSA::reoriginate(int forced)
102 {
103     SpfIfc *ip;
105     if ((ip = ospf->find_ifc(ls_id())) == 0 ||
106         ip->area() != lsa_ap)
107         lsa_flush(this);
108     else
109         ip->nl_orig(forced);
110 }
```

netlsa.C

Figure 7.10 `LSA::reoriginate()`, specialized for network-LSAs.

105-107   If we are supposed to reoriginate this network-LSA, we should have an interface
with an IP address equal to the network-LSA's Link State ID, and the interface must
attach to the same area to which the network-LSA belongs. If one of these conditions is
false, we simply flush the current database copy.

109   We call `SpfIfc::nl_orig()` for the matching interface.

7.6   Refreshing LSAs

An OSPF router periodically reoriginates all its self-originated LSAs (called *refreshing*),
for reasons of robustness. This minimizes the damage that corruption of one or more of
the router's self-originated LSAs can cause in its own database or in other routers' databases. The reoriginated LSA overwrites the corrupted data with a new, clean copy of the
LSA.

The specification mandates that each LSA be reoriginated at least every LSRefresh-
Time, which is equal to 30 minutes. The mechanism is similar to that just discussed for
deferred originations. The database aging procedure calls `OSPF::refresh_lsas()`,
which looks at all the LSAs with LS Age equal to LSRefreshTime and reoriginates any
LSAs marked as self-originated, by calling their `LSA::reoriginate()` method.

This implementation also supports the configuration of the refresh rate, or the elim-
ination of LSA refresh altogether, through the setting of the DoNotAge bit. See Section
6.5 for details.

Note that refreshing the LSA by calling `LSA::reoriginate()` rebuilds the contents
of the LSA from first principles. Another way of refreshing the LSA would be to simply
increase its LS Sequence Number and reflood. However, if the router's own copy of the
LSA had become corrupted, that (simpler) procedure would allow the corruption to
persist indefinitely.

7.7   LS Sequence Number Rollover

The LS Sequence Number space for OSPF LSAs is linear (see Section 4.2.2 of [67]). At
first, an LSA is originated with an LS Sequence Number of `InitLSSeq` (0x80000001), the
smallest negative signed 32-bit integer. An LSA's LS Sequence Number then increments
with each successive reorigination of the LSA, until the maximum value of `MaxLSSeq`
(0x7fffffff) is reached. At this point, in order to reoriginate the LSA, we will again use the
smallest LS Sequence Number `InitLSSeq` (this is called sequence number rollover, or
wrap). However, in order to get the rest of the routers to accept this new LSA, we must
first flush the instance with LS Sequence Number of `MaxLSSeq` from the routing domain.

Just as the OSPF implementation checks to make sure that the minimum interval
between successive originations is met when getting the next LS Sequence Number for a
reorigination (Section 7.1.1), we also check to see whether the current LS Sequence

Number is `MaxLSSeq`. If it is, we set `LSA::rollover`, begin the process of flushing the database copy from the routing domain (Section 7.8), and return the invalid LS Sequence Number `InvalidLSSeq`, terminating the present attempt at reoriginating the LSA.

When the flushing of LSA completes and we are ready to remove the LSA from our database (Section 6.2.4), we notice that `LSA::rollover` is set. As a result, instead of removing the LSA from the database, we reoriginate the LSA. However, in this case, instead of calling `LSA::reoriginate()` directly, as was done for deferred originations, we call the intermediary routine `LSA::refresh()` (Figure 7.11), which allows us to specify the LS Sequence Number (namely, `seqno` + 1) to be used in the reorigination. To wrap the LS Sequence Number, we call `LSA::refresh()` with the argument `InvalidLSSeq`, which causes the reorigination to use the LS Sequence Number `InvalidLSSeq+1` = `InitLSSeq`.

```
                                                          ───── spforig.C
114 int LSA::refresh(seq_t seqno)
116 {
117     lsa_seqno = seqno;
118     reoriginate(true);
119     return(true);
120 }
                                                          ───── spforig.C
```

Figure 7.11 Forcing a reorigination with a particular LS Sequence Number: `LSA::refresh()`.

7.8   Premature Aging

In order to delete an LSA from the link-state database, a router sets the LSA's LS Age to MaxAge and refloods it, a procedure called *premature aging*. Only when the flood of a MaxAge LSA has been acknowledged by all of a router's adjacent neighbors is the LSA removed from the router's link-state database.

It's a bad idea to prematurely age an LSA that has been originated by another router. Why? Because the other router may disagree with your decision, immediately reoriginating the LSA, with a possible continual loop of flushes and reoriginations ensuing. And contrary to intuition, even if your routing calculation indicates that a particular router is unreachable, that router may indeed be participating in flooding. So the OSPF specification states that you can prematurely age only your *self-originated LSAs*, with a couple of exceptions made for those LSAs with the DoNotAge bit set (Section 6.5). Our implementation obeys these rules.

Premature aging of an LSA is accomplished by `OSPF::age_prematurely()`, shown in Figure 7.12.

—— spforig.C

```
210 void OSPF::age_prematurely(LSA *lsap)
212 {
213     LShdr *hdr;
214     LSA *nlsap;
215     age_t oldage;
216     int msgno;
217
218     hdr = ospf->BuildLSA(lsap);
219     oldage = ntoh16(hdr->ls_age);
220     hdr->ls_age = hton16(MaxAge);
221     hdr->generate_cksum();
222
223     msgno = (oldage == MaxAge ? LOG_LSAMAXAGE : LOG_LSAFLUSH);
224     if (spflog(msgno, 3))
225         log(hdr);
226
227     // Add to database and flood
228     // lsap may be deleted after this line
229     nlsap = AddLSA(lsap->area(), lsap, hdr, true);
230     nlsap->flood(0, hdr);
231 }
```

—— spforig.C

Figure 7.12 Flushing an LSA from the routing domain: OSPF::age_prematurely().

218-221   After converting the internally parsed version of the LSA back into the network format, we set its LS Age field to MaxAge to indicate to the other routers that the LSA should be removed from their databases after reflooding.

229   Although the body of the LSA has not changed, setting its age to MaxAge means that we are now dealing with a new instance of the LSA. Therefore, we reinstall it in the database, which as a side effect will schedule the appropriate routing calculations.

230   We start the flooding of the new LSA instance. Later, when the routine OSPF::free_maxage_lsas() (Section 6.2.4) runs as part of the database aging process and notices that the MaxAge LSA has been acknowledged by all adjacent neighbors, the LSA will be removed from the router's link-state database.

Exercises

7.1   Implement a configurable option to advertise a stub link for a point-to-point network's subnet, instead of advertising a link to the IP address of the router on the other end of the link (see Section 7.2).

8

Neighbor Maintenance

In this chapter, we discuss the handling of neighbor relationships by the OSPF implementation: their discovery, the initial database synchronization performed after discovery, and the continued monitoring of neighbor liveness. This subject naturally encompasses both the OSPF neighbor and the interface finite state machines.

A number of small enhancements have been made to OSPF's Hello Protocol, to speed up neighbor discovery and to minimize its bandwidth consumption. These are discussed in Section 8.2.

The `ospfd` software also contains enhancements reducing resource consumption during initial database synchronization, the so-called Database Exchange process. These enhancements include limiting the number of concurrent Database Exchange sessions and are discussed in Section 8.3.

8.1 Neighbor State Machine

The purpose of the OSPF neighbor state machine is to ensure that a router finds the neighbors with which it needs to maintain link-state database synchronization and that with these neighbors, it performs an initial database synchronization before advertising the neighbor connections in LSAs. The OSPF protocol's database synchronization requirements minimize the chance of routing loops, as discussed in Section 4.7.1 of [67].

Each neighbor is represented by a `class SpfNbr` (Section 3.2.5). The state of the communication with a neighbor is stored in the variable `SpfNbr::n_state` and takes one of the enumerated values prefixed by **NBS_** in Figure 8.1. When a neighbor is first allocated, its initial state is set to **NBS_DOWN**, indicating that the router and the neighbor are not currently communicating. However, the usual reason for allocating a neighbor structure is that a Hello packet has been received from the neighbor, in which case the neighbor state immediately transitions to **NBS_INIT**. If then some time later, Hello packets cease to be received from the neighbor, the neighbor transitions back to the **NBS_DOWN** state and is freed by the routine **OSPF::delete_down_neighbors()**.

```
                                                                    nbrfsm.h
37 enum {
38      NBS_DOWN = 0x01,      // Neighbor down
39      NBS_ATTEMPT = 0x02,   // Attempt to send hellos (NBMA)
40      NBS_INIT = 0x04,      // 1-Way communication
41      NBS_2WAY = 0x08,      // 2-Way communication
42      NBS_EXST = 0x10,      // Negotiate Master/Slave
43      NBS_EXCH = 0x20,      // Start sending DD packets
44      NBS_LOAD = 0x40,      // DDs done, now only LS reqs
45      NBS_FULL = 0x80,      // Full adjacency
46
47      NBS_ACTIVE = 0xFE,    // Any state but down
48      NBS_FLOOD = NBS_EXCH | NBS_LOAD | NBS_FULL,
49      NBS_ADJFORM = NBS_EXST | NBS_FLOOD,
50      NBS_BIDIR = NBS_2WAY | NBS_ADJFORM,
51      NBS_PRELIM = NBS_DOWN | NBS_ATTEMPT | NBS_INIT,
52      NBS_ANY = 0xFF,       // All states
53 };
                                                                    nbrfsm.h
```

Figure 8.1 List of possible neighbor states reported in **SpfNbr::n_state**.

The other reason for allocating a neighbor is when a neighbor is statically configured. Each configured neighbor is represented as a **class StaticNbr**, which is a superclass of **class SpfNbr**. Neighbors are statically configured on nonbroadcast networks, where some configuration information is necessary to bootstrap OSPF's Hello Protocol (see Sections 5.3 and 5.4 of [67]). On these networks, a neighbor that the router has not heard Hellos from recently can be in either **NBS_DOWN** or **NBS_ATTEMPT** state. In either state, the router may attempt to send Hello packets to the neighbor, although at different rates—every PollInterval seconds for neighbors in state Down and the faster rate of one Hello every HelloInterval seconds while the neighbor is in Attempt state. Lack of received Hellos again causes the neighbor to fall back to **NBS_DOWN** state, although configured neighbors are never freed.

Communication with a neighbor progresses until it has been determined that the link between the router and the neighbor is bidirectional (state **NBS_2WAY**). At that point, the neighbor FSM (finite state machine) determines whether a full adjacency with the neighbor is required (see Chapter 5 of [67]). If not, the neighbor state remains at

`NBS_2WAY`. If a full adjacency with the neighbor is required, the Database Exchange process (Section 8.3) eventually brings the neighbor state to `NBS_FULL`.

8.1.1   Finite State Machine Mechanism

Changes in neighbor state are triggered by certain events, listed in Figure 8.2. When an event occurs for a particular neighbor, the routine `SpfNbr::nbr_fsm()` is called, passing the event as the only argument. This routine consults the table shown in Figure 8.3, choosing an action and a new state, depending on the neighbor's current state and the event that has just occurred (`OSPF::run_fsm()`).

```
                                                            ───────── nbrfsm.h
59 enum {
60      NBE_HELLO = 1,        // Hello Received
61      NBE_START,            // Start sending hellos
62      NBE_2WAY,             // Bidirectional indication
63      NBE_NEGDONE,          // Negotiation of master/slave, seq #
64      NBE_EXCHDONE,         // All DD packets exchanged
65      NBE_BADLSREQ,         // Bad LS request received
66      NBE_LDONE,            // Loading Done
67      NBE_EVAL,             // Evaluate whether should be adjacent
68      NBE_DDRCVD,           // Received valid DD packet
69      NBE_DDSEQNO,          // Bad sequence number in DD process
70      NBE_1WAY,             // Only 1-way communication
71      NBE_DESTROY,          // Destroy the neighbor
72      NBE_INACTIVE,         // No hellos seen recently
73      NBE_LLDOWN,           // Down indication from link level
74      NBE_ADJTMO,           // Adjacency forming timeout
75 };
                                                            ───────── nbrfsm.h
```

Figure 8.2 Events triggering neighbor state changes.

The table implements state transitions in the following way. In the table, the first line is found that matches the current state (first column) and the trigger event (second column)—one line can match multiple states, because we represent states as individual nonoverlapping bits. The matching table entry then indicates the action (third column) and the new neighbor state (fourth column). A new neighbor state of 0 indicates that the neighbor state has not changed or that the action routine will set the new state.

As an example, suppose that a Database Description packet has just been received (event `NBE_DDRCVD`) from a neighbor that we have previously seen a Hello from but to which bidirectional communication had not previously been proved (state `NBS_INIT`); `np->nbr_fsm(NBE_DDRCVD)` will be called. The first matching line in `NbrFsm[]` is line 43, specifying an action of `NBA_EVAL2`. Then, `SpfNbr::nbr_fsm()` executes a switch

nbrfsm.C

```
34 FsmTran NbrFsm[] = {
35      { NBS_ACTIVE,  NBE_HELLO,      NBA_RST_IATIM,  0},
36      { NBS_BIDIR,   NBE_2WAY,       0,              0},
37      { NBS_INIT,    NBE_1WAY,       0,              0},
38      { NBS_DOWN,    NBE_HELLO,      NBA_ST_IATIM,   NBS_INIT},
39      { NBS_DOWN,    NBE_START,      NBA_START,      NBS_ATTEMPT},
40      { NBS_ACTIVE,  NBE_START,      NBA_START,      0},
41      { NBS_ATTEMPT, NBE_HELLO,      NBA_RST_IATIM,  NBS_INIT},
42      { NBS_INIT,    NBE_2WAY,       NBA_EVAL1,      0},
43      { NBS_INIT,    NBE_DDRCVD,     NBA_EVAL2,      0},
44      { NBS_2WAY,    NBE_DDRCVD,     NBA_EVAL2,      0},
45      { NBS_EXST,    NBE_NEGDONE,    NBA_SNAPSHOT,   NBS_EXCH},
46      { NBS_EXCH,    NBE_EXCHDONE,   NBA_EXCHDONE,   0},
47      { NBS_LOAD,    NBE_LDONE,      0,              NBS_FULL},
48      { NBS_2WAY,    NBE_EVAL,       NBA_EVAL1,      0},
49      { NBS_ADJFORM, NBE_EVAL,       NBA_REEVAL,     0},
50      { NBS_PRELIM,  NBE_EVAL,       NBA_HELLOCHK,   0},
51      { NBS_ADJFORM, NBE_ADJTMO,     NBA_RESTART_DD, NBS_2WAY},
52      { NBS_FLOOD,   NBE_DDSEQNO,    NBA_RESTART_DD, NBS_2WAY},
53      { NBS_FLOOD,   NBE_BADLSREQ,   NBA_RESTART_DD, NBS_2WAY},
54      { NBS_ANY,     NBE_DESTROY,    NBA_DELETE,     NBS_DOWN},
55      { NBS_ANY,     NBE_LLDOWN,     NBA_DELETE,     NBS_DOWN},
56      { NBS_ANY,     NBE_INACTIVE,   NBA_DELETE,     NBS_DOWN},
57      { NBS_BIDIR,   NBE_1WAY,       NBA_CLR_LISTS,  NBS_INIT},
58      { 0,           0,              -1,             0},
59 };
```

nbrfsm.C

Figure 8.3 Neighbor state transitions: `FsmTran NbrFsm[]`.

statement on the action, calling, in this case, the routine `SpfNbr::nba_eval2()`, which transitions the state to `NBS_EXST` and begins the Database Exchange process if an adjacency is wanted and resources are available (Section 8.3); or, it simply sets the neighbor state to `NBS_2WAY`.

A new neighbor state may require other protocol actions, regardless of the trigger event. These actions are gathered together at the bottom of `SpfNbr::nbr_fsm()`, as shown in Figure 8.4. The only way that we get to the listed code is if the state of the neighbor has changed, due either to the table lookup or to the FSM action routine. Just prior to the code shown, a state change has been logged, with state regressions and the attainment of one of the stable states (`NBS_2WAY` or `NBS_FULL`) being logged with a higher priority.

229-238   The neighbor is now fully adjacent. We increment the count of fully adjacent neighbors attached to the associated interface, `SpfIfc::if_nfull`; this count determines how router-LSAs, network-LSAs, and group-membership-LSAs will describe the inter-

```
                                                                    nbrfsm.C
225      // Maintain count of adjacencies that we are
226      // currently attempting
227      tap = n_ifp->transit_area();
228      // now Full
229      if (n_state == NBS_FULL) {
230          if (n_ifp->if_nfull++ == 0)
231              n_ifp->reorig_all_grplsas();
232          ospf->n_dbx_nbrs--;
233          n_progtim.stop();
234          exit_dbxchg();
235          if (tap && tap->n_VLs++ == 0)
236              tap->rl_orig();
237          ap->rl_orig();
238      }
239      // beginning exchange
240      else if (n_ostate <= NBS_EXST && n_state > NBS_EXST)
241          ospf->n_dbx_nbrs++;
242      // Never go from Full state immed back into dbxchng
243      else if (n_ostate == NBS_FULL) {
244          if (n_ifp->if_nfull-- == 1)
245              n_ifp->reorig_all_grplsas();
246          if (tap && tap->n_VLs-- == 1)
247              tap->rl_orig();
248          ap->rl_orig();
249      }
250      else if (n_state <= NBS_2WAY && n_ostate >= NBS_EXST) {
251          exit_dbxchg();
252          if (n_ostate > NBS_EXST)
253              ospf->n_dbx_nbrs--;
254      }
255
256      // (Re)originate network-LSA if we're DR
257      if (n_ifp->state() == IFS_DR)
258          n_ifp->nl_orig(false);
259
260      // If necessary, run Interface state machine with event
261      // NeighborChange
262      if ((n_state >= NBS_2WAY && n_ostate < NBS_2WAY) ||
263          (n_state < NBS_2WAY && n_ostate >= NBS_2WAY))
264          n_ifp->run_fsm(IFE_NCHG);
265 }
                                                                    nbrfsm.C
```

Figure 8.4 Processing based on new neighbor state, in `SpfNbr::nbr_fsm()`.

face and its attached subnet. We have now successfully exited the Database Exchange procedure and so have to clean up appropriately (lines **232-234**, described further in Section 8.3.2).

235-236   If this is the first fully adjacent virtual link for its associated area (`SpfIfc::transit_area()`), we have to reoriginate the router-LSA for that area with its V bit set. This will tell all the other area border routers attached to that area that the area is being used for transit traffic, and they will adjust their routing table calculations appropriately (Section 11.2.7).

237, 248   Aside from changes to the V bit setting, the only time that the contents of a router-LSA need to change, accomplished by calling `SpfArea::rl_orig()`, is when there is a change in the collection of fully adjacent neighbors.

240-241   The neighbor is starting the Database Exchange procedure. We keep track of the number of neighbors currently undergoing Database Exchange (`OSPF::n_dbx_nbrs`) because while one or more neighbors are in Database Exchange, we cannot remove MaxAge LSAs from our link-state database (Section 9.2.1).

243-249   The neighbor was formerly fully adjacent. We have to perform the mirror image of the operations that were done when the neighbor first became fully adjacent, reducing the count of fully adjacent neighbors and, if the neighbor is virtual, revoking the associated area's transit status, if necessary.

250-254   The Database Exchange process stopped before it could complete. Appropriate cleanup actions are taken, again as described in Section 8.3.2.

257-258   If the router is Designated Router on the attached network segment, any neighbor state changes cause it to reoriginate the segment's network-LSA by calling `SpfIfc::nl_orig()`. This is overkill because only certain state changes cause a change of contents to the network-LSA. However, it doesn't hurt to call `SpfIfc::nl_orig()`, because if the contents of the network-LSA don't change, it won't be reoriginated (Section 7.1.2).

262-265   OSPF has two state machines: the neighbor state machine, which we have been discussing; and a separate state machine that controls an interface's state. These two state machines are intertwined; certain state changes in the neighbor state machine cause events to be passed to the interface state machine, and vice versa. Changes in the collection of bidirectional neighbors are passed to the interface state machine as the event `IFE_NCHG`, which will force a recalculation of the attached segment's Designated Router. *Note:* The OSPF specification takes care to require that any invocations of the interface state machine from within the neighbor state machine are *scheduled* for later execution. This requirement allows the programmer to implement the state machines as nonreentrant code and is met by our implementation simply by delaying such cross-invocations until the end of `SpfNbr::nbr_fsm()`, after any neighbor state changes and action routines have already been executed. The interface state machine is discussed further in Section 8.4.

8.1.2   Neighbor State Transitions

In this section, we examine the neighbor state machine in Figure 8.3 in more detail. First note that the state table must always end with an entry specifying a matching state of `0` (line `58`). If this entry is reached by a call to `SpfNbr::nbr_fsm()`, no processing has been specified for the given event and current neighbor state; the event and current neighbor state are simply logged, and no state change or action routine is executed. Most of the entries in the state table are associated either with OSPF's Hello Protocol, which takes care of neighbor discovery and maintenance, or with the Database Exchange process, which performs the initial database synchronization with the neighbor.

As mentioned, the neighbor state machine is intertwined with the interface state machine (Section 8.4). In particular, the interface state machine can generate the following events for the neighbor state machine: `NBE_START`, indicating that an NBMA interface has just become operational and causing Hellos to be sent to the appropriate neighbors; `NBE_EVAL`, indicating an interface state change that causes a reevaluation of which neighbors should become fully adjacent; and `NBE_DESTROY`, indicating that an interface has failed, which causes its associated neighbors to be deleted.

Lines `35-42`, `50`, `56`, and `57` of the state machine in Figure 8.3 implement OSPF's Hello Protocol. This part of the state machine has been taken right out of Section 10.3 of the OSPF specification [75], with the addition of line `50`, which allows us to control the sending of Hello packets to NBMA neighbors completely through the state machine. The Hello Protocol is discussed further in Section 8.2.

Lines `42-49` and `51-53` of the state machine implement OSPF's Database Exchange procedure. This part of the state machine is also taken from the OSPF specification, with the following modifications. A new event `NBE_DDRCVD` has been added, allowing us to distinguish whether the neighbor is starting the Database Exchange or whether we are, as the result of an `NBE_EVAL` event; this is used to avoid deadlock situations when limiting the number of neighbors concurrently undergoing Database Exchange. Because Database Exchange sessions then become a precious resource, a new event `NBE_ADJTMO` is added to indicate that a neighbor is not progressing through the Database Exchange process, causing us to terminate Database Exchange with the neighbor and to, potentially, give another neighbor the chance to synchronize.

Lines `54-56` cause a neighbor to be deleted, although configured neighbors are instead simply put back into the Down state. Event `NBE_DESTROY` indicates that the corresponding interface has become inoperational. Event `NBE_LLDOWN` is generated when the data-link layer has provided an indication that a particular neighbor is now inoperational—for example, on a connection-oriented network segment, such as ATM or X.25, this could be indicated by a particular Call clearing diagnostic code. Event `NBE_INACTIVE` means that OSPF Hellos have not been heard from the neighbor for the past RouterDeadInterval seconds.

8.2   Neighbor Discovery

In OSPF, neighbors are discovered and their continued operation ensured through the sending and receiving of OSPF Hello packets. Reception of Hellos is handled by the single routine `SpfIfc::recv_hello()`. Sending of Hellos is performed by `SpfIfc::send_hello()` on broadcast and point-to-point interfaces, where Hellos are periodically multicast out the interface, and by `SpfNbr::send_hello()` on nonbroadcast interfaces, where Hellos are sent separately to each neighbor.

8.2.1   Receiving Hello Packets: `SpfIfc::recv_hello()`

Reception of Hellos is implemented pretty much by the book, following Section 10.5 of the OSPF specification [75]. The only variances are as follows.

- Because you have to wait for bidirectional communication with a neighbor to be established before you can start forming an adjacency, it usually takes at least one full HelloInterval before you can start using the neighbor for forwarding. To shorten this time, we respond immediately to a received Hello by sending a Hello of our own if both (1) this is the first Hello received from the neighbor *and* (2) the neighbor doesn't yet think that communication is bidirectional.

- Although not explicitly mentioned in Section 10.5 of [75], if the received Hello indicates that the neighbor's Router ID has changed and the router itself is Designated Router for the attached network segment, the router must reoriginate the network-LSA for the segment, as its contents, namely, the Router IDs of all fully adjacent neighbors, may have changed.

Received Hello packets create the neighbor structure in the first place, negotiate the demand status of the attached link, and ensure agreement on the basic link parameters (HelloInterval, RouterDeadInterval, subnet mask, and the ability to flood AS-external-LSAs) by rejecting Hellos with conflicting settings. Agreement on a further link parameter, namely, its MTU, is ensured when Database Description packets are received.

The rest of `SpfIfc::recv_hello()` proceeds in standard fashion, generating events for the neighbor state machine described in Section 8.1. Received Hellos generate the **NBE_HELLO** event, which keeps the neighbor relationship alive. If the router sees itself listed in the body of the received Hello, the event **NBE_2WAY** possibly paves the way toward establishing a full adjacency; the failure to see itself listed destroys the adjacency via the event **NBE_1WAY**. If the received Hello indicates the existence of a Backup Designated Router for the attached segment or conclusively indicates the lack of one, the router may run the Designated Router election for the first time by generating the event **IFE_BSEEN**. Alternatively, changes in a bidirectional neighbor's Router ID, declaration of Designated Router or Backup Designated Router, and/or Router Priority cause the Designated Router election to be rerun via the event **IFE_NCHG**.

8.2.2 Sending Hellos on Broadcast Interfaces: `SpfIfc::send_hello()`

On broadcast interfaces, point-to-point interfaces, and virtual links, the sending of Hellos is very simple. A Hello packet is sent out the interface when the interface first becomes operational and then is sent periodically on the firing of the interval timer `HelloTimer SpfIfc::if_htim`.

The building and sending of Hellos on these interface types is accomplished by the routine `SpfIfc::send_hello()`, shown in Figure 8.5.

```
────────────────────────────────────────────────────  spfhello.C
47  void SpfIfc::send_hello(bool empty)
49  {
50      NbrIterator iter(this);
51      SpfNbr *np;
52      uns16 size;
53      Pkt pkt;
54      HloPkt *hlopkt;
55      rtid_t *hlo_nbrs;
56
57      if (passive)
58          return;
60      size = sizeof(HloPkt);
61      while((np = iter.get_next())) {
62          if (np->state() >= NBS_INIT)
63              size += sizeof(rtid_t);
64      }
66      if (build_hello(&pkt, size) == 0)
67          return;
69      // Fill in the neighbors recently heard from
70      iter.reset();
71      hlopkt = (HloPkt *) (pkt.spfpkt);
72      hlo_nbrs = (rtid_t *) (hlopkt + 1);
73      // If shutting down, send empty hellos
74      while(!empty && (np = iter.get_next())) {
75          if (np->state() >= NBS_INIT) {
76              *hlo_nbrs++ = hton32(np->id());
77              pkt.dptr += sizeof(rtid_t);
78          }
79      }
80
81      if_send(&pkt, AllSPFRouters);
82  }
────────────────────────────────────────────────────  spfhello.C
```

Figure 8.5 Sending Hello packets on broadcast interfaces: `SpfIfc::send_hello()`.

47   The routine is not called if Hellos should be suppressed, which would be the case for interfaces attaching to demand circuits. The argument **empty** is set when the router is sending out one last Hello before shutting down the interface. If the argument is set, the router omits all neighbors from the body of the Hello, which will immediately destroy any adjacencies on receipt of the Hello by the router's neighbors.

57-58   On passive interfaces, we do not process OSPF protocol packets. However, simply suppressing all sending and receiving of Hellos is sufficient, because without Hellos, no other OSPF packet exchanges can get started.

61-64,   We put the Router IDs of all neighbors that we have seen Hellos from recently in the
70-79   body of the Hello packet, so that the neighbors will know that communication is bidirectional. First, we determine how many neighbors are active, so we know how large a Hello to allocate, and then we fill in the Hello body with their Router IDs.

66   **SpfIfc::build_hello()** will allocate the Hello packet and fill in the configured parameters for the attached network segment (subnet mask, HelloInterval, and Router-DeadInterval), the parameters that the neighbors will need for their Designated Router calculations (our configured Router Priority and our current view as to the segment's Designated Router and Backup Designated Router), and the optional OSPF capabilities the we are supporting on the interface.

81   Sending a packet out an interface is performed by **SpfIfc::if_send()**, which is a virtual function, depending on interface type. For unnumbered point-to-point interfaces, it checks to see that we have an IP address to use as the source address in the Hello before sending. For virtual links, it sends all packets to the virtual neighbor's IP address.

8.2.3 Sending Hellos on Nonbroadcast Interfaces: SpfNbr::send_hello()

On nonbroadcast networks, either NBMA or Point-to-MultiPoint segments, Hellos are sent separately to each neighbor. Hellos are sent by using **SpfNbr::send_hello()**; the only real difference between this routine and the previously described **SpfIfc::send_hello()** is that (1) Hellos are smaller—because the Hello is being sent to one neighbor only, at most that neighbor's Router ID appears in the body of the Hello; and (2) the packet is transmitted by using **SpfIfc::nbr_send()**, which transmits the packet directly to the neighbor.

Depending on the state and the configuration of the interface and the neighbor, Hellos are sent to the neighbor (1) periodically on the timer **SpfNbr::n_htim**, (2) in response to Hellos received on NBMA interfaces (**NBMAIfc::send_hello_response()**), or (3) not at all. These situations are described in detail in Chapter 5 of [67]. The decision as to which neighbors should receive timed Hellos is made by the routine **SpfIfc:: ifa_nbr_start()**.

8.3   Database Exchange

Database Exchange is the process of initially synchronizing the link-state database with a neighbor. The process proceeds as shown in Figure 8.6. The Database Exchange process starts when bidirectional communication is established *and* the router determines that a full adjacency with the neighbor is desired *and* the router has not yet reached its limit of concurrent Database Exchanges. If the Database Exchange starts with the reception of a Database Description packet from the neighbor, the exchange is *remotely initiated*; the current number of these is given by `OSPF::n_rmt_inits`. If the router instead starts the exchange by sending a Database Description packet to the neighbor, the exchange is *locally initiated* and is counted by `OSPF::n_lcl_inits`. Both the number of remotely initiated and the number of locally initiated exchanges are limited to `OSPF::max_dds`, bringing the total number of concurrent Database Exchanges to `2*OSPF::max_dds`.

The neighbors that the router would like to synchronize with but has not yet done so because of the limit on the number of concurrent exchanges are kept on the queue whose head is `OSPF::g_adj_head` and tail is `OSPF::g_adj_tail`. Periodically, the router checks to see whether there is now room to start the exchange process with one or more of these neighbors.

The Database Exchange process starts by taking a snapshot of the link-state database. This snapshot is contained in `LsaList SpfNbr::n_ddlst` and provides the contents for the Database Description packets sent to the neighbor in `SpfNbr::send_dd()`. Note that the contents of the snapshot depend on the OSPF extensions supported by the neighbor, if any, as learned from the initial Database Description packet received from the neighbor and stored in `SpfNbr::n_opts`.

The contents of received Database Description packets are processed by `SpfNbr::process_dd_contents()`. Those LSAs mentioned by the neighbor and that are more recent than the router's own copies are added to the link-state request list `LsaList SpfNbr::n_rqlst`. The router requests these LSAs from the neighbor in Link State Request packets, and the neighbor responds by flooding back the requested LSAs in Link State Update packets.

The Database Exchange process ends successfully when both the router and the neighbor have sent their full set of Database Description packets and all the router's link-state requests have been satisfied. The process can terminate in failure when an error is discovered (not shown in Figure 8.6), in which case the exchange will be re-attempted at a future date.

The count of neighbors with which the router is currently undergoing Database Exchange is kept in `OSPF::n_dbx_nbrs`. When this count is nonzero, the router will hold all MaxAge LSAs in its database instead of freeing them to the heap, for reasons discussed in Chapter 8 of [67].

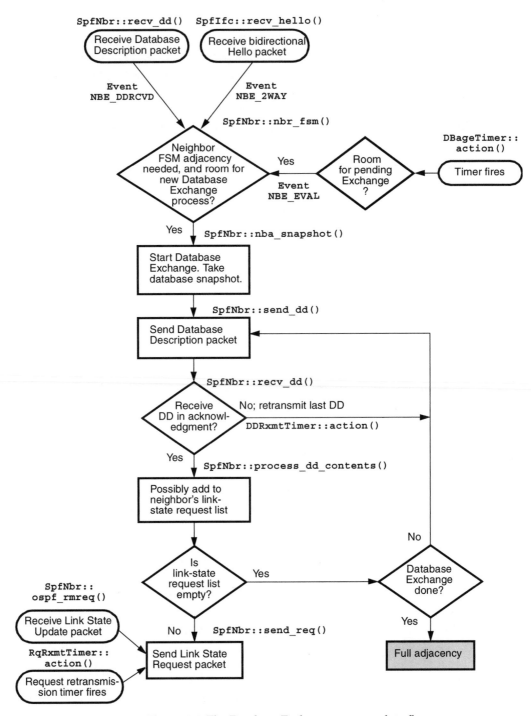

Figure 8.6 The Database Exchange process: data flow.

8.3.1   Enhancements above RFC 2328

The Database Exchange code in this implementation has three enhancements beyond the standard OSPFv2 specification [75], all in the area of reducing resources consumed by Database Exchange.

1. The first reduction is in the way we store the database snapshot produced at the start of Database Exchange. Rather than copy the database into a complete sequence of Database Description packets, we simply create a list of LSAs, `SpfNbr::n_ddlst`, which references each LSA currently in the database. This has two advantages. First, it consumes less space. Second, if an LSA is overwritten in the database before we have had a chance to send the LSA to the neighbor in a Database Description packet, we don't bother sending the LSA, as it will be marked in the list as `!LSA::valid()` (see `SpfNbr::send_dd()`).

2. We restrict the number of concurrent Database Exchanges to `2*OSPF::max_dds`. Half of these are allowed to be Database Exchanges that we initiate—in other words, we send the first Database Description packet—and half those started by receiving a Database Description from a neighbor. We split the limit in this manner to avoid possible deadlocks. As a simple deadlock example, suppose that our limit logic allowed only a single Database Exchange at any one time. Then in the network diagram on the flyleaf, you could have the triangle of routers A, B, and D getting stuck, with A trying to synchronize with B, B with D, and D with A.

    When limiting the number of Database Exchanges, you also have to make sure that neighbors having problems completing Database Exchange don't prevent the router from synchronizing with better-implemented neighbors. For this reason, we time out neighbors that fail to make progress in Database Exchange (`SpfNbr::n_progtim`), terminating their current exchange and relegating them to the end of the queue of neighbors waiting to undergo Database Exchange (`OSPF::g_adj_tail`).

3. We also limit the size of the list of LSAs that need to be requested from the neighbor (`SpfNbr::n_rqlst`), by requiring that all current requests be satisfied (that is, the size of the request list going to 0) before the next Database Description packet is transmitted to the neighbor.

8.3.2   Termination of Database Exchange

A successful end to the Database Exchange process produces a full adjacency, which is used for flooding and is advertised in the link-state database. The router knows that Database Description has finished when both (1) the router and its neighbor have sent a full set of Database Description packets and (2) the neighbor has satisfied all the router's

requests for more recent LSAs. In the code, this can occur either (1) with the
NBE_EXCHDONE event generated as the result of receiving (`SpfNbr::recv_dd()`) or sending (`SpfNbr::send_dd()`) the last Database Description packet; or (2) afterward, with
the **NBE_LDONE** event signifying that the last outstanding request has been satisfied in
`SpfNbr::ospf_rmreq()`.

Unsuccessful ends to the Database Exchange process can be due to errors encountered or to an indication that communication with the neighbor is no longer bidirectional. In these cases, the state associated with the Database Exchange must be cleaned
up, as can be seen in `SpfNbr::nba_clr_lists()`.

8.4   Interface State Changes

One reason for the OSPF interface state machine is to invoke the proper actions as an
interface becomes activated or deactivated; for example, how should the interface be
advertised in router-LSAs, if at all? Another reason is to control which adjacencies
should form over the interface, partially driven by the Designated Router calculation for
the attached segment.

Each OSPF interface is represented by a **class SpfIfc**. The interface's current state
is stored in **SpfIfc::if_state**, which can take any of the values shown in Figure 8.7.
These states are all defined in Section 9.1 of the OSPFv2 specification [75]. When an
event occurs, the interface state machine is invoked as **SpfIfc::run_fsm(int event)**,
which uses the same mechanism as the neighbor state machine described in Section 8.1.
The events also come straight out of the OSPFv2 specification and are encoded as in
Figure 8.8.

```
                                                                   ifcfsm.h
 36 enum {
 37     IFS_DOWN = 0x01,     // Interface is down
 38     IFS_LOOP = 0x02,     // Interface is looped
 39     IFS_WAIT = 0x04,     // Waiting to learn Backup DR
 40     IFS_PP   = 0x08,     // Terminal state for P-P interfaces
 41     IFS_OTHER = 0x10,    // Mult-access: neither DR nor Backup
 42     IFS_BACKUP = 0x20,   // Router is Backup on this interface
 43     IFS_DR   = 0x40,     // Router is DR on this interface
 44
 45     N_IF_STATES = 7,     /* # OSPF interface states */
 47     /* Terminal multi-access states */
 48     IFS_MULTI = (IFS_OTHER | IFS_BACKUP | IFS_DR),
 49     IFS_ANY = 0x7F,      /* Matches all states */
 50 };
                                                                   ifcfsm.h
```

Figure 8.7 Encoding OSPF interface state.

```
                                                                  ─── ifcfsm.h
 58 enum {
 59     IFE_UP   = 1,         // Interface has come up
 60     IFE_WTIM,             // Wait timer has fired
 61     IFE_BSEEN,            // Backup DR has been seen
 62     IFE_NCHG,             // Associated neighbor has changed state
 63     IFE_LOOP,             // Interface has been looped
 64     IFE_UNLOOP,           // Interface has been unlooped
 65     IFE_DOWN,             // Interface has gone down
 66     // # OSPF interface events
 67     N_IF_EVENTS = IFE_DOWN,
 68 };
                                                                  ─── ifcfsm.h
```

Figure 8.8 Encoding of interface events.

8.4.1 `SpfIfc::run_fsm(int event)`

When an interface's state has changed, certain actions must be taken. These actions are implemented at the bottom of `SpfIfc::run_fsm(int event)`, displayed in Figure 8.9.

144   `SpfIfc::if_faddr` is the IP address to which Link State Update packets and Link State Acknowledgment packets will be sent on this interface. The Designated Router and the Backup Designated Router send these packets to all routers on the attached segments (`AllSPFRouters`), whereas the other routers send only to the Designated Router and its Backup (`AllDRouters`).

146-149   `SpfArea::IfcChange()` keeps track of the number of interfaces actively attached to an area. That routine determines whether the router is an area border router and deletes the area's link-state database when interfaces are no longer attaching to it.

151-154   Designated Routers and Backup Designated Routers must listen to the extra multicast group `AllDRouters`.

158   If the state of the interface changes, so might its representation in the router's router-LSA.

159-162   It is the responsibility of the Designated Router—and the Designated Router only—to originate a network-LSA for the attached segment and to advertise the attached segment's multicast group membership in group-membership-LSAs.

164-178   Interface state changes are logged, with state regressions logged at the highest priority, ascensions into possibly terminal states at the next highest, and then pass-through states at the lowest priority.

```
                                                                  ─── ifcfsm.C
141    if (if_ostate == if_state)
142        return;
143    // Set address to use when flooding
144    if_faddr = (if_state == IFS_OTHER) ? AllDRouters : AllSPFRouters;
145    // Newly up or down
146    if (if_ostate == IFS_DOWN)
147        if_area->IfcChange(1);
148    else if (if_state == IFS_DOWN)
149        if_area->IfcChange(-1);
150    // Want AllDRouters now?
151    if (if_state > IFS_OTHER && if_ostate <= IFS_OTHER)
152        ospf->app_join(if_phyint, AllDRouters);
153    else if (if_state <= IFS_OTHER && if_ostate > IFS_OTHER)
154        ospf->app_leave(if_phyint, AllDRouters);
155    // (Re)originate appropriate LSAs
156    // Always do router-LSA, and do network-LSA if we've
157    // transitioned to/from Designated Router
158    if_area->rl_orig();
159    if (if_state == IFS_DR || if_ostate == IFS_DR) {
160        nl_orig(false);
161        reorig_all_grplsas();
162    }
163
164    // Log significant events
165    if (if_state < if_ostate)
166        llevel = 5;
167    else if (if_state >= IFS_PP)
168        llevel = 4;
169    else
170        llevel = 1;
171    if (ospf->spflog(IFC_STATECH, llevel)) {
172        ospf->log(ifstates(if_state));
173        ospf->log("<-");
174        ospf->log(ifstates(if_ostate));
175        ospf->log(" event ");
176        ospf->log(ifevents(event));
177        ospf->log(this);
178    }
179 }
                                                                  ─── ifcfsm.C
```

Figure 8.9 Actions taken as a result of interface state changes: `SpfIfc::run_fsm(int event)`.

8.4.2 Passive Interfaces

Passive interfaces are those that you want the router to advertise in its LSAs so that IP connectivity to the attached network segment will be established but on which you want to disable OSPF protocol exchanges. Why would you want to disable OSPF protocol exchanges on the interface? Perhaps you know that no other routers are attached to the network segment and that (1) you want to reduce the traffic on the network segment by omitting the periodic OSPF Hello packets, or (2) some hosts on the attached network segment are disturbed by the presence of OSPF Hellos. (Because OSPF uses data-link multicast for its Hello packets, host disturbance is most likely on those network segments having little or no multicast support, such as IBM token rings [83].) Or, you may have a network segment that has multiple attached routers but over which you want to prevent transit traffic. Configuring the interfaces to such a segment to be passive will cause the attached routers to advertise the segment as a stub network, preventing any transit traffic from being forwarded over the segment.

Configuration of passive interfaces is performed by setting the interface configuration parameter `CfgIfc::passive`. By default, this parameter is set to `0`, but setting it to `1` puts the interface in passive mode.

When we are dynamically changing an interface to be passive, we want to immediately drop all neighbor conversations on the interface and to start advertising the attached network as a stub network in our LSAs. This is accomplished by restarting the interface whenever it enters or leaves passive state (see Section 13.2).

Implementation of passive interfaces is very simple. We simply inhibit the sending (`SpfIfc::send_hello()`) and receiving of Hello packets (`SpfIfc::recv_hello()`) on the passive interface. This ensures that no neighbor relationships will form over the interface, as neighbor relationships always start with their discovery through the sending and reception of Hellos.

Whether an interface is passive does not alter the operation of the interface state machine. In particular, on passive interfaces to broadcast or NBMA networks, the router will elect itself as Designated Router. However, it will still advertise the network segment as a stub, as there are no associated neighbors (see Section 12.4.1.1 of [75]).

Note that it makes little sense to configure point-to-point interfaces as passive, as the lack of neighbors will prevent any part of the interface from being advertised, and they will act just as if they didn't exist at all.

Exercises

8.1   Add a global configuration option so that a subnet will be assigned to and advertised for each point-to-point link. Does it now make any sense to configure a point-to-point interface as passive?

8.2   Implement the functionality outlined in Appendix F of [75], enabling a router to have two or more interfaces attaching to the same IP subnet.

8.3   Modify the `ospfd` software so that Hellos are sent to the address AllDRouters when the associated broadcast interface's DR Priority has been configured as `0`. What is the advantage of doing so?

8.4   Fix the following two bugs in the implementation of host routes, which show up when you dynamically reconfigure an `ospfd` that has had one or more host routes defined. (1) A loopback interface (`class LoopIfc`) is allocated for each host route for convenience of the routing calculation, but these interfaces should not be counted as active interfaces to an area; nor should they undergo interface state machine processing. (2) When the configuration of a host route is updated, its loopback interface must also be marked as updated, or it will be deleted by `OSPF::cfgDone()`.

8.5   In a similar vein, fix the following bug in `OSPF::cfgIfc()`. When configuration of an interface implicitly creates an OSPF area, make sure that the area's `class SpfArea` has `SpfArea::updated` set to `true` whenever the interface's configuration is refreshed.

8.6   Fix the following bug. When a Database Description packet is received indicating that the neighbor's link MTU is larger than the router's own, the Database Description packet should be discarded without further processing.

8.7   Figure 8.6 is not exactly correct, in that the database snapshot is not taken until the first Database Description packet is received from the neighbor. Draw a more correct figure.

9

Flooding

Flooding is the procedure by which a link-state protocol, such as OSPF, maintains database synchronization between routers. Database synchronization is the most crucial function in a link-state protocol. Without a synchronized database, routers might calculate incompatible routes, leading to unreachable destinations and routing loops. It is also important that flooding happen quickly, so that changes in network topology are recognized soon and so that new routes are calculated, taking the changes into account.

Figure 9.1 diagrams the flooding procedure in a single router. Flooding starts when a router receives a Link State Update packet from an adjacent neighbor. The router examines and acknowledges each LSA in the Update packet. The router identifies the more recent LSAs, installs them in its link-state database, adds them to all other adjacent routers' link-state retransmission lists, and encapsulates them in Link State Update packets to be sent out all interfaces, with the possible exception of the interface on which that LSA was initially received.

The LSAs that the router itself originates are also flooded to its adjacent neighbors. The flooding logic used is, beginning with the installation of the LSAs into the database, identical to the flooding procedure for LSAs received in Link State Updates.

A router periodically retransmits LSAs on the link-state retransmission list for an adjacent neighbor to that neighbor. The router removes LSAs from the link-state retransmission list when the neighbor acknowledges receipt of the LSA by responding with a Link State Acknowledgment packet.

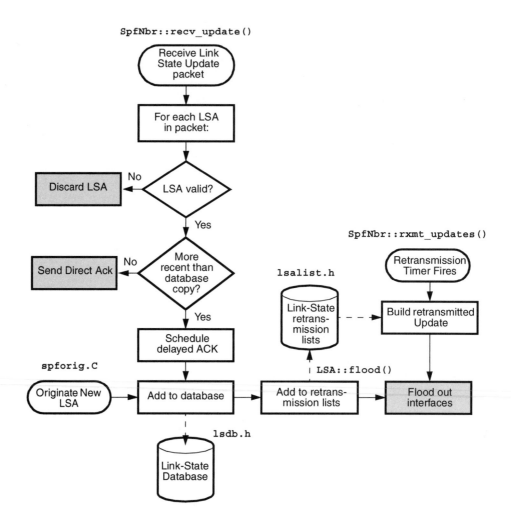

Figure 9.1 Data flow of flooding in a single router. Shaded rectangles
indicate disposition of the received LSA.

The routines that implement the reception and transmission of Link State Update
packets are in the file **spflood.C**. The routines that implement the building and reception of Link State Acknowledgment packets, and the retransmission of LSAs, are in the
file **spfack.C**.

Flooding is only part of the synchronization story. Flooding is responsible for maintaining synchronization, but it does not cover the building of adjacencies or the initial
database synchronization that is performed over the adjacency. This latter procedure is
called the Database Exchange process, described in Section 8.3.

9.1   Data Structures

Most of the state of the flooding algorithm is associated with each adjacent neighbor. This state is stored in the **SpfNbr** class representing the neighbor, as shown in Figure 9.2. In this section, we describe this state information in detail. Flooding state is also spread over a number of other data structures: the global **OSPF** class and the area and interface classes. We defer the description of the relevant portions of these classes until detailed examination of the individual flooding procedures later in the chapter.

```
────────────────────────────────────────────────── spfnbr.h
130 class SpfNbr {
135     int n_state;         // Current neighbor state
137     byte n_opts;         // Options advertised by neighbor

148     // Four-part retransmission list
149     LsaList n_pend_rxl;  // LSAs recently retransmitted
150     LsaList n_rxlst;     // Flooded, but not time to rxmt
151     LsaList n_failed_rxl; // Failed retransmissions
152     uns32 rxmt_count;    // Count of all rxmt queues together
153     uns16 n_rxmt_window; // # consecutive retransmissions allowed

156     LsaList n_rqlst;     // Request list

159     Pkt n_update;        // Pending update
160     Pkt n_imack;         // Immediate acks to send to nbr
167     LsaRxmtTimer n_lsarxtim; // LSA retransmit timer
255 };
────────────────────────────────────────────────── spfnbr.h
```

Figure 9.2 Flooding state in **class SpfNbr**.

In OSPF, the adjacency is the basic unit of database synchronization. A subset of an interface's neighbor relationships become adjacencies, depending on interface type and current state (**SpfIfc::adjacency_wanted()**). Although routers generally send and receive Link State Updates per interface, they maintain link-state retransmission lists per adjacency, which ensures database synchronization.

135   Adjacencies are those neighbor relationships whose **n_state** has reached Exchange (encoded as **NBS_EXCH** in file **nbrfsm.h**) or higher. It is in Exchange state that a router takes a snapshot of the database for the neighbor, to begin the Database Exchange process, described in Section 8.3. At the same time, flooding begins to/from the neighbor, as we start accepting/sending Link State Update packets from/to the neighbor.

137   The Options field that the neighbor has advertised in its Database Description packets is stored in **n_opts**. For optional LSA types, the **n_opts** field indicates whether the

LSA should be transmitted to the neighbor. For example, group-membership-LSAs are flooded to the neighbor only if the **SPO_MC** bit is set in the neighbor's **n_opts** field.

148-152   The link-state retransmission list for the neighbor is split into four parts. The number of LSAs that have been flooded to the neighbor but not yet acknowledged is **rxmt_count**. Each of these unacknowledged LSAs is on one, and only one, of the LSA lists **n_pend_rxl**, **n_rxlst**, and **n_failed_rxl**. The LSAs that we have recently sent to the neighbor but have not yet been forced to retransmit are on the list **n_rxlst**. We expect that most LSAs will be added to **n_rxlst** and then removed when appropriate Link State Acknowledgment packets are received (see Section 9.4). If we have to retransmit an LSA, it is moved to the **n_pend_rxl** list. Those LSAs that we have retransmitted and *still* not received acknowledgments for are put on the **n_failed_rxl** list. This organization of the unacknowledged LSAs into multiple lists allows us to implement more sophisticated retransmission logic. See Section 9.5 for details.

153   The number of back-to-back Link State Update packets containing LSA retransmissions that we are currently willing to send to the neighbor is **n_rxmt_window**. This value varies dynamically, using logic similar to TCP's slow-start [41]; see Section 9.5 for details.

156   The headers of LSAs that the neighbor has in its database and that are more recent than the router's own database copies are stored in **n_rqlst**. The router uses **n_rqlst** during the flooding process to (1) verify that Link State Update packets received from the neighbor are consistent and (2) avoid unnecessarily flooding LSAs to a neighbor when it knows that the neighbor already has the same or a more recent instance. See Sections 9.2 and 9.3, respectively.

159   The Link State Update packet under construction that the router will send back to the neighbor is **n_update**. This update can be a result of receiving either (1) a less recent LSA from the neighbor in a Link State Update packet (see Section 9.2) or (2) a Link State Request packet from the neighbor (see Chapter 8, Neighbor Maintenance), or a packet of retransmitted LSAs for the neighbor (Section 9.5).

160   The Link State Acknowledgment packet under construction that the router will unicast back to the neighbor as a result of receiving duplicate LSAs from the neighbor is **n_imack**. See Section 9.2 for details.

167   The LSA retransmission timer is **n_lsarxtim**. It will be set whenever the neighbor's link-state retransmission list is nonempty and will be scheduled to go off when the next LSA, if still not acknowledged, would need to be retransmitted.

9.2   Receiving Link State Updates: `SpfNbr::recv_update()`

A Link State Update packet can contain many LSAs. When a router receives a Link State Update packet, it examines each LSA in turn. The router selects the LSAs that are of known type, of valid content, and more recent than the current database copy. The router installs the selected LSAs in the database, floods them out some set of interfaces, and then acknowledges them. The routine **`SpfNbr::recv_update()`** handles the reception of Link State Update packets, as shown in Figure 9.3.

47   Routers receive and transmit Link State Update packets only over adjacencies. Adjacencies are neighbor relationships whose state is Exchange (coded as **`NBS_EXCH`** in file **`nbrfsm.h`**) or greater.

The following lines of code pertain to LSA verification.

58-184   The router examines each of the LSAs within the Link State Update packet in turn.

75-76   The router checks to see whether the packet ends prematurely, in the middle of an LSA. This should not happen. If it does, it indicates an error in the sending neighbor; the router stops processing the packet, although all previous LSAs in the packet will have been processed.

78-79   All LSAs are covered by a checksum (the ISO Fletcher checksum, to be exact). The checksum enables the router to check that the contents of the LSA have not been corrupted. If the checksum fails, presumably the LSA has been damaged in transit, although it could have been transmitted incorrectly by the neighbor. In any case, the router silently discards any LSAs failing the checksum, in hopes that the retransmitted LSA will be in better shape.

80-81   In OSPF, a router does not have to store and/or forward LSAs whose contents it does not understand. A router silently drops unrecognized LSA types. Five LSA types are mandatory in OSPF: router-LSAs, network-LSAs, type-3 summary-LSAs, type-4 summary-LSAs, and AS-external-LSAs. All other LSA types are optional; a router indicates that it understands an optional LSA type by setting the appropriate bits in the Options field of its Database Description packets. Because Link State Update packets are often multicast, a router may receive unknown LSA types, but its neighbors know better than to retransmit them.

82-83   Routers do not flood AS-external-LSAs into or throughout stub areas, in order to keep the size of the stub areas' databases small.

84-85   A router must store and forward group-membership-LSAs only when it is running MOSPF. (It indicates this to its neighbors by setting the MC bit in the Options field of its Database Description packets.) This behavior creates problems for MOSPF on broadcast and NBMA networks: Unless the Designated Router or the Backup Designated Router runs MOSPF, group-membership-LSAs will not be flooded over the network.

110-112   The router locates the database copy of the received LSA, **`olsap`**. If it is equal to **`0`**, no instance of the received LSA is currently in the database.

The following lines of code pertain to receiving MaxAge LSAs.

119-122   If the age of the received LSA is equal to MaxAge, the LSA is being flushed from the routing domain. If the router has no database copy, the router almost always simply acknowledges the LSA and continues.

In one case, however, the router must store the MaxAge LSA in the database: when the Database Exchange procedure is in progress with one or more neighbors. Some

OSPF implementations (although not the one in this book) prebuild the entire sequence of Database Description packets as soon as the neighbor relationship enters Exchange state. If the neighbor is one of those implementations, when the router receives the Database Description packet from the neighbor, it might contain old information. In particular, the packet might contain LSAs that have since been flushed from the database. If the router had not held the MaxAge LSA in this case, it would instead generate a Link State Request that could not be satisfied by the neighbor, which would cause the entire Database Exchange procedure to be repeated. This scenario is shown in Figure 9.4.

The decision to store the MaxAge LSA even when there is no database copy is made by the routine `OSPF::maxage_free()`, which is shown in Figure 9.5. This routine returns **false** if the MaxAge LSA must be stored and **true** if it can be freed. The number of neighbors undergoing Database Exchange is kept in `OSPF::n_dbx_nbrs`; if no neighbors are undergoing Database Exchange, the MaxAge LSA can always be freed. If neighbors are undergoing Database Exchange, we still free the LSA in one exceptional condition: The LSA is an AS-external-LSA and we are in Database Overflow state. In this condition, we must free MaxAge AS-external-LSAs in order to get back under the limit of nondefault AS-external-LSAs, and this concern takes precedence over the integrity of the Database Exchange process described previously.

The following line of code is used to compare against the database LSA copy.

125   If a copy of the LSA is currently in the database, the router uses `LSA::cmp_instance()` to compare the two LSA instances to see which one is more recent. We then process three separate cases: the received LSA is newer than the database copy, the same instance as the database copy, or less recent than the database copy.

9.2.1 Handling More Recent LSA Instances

Continuing with the routine `SpfNbr:recv_update()`, we examine the processing when either the LSA just received is more recent than the database copy or there is no database copy (lines **128-162**).

131-140   If the current database copy has been in the database for less than 1 second (the value of **MinArrival**), the router silently discards the new LSA. This behavior protects against neighbors that disregard the restriction that LSA updates must be spaced 5 (MinLSInterval) or more seconds apart; the excess originations would affect routers one hop away, but no further, from the misbehaving router. (This clause in the OSPF specification is sometimes called the Tsuchiya fix, after the person who suggested it.)

142   `LSA::cmp_contents()` indicates whether the contents of the received LSA have changed when compared to the current database copy or whether the received LSA is a simple refresh. Simple refreshes do not cause new routing calculations; nor are they flooded over demand circuits (see Section 9.3). The following are all considered changes

```
                                                              ———— spflood.C
37 void SpfNbr::recv_update(Pkt *pdesc)
38
39 {
40     SpfIfc *ip;
41     SpfArea *ap;
42     int count;
43     UpdPkt *upkt;
44     LShdr *hdr;
45     byte *end_lsa;
46
47     if (n_state < NBS_EXCH)
48         return;
49
50     ip = n_ifp;
51     ap = ip->area();
52     upkt = (UpdPkt *) pdesc->spfpkt;
53     ip->in_recv_update = true;
54
55     count = ntoh32(upkt->upd_no);
56     hdr = (LShdr *) (upkt+1);
57
58     for (; count > 0; count--, hdr = (LShdr *) end_lsa) {
59         int errval=0;
60         int lslen;
61         int lstype;
62         lsid_t lsid;
63         rtid_t orig;
64         age_t lsage;
65         LSA *olsap;
66         int compare;
67         int rq_cmp;
68
69         lstype = hdr->ls_type;
70         lsage = ntoh16(hdr->ls_age);
71         if ((lsage & ~DoNotAge) >= MaxAge)
72             lsage = MaxAge;
73         lslen = ntoh16(hdr->ls_length);
74         end_lsa = ((byte *)hdr) + lslen;
75         if (end_lsa > pdesc->end)
76             break;
77
78         if (!hdr->verify_cksum())
79             errval = ERR_LSAXSUM;
80         else if (!ospf->FindLSdb(ap, lstype))
81             errval = ERR_BAD_LSA_TYPE;
```

(Continued)

```
82              else if (lstype == LST_ASL && ap->is_stub())
83                  errval = ERR_EX_IN_STUB;
84              else if (lstype == LST_GM && !ospf->mospf_enabled())
85                  continue;
86
87              if (errval != 0) {
88                  if (ospf->spflog(errval, 5)) {
89                      ospf->log(hdr);
90                      ospf->log(this);
91                  }
92                  continue;
93              }

109             /* Find current database copy, if any */
110             lsid = ntoh32(hdr->ls_id);
111             orig = ntoh32(hdr->ls_org);
112             olsap = ospf->FindLSA(ap, lstype, lsid, orig);

119             if (lsage == MaxAge && (!olsap) && ospf->maxage_free(lstype)){
120                 build_imack(hdr);
121                 continue;
122             }
123
124             /* Compare to database instance */
125             compare = (olsap ? olsap->cmp_instance(hdr) : 1);
126
127             /* If received LSA is more recent */
128             if (compare > 0) {
129                 bool changes;
130                 LSA *lsap;
131                 if (olsap && olsap->since_received() < MinArrival) {
132                     // One time grace period
133                     if (olsap->min_failed) {
134                         if (ospf->spflog(LOG_MINARRIVAL, 4)) {
135                             ospf->log(hdr);
136                             ospf->log(this);
137                         }
138                         continue;
139                     }
140                 }
141                 // If self-originated forces us to re-originate
142                 changes = (olsap ? olsap->cmp_contents(hdr) : true);
143                 if (changes && ospf->self_originated(ap, hdr, olsap))
144                     continue;
```

(Continued)

```
151                    if ((!olsap) && lstype == LST_ASL &&
152                        lsid != DefaultDest &&
153                        ospf->ExtLsdbLimit &&
154                        ospf->n_exlsas >= ospf->ExtLsdbLimit) {
155                        continue;
156                    }
158                    if (ospf->spflog(LOG_RXNEWLSA, 1))
159                        ospf->log(hdr);
160                    lsap = ospf->AddLSA(ap, olsap, hdr, changes);
161                    lsap->flood(this, hdr);
162                }
163                else if (ospf_rmreq(hdr, &rq_cmp)) {
165                    nbr_fsm(NBE_BADLSREQ);
166                }
167                else if (compare == 0) {
169                    if (!remove_from_rxlist(olsap))
170                        build_imack(hdr);
171                }
172                else {
173                    LShdr *ohdr;
175                    if (olsap->ls_seqno() == MaxLSSeq)
176                        continue;
177                    if (olsap->sent_reply)
178                        continue;
179                    ohdr = ospf->BuildLSA(olsap);
180                    add_to_update(ohdr);
181                    olsap->sent_reply = true;
182                    ospf->replied_list.addEntry(olsap);
183                }
184        }
185
187        ip->if_send_update();
189        ospf->send_updates();
190        ip->nbr_send(&n_imack, this);
191        ip->nbr_send(&n_update, this);
192        ip->in_recv_update = false;
194        if (n_rqlst.count() && n_rqlst.count() <= rq_goal) {
195            n_rqrxtim.restart();
196            send_req();
197        }
198 }
```

—— spflood.C

Figure 9.3 Receiving Link State Update packets: SpfNbr::recv_update().

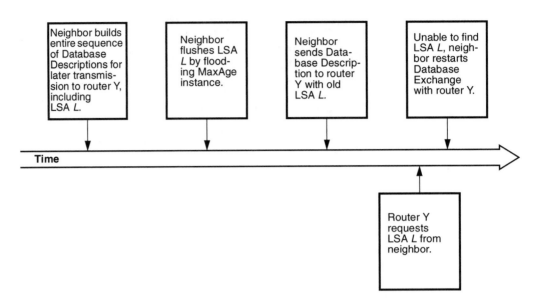

Figure 9.4 Possible race condition in the Database Exchange procedure, involving a hypothetical LSA *L*, a router Y, and its neighbor. OSPF avoids the race by requiring the router to hold MaxAge LSAs received from neighbor during the Database Exchange procedure.

```
                                                               ─ spflood.C
678 bool OSPF::maxage_free(byte lstype)
679
680 {
681     if (n_dbx_nbrs == 0)
682         return(true);
683     else if (!OverflowState)
684         return(false);
685     else if (lstype == LST_ASL)
686         return(true);
687     else
688         return(false);
689 }
                                                               ─ spflood.C
```

Figure 9.5 Deciding whether to free or to store a MaxAge LSA: `OSPF::maxage_free()`.

in contents: (1) any differences in the body of the LSA (that part past the 20-byte LSA header), (2) one but not both of the LSAs having LS Age equal to MaxAge, or (3) a change in LSA's LS Options field.

143-144   The `OSPF::self_originated()` routine (Section 7.4) indicates whether the received LSA is one that the router itself has originated. If the LSA is self-originated, either LSAs that the router originated before its last restart are in the routing domain, or, less likely, another router with the same OSPF Router ID is in the routing domain. In the former case, the router must ensure that any old information present in the received LSA is replaced, by originating a new LSA in the function `OSPF::self_originated()`. This action is necessary only if the contents would be different. The case of duplicate Router IDs must be handled by the network's administrator.

151-156   This is the OSPF Database Overflow logic. The system administrator can enable this logic and configure a ceiling on the number of nondefault AS-external-LSAs (`OSPF::ExtLsdbLimit`); routers simply discard any LSAs received in excess of the limit. The first time that the router senses that the limit of nondefault AS-external-LSAs has been reached, the router goes into Overflow State and flushes all its self-originated nodefault AS-external-LSAs. This logic is located in the function `ASextLSA::parse()` and is described in Section 10.3.4.

160   The router adds the received LSA to the database, replacing any existing database copy. This action might cause one of several routing calculations to be invoked or scheduled, as implemented in function `OSPF::rtsched()` and described in Section 11.1.

161   The router calls `LSA::flood()` to flood the newly added LSA out the appropriate interfaces. We describe this behavior in detail in Section 9.3.

163-166   If instead of being newer, the received LSA is either the same instance or even older than the copy of the LSA presently in the router's database, the router should not be expecting to see a more recent LSA from the neighbor. If `SpfNbr::ospf_rmreq()` indicates that the router is expecting a more recent LSA, the router restarts the Database Exchange procedure with the neighbor (via the neighbor FSM), to remove the synchronization roadblock. Note that this step would not be necessary when dealing with bug-free OSPF implementations but has proved useful in bake-offs over the years.

9.2.2 Handling Duplicate LSAs: `SpfNbr::recv_update` Continued

In lines **167-171** of `SpfNbr::recv_update()`, we are processing a received LSA that is the same instance as our database copy.

169-170   If the router is not expecting an acknowledgment from the neighbor for this LSA, the router sends an immediate direct acknowledgment to the neighbor via the function `SpfNbr::build_imack()`. Otherwise, receipt of the duplicate LSA is treated as an implied acknowledgment, just as if an appropriate Link State Acknowledgment were received: The LSA is removed from the link-state retransmission list for the neighbor in the call to `SpfNbr::remove_from_rxlist()`.

9.2.3   Receiving Old LSA Instances: `SpfNbr::recv_update` **Continued**

In lines 172-183 of `SpfNbr::recv_update()`, the received LSA has been found to be less recent than our database copy. Unless this is an LS Sequence Number rollover situation, the router responds by flooding the database copy back to the neighbor by calling `SpfNbr::add_to_update()`. This behavior speeds up database synchronization when old MaxAge LSAs are getting stuck on long interface output queues, and it is also necessary when two halves of a routing domain are separated by a demand circuit (see Section 2.4 of [64]). OSPF treats LS Sequence Number rollovers differently, because the LSA's source must wait until the MaxSequenceNumber LSA is flushed from the routing domain; in all other cases, the source can respond to the flood back of the MaxAge LSA by incrementing the LS Sequence Number and immediately originating the LSA with its new contents.

9.2.4   Postprocessing of Updates: `SpfNbr::recv_update` **Completed**

In lines 187-197 of `SpfNbr::recv_update()`, the processing of a received Link State Update packet is completed by flooding new LSAs out the router's other interfaces and sending any immediate acknowledgments.

187   The Designated Router may have to flood new LSAs back out the receiving interface by calling `SpfIfc::if_send_update()`.

189   The `OSPF::send_updates()` function floods new LSAs out all interfaces other than the receiving interface.

190-191   Immediate acknowledgments and Link State Updates caused by the reception of old LSAs are sent directly to the neighbor from which the Update was received.

194-197   If this Update has satisfied all the pending Link State requests, the router sends a new set of requests to the neighbor to keep the Database Exchange procedure moving forward. See Section 8.3 for more details.

9.3   Flooding LSAs: `LSA::flood()`

Routers must flood new LSAs, either received from a neighbor in a Link State Update or originated by the router itself, out appropriate interfaces. Routers ensure reliable flooding by adding the LSA to appropriate link-state retransmission lists in the flooding process. The `LSA::flood()` routine accomplishes all this flooding, as shown in Figure 9.6.

226-227   If the LSA has not yet been formatted to send in a Link State Update packet, `OSPF::BuildLSA()` is called to produce the network representation.

229-286   The router considers each OSPF interface in turn, to see whether the LSA should be flooded out the interface.

```
                                                            ─ spflood.C
211 void LSA::flood(SpfNbr *from, LShdr *hdr)
212
213 {
214     IfcIterator ifcIter(ospf);
215     SpfIfc *r_ip;
216     SpfIfc *ip;
217     byte lstype;
218     int scope;
219     bool flood_it=false;
220     bool on_demand=false;
221     bool on_regular=false;
222
223     lstype = hdr->ls_type;
224     scope = flooding_scope(lstype);
225     r_ip = (from ? from->ifc() : 0);
226     if (!hdr)
227         hdr = ospf->BuildLSA(this);
228
229     while ((ip = ifcIter.get_next())) {
230         SpfArea *ap;
231         SpfNbr *np;
232         NbrIterator nbrIter(ip);
233         int n_nbrs;
234
235         ap = ip->area();
236         if (ip->demand_flooding(lstype) && !changed)
237             continue;
238         if (lstype == LST_ASL && ap->is_stub())
239             continue;
240         if (lstype == LST_ASL && ip->is_virtual())
241             continue;
242         if (scope == AreaScope && ap != lsa_ap)
243             continue;
244
245         n_nbrs = 0;
246         while ((np = nbrIter.get_next())) {
247             int rq_cmp;
248
249             if (np->state() < NBS_EXCH)
250                 continue;
251             if (np->ospf_rmreq(hdr, &rq_cmp) && rq_cmp <= 0)
252                 continue;
```

(Continued)

```
253              if (np == from)
254                  continue;
255              if (lstype == LST_GM && (!np->supports(SPO_MC)))
256                  continue;
259              n_nbrs++;
260              np->add_to_rxlist(this);
261          }
264          if (ip == r_ip &&
265              (ip->state() == IFS_DR && !from->is_bdr() && n_nbrs != 0)) {
266              ip->add_to_update(hdr);
267          }
268          else if (r_ip == 0 && ip->in_recv_update && n_nbrs != 0)
269              ip->add_to_update(hdr);
270          else if (ip != r_ip) {
271              if (n_nbrs == 0)
272                  continue;
273              flood_it = true;
274              if (scope == AreaScope)
275                  ip->area_flood = true;
276              else
277                  ip->global_flood = true;
278              if (ip->demand_flooding(lstype))
279                  on_demand = true;
280              else
281                  on_regular = true;
282          }
284          else
285              ip->if_build_dack(hdr);
286      }
289      if (!flood_it)
290          return;
291      else if (scope == AreaScope) {
292          if (on_regular)
293              lsa_ap->add_to_update(hdr, false);
294          if (on_demand)
295              lsa_ap->add_to_update(hdr, true);
296      }
297      else {        // AS scope
298          if (on_regular)
299              ospf->add_to_update(hdr, false);
300          if (on_demand)
301              ospf->add_to_update(hdr, true);
302      }
303 }
```

—— `spflood.C`

Figure 9.6 Sending Link State Update packets: `OSPF:ospf_flood()`.

236-237   If `ip` connects to a demand circuit and the LSA is a simple refresh (that is, the LSA's contents haven't changed but only its LS Sequence Number), the router does not flood the LSA out the interface.

238-241   Routers do not flood AS-external-LSAs into or throughout stub areas. AS-external-LSAs are also not flooded across virtual links, as they are flooded through the virtual link's transit area anyway.

242-243   All LSAs except AS-external-LSAs are specific to a single area, so routers must flood them only within their area of origin.

246-261   At this point, the LSA may be flooded out the interface `ip`. The router scans the interface's list of neighbors, deciding whether any of them should receive the LSA.

The following lines of code pertain to deciding whether to flood to a neighbor.

249-250   The link-state database is synchronized only across adjacencies, which are neighbor relationships in state Exchange or greater.

251-252   The reception of Link State Updates is a natural part of the initial synchronization with the neighbor called Database Exchange (see Section 8.3). When the router receives Link State Updates, it sometimes depletes the link-state request list, thereby allowing the neighbor eventually to become fully adjacent (neighbor state `NBS_FULL`). This logic is implemented by the `SpfNbr::ospf_rmreq()` routine. If that routine indicates that the router is requesting from the neighbor an instance of the LSA that is equal to or more up-to-date than the LSA the router is flooding, indicated by the sign of the `rq_cmp` argument, there is no point in sending the LSA to the neighbor.

253-254   The router does not need to send an LSA back to the neighbor that sent it.

255-256   The OSPF philosophy for optional LSA types is that routers that do not understand LSAs should not have to store or to forward them. In particular, routers should send group-membership-LSAs only to neighbors that are running MOSPF, as indicated by the Options field of the neighbors' Database Description packets.

260   At this point, the router should send the LSA to the neighbor. The router adds the LSA to the link-state retransmission list for the neighbor, using `SpfNbr::add_to_rxlist()` so that flooding will be reliable: The router will retransmit the LSA at intervals until it is acknowledged by the neighbor (see Section 9.5).

We are going to flood the LSA out the interface if both (1) the interface is different from the receiving interface or the interface is the receiving interface and the router is its Designated Router, and (2) one or more neighbors that we wanted to flood the LSA to are attached to the receiving interface (lines `264-269`). However, we do not build a separate Link State Update packet to be sent out each interface. Instead, we build four separate packets.

- `SpfArea::a_update` is the Link State Update packet that will contain all area-scoped LSAs to be flooded out the area's nondemand interfaces.

- **SpfArea::a_demand_upd** is the **SpfArea::a_update** subset that will be sent out the area's demand interfaces. It contains area-scoped LSAs whose contents have changed.

- **OSPF::o_update** is the packet containing new AS-external-LSAs to be flooded out all interfaces.

- **OSPF::o_demand_upd** is the subset of the new AS-external-LSAs that should be flooded out all demand interfaces.

274-282   When the LSA is to be flooded out an interface other than the receiving interface, flags are set to control which of the four packets the LSA should be placed into. If the LSA is to be flooded back out the receiving interface (lines **266**, **269**) the LSA is put instead into the packet **SpfIfc::if_update**.

284-285   If the router does not flood the LSA back out the receiving interface, a delayed Link State Acknowledgment is scheduled by calling **SpfIfc::if_build_dack()**. The implementation will delay the acknowledgment for up to 1 second. This delay allows multiple LSAs to be acknowledged by a single Link State Acknowledgment packet, improving efficiency.

291-302   The LSA is placed in the appropriate outgoing Link State Update packets. For example, a new router-LSA with changed contents will be placed in both **SpfArea::a_update** and **SpfArea::a_demand_upd**. Placement into Link State Update packets is done by calling the appropriate **add_to_update()** routine.

The routine **OSPF::send_updates()** goes through the list of interfaces and floods out each interface whichever of the four packets is appropriate. The checksum of the packet bodies is precalculated, so that only packet header checksums are calculated for each interface. This logic saves much copying and checksumming when the router has many interfaces, but at a cost. First, whereas before you may have sent only one Link State Update packet out an interface, now you may send two (one with area-scoped LSAs and one with AS-external-LSAs). In addition, interfaces that may not necessarily want an LSA may get the LSA anyway—for example, the LSA may be a group-membership-LSA and the interface may have no MOSPF routers.

In addition, for those interfaces running MD5 authentication, there is no way to avoid running the MD5 digest calculation on the whole packet for each interface unless, of course, the interfaces use the same keys, an anomaly that the code does not check for.

9.4   Receiving Acknowledgments: SpfNbr::recv_ack()

It is a simple matter for a router to handle Link State Acknowledgments. A neighbor acknowledges an LSA sent by the router by listing the LSA's 20-byte link-state header in a Link State Acknowledgment packet. On receiving the acknowledgment, the router removes any matching LSA instance from the link-state retransmission list for the neighbor. It is important that the acknowledgment specify the correct instance; the router ignores any acknowledgments of old instances or, in rare cases, acknowledgments of future instances.

The `SpfNbr::recv_ack()` routine performs receive processing for Link State Acknowledgment packets. See Figure 9.7.

49-50   Routers perform flooding and, in particular, perform the exchange of Link State Update and Link State Acknowledgment packets only over adjacencies. Adjacencies are the subset of neighbor relationships in state Exchange or greater.

57-91   Multiple LSAs can be acknowledged by a single Link State Acknowledgment packet, and we go through a loop to process each individual LSA acknowledgment in turn.

68   We find the database copy of the LSA that is being acknowledged.

71-83   If the acknowledgment is for a different instance of the LSA than the one we have in our database, we take no action other than to log an unusual event.

85-90   Because the neighbor is acknowledging the correct, current instance of the LSA, we attempt to remove the LSA from the neighbor's link-state retransmission list by calling `SpfNbr::remove_from_rxlist()`. This ensures that we will not retransmit the LSA to the neighbor. If the LSA was not on the retransmission list, we again log an unusual event but take no other action.

9.5   Retransmitting LSAs: `SpfNbr::rxmt_update()`

As mentioned earlier in this chapter, the link-state retransmission list for a neighbor is composed of multiple lists. The LSAs that we have recently sent to the neighbor but have not yet been forced to retransmit are on the list `SpfNbr::n_rxlst`. The LSAs that we have recently retransmitted to the neighbor are on the list `SpfNbr::n_pend_rxl`. The LSAs that we have previously retransmitted and *still* have not received acknowledgments for are put on the list `SpfNbr::n_failed_rxl`.

An LSA is originally put on a neighbor's link-state retransmission list during the reliable-flooding procedure, by calling the `SpfNbr::add_to_rxlist()` routine. This routine inserts the LSA on the tail of the `SpfNbr::n_rxlst` list and starts the retransmission timer `SpfNbr::n_lsarxtim` if it has not already been started.

When the retransmission timer fires, its action routine `LsaRxmtTimer::action()` gets called. At this point, we are going to transmit some of the LSAs that the neighbor has not acknowledged in a timely fashion (that is, within ospfIfRetransInterval seconds of receiving the LSA). But we might not retransmit all the LSAs that the neighbor has failed to acknowledge, because we are allowed to send only a window of retransmissions (`SpfNbr::n_rxmt_window` packets) at any one time, so as not to overwhelm the neighbor. The neighbor's retransmission window varies dynamically between **1** and the configured maximum `OSPF::max_rxmt_window`, similarly to the TCP window in TCP's slow-start congestion control scheme [41]. When the retransmission timer fires and

---
spfack.C

```
41 void SpfNbr::recv_ack(Pkt *pdesc)
43 {
44     SpfIfc *ip;
45     SpfArea *ap;
46     AckPkt *apkt;
47     LShdr *hdr;
49     if (n_state < NBS_EXCH)
50         return;
52     ip = n_ifp;
53     ap = ip->area();
54     apkt = (AckPkt *) pdesc->spfpkt;
55     hdr = (LShdr *) (apkt+1);
57     for (; ((byte *)(hdr+1)) <= pdesc->end; hdr++) {
58         int lstype;
59         lsid_t lsid;
60         rtid_t orig;
61         LSA *lsap;
62         int compare;
64         lstype = hdr->ls_type;
65         lsid = ntoh32(hdr->ls_id);
66         orig = ntoh32(hdr->ls_org);
68         lsap = ospf->FindLSA(ap, lstype, lsid, orig);
69         compare = lsap ? lsap->cmp_instance(hdr) : 1;
71         if (compare > 0) {
72             if (ospf->spflog(ERR_NEWER_ACK, 5)) {
73                 ospf->log(hdr);
74                 ospf->log(this);
75             }
76         }
78         else if (compare < 0) {
79             if (ospf->spflog(ERR_OLD_ACK, 4)) {
80                 ospf->log(hdr);
81                 ospf->log(this);
82             }
83         }
85         else if (!remove_from_rxlist(lsap)) {
86             if (ospf->spflog(DUP_ACK, 1)) {
87                 ospf->log(hdr);
88                 ospf->log(this);
89             }
90         }
91     }
92 }
```

---
spfack.C

Figure 9.7 Receiving acknowledgments: `SpfNbr::recv_ack()`.

LSAs require retransmission (that is, have not been acknowledged by the neighbor in a timely fashion), the retransmission window is set to `1`. If the neighbor then acknowledges the full window of retransmissions before the retransmission timer fires again, the retransmission window is doubled, and another window of retransmissions is sent immediately if any additional LSAs remain to be retransmitted. This procedure of continually adjusting is an attempt to discover the rate at which the neighbor can absorb the unacknowledged LSAs.

LSAs are removed from the retransmission list when an acknowledgment, either explicit or implicit, is received from the neighbor. Removal is accomplished by calling `SpfNbr::remove_from_rxlist()`. The LSA could appear on any of the three components of the retransmission list. If the LSA was the last on the list of recently retransmitted LSAs, `SpfNbr::n_pend_rxl`, we immediately send another set of LSAs requiring retransmission instead of waiting for the retransmission timer again. Both this logic and the retransmission timer call the same routine, `SpfNbr::rxmt_update()`, to pack the retransmitted LSAs into Link State Update packets and send them to the neighbor.

Figure 9.8 shows `SpfNbr::rxmt_update()`, the routine used to retransmit LSAs to an adjacent neighbor.

280   We call `SpfNbr::get_next_rxmt()` to get the next LSA that requires retransmission. This LSA will be on the list of LSAs that either have recently been received (`SpfNbr::n_rxlst`) or have been previously retransmitted but still not acknowledged (`SpfNbr::n_failed_rxl`). We send the LSAs on the former list first. In the past, I have encountered implementation bugs where certain LSAs are never acknowledged by the neighbor, and we don't want these problem LSAs (which will gravitate to `SpfNbr::n_failed_rxl`) to inhibit the flooding of other LSAs.

If no LSA is currently requiring retransmission, `SpfNbr::get_next_rxmt()` returns in `nexttime` the number of seconds before another LSA will need to be retransmitted. This information is used to restart the retransmission timer in lines **304-306**. For a detailed description of the `SpfNbr::get_next_rxmt()` function, see Section 6.3.

281-288   The LSA requiring retransmission is added to a Link State Update packet but only if the current retransmission window still has room available.

289-290   The LSA is moved to the "pending" retransmission list `SpfNbr::n_pend_rxl`. This accomplishes two things. It allows us to determine whether the neighbor has acknowledged the current window of retransmission, by seeing whether the pending list becomes empty after an acknowledgment is received. It also ensures that we will retransmit any particular LSA no more often than `SpfIfc::rxmt_interval()` seconds (line **302**): LSAs on the pending list are not retransmitted again until the retransmission timer fires.

300-302   The router unicasts the Link State Update packet to the neighbor. The retransmission timer is set to its maximum value. As long as the neighbor acknowledges the current set of LSAs that we have just sent, we will continue to send the rest of the LSAs that require retransmission, without waiting for the retransmission timer to fire. Another way of looking at this is that further retransmissions will be clocked out by received Link State Acknowledgment packets.

```
266 void SpfNbr::rxmt_updates()
267
268 {
269     int space;
270     LSA *lsap;
271     LShdr *hdr=0;
272     int npkts;
273     LsaList *list;
274     uns32 nexttime;
275
276     space = 0;
277     npkts = 0;
278
279     // Fill in packet from the "Link state retransmission list"
280     while ((lsap =  get_next_rxmt(list, nexttime))) {
281         bool full;
282         // Sent entire window?
283         full = space < lsap->ls_length();
284         if (full && ++npkts > n_rxmt_window)
285             break;
286         // Add to update packet
287         hdr = ospf->BuildLSA(lsap);
288         space = add_to_update(hdr);
289         // Move LSA to pending list
290         list->remove(lsap);
291         n_pend_rxl.addEntry(lsap);
292     }
293
294     if (npkts > 0) {
295         if (ospf->spflog(LOG_RXMTUPD, 4)) {
296             ospf->log(hdr);
297             ospf->log(this);
298         }
299         // Send the retransmitted update
300         n_ifp->nbr_send(&n_update, this);
301         // Restart retransmission timer
302         n_lsarxtim.start(n_ifp->rxmt_interval()*Timer::SECOND);
303     }
304     else if (nexttime) {
305         n_lsarxtim.start(nexttime*Timer::SECOND);
306     }
307 }
```

Figure 9.8 Retransmitting LSAs: SpfNbr::rxmt_update().

9.6   Building Update Packets

To add an LSA to a Link State Update packet in order to transmit the LSA out one or more interfaces, you call `SpfNbr::add_to_update()`, `SpfArea::add_to_update()`, or `OSPF::add_to_update()`, depending on whether you want to send the LSA to a particular neighbor, out all interfaces to an area, or out all the router's interfaces, respectively. The respective `add_to_update()` routine chooses the correct Link State Update packet to add the LSA to and makes sure that there is enough room for the LSA in the current, if any, Link State Update packet. If there is insufficient room, the current Link State Update is flooded. The Link State Update packet is then formatted by calling `OSPF::build_update()`.

Figure 9.9 shows `OSPF::build_update()`, the routine used to add an LSA to an existing Link State Update packet.

491-499   If no buffer is associated with the current Link State Update packet, we allocate one. The size of the buffer is equal to the `mtu` argument, which is the minimum MTU over all the interfaces out which the packet will be sent. If the buffer is not large enough to hold the LSA that we're adding, we instead make the buffer size just large enough to hold the LSA.

509-512   We increment the age of the LSA by 1 when copying it into the Link State Update packet. This is protection against flooding loops, as described in Section 4.7.3 of [67]. We are supposed to increment the LS Age field on a per interface basis, by the interface's ospfIfTransitDelay, but because we are potentially sending the same packet out multiple interfaces, incrementing by 1 suffices here.

513-514   If the LSA is being flooded out a demand interface, we set its DoNotAge bit. If the DoNotAge bit was already set in the LSA, we keep it set. For more information on the DoNotAge bit and the demand circuit extensions to OSPF, see [64] and Section 7.3 of [67].

Exercises

9.1   Modify the function `SpfNbr::recv_update()` to enable the flooding of an NSSA area's type-7 LSAs. These LSAs should be flooded only within NSSA areas. See Section 7.4 of [67] for details.

9.2   Modify the functions `SpfNbr::recv_update()` and `LSA::ospf_flood()` to enable the flooding of external-attributes-LSAs (LS type 8). External-attributes-LSAs are similar to MOSPF's group-membership-LSAs—routers flood external-attributes-LSAs only to neighbors claiming to understand them, by setting the appropriate Options bit in Database Description packets.

─── spflood.C

```
481 void OSPF::build_update(Pkt *pkt, LShdr *hdr, uns16 mtu, bool demand)
482
483 {
484     int lsalen;
485     UpdPkt *upkt;
486     age_t c_age, new_age;
487     LShdr *new_hdr;
488     int donotage;
489
490     lsalen = ntoh16(hdr->ls_length);
491     if (!pkt->iphdr) {
492         uns16 size;
493         size = MAX(lsalen+sizeof(InPkt)+sizeof(UpdPkt), mtu);
494         if (ospf_getpkt(pkt, SPT_UPD, size) == 0)
495             return;
496         upkt = (UpdPkt *) (pkt->spfpkt);
497         upkt->upd_no = 0;
498         pkt->dptr = (byte *) (upkt + 1);
499     }
500     /* Get pointer to link state update packet. Increment count
501      * of LSAs, copy in the current LSA and increment the
502      * buffer point.
503      */
504     upkt = (UpdPkt *) (pkt->spfpkt);
505     upkt->upd_no = hton32(ntoh32(upkt->upd_no) + 1);
506     new_hdr = (LShdr *) pkt->dptr;
507     // Increment age by interface's transmission delay
508     // Set DoNotAge if demand interface
509     c_age = ntoh16(hdr->ls_age);
510     donotage = (c_age & DoNotAge) != 0;
511     c_age &= ~DoNotAge;
512     new_age = MIN(MaxAge, c_age + 1);
513     if (new_age < MaxAge && (donotage || demand))
514         new_age |= DoNotAge;
515     new_hdr->ls_age = hton16(new_age);
516     // Copy rest of LSA into update
517     memcpy(&new_hdr->ls_opts, &hdr->ls_opts, lsalen - sizeof(age_t));
518     pkt->dptr += lsalen;
519 }
```

─── spflood.C

Figure 9.9 Building a Link State Update packet: SpfIfc::if_build_update().

10

OSPF Hierarchy

The OSPF protocol supports multiple levels of hierarchy, first allowing the OSPF routing domain to be broken up into regions, or areas, and then allowing external routing information to be imported into the OSPF routing domain in AS-external-LSAs. This chapter discusses OSPF area routing: the rules for configuring areas, aggregation of routing information at area boundaries, virtual links, and the interaction of summary-LSAs and the OSPF routing calculations. We also discuss the handling of external routing information, including the origination of AS-external-LSAs, the external routing calculation, and the interaction between OSPF areas and external routes.

10.1 Guidelines for Area Boundaries

Many people are confused about what constitutes a legal OSPF area configuration, which traditionally has been stated as follows: *Area 0.0.0.0, the so-called backbone area, is the area to which all other areas must connect either directly or via virtual links.* However, the following formulation may be easier to understand:

 Definition 1: An *area border router* is an OSPF router that has operational interfaces belonging to two or more areas.

 Definition 2: A *backbone network segment* is either an IP subnet belonging to area 0.0.0.0 or an OSPF virtual link.

 Area configuration requirement: You must be able to get from any area border router to any other area border router by traversing only backbone network segments.

Equivalently, the collection of area border routers and backbone network segments must form a connected graph.

Let us use the network diagram shown on the flyleaf as an example. The six area border routers are A, B, C, D, E, and F. Physical backbone network segments interconnect routers A through D. However, to meet the area configuration requirement, virtual links have been configured between routers D and E and between routers D and F. The resulting graph of the backbone area 0.0.0.0 is shown in Figure 10.1.

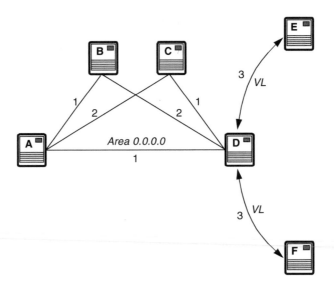

Figure 10.1 The backbone graph resulting from the network configuration in the diagram on the flyleaf.

Virtual links are configured through a given *transit area* but are not tied to any given physical path. In the network diagram on the flyleaf, both virtual links have been configured to use area 0.0.0.3 as their transit area. As long as a path through area 0.0.0.3 exists between each virtual link's endpoints, the virtual link remains operational. For example, if the physical link between routers D and E fails, the virtual link remains operational because of the existence of the area 0.0.0.3 path router E↔F↔D.

Any configuration of virtual links that maintains connection of the collection of area border routers is acceptable. For example, in the network diagram on the flyleaf, we could configure a virtual link between E and F instead of between D and E and still meet the area configuration requirements.

The backbone graph must also remain connected when network components fail; you may want to configure extra virtual links for redundancy. The configuration in the network diagram on the flyleaf is not optimal when router D fails. After the failure, router F can no longer reach routers A through D, no matter how many virtual links are configured. However, routers E and F would still be able to form their own connected backbone if a virtual link were configured between routers E and F, which would enable areas 0.0.0.5 and 0.0.0.4 to exchange user data even during router D failures.

Q: *What happens when the area configuration guidelines are violated?*

A: In general, some destinations will become unreachable. For example, in the network diagram on the flyleaf, if router D fails, the area connectivity rules are violated between area border routers E and F, and sources within area 0.0.0.5 will not be able to access destinations in area 0.0.0.4 (and vice versa). However, violation of the area configuration guidelines will not cause routing loops.

Q: *May separate OSPF areas have the same OSPF Area ID?*

A: Yes, two physically separate regions having the same OSPF Area ID will form two separate areas. For example, in the network diagram on the flyleaf, areas 0.0.0.2, 0.0.0.4, and 0.0.0.5 could equally well have been configured to use Area IDs 0.0.0.1, and there would still be five separate nonbackbone areas. However, if area 0.0.0.3 also changed to Area ID 0.0.0.1, the three areas on the right of the diagram would all form a single, larger area.

   This fact can be used to advantage when changing a single-area OSPF configuration into multiple areas. Suppose that the network diagram on the flyleaf was originally configured as a single OSPF area 0.0.0.1. To be reconfigured into the five nonbackbone areas pictured, you would have to reconfigure only the Area ID assignments of the backbone network links and the links in area 0.0.0.3, together with the addition of the two virtual links.

Q: *Might I want to configure additional virtual links to further influence the paths that data traffic takes?*

A: Sometimes, yes. Once data traffic reaches a transit area (that is, an area containing one or more virtual links), it will always take the shortest path across the area, thanks to the calculation in Section 16.3 of [75]. Sometimes, however, to attract data to the transit area in the first place, additional virtual links will have to be configured. As an example, suppose that we modify the network diagram on the flyleaf as follows. First, we add a physical area 0.0.0.0 link between routers A and F, with a cost of 10. Then, because it is no longer required by the area configuration rules, we delete the virtual link between routers D and F.

   As a result, data traffic between areas 0.0.0.2 and 0.0.0.5 will take the costlier physical link between routers A and F instead of the cheaper path through area 0.0.0.3. In order to force the traffic through area 0.0.0.3, the virtual link between routers D and F would have to be reconfigured.

Additional questions about OSPF areas are addressed in Chapters 6 and 8 of [67].

10.2   Implementing Area Routing

OSPF areas are collections of network segments, not collections of routers. A network segment belongs to one, and only one, OSPF area, whereas an OSPF router participates in all the OSPF areas to which it directly connects. The configuration of OSPF areas consists of assigning an OSPF Area ID to each network segment; in practice, and also in our OSPF implementation, this amounts to configuring the OSPF area to which each router interface connects (`CfgIfc::area_id`; see Section 13.2).

The basic OSPF operations execute separately on each area. In our implementation, each area is represented by a `class SpfArea`. Each area has its own link-state database (Section 6.1.2), which the flooding algorithm synchronizes with the databases of the other routers participating in the area and serves as the raw input to the intra-area routing calculation (Section 11.2.1).

Area border routers (ABRs) connect to two or more areas and so are, in essence, running multiple copies of the basic OSPF algorithm. The job of an area border router is to advertise the network segments in any one of its areas to its other attached areas, through the origination of summary-LSAs (Section 10.2.1). An area border router can be configured to aggregate multiple segments in a single summary-LSA (`struct CfgRnge`; see Sections 10.2.2 and 13.5).

To propagate routing information through multiple area hops, an area border router is allowed to calculate routing table entries based on summary-LSAs received from the backbone OSPF area 0.0.0.0 (Section 11.2.6). The ABR then distributes the resulting routing information to its attached nonbackbone areas, again through summary-LSAs. OSPF requires that all nonbackbone areas be attached directly to area 0.0.0.0 through either an area border router or a sequence of virtual links. For example, in the network diagram on the flyleaf, area 0.0.0.1 is connected to the backbone by router B (and/or router C), whereas area 0.0.0.4 is connected to the backbone by the virtual link between routers D and E. This area requirement implies that the distribution of routing information goes from a segment's area to the backbone and then to all other areas not directly connected to the segment's home area.

Virtual links are configured between area border routers (`struct CfgVL`; see Section 13.6). Operation of OSPF over virtual links is described in Section 10.2.3. When a fully adjacent virtual link has been established through a nonbackbone area, the endpoints of the virtual link advertise the area as a "transit area" by setting the V bit in their router-LSAs (see Sections 7.2 and 11.2). Transit areas are those areas willing to carry traffic that neither originates in nor is destined for the area itself. The routing calculation then calculates shortcut routes through the transit area, as described in Section 11.2.7.

Network operators can reduce the size of an area's link-state database and routing table by configuring the area as a "stub area" (`struct CfgArea`; see Section 13.4). Stub areas omit all external routing information, routing to external destinations instead via a default route, and can have their link-state database size reduced even further by inhibiting the origination of summary-LSAs by their area border routers.

10.2.1 Originating Summary-LSAs

An area border router advertises its intra-area and inter-area routes in the form of summary-LSAs. The data flow for summary-LSA origination is pictured in Figure 10.2. The function that builds the summary-LSA is `OSPF::sl_orig(INrte *rte, bool transit_changes_only)`. It creates the summary-LSA, based on the contents of the routing table entry `rte`, thereby enforcing the general principle that a router should

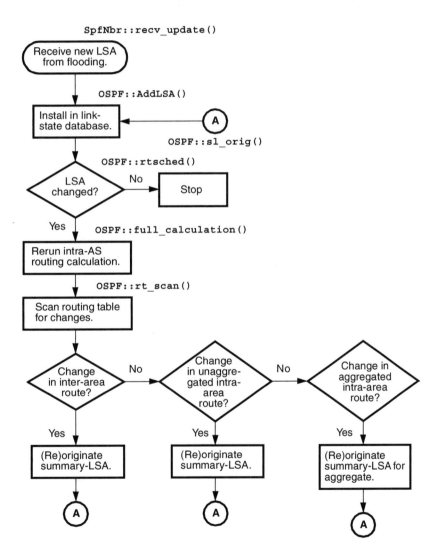

Figure 10.2 Data flow of summary-LSA (re)origination.

advertise only those paths that it is using in forwarding. The routing table entry itself is built from the link-state database—the router-LSAs, network-LSAs, and summary-LSAs that have been received from flooding. The summary-LSA that the router will originate will also be installed in the link-state database, but a feedback loop is avoided because the router does not use self-originated summary-LSAs in its routing table calculation (Section 11.2.6).

Summary-LSAs have "area scope," meaning that they are associated with a single area only. The function `OSPF::sl_orig(INrte *rte, bool transit_changes_only)` originates separate summary-LSAs for each of the router's attached areas by calling `SpfArea::sl_orig()` for each area. If `transit_changes_only` is set, summary-LSAs are reoriginated only into those areas whose transit status has changed. The OSPF protocol prohibits aggregation of routes into transit areas, so when an area's transit status changes, the router must either reaggregate or deaggregate its summary-LSAs.

`SpfArea::sl_orig()` must address two main issues. One is the cost to advertise in the summary-LSA. This cost is determined by the function `SpfArea::sl_cost()`. The second issue is the question of which Link State ID to use for the summary-LSA. The procedure here is the same as that used for AS-external-LSAs and is addressed in detail in Section 10.3.3.

The cost that the router should advertise in its summary-LSAs is determined by `SpfArea::sl_cost()`, shown in Figure 10.3.

121   We are calculating the cost of the summary-LSA for the specified area (`this`) and destination (`rte`). It may be the case that no summary-LSA should be originated for this combination of area and destination—for example, an intra-area destination is not advertised back to its own area, or the destination may not be reachable through intra-area or inter-area paths. In these cases, a cost of `LSInfinity` is returned, telling the caller not to advertise the summary-LSA and to flush any summary-LSA that the router had originated previously.

128-133   In stub areas, area border routers (and only area border routers) advertise summary-LSAs specifying a default route (lines **129-130**). The cost of this default advertisement is the configured value `SpfArea::a_dfcst`. The origination of all other summary-LSAs into a stub area can be disabled by setting `SpfArea::a_import` to `false` (lines **131-132**).

135-147   If `INrte::is_range()` returns `true`, the destination is a configured aggregate. We allow the same aggregate to be configured for multiple areas. In that case, we aggregate the area that would advertise the smallest cost for the aggregate; the aggregation data for this area (`class Range *rp`) is returned by `OSPF::GetBestRange()`. We are going to advertise a cost for the aggregate equal to the distance to the farthest intra-area component of the aggregate (stored in `Range::r_cost`), with the following provisos: (1) we don't advertise aggregates having no intra-area components, as indicated by `Range::r_active`; (2) backbone routes are not aggregated into transit areas (line **139**);

```
                                                              ——— summlsa.C
121 uns32 SpfArea::sl_cost(INrte *rte)
123 {
124     aid_t home;
125     uns32 cost;
126
128     if (a_stub) {
129         if (rte == default_route)
130             return((ospf->n_area > 1) ? a_dfcst : LSInfinity);
131         else if (!a_import)
132             return(LSInfinity);
133     }
135     if (rte->is_range()) {
136         Range   *rp;
137         if ((rp = ospf->GetBestRange(rte)) &&
138             (rp->r_active) &&
139             (!a_transit || rp->r_area != BACKBONE)) {
140             if (rp->r_suppress)
141                 return(LSInfinity);
142             else if (rp->r_area == a_id)
143                 return(LSInfinity);
144             else
145                 return(rp->r_cost);
146         }
147     }
149     if (rte->type() == RT_SPFIA) {
150         home = rte->area();
151         cost = rte->cost;
152     }
153     else if (rte->type() != RT_SPF)
154         return(LSInfinity);
155     else if (rte->r_mpath->all_in_area(this))
156         return(LSInfinity);
157     else if ((!a_transit || rte->area() != BACKBONE) &&
158             rte->within_range())
159         return(LSInfinity);
160     else {
161         home = rte->area();
162         cost = rte->cost;
163     }
166     if (a_id == home)
167         return(LSInfinity);
169     return(cost);
170 }
                                                              ——— summlsa.C
```

Figure 10.3 Determining the cost to advertise in a summary-LSA: `SpfArea::sl_cost()`.

(3) advertising of an aggregate can be inhibited through configuration (`Range::`
`r_suppress`). An area's routes are never aggregated back into itself (lines `142-143`).

149-152   Inter-area destinations are never aggregated.

153-154   Summary-LSAs are originated only for intra-area and inter-area destinations.

155-156   This is the split-horizon logic. If packets destined for the destination are always forwarded into a given area, we do not originate a summary-LSA into that area. For the
base OSPF protocol, this logic is simply an optimization, as such a summary-LSA would
not be used in any routers' calculations anyway. However, this logic is necessary for
inter-area MOSPF forwarding to work correctly.

157-159   If we are allowed to aggregate routes into the area and the intra-area destination
falls into a configured aggregate, as determined by `INrte::within_range()`, origination of the more-specific summary-LSA is inhibited.

166-167   For an intra-area destination, summary-LSAs are not originated into the destination's area. Summary-LSAs for inter-area destinations are not originated back into the
backbone area, from which they were originally learned.

10.2.2 Area Aggregates

The subject of aggregating an OSPF area's routing information before advertising it to
other areas is addressed in various sections scattered throughout the book. In this section, we gather together references to those sections.

- Aggregates are configured via `OSPF::cfgRnge(struct CfgRnge *msg, int status)`, as described in Section 13.5.

- A configured aggregate is stored in a `class Range`. In particular, you can tell
whether a range is currently being advertised in summary-LSAs (that is, is
active and not suppressed) by the values of `Range::r_active` and
`Range::r_suppress`. All the aggregates associated with a particular area are
organized into `SpfArea::ranges`.

- Configuration of area aggregates modifies the collection of summary-LSAs that
the router originates (Section 10.2.1).

- Whether an area aggregate is active and, if so, the cost to advertise for an aggregate, is calculated during the intra-AS routing calculation (Section 11.2.5). First,
aggregates are set to an unadvertised state by `OSPF::invalidate_ranges()`.
Then, as `OSPF::rt_scan()` scans the routing table after the Dijkstra algorithm
has calculated all intra-area routes, the cost of each aggregate is updated, using
`OSPF::update_area_ranges()`. Note that when an intra-area route matches
multiple configured aggregates, only the cost of the most specific aggregate is
updated.

10.2.3 Virtual Links

OSPF virtual links can be configured by the network administrator in order to attach nonbackbone areas to OSPF's backbone area 0.0.0.0 and to ensure connectivity of the backbone area. For a description of how virtual links are used in OSPF area configurations, see Section 6.1.2 of [67].

In our OSPF implementation, a virtual link is modeled as a special kind of OSPF point-to-point interface. Virtual links are configured by calling the routine `OSPF::cfgVL()`, described in Section 13.6. Each virtual link configured in the router is represented by a `class VLIfc`, which inherits from the base point-to-point interface `class PPIfc`. The other endpoint of the virtual link is specified by a remote OSPF router's Router ID (`VLIfc::if_nbrid`). The virtual link is configured to use the services of a particular nonbackbone OSPF area, called the virtual link's *transit area* (`VLIfc::if_tap`).

The behavior of a virtual link is specialized by virtual functions in `class VLIfc`. `VLIfc::rl_insert()` inserts a link description into the router's backbone router-LSA for the virtual link; this description is similar to that of an unnumbered point-to-point link but sets the description's Type field to "Virtual link." OSPF protocol packets are sent over the virtual link by `VLIfc::if_send()` and `VLIfc::nbr_send()`, both of which send the packet directly to the IP address of the virtual link endpoint (`VLIfc::if_rmtaddr`).

Unlike other interfaces, the viability of a virtual link is not determined by the operational state of its underlying physical interface. In fact, `VLIfc::if_phyint` is set to `-1`, indicating that the underlying physical interface is unspecified. Instead, a virtual link is declared operational when the Dijkstra calculation for the virtual link's transit area finds that the remote endpoint is reachable. At this point, the function `VLIfc::update()` is called to invoke the interface state machine and to calculate the IP address of the remote router.

The function `VLIfc::update(class RTRrte *endpt)` is illustrated in Figure 10.4. The endpoint of a virtual link is represented by the routing table entry for the remote router in the transit area (`endpt`). `VLIfc::update()` is called when the route to the endpoint changes. It is also called when updated LSAs are received that change the bidirectional status of some of the remote router's interfaces, as this may change the calculation of the remote router's IP address.

139-142   If the endpoint is not reachable through the transit area, the virtual link is declared inoperational. In addition, virtual links are not allowed to use stub areas as transit areas.

148-150   The router calculates the source IP address to be used for the virtual link. This will be one of the router's own IP addresses. First, it tries to use the IP address of the outgoing interface used to send packets to the virtual link endpoint (line **148**). If the first byte of this address is `0`, we assume that the outgoing interface is an unnumbered point-to-point link. The router then looks for any other address belonging to the transit area, by calling `SpfArea::id_to_addr(rtid_t id)`. That function finds an IP address

```
                                                         —————————— spfvl.C
131 void VLIfc::update(class RTRrte *endpt)
133 {
134     SpfArea *ap;
135
136     ap = endpt->ap;
139     if (endpt->type() != RT_SPF || ap->is_stub()) {
140         run_fsm(IFE_DOWN);
141         return;
142     }
143
148     if_addr = endpt->ifc()->if_addr;
149     if (byte0(if_addr) == 0)
150         if_addr = ap->id_to_addr(ospf->my_id());
151     if_rmtaddr = ap->id_to_addr(endpt->rtrid());
152     if (byte0(if_addr) == 0 || byte0(if_rmtaddr) == 0) {
153         run_fsm(IFE_DOWN);
154         return;
155     }
156
160     if (if_cost != endpt->cost) {
161         SpfArea *a;
162         a = ospf->FindArea(BACKBONE);
163         if_cost = endpt->cost;
164         a->rl_orig(0);
165     }
166
167     run_fsm(IFE_UP);
168 }
                                                         —————————— spfvl.C
```

Figure 10.4 Calculating the operational parameters of a virtual link: `VLIfc::update()`.

belonging to a router with OSPF Router ID `id`. The function does so by finding `id`'s router-LSA in the area's link-state database and then looking at the link descriptions therein. A host route advertised with a cost of `0`, the Link Data field of a link to a network, or a Link Data field with nonzero high byte in a link to a router are all assumed to be IP addresses belonging to `id`.

151   The IP address of the remote router is also calculated by using `SpfArea:: id_to_addr()`. Note that this function gives preference to the IP address in the remote router that points back along the shortest path from the calculating router. This is the address that the OSPF specification says to use, although the other ones returned by `SpfArea::id_to_addr()` will also work.

152-155   If the source and the destination addresses of the virtual link are not both valid, the virtual link is declared invalid. This should happen only if one of the router endpoints has no IP addresses belonging to the transit area.

160-165   The cost of the virtual link is the cost of the path through the transit area to the remote router endpoint. If the cost changes, the router's backbone router-LSA must be reoriginated.

167   At this point, the remote endpoint of the virtual link is reachable through the transit area. The transit area is not a stub area, and source and destination IP addresses have been discovered for the virtual link. Therefore, we declare the virtual link up. (It may already be up, in which case the interface state machine does nothing with the **IFE_UP** event.)

10.3   Implementing External Routing

The data flow for the calculation of external routes and the origination of external routing information is shown in Figure 10.5. External routing information can be imported into an OSPF routing domain in AS-external-LSAs. When calculating a routing table entry for which it has AS-external-LSAs, an OSPF router looks at other sources of routing information as well—statically configured routes, routes learned from other routing protocols, such as BGP and RIP, and so on. The router then decides which source of routing information should take precedence. If received AS-external-LSAs provide the best route, the router installs a routing table entry of type **RT_EXTT1** or **RT_EXTT2**. Otherwise, the router installs a route of type **RT_STATIC** and originates an AS-external-LSA to tell the rest of the routing domain about its external route.

Routes available to the router but learned through non-OSPF sources, such as static configuration or other routing protocols, such as BGP, are conveyed to the OSPF implementation though the API routine **OSPF::cfgExRt(struct CfgExRt *msg, int status)**. This routine is discussed in detail in Section 13.9. Note, however, that before the route is passed to OSPF, a cost must be calculated so that the route can be compared to routes that the OSPF router learns through the reception of AS-external-LSAs. This cost has two components: (1) whether the route is equivalent to an OSPF external type-1 or type-2 metric (**CfgExRt::type2**), and (2) the cost of the route in terms of this metric (**CfgExRt::cost**). After being passed to OSPF through the API, the external routing information is stored in a **class ExRtData**, a pointer to which is stored in the matching routing table entry (**INrte::exdata**).

Calculating the preferred path from among the non-OSPF routing sources and the AS-external-LSAs that have been received during flooding is implemented by **INrte::run_external()** and is discussed in detail in Section 11.6. When non-OSPF sources take precedence, the router uses **OSPF::ase_schedule()** to schedule origination of an AS-external-LSA, which imports the external routing information into the OSPF routing domain. Scheduling the origination enables us to rate-limit the introduction of AS-external-LSAs into the routing domain; see Section 10.3.2 for details.

AS-external-LSAs have global flooding scope. This means that they are flooded across area boundaries into all areas except those that have been configured as stub

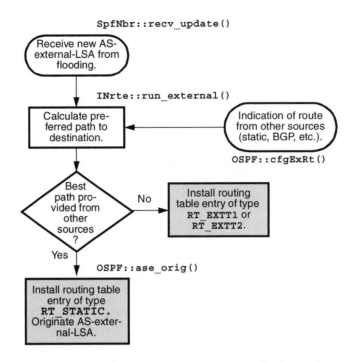

Figure 10.5 Data flow of external route processing. Shading indicates installation of routing table entries into the system kernel.

areas (Section 10.3.5). When trying to calculate a routing table entry, based on an AS-external-LSA originated by a router in a remote area, a router must know the cost of reaching that remote router. For example, in the network diagram on the flyleaf, router J may have in its link-state database an AS-external-LSA originated by router G, but in order to calculate the cost of using this AS-external-LSA, router J must know the cost of the path to the ASBR router G.

In our implementation, the best path to an ASBR is stored in a **class ASBRrte**. In order for routers to discover the best path to an ASBR in a remote area, ASBR-summary-LSAs are originated to advertise ASBRs across area boundaries. In our example, router A advertises an ASBR-summary-LSA for router G into area 0.0.0.0, and router E then advertises an ASBR-summary-LSA for G into area 0.0.0.4. The origination of ASBR-summary-LSAs is covered in Section 10.3.1.

The best path to an ASBR is then calculated, based on any intra-area paths to the ASBR that the Dijkstra algorithm discovers, together with the inter-area paths that are learned via the received ASBR-summary-LSAs. This calculation is described in Section 11.5.

10.3.1 Originating ASBR-summary-LSAs

Originating ASBR-summary-LSAs is similar to originating summary-LSAs (Section 10.2.1) but is easier, as you don't have to deal with aggregation. Origination of summary-LSAs is handled by the routine `SpfArea::asbr_orig()`. ASBR-summary-LSAs are (re)originated by an area border router when (1) the cost to an ASBR changes, (2) the area border router becomes attached to a new area, or (3) the ability of the OSPF routing domain to support DoNotAge-LSAs changes (Section 6.5.5).

The majority of the routine `SpfArea::asbr_orig()` is given in Figure 10.6.

69   The routine originates an ASBR-summary-LSA into the area specified by `this`. As with summary-LSAs and AS-external-LSAs, the router advertises the path that it is using for forwarding, which is stored in `rte`. If `forced` is nonzero, an ASBR-summary-LSA will be reoriginated even if the database already contains an LSA with the same contents.

81-83   The Link State ID used for the ASBR-summary-LSA, `ls_id`, is the ASBR's Router ID. We perform a lookup in the link-state database to see whether the router has already originated an ASBR-summary-LSA (`olsap`) for the ASBR.

85-101   We determine the `cost` to advertise in the ASBR-summary-LSA. If `cost` is set to `LSInfinity`, we will not advertise an ASBR-summary-LSA and will flush any ASBR-summary-LSA that we have previously advertised for the ASBR.

85-89   We advertise an ASBR-summary-LSA for ourselves only when we are signaling the lack of DoNotAge capability across area borders. This signaling is performed by using so-called *indication-LSAs*: ASBR-summary-LSAs specifying the router's own Router ID, with a cost of `LSInfinity`, and the DC bit off. The function `SpfArea::needs_indication()` implements the tiebreakers from Section 2.5.1.1 of [64] to ensure that only the minimum number of indication-LSAs are originated.

90-91   ASBR-summaries are not originated into stub areas, as they don't receive AS-external-LSAs and so don't need to keep track of the location of ASBRs.

92-93   If the ASBR is unreachable, the ASBR-summary is not originated.

94-95   This is the split-horizon logic. If the best path(s) to the ASBR go through an area A, the ASBR-summary is not originated into area A itself.

96-101   The path to the ASBR must be either an intra-area or an inter-area path.

104-107   If the best path(s) to the ASBR are learned from area A, the ASBR-summary-LSA is not originated into area A. Note, by example, the difference between this test and the test in line **94**. In the network diagram on the flyleaf, the best path from router D to the ASBR router H is associated with area 0.0.0.0 but has next hops belonging to area 0.0.0.3. As a result, router D does not originate an ASBR-summary-LSA for H into area 0.0.0.0 or into area 0.0.0.3. If the ASBR-summary should not be originated, the call to `OSPF::lsa_flush()` removes any ASBR-summary-LSA that may have been previously originated.

110   The only reasons for failing to get an LS Sequence Number to use in the LSA are (1) the LSA has been updated within the last MinLSInterval seconds or (2) the current LS

─── asbrlsa.C

```
 69 void SpfArea::asbr_orig(ASBRrte *rte, int forced)
 71 {
 72     asbrLSA *olsap;
 73     uns16 length;
 74     LShdr *hdr;
 75     SummHdr *summ;
 76     lsid_t ls_id;
 77     aid_t home=0;
 78     uns32 cost;
 79     seq_t seqno;
 81     ls_id = rte->rtrid();
 82     length = sizeof(LShdr) + sizeof(SummHdr);
 83     olsap = (asbrLSA *) ospf->myLSA(this, LST_ASBR, ls_id);
 85     if (ls_id == ospf->my_id()) {
 86         cost = LSInfinity;
 87         if (needs_indication())
 88             goto get_seqno;
 89     }
 90     else if (a_stub)
 91         cost = LSInfinity;
 92     else if (!rte->valid())
 93         cost = LSInfinity;
 94     else if (rte->r_mpath->all_in_area(this))
 95         cost = LSInfinity;
 96     else if (rte->type() == RT_SPF || rte->type() == RT_SPFIA) {
 97         home = rte->area();
 98         cost = rte->cost;
 99     }
100     else
101         cost = LSInfinity;
104     if (cost == LSInfinity || a_id == home) {
105         lsa_flush(olsap);
106         return;
107     }
109 get_seqno:
110     if ((seqno = ospf->ospf_get_seqno(olsap, length, forced)) ==
            InvalidLSSeq)
111         return;
112
113     // Fill in LSA contents
114     // Header
```

─── asbrlsa.C

Figure 10.6 Originating ASBR-summary-LSAs: `SpfArea::asbr_orig()`.

Sequence Number is equal to MaxSequenceNumber and must be rolled over. In either case, origination of the LSA will be rescheduled by `OSPF::ospf_get_seqno()`.

The rest of the routine simply fills in the contents of the ASBR-summary-LSA and then calls `OSPF::lsa_reorig()` to install the LSA into the router's own database and to start flooding the LSA to the router's neighbors. Note that if the contents of the LSA are the same as the current database copy and `forced` is set to `false`, `OSPF::lsa_reorig()` will *not* perform the reorigination.

10.3.2 Originating AS-external-LSAs

The origination of an AS-external-LSA is scheduled by calling `OSPF::ase_schedule()`. We schedule originations instead of doing them immediately, in order to rate-limit the number of AS-external-LSA originations to `CfgGen::new_flood_rate` per second, distributing the control traffic load over time even when many thousands of AS-external-LSAs must be originated. More information on the rate-limiting of AS-external-LSA origination can be obtained in the discussion of `LocalOrigTimer::action()` later.

The (re)origination of one or more AS-external-LSAs must be scheduled on the following events.

- A routing table entry is changed to reflect routing information obtained from a non-OSPF source, or non-OSPF data is withdrawn or overridden by a received AS-external-LSA. This condition is detected by `INrte::type()` changing to or from `RT_STATIC`.

- When the router enters Overflow State (Section 10.3.4), all nondefault AS-external-LSAs that the router had originated should be flushed. On leaving Overflow State, those same AS-external-LSAs should be reoriginated.

- When the router notices that some of the routers in the OSPF routing domain are incapable of DoNotAge processing (Section 6.5), any AS-external-LSAs that the router had originated with DoNotAge set must be reoriginated with DoNotAge clear (`OSPF::flush_donotage()`).

Determining AS-external-LSA Contents: `OSPF::ase_orig()`

The routine that builds an AS-external-LSA for a prefix, installs it in the router's link-state database, and starts its flooding throughout the OSPF routing domain is `OSPF::ase_orig()`, the beginning and end of which are shown in Figures 10.7 and 10.8.

271 The `exdata` argument is the non-OSPF information that has been associated with the prefix through a previous call to `OSPF::cfgExRt()`. If this information does not exist, the router will not originate an AS-external-LSA for the prefix. However, the router may want to flush a previously advertised AS-external-LSA; to do so, the routine

── asexlsa.C

```
271  void OSPF::ase_orig(ExRtData *exdata, int forced)
273  {
274      ASextLSA *olsap;
275      lsid_t ls_id;
276      INrte *o_rte;
277      ASextLSA *nlsap;
278      uns16 length;
279      LShdr *hdr;
280      ASEhdr *ase;
281      seq_t seqno;
282      INrte *rte;
283      FWDrte *faddr;

285      o_rte = 0;
287      rte = exdata->rte;
288      exdata->forced = false;
290      if ((olsap = rte->my_ase_lsa()))
291          ls_id = olsap->ls_id();
292      else if (!ospf->get_lsid(rte, LST_ASL, 0, ls_id))
293          return;
296      if ((olsap = (ASextLSA *)ospf->myLSA(0, LST_ASL, ls_id))) {
297          o_rte = olsap->orig_rte;
298          olsap->orig_rte = rte;
299      }
301      length = sizeof(LShdr) + sizeof(ASEhdr);
303      if (exdata->cost == LSInfinity ||
304          rte->type() != RT_STATIC ||
305          exdata->noadv != 0) {
306          lsa_flush(olsap);
307          if (exdata->cost == LSInfinity) {
308              rte->exdata = 0;
309              delete exdata;
310              if (--(ospf->n_extImports) == 0)
311                  ospf->rl_orig();
312          }
313          return;
314      }
315      if (ospf->OverflowState && rte != default_route) {
316          lsa_flush(olsap);
317          return;
318      }
```

── asexlsa.C

Figure 10.7 Starting to originate an AS-external-LSA in OSPF::ase_orig().

```
                                                              ──── asexlsa.C
345        nlsap = (ASextLSA *) ospf->lsa_reorig(0, olsap, hdr, forced);
346        if (nlsap)
347            nlsap->orig_rte = rte;
348
349        // If bumped another LSA, reoriginate
350        if (o_rte && (o_rte != rte)) {
351            // Print log message
352            ase_orig(o_rte, false);
353        }
354 }
                                                              ──── asexlsa.C
```

Figure 10.8 Completion of AS-external-LSA origination in `OSPF::ase_orig()`.

`OSPF::ase_orig(INrte *rte, int forced)` would be called instead. As always, the
`forced` argument indicates whether the LSA should be reoriginated regardless of
whether it has changed.

287   The routing table entry for the prefix is `rte`. Its type (`rte->type()`) must equal
`RT_STATIC` in order for an AS-external-LSA to be originated (line **304**).

288   `ExRtData::forced` is set to `true` when changes to the non-OSPF information do
not change the routing table entry but would change the contents of the AS-external-
LSA originated for the prefix. One example is a change in the external route tag
`ExRtData::tag`.

290-294   An attempt is made in `INrte::my_ase_lsa()` to find the current AS-external-LSA
that the router is advertising for the prefix. If the LSA is found, the router reuses its Link
State ID. Otherwise, the Link State ID is chosen as described in Section 10.3.3.

296-299   The router finds the AS-external-LSA (`olsap`) that it has previously originated with
the chosen Link State ID, if any. This LSA may have been originated describing a route
for a different prefix (see Section 10.3.3). If so, because we are going to bump this advertisement, the previously described prefix is remembered in `o_rte`. At the end of the routine (lines **350-353**), we will replace this LSA with one having a different Link State ID.
We note the new prefix that the LSA will describe in `ASextLSA::orig_rte`—then even
if the reorigination of the LSA is postponed in lines **319-321**, the LSA will not revert to
its old prefix.

303-314   In these lines, the router has decided to flush the LSA instead of reoriginating it. If
`ExRtData::noadv` is `true`, the non-OSPF information is supposed to be installed in the
router's routing table but *not* imported into the OSPF routing domain. When non-OSPF
information is to be withdrawn from the OSPF routing domain, the implementation first
sets `ExRtData::cost` to `LSInfinity`; then, after the flush of the LSA has begun, the
non-OSPF information is deleted (lines **308-309**). This delayed deletion is necessary
because the `class ExRtData` needs to be kept around as an argument to the routine we
are examining. `OSPF::n_extImports` is the number of AS-external-LSAs that the router
is currently originating. The router is an ASBR if and only if this number is nonzero.

315-318   When in Overflow State, only AS-external-LSAs for the default route 0/0 can be originated (see Section 10.3.4).

345-347   `OSPF::lsa_reorig()` returns the LSA that it has just (re)originated, if any. The router marks it with the prefix that is being advertised.

350-353   If the choice of Link State ID for the current prefix (`rte`) has bumped a less specific prefix (`o_rte`), the router immediately reoriginates an AS-external-LSA for the less specific prefix. This one will have a larger Link State ID than it had previously.

Rate-Limiting AS-external-LSA Origination: `LocalOrigTimer::action()`

The OSPF implementation rate-limits the number of AS-external-LSAs that the router imports. In some OSPF routing domains, many thousands of external routes are imported, and rate-limiting the importation spreads out over time the demands on router CPU and network bandwidth—even if the external routes are discovered all at once through an initial set of received BGP updates or by reading a configuration file of static routes or through other means.

The rate-limit is configurable, importing a maximum number of `CfgGen::new_flood_rate` (stored internally as `OSPF::new_flood_rate`) AS-external-LSAs per second. If not specified, the rate defaults to 1,000 AS-external-LSAs per second (see `CfgGen::set_defaults()`).

For the purpose of rate-limiting, time is broken into 100-millisecond intervals. The origination of AS-external-LSAs is scheduled by calling `OSPF::ase_schedule()`. That routine first checks to see whether the maximum number of AS-external-LSAs have been imported in the current 100-millisecond interval. If not, origination of the AS-external-LSA is performed immediately by calling `ospf->ase_orig()` (see Section 10.3.2). Otherwise, the external routing information that will lead to the AS-external-LSA is appended to the singly linked list whose head is `OSPF::ases_pending` and tail is `OSPF::ases_end`. This list will then be processed by the timer `class LocalOrigTimer`, which expires at the end of each 100-millisecond interval.

The action routine that is executed on timer expiration, `LocalOrigTimer::action()`, is displayed in Figure 10.9.

211   We keep track of whether any more AS-external-LSAs are pending origination in the variable `more_todo`. If the routine finds that all AS-external-LSAs have been originated, the `LocalOrigTimer` is canceled in lines **262-263**.

213   `OSPF::n_local_flooded` counts the number of AS-external-LSAs that have been originated this 100-millisecond interval. Because we are starting a new interval, we zero the count.

214-222   Here, the router has an AS-external-LSA to originate that fits under the rate-limit. The external information that will control the contents of the AS-external-LSA is stored in `exdata`. We remove the AS-external-LSA's information from the pending origination

```
                                                                  asexlsa.C
205 void LocalOrigTimer::action()
207 {
208     ExRtData *exdata;
209     AreaIterator iter(ospf);
210     SpfArea *a;
211     bool more_todo=false;
213     ospf->n_local_flooded = 0;
214     while (ospf->n_local_flooded < ospf->new_flood_rate/10 &&
215             (exdata = ospf->ases_pending)) {
216         if (!(ospf->ases_pending = exdata->sll_pend))
217             ospf->ases_end = 0;
218         ospf->n_local_flooded++;
219         exdata->sll_pend = 0;
220         exdata->orig_pending = false;
221         ospf->ase_orig(exdata, false);
222     }
224     // Flush unsupported DoNotAge LSAs w/ area scope
225     while ((a = iter.get_next())) {
226         LsaListIterator iter(&a->a_dna_flushq);
227         LSA *lsap;
228         if (a->donotage()) {
229             a->a_dna_flushq.clear();
230             continue;
231         }
232         while (ospf->n_local_flooded < ospf->new_flood_rate/10 &&
233                 (lsap = iter.get_next())) {
234             if (lsap->valid()) {
235                 ospf->n_local_flooded++;
236                 lsa_flush(lsap);
237             }
238             iter.remove_current();
239         }
240         a->a_dna_flushq.garbage_collect();
241         if (!a->a_dna_flushq.is_empty())
242             more_todo = true;
243     }
245     // Flush unsupported DoNotAge AS-external-LSAs
246     if (ospf->donotage())
247         ospf->dna_flushq.clear();
248     else {
249         LsaListIterator iter(&ospf->dna_flushq);
250         LSA *lsap;
```

(Continued)

```
251              while (ospf->n_local_flooded < ospf->new_flood_rate/10 &&
252                  (lsap = iter.get_next())) {
253                if (lsap->valid()) {
254                    ospf->n_local_flooded++;
255                    lsa_flush(lsap);
256                }
257                iter.remove_current();
258              }
259              ospf->dna_flushq.garbage_collect();
260            }
261
262            if (!ospf->ases_pending && ospf->dna_flushq.is_empty() &&
                   !more_todo)
263              ospf->origtim.stop();
264  }
```
——— asexlsa.C

Figure 10.9 Rate-limiting AS-external-LSA origination: `LocalOrigTimer::action()`.

list in lines `216-217`, taking care to zero the tail pointer when the list becomes empty.
`ExRtData::orig_pending` is cleared, indicating that the AS-external-LSA is no longer
pending. The origination is then performed by calling `OSPF::ospf->ase_orig()`.

225-243   When an area no longer supports DoNotAge LSAs (Section 6.5), all DoNotAge
LSAs must be flushed from the area's link-state database. These LSAs are also covered
under the AS-external-LSA rate-limit, as again, a potentially large number of LSAs will
be scheduled for reorigination at the same time.

226   When the area becomes DoNotAge-incapable, all the DoNotAge LSAs are
enqueued on `SpfArea::a_dna_flushq` by the routine `OSPF::donotage_changes()`.

228-231   It is possible that the area is again DoNotAge-capable, before all the DoNotAge-
LSAs have been flushed. If so, we just remove the remaining DoNotAge-LSAs from the
"pending flush" queue, as the flush is no longer necessary.

232-239   Otherwise, we flush all the DoNotAge LSAs that fit under the rate-limit.

240   Some of the remaining DoNotAge LSAs still on the pending flush queue may
already have been removed from the database. Calling `LsaList::garbage_collect()`
allows such LSAs to be freed to the heap (see Section 6.3).

245-260   When the entire OSPF routing domain becomes incapable of DoNotAge processing,
all DoNotAge AS-external-LSAs must be flushed. Again, the flushing of these LSAs is
forced to obey the rate-limit and follows similar logic to the preceding per-area case.
When the OSPF routing domain becomes DoNotAge-incapable, the DoNotAge AS-
external-LSAs have been enqueued onto `OSPF::dna_flushq` by `OSPF::`
`donotage_changes()`.

10.3.3 Assigning Link State IDs

For each prefix it advertises in an AS-external-LSA (and also for prefixes advertised in summary-LSAs), the implementation must decide which Link State ID to use for the advertisement. The implementation first tries to use the prefix's network number as Link State ID, but this may collide with an LSA that the router has previously originated. For example, if the router tries to originate AS-external-LSAs for both 10/8 and 10.0/16, it cannot use the Link State ID of 10.0.0.0 for both.

Appendix E of the OSPF specification [75] provides an algorithm for assigning Link State IDs. However, Link State ID assignment is a local problem: Each router may choose its own algorithm to distinguish its own LSAs. In our implementation, we have chosen a very simple Link State ID assignment strategy.

1. Start by trying to assign the Link State ID equal to the network number.

2. When two prefixes contend for the same Link State ID, the most specific prefix wins. The loser then tries to grab the next Link State ID in sequence (that is, the previous Link State ID plus 1).

3. If there is contention for the next Link State ID in sequence, step 2 is repeated.

In our example, this algorithm chooses a Link State ID of 10.0.0.0 for 10.0/16 and 10.0.0.1 for 10/8. In a second example, if trying to advertise AS-external-LSAs for 10/8, 10.0/16, 10.0.0.1/32, and 10.0.0.2/32, Link State IDs 10.0.0.3, 10.0.0.0, 10.0.0.1, and 10.0.0.2 are used, respectively.

This Link State ID assignment algorithm works *unless* you are trying to advertise a subnet and all its constituent host routes. However, in this case, the algorithm will simply fail to assign a Link State ID to the subnet, leading to a failure to advertise it in an AS-external-LSA, which is probably what you would want anyway, as the subnet advertisement would always be overridden by one of the host routes. The Link State ID assignment does require you to sometimes reoriginate one or more existing AS-external-LSAs when a new, more specific prefix needs to be advertised—for example, see what happens in the second example when you want to advertise 10.0.0.0/32. However, this undesirable property is also present in the algorithm in Appendix E of [75].

Choosing a Link State ID for an AS-external-LSA or a summary-LSA is performed by the function `OSPF::get_lsid()`, which is shown in Figure 10.10.

177   The `rte` argument is the prefix to be advertised. This same routine is used to choose Link State IDs for both AS-external-LSAs and summary-LSAs. In the former case, `lstype` is set to `LST_ASL`. In the latter case, `lstype` is set to `LST_SUMM`, and `ap` is set to point to the area that the summary-LSA will belong to. The Link State ID will be returned in (call by reference) argument `ls_id`. The routine returns `true` if and only if the Link State ID assignment has been successful.

182   The router first tries to assign the Link State ID equal to the prefix's network number.

—— spforig.C

```
177 int OSPF::get_lsid(INrte *rte, byte lstype, SpfArea *ap, lsid_t &ls_id)
178
179 {
180     uns32 end;
181
182     ls_id = rte->net();
183     end = rte->broadcast_address();
184
185     for (; ls_id <= end; ls_id++) {
186         rteLSA *lsap;
187         INrte *o_rte;
188         if (!(lsap = (rteLSA *) myLSA(ap, lstype, ls_id)))
189             return(true);
190         else if (!(o_rte = lsap->orig_rte))
191             return(true);
192         else if (rte->mask() >= o_rte->mask())
193             return(true);
194     }
195
196     return(false);
197 }
```

—— spforig.C

Figure 10.10 Choosing a Link State ID for AS-external-LSAs: `OSPF::get_lsid()`.

183   In any case, the Link State ID masked with the prefix's network mask must equal the prefix's network number. The largest Link State ID satisfying this constraint is given by **end**.

185-194   The possible Link State IDs are examined, from lowest (most desirable) to highest. The first Link State that either (1) the router has not yet used in an LSA of the same LS type and area (lines **188-189**) or (2) is being used for a less specific LSA (lines **192-193**) is returned. The variable `rteLSA::orig_rte` points to the routing table entry of the prefix that the router is advertising in the LSA. If set to **0** (lines **190-191**), the router is in the process of withdrawing the advertisement, and so the Link State ID can be reused.

196   If none of the possible Link State IDs can be used, a failure indication is returned.

10.3.4 Database Overflow

Following the algorithms in *OSPF Database Overflow* [68], the implementation allows you to configure a maximum number of nondefault AS-external-LSAs that will be carried by the OSPF routing domain. This maximum must be configured identically in all the routers belonging to the routing domain; in this implementation, it is configured by `OSPF::cfgOspf()` (Section 13.1) and is stored in `OSPF::ExtLsdbLimit`.

The router first enters Overflow State when a new, nondefault AS-external-LSA is added to the link-state database (`ASextLSA::parse()`), bringing the count of such LSAs up to `OSPF::ExtLsdbLimit`. At this point, the function `OSPF::EnterOverflowState()` is called.

`OSPF::EnterOverflowState()`

The function `OSPF::EnterOverflowState()` is shown in Figure 10.11.

```
────────────────────────────────────────────────── asexlsa.C
481 void OSPF::EnterOverflowState()
482
483 {
484     if (OverflowState)
485         return;
486     // Enter overflow state
487     OverflowState = true;
488     // Flush locally-originated LSAs
489     reoriginate_ASEs();
490     // Start exit overflow timer
491     if (ExitOverflowInterval)
492         oflwtim.start(ExitOverflowInterval*Timer::SECOND);
493 }
────────────────────────────────────────────────── asexlsa.C
```

Figure 10.11 Entering Overflow State: `OSPF::EnterOverflowState()`.

484-487 This routine handles the transition from normal state into Overflow State. When in Overflow State, `OSPF::OverflowState` is set to `true`.

489 The routine `OSPF::reoriginate_ASEs()` will force the router to reexamine all the AS-external-LSAs that the router itself has originated. Because the router is now in Overflow State, that routine will set the age of its self-originated nondefault AS-external-LSAs to MaxAge and reflood them, flushing them from the routing domain.

491-492 If `OSPF::ExitOverflowInterval` is nonzero, it specifies the length of time before the router will try to return to normal operation. When the router does return to normal operation (`ExitOverflowTimer::action()`), it will attempt to reoriginate all the AS-external-LSAs that it was forced to flush when it entered Overflow State.

Behavior while in Overflow State

When in Overflow State (`OSPF::OverflowState = true`), the OSPF implementation's behavior is changed in the following ways.

- Any attempt by the router to originate new, nondefault AS-external-LSAs is deferred until after the router exits Overflow State (`OSPF::ase_orig()`).

- Nondefault AS-external-LSAs received during flooding in excess of the configured limit (`OSPF::ExtLsdbLimit`) are discarded by `SpfNbr::recv_update()`.

- When in Overflow State, nondefault AS-external-LSAs with LS Age equal to MaxAge are removed from the link-state database even if neighbors are currently undergoing Database Exchange (Section 8.3). Convergence of the algorithm specified by *OSPF Database Overflow* [68] takes precedence over the acquiring of new adjacencies.

10.3.5 Stub Areas

A network administrator configures an area as a stub area in order to reduce the size of its link-state database and routing table—AS-external-LSAs are not flooded into stub areas, and stub areas route to external destinations based on a default route advertised by the area's border routers. For more information on stub areas, see Section 7.2 of [67]. Here, we gather together information about the implementation of stub areas.

- Stub areas are configured by using `OSPF::cfgArea()`, as described in Section 13.4. Within the implementation, stub areas are detected by `SpfArea::is_stub()` (or sometimes by `SpfArea::a_stub == true`).

- All routers in a stub area are required to agree that the area is a stub. This is enforced during the acquisition of neighbors by OSPF's Hello Protocol (Section 8.2).

- AS-external-LSAs are not flooded into stub areas (Section 9.3). An AS-external-LSA received on an interface belonging to a stub area is discarded without being acknowledged (Section 9.2).

- A stub area's border routers advertise a summary LSA for 0.0.0.0/0 (the default route) into stub areas, with a configured cost of `SpfArea::a_dfcst` (Section 10.2.1).

- As an additional configuration option, a stub area's border routers can be inhibited from originating any summary-LSAs into the stub area other than the default summary-LSA. This behavior is dictated by `SpfArea::a_import` and is described in Section 10.2.1.

- Virtual links cannot be configured to have stub areas as their transit area (Section 10.2.3).

- When determining the best path to an ASBR, which will be used when calculating external routing table entries and when originating ASBR-summary-LSAs, paths through stub areas are not considered (Section 11.5).

11

Routing Calculations

In this chapter, we examine the OSPF routing calculations that produce the IP routing table from the raw topology data contained in the link-state database. We follow the traditional division of the routing calculations into intra-area, inter-area, and external route calculations, devoting a section to each. No discussion of routing table calculations would be complete without an explanation of when and how the calculations are scheduled, which is the subject of the first section of this chapter.

11.1 Triggering the Routing Calculation: `OSPF::rtsched()`

All routing calculations are triggered by a change in the contents of the link-state database as a new or an updated LSA is installed in the database. This new LSA must be semantically different from the previous instance, if any, found in the database—simple refreshes do not cause routing calculations. Semantic differences include significant changes in LS age (to or from MaxAge), changes in LS options, or changes in the body of the LSA, as determined by `LSA::cmp_contents()`.

When an LSA has been found to be different, the correct routing calculation is performed or scheduled by calling `OSPF::rtsched(LSA *newlsa, RTE *old_rte)`, whose data flow is diagrammed in Figure 11.1. This function takes two arguments: the new LSA and the routing table entry referenced by the previous LSA instance. For summary-LSAs and AS-external-LSAs, a new instance of the LSA may reference a routing table entry different from the previous instance, as the network mask in the body of the LSA may have changed. In this case, the routing table calculations for both the old and the new routing table entries must be rerun.

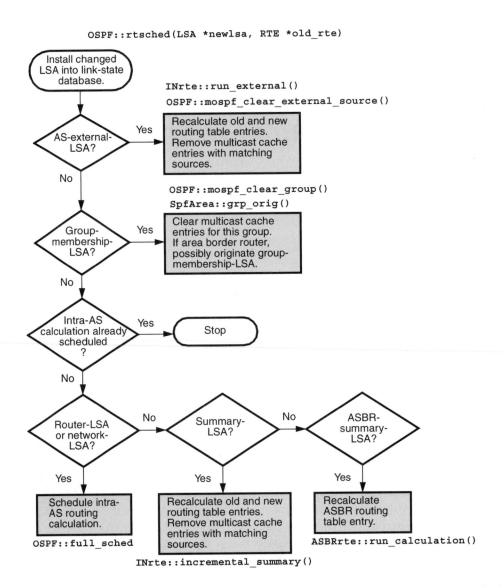

Figure 11.1 Triggering recalculation of routing table entries: `OSPF::rtsched()`. Shaded rectangles indicate calculations executed or scheduled.

The implementation splits the routing calculation into three parts:

1. The intra-AS routing calculation, including intra-area and inter-area routes. This calculation is triggered by changes in router-LSAs or network-LSAs and is scheduled by setting `OSPF::full_sched`. The calculation itself is then performed inside the periodic timer `DBageTimer::action()`, thereby imposing a rate-limit on the intra-AS routing calculation of one per second. See Section 11.2 for more details about the intra-area routing calculation.

2. The calculation of AS external routes. If `OSPF::ase_sched` is set, the complete set of AS-external routes will be recalculated inside `DBageTimer::action()`. The external routing calculation will be scheduled in this way when (a) the path to an AS boundary router changes (`ASBRrte::run_calculation()`), (b) the operational status of a physical interface changes (`OSPF::phy_down()` and `OSPF::phy_up()`), (c) an intra-AS route disappears and is referenced by one or more AS-external-LSAs (`INrte::declare_unreachable()`), and (d) the path to an AS-external-LSA's forwarding address changes (`FWDtbl::resolve()`).

3. The calculation of MOSPF multicast cache entries. These are calculated one at a time when matching multicast datagrams are received and must be forwarded, through the API entry point `OSPF::mclookup()`. Recalculation of particular entries can be forced simply by deleting them, which is what the various `OSPF::mospf_clear_XXX()` routines do. For example, reception of a new group-membership-LSA deletes all multicast cache entries for the specified group by calling `OSPF::mospf_clear_group(InAddr group)`. See Chapter 12, MOSPF Implementation, for more information on MOSPF's routing calculations.

If the corresponding full calculation has not already been scheduled, a changed LSA may cause an immediate recalculation of single routing table entries, also called incremental routing calculations.

If the intra-AS routing calculation has not been scheduled, a changed summary-LSA forces recalculation of one or two routing table entries by reexamining the summary-LSAs for the old and new routing table entries in the function `INrte::incremental_summary()`. See Section 11.2.6 for details about the calculation of inter-area routes.

The external routing calculation uses the results of the intra-AS routing calculation, namely, the paths to ASBRs, each stored in a `class ASBRrte`, and the paths to the AS-external-LSAs' forwarding addresses, each stored in a `class FWDrte`. When a changed ASBR-summary-LSA is received and the intra-AS calculation has not been scheduled, the path to that ASBR is immediately recalculated by `ASBRrte::run_calculation()`. When a changed AS-external-LSA is received, one or two routing table entries are recalculated immediately by reexamining their AS-external-LSAs in `INrte::run_external()`.

11.2   The Intra-AS Routing Calculation: `OSPF::full_calculation()`

The routine that implements the complete recalculation of all intra-AS routes, `OSPF::full_calculation()`, is shown in Figure 11.2.

```
────────────────────────────────────────────────────────── spfcalc.C
101 void OSPF::full_calculation()
102
103 {
104     full_sched = false;
105     // Dijkstra, all areas at once
106     dijkstra();
107     // Update ABRs
108     update_brs();
109     // Scan of routing table
110     // Delete old intra-area routes
111     // then process summary-LSAs and AS-external-LSAs
112     // Originates summary-LSAs when necessary
113     invalidate_ranges();
114     rt_scan();
115     advertise_ranges();
116     // Clear MOSPF cache on next timer tick
117     clear_mospf = true;
118     // Update ASBRs and
119     // recalculate forwarding addresses
120     update_asbrs();
121     fa_tbl->resolve();
122     // ASE calculation will run later, if necessary
123 }
────────────────────────────────────────────────────────── spfcalc.C
```

Figure 11.2 Recalculating the complete IP routing table: `OSPF::full_calculation()`.

104   The flag `OSPF::full_sched` telling the timer routine `DBageTimer::action()` to execute the complete intra-AS calculation is reset.

106   The router recalculates all its intra-area routes by running the Dijkstra algorithm on all areas' link-state databases at once, using `OSPF::dijkstra()` (Section 11.2.1). We do not restrict the Dijkstra calculation to only the changed areas. The reason is that the Dijkstra calculation is inexpensive, and trying to run it on only the affected areas involves potentially error-prone bookkeeping. Intra-area routes are calculated to both networks (`class INrte`) and routers (`class RTRrte`).

108   The router keeps track of the best paths to all other routers in its attached areas. If a router is reachable through two separate areas, each area will be accounted for separately. The path to each router is stored in a `class RTRrte`. As an example, router B in the network diagram on the flyleaf will have ten of these classes, four associated with

area 0.0.0.1 and six associated with area 0.0.0.0, with itself and router C being counted twice. The routine `OSPF::update_brs()` checks to see whether the intra-area routing calculation has changed the best path to any of the area border routers. If it has and if the area border router is the endpoint of a virtual link, `VLIfc::update()` is called to process any resulting changes to the virtual link's operational state or cost.

113   If the router is an area border router, it may be configured to aggregate one area's routes before advertising them into other areas. The cost advertised for these aggregates is based on the intra-area paths calculated to the aggregate's constituent subnets. In preparation for the recalculation of the advertised cost, `OSPF::invalidate_ranges()` sets all configured aggregates to "do not advertise."

114   `OSPF::rt_scan()` iterates through the router's IP routing table, performing the following bookkeeping functions: (1) deleting old intra-area routes that were not updated by the latest Dijkstra calculation, (2) calculating inter-area routes to network segments in remote areas, (3) modifying the system's kernel routing table to reflect any changes in intra-AS routing, (4) accumulating the cost to advertise for configured area aggregates, and (5) updating any nonaggregated summary-LSAs that the router should/should not be originating. We examine `OSPF::rt_scan()` in more detail in Section 11.2.5.

115   The router reoriginates/flushes any aggregated summary-LSAs whose cost or advertisability has changed.

117   The paths of multicast datagrams may have changed due to changes in intra-AS routing. Rather than trying to figure out exactly which ones have changed, we delete all MOSPF cache entries, forcing them to be recalculated when needed.

120   `OSPF::update_asbrs()` takes the previously calculated intra-area paths to the routers, together with the ASBR-summary-LSAs in the link-state database, and calculates the preferred path to each ASBR according to the rules in Section 16.4.1 of [75]. See Section 11.5 for more details on this process. If the preferred path to any ASBR has changed, the AS-external routing calculation (Section 11.6) is scheduled.

121   The best paths to all the AS-external-LSAs' forwarding addresses are recalculated. If the best path to any forwarding address has changed, the AS-external routing calculation (Section 11.6) is scheduled.

11.2.1 Intra-Area Routing Calculation: `OSPF::dijkstra()`

`OSPF::dijkstra()` calculates all the router's intra-area routes, using Dijkstra's Shortest Path First algorithm. OSPF's use of the Dijkstra algorithm is described in detail in Section 4.8 of [67]. A single run of the algorithm finds the shortest path to each router-LSA and network-LSA in the router's attached areas.

In a nutshell, OSPF's Dijkstra algorithm iterates through the following loop. There is a candidate list consisting of those router-LSAs and network-LSAs to which paths have been found, but possibly not optimal paths. At the beginning of each loop, the path to the closest remaining candidate is guaranteed to be optimal (that is, the shortest possible), and so the candidate is removed from the candidate list and added to the tree of shortest paths. The just-removed candidate's neighboring LSAs are then examined, possibly being added to or having their position adjusted on the candidate list. The loop then begins again, with the algorithm terminating when the candidate list becomes empty.

The candidate LSAs are implemented by using the `class TNode`. The candidate status of an LSA is then indicated by `TNode::t_state`. If set to `DS_ONCAND`, the LSA is currently on the candidate list; `DS_ONTREE`, the shortest path to the LSA has already been found; and `DS_UNINIT`, no path has been found yet for the LSA. The candidates must be sorted by distance, and for this we use a priority queue: `class TNode` inherits from `class PriQElt`, which is described in Chapter 5, Building Blocks.

When an LSA is added to the tree of shortest paths, the routing entry associated with the LSA is updated by calling `RTE::new_intra()`. If the LSA is a network-LSA, the routing table entry for the network's prefix is updated. For router-LSAs, the entry for the router (a `class RTRrte`) is updated, and then the stub network link descriptions in the router-LSA are processed, making repeated calls to `RTE::new_intra()` in order to update their routing table entries. `RTE::new_intra()` discards paths when shorter paths have already been found and keeps multiple shortest paths when they exist.

Other significant facts about `OSPF::dijkstra()` follow.

- All areas' intra-area paths are calculated in a single Dijkstra calculation. There is no speed advantage to doing so, however; if anything, it's a little bit slower than doing a separate Dijkstra calculation for each area, because in the former case, the sorted candidate list gets larger.

- Initialization of the candidate list differs, depending on whether `ospfd` is running as a router or as a host. See Sections 11.2.3 and 11.2.4.

- The cost used to determine which path is optimal has two components. The first and most significant component, stored in `PriQElt::cost0`, is the normal sum of link costs from the calculating router to the LSA. The second component, `PriQElt::tie1`, is the LSA's LS Type. For the second component, larger costs are considered better. That logic forces network-LSAs onto the tree of shortest paths first, which in turn guarantees that all equal-cost paths are found during the Dijkstra calculation.

- You'll notice that there are no link-state database lookups during the Dijkstra calculation; nor are there any bidirectional checks, thereby enabling the Dijkstra algorithm to run more quickly. These operations have been performed beforehand when the LSAs were first installed in the database (Section 11.4).

- Next hops are calculated when an LSA is first added to the candidate list or when its position on the candidate list is changed due to the discovery of a shorter path. Next-hop calculation is performed by `TNode::add_next_hop()` and is the subject of Section 11.2.2.

- Along with its main job of calculating intra-area routes, the Dijkstra calculation also performs a number of bookkeeping functions. It determines which areas are transit areas (that is, the areas supporting active virtual links, indicated by **SpfArea::a_transit**) by looking at the V bit in the router-LSAs it encounters. The Dijkstra algorithm also keeps track of the number of reachable routers in the area, **SpfArea::n_routers**, which includes the calculating router itself.

11.2.2 Calculating Next Hops

When a shorter path to an LSA (router-LSA or network-LSA) is found during the Dijkstra calculation, its next hop is recalculated by using the LSA's **TNode:: add_next_hop()** method given in Figure 11.3.

476   The LSA whose next hop we are trying to calculate is **this**. The **v** argument is the immediately preceding router-LSA or network-LSA on the path back to the calculating router, which we also called the LSA's *parent*. In most cases, the LSA's next hop will simply be inherited from **v**. One of the link descriptions in **v**'s LSA points to **this**; the index of this link description in **v**'s LSA is indicated by **_index**.

484-492   In this case, the LSA whose next hop we are trying to calculate is directly connected to the calculating router. This is the most difficult case. The calculating router's router-LSA does not have enough information to determine the correct outgoing interface to use. To enable this calculation, when we originated our router-LSA, we stored in **SpfArea::ifmap** a mapping from the link descriptions in the router-LSA to the matching router interface (line **485**).

For directly connected network segments, we set the next hop to 0.0.0.0 (lines **487- 488**). For directly connected routers, we try to find the IP address of the neighboring router by calling the neighbor's **TNode::ospf_find_gw()** method (lines **489-490**). This method goes through the neighbor's router-LSA, looking for a link description pointing back to the calculating router and then sets the next-hop address to the Link Data field in that description. Note that for unnumbered links, this will yield an IfIndex instead of an IP address, but that's OK, because for directly connected routers, the next-hop IP address is unnecessary for forwarding and is being calculated here only for display purposes.

494-495   If one or intermediate routers are between the calculating router and the LSA, the LSA simply inherits the next hops from its parent, **v**.

497-502   In this case, the LSA is a router-LSA, one that attaches to the calculating router through a single network segment, **v**. We find the router-LSA's address on this common segment (line **500**) and use this, together with the outgoing interface which has already been calculated for **v** (line **501**).

504   If the new path to the LSA is shorter than the previously calculated path, the caller will have zeroed out **TNode::t_mpath**. If the new path is the same cost as previously discovered paths, the new next hop(s) are merged with the previously discovered ones.

─── spfcalc.C

```
476 void TNode::add_next_hop(TNode *V, int _index)
477
478 {
479     MPath *new_nh;
480     SpfIfc *t_ifc;
481     InAddr t_gw;
482
483     // If parent is the root
484     if (V == lsa_ap->mylsa) {
485         if (!(t_ifc = lsa_ap->ifmap[_index]))
486             return;
487         if (lsa_type == LST_NET)
488             t_gw = 0;
489         else
490             t_gw = ospf_find_gw(V, t_ifc->net(), t_ifc->mask());
491         new_nh = MPath::create(t_ifc, t_gw);
492     }
493     // Not adjacent to root, simply inherit
494     else if (!V->t_direct || V->ls_type() != LST_NET)
495         new_nh = V->t_mpath;
496     // Directly connected to root through transit net
497     else {
498         INrte *rte;
499         rte = (INrte *) V->t_dest;
500         t_gw = ospf_find_gw(V, rte->net(), rte->mask());
501         new_nh = MPath::addgw(V->t_mpath, t_gw);
502     }
503
504     t_mpath = MPath::merge(t_mpath, new_nh);
505 }
```

─── spfcalc.C

Figure 11.3 Calculating the next hops toward a network or router: `TNode::add_next_hop()`.

11.2.3 Dijkstra Initialization

The Dijkstra algorithm is initialized by clearing the candidate list and shortest-path tree, which is accomplished by setting the `TNode::t_state` of each router-LSA and network-LSA to `DS_UNINIT` (which stands for "Dijkstra state uninitialized"). The routine `OSPF::dijk_init()` (Figure 11.4) is then called to place the router's own router-LSA on the candidate list, where it will be the first thing removed by the main loop of the Dijkstra algorithm.

128   The empty candidate list is passed as the argument `cand`.

─── spfcalc.C

```
128 void OSPF::dijk_init(PriQ &cand)
129
130 {
131     AreaIterator iter(ospf);
132     SpfArea *ap;
133
134     // Put all our own router-LSAs onto candidate list
135     while ((ap = iter.get_next())) {
136         rtrLSA *root;
137         root = (rtrLSA *) myLSA(ap, LST_RTR, myid);
138         if (root == 0 || !root->parsed || ap->ifmap == 0)
139             continue;
140         root->cost0 = 0;
141         root->cost1 = 0;
142         root->tie1 = root->lsa_type;
143         cand.priq_add(root);
144         root->t_state = DS_ONCAND;
145         ap->mylsa = root;
146     }
147 }
```

─── spfcalc.C

Figure 11.4 Seeding the Dijkstra algorithm's candidate list with the router's own router-LSA:
`OSPF::dijk_init()`.

135   We run the Dijkstra algorithm for all areas simultaneously. (Running all areas at once does not gain any efficiency; it just makes for a little more compact code.) We go through all the router's attached areas, installing our own router-LSA for each area onto the candidate list. As an example, router C in the network diagram on the flyleaf would insert two router-LSAs onto the candidate list: its own router-LSAs for areas 0.0.0.0 and 0.0.0.1.

137-139   If the router has originated a router-LSA for the area, we should be able to find it in the database, it should be preparsed and ready for the routing calculation, and the list of interfaces reported in the router-LSA (`SpfArea::ifmap`) should be set. If any of these conditions fails, probably due to a lack of active interfaces attaching to the area, we don't run the shortest-path calculation in the area.

140-144   We add our router-LSA to the candidate list, with a cost of 0. Use of the LSA's LS Type as a tiebreaker (line **142**) allows us to put network-LSAs onto the SPF (shortest-path first) tree before router-LSAs, which is both required by MOSPF and necessary in order to find all equal-cost paths to a given destination (see Section 16.1 of [75]).

145   We note our own router-LSA for the area in `SpfArea::mylsa`, for later use in calculating next-hop router addresses (Section 11.2.2).

11.2.4 Host Mode Initialization

When the router is running OSPF in host mode (Section 13.12), the only difference in the routing calculation is in the intra-area routing calculation's initialization of the Dijkstra algorithm's candidate list. Instead of using the routine `OSPF::dijk_init()`, the routine `OSPF::host_dijk_init()` (Figure 11.5) is used to initialize the candidate list.

```
─────────────────────────────────────────────────────── hostmode.C
34 void OSPF::host_dijk_init(PriQ &cand)
35
36 {
37     AreaIterator iter(ospf);
38     SpfArea *ap;
39
40     // Put all adjacent nodes onto candidate list
41     while ((ap = iter.get_next())) {
42         IfcIterator iiter(ap);
43         SpfIfc *ip;
44         ap->mylsa = 0;
45         while ((ip = iiter.get_next()))
46             ip->add_adj_to_cand(cand);
47     }
48 }
─────────────────────────────────────────────────────── hostmode.C
```

Figure 11.5 Initializing the Dijkstra algorithm's candidate list when in host mode: `OSPF::host_dijk_init()`.

In host mode, the router has no self-originated router-LSAs and so must initialize the candidate list with the LSAs associated with directly attached network segments or routers.

41   Again, we are running the Dijkstra algorithm over all areas at once.

44   `SpfArea::mylsa` is set to 0 to indicate that the host has not originated a router-LSA.

45-46   For each interface, we call the virtual function `SpfIfc::add_adj_to_cand()` to add the neighboring LSAs to the candidate list. In addition, for some interface types, routes to directly connected network segments are added to the routing table by calling the function `RTE::host_new_intra()`, which is the host mode equivalent of `RTE::new_intra()`. For the various interface types, the adding of neighboring LSAs proceeds as follows.

- `PPIfc::add_adj_to_cand()`. For point-to-point interfaces, we add the neighboring router's router-LSA as long as the router is fully adjacent. In addition, for numbered links, we add the neighboring router's interface address to the routing table.

- **DRIfc::add_adj_to_cand()**. Used for broadcast and NBMA links, this routine is shown in Figure 11.6. If we are fully adjacent to the link's Designated Router (lines **117-118**), we add the link's network-LSA to the candidate list (lines **122-124**). Otherwise, we add a route for the network segment directly to the routing table (lines **129-133**).

```
                                                                    ─ hostmode.C
113 void DRIfc::add_adj_to_cand(class PriQ &cand)
114
115 {
116    // If there is a network-LSA, put on candidate list
117      if (if_state == IFS_OTHER &&
118          if_dr_p && if_dr_p->state() == NBS_FULL) {
119          lsid_t lsid;
120          TNode *node;
121          lsid = if_dr;
122          node = (TNode *) if_area->netLSAs.previous(lsid+1);
123          if (node != 0 && node->ls_id() == lsid) {
124              ospf->add_cand_node(this, node, cand);
125              return;
126          }
127      }
128      // Otherwise add route for directly attached network
129      if (if_state != IFS_DOWN) {
130          INrte *rte;
131          rte = inrttbl->add(net(), mask());
132          rte->host_new_intra(this, if_cost);
133      }
134 }
                                                                    ─ hostmode.C
```

Figure 11.6 Initializing the candidate list with a broadcast or NBMA segment's network-LSA: DRIfc::add_adj_to_cand().

- **P2mPIfc::add_adj_to_cand()**. For Point-to-MultiPoint interfaces, we add the router-LSAs of any fully adjacent neighboring routers to the candidate list.

As an example of initializing the Dijkstra candidate list when in host mode, suppose that node I in the network diagram on the flyleaf is running in host mode. It would then add the network-LSA of the segment that it shares with router J to the Dijkstra candidate list with a cost of **1** and the router-LSA of router E with a cost of **3**.

11.2.5 Postprocessing the Intra-Area Calculation: `OSPF::rt_scan()`

Postprocessing of the results of the Dijkstra calculation is performed by the routing table scan routine `OSPF::rt_scan()` (Figure 11.7).

574-578   The router is determining whether the transit status of any of its attached areas has changed. A transit area is one that is currently supporting one or more virtual links, which is determined by examining the V bit in the router-LSAs encountered during the Dijkstra calculation. Changes in transit status are important because the set of summary-LSAs that the router imports into the area depends on the area's transit status.

580   The router iterates through all the entries in its IP routing table. These are all routes to network segments; routes to routers are kept in a separate table.

582-586   The counter `OSPF::n_dijkstras` is incremented every time the router runs the Dijkstra calculation, thus indicating how many times the Dijkstra calculation has been run and identifying the current run. When an IP routing table entry has been referenced by the Dijkstra calculation, its `INrte::dijk_run` is set equal to the parity of the current run. So at this point, routing table entries with the wrong parity should be deleted, as no routes to these subnets were found by the latest Dijkstra calculation.

588-589   If there was an inter-area route to the network segment or if there are summary-LSAs for the segment (`INrte::summs`) in the link-state database, we examine all the summary-LSAs again, refreshing, adding, or deleting an inter-area route. See Section 11.2.6 for more details.

591-595   For backbone intra-area and inter-area routes, we have to see whether there are any shorter paths if the resources of the attached transit areas are used, as specified by Section 16.3 of [75]. In particular, if the previous calculations have found only virtual links for next hops, this calculation must update the routing table entry with real next hops, or the entry is declared unreachable.

597-600   If the network segment belongs to one of the router's attached areas, the cost of the most specific matching aggregate is updated (see Section 10.2.2).

603-608   If the route has changed, the router updates the system's kernel routing table entry (`INrte::sys_install()`); if the network is not also a configured aggregate, updated summary-LSAs may be originated/flushed by `OSPF::sl_orig()` (Section 10.2.1). The router hasn't finished calculating the cost of area aggregates, so summary-LSAs for those routing table entries must be originated/flushed by the caller.

A word should be said here about the detection of changed routing table entries. Before modifying a routing table entry, the entry's current state can be saved by calling `RTE::save_state()` (this works for both network and router routing table entries). Later, you can detect whether the entry has really changed, by calling `RTE::state_changed()`. This mechanism catches changes to an entry's next hop(s) and cost. However, more significant changes, such as changes in the entry's associated OSPF area, or a change in the routing table entry's type, as from intra-area to inter-area, must be indicated directly by setting `RTE::changed`.

spfcalc.C

```
564 void OSPF::rt_scan()
566 {
567     INrte *rte;
568     INiterator iter(inrttbl);
569     AreaIterator a_iter(ospf);
570     SpfArea *ap;
571     bool transit_changes;
574     transit_changes = false;
575     while ((ap = a_iter.get_next())) {
576         if (ap->was_transit != ap->a_transit)
577             transit_changes = true;
578     }
580     while ((rte = iter.nextrte())) {
582         if (rte->intra_area() &&
583             ((n_dijkstras & 1) != rte->dijk_run)) {
584             rte->declare_unreachable();
585             rte->changed = true;
586         }
588         if (rte->inter_area() || rte->summs)
589             rte->run_inter_area();
591         if (rte->intra_AS() && rte->area() == BACKBONE)
592             rte->run_transit_areas(rte->summs);
594         if (rte->intra_AS() && rte->r_mpath == 0)
595             rte->declare_unreachable();
597         if (rte->intra_area()) {
598             rte->tag = 0;
599             update_area_ranges(rte);
600         }
603         if (rte->changed || rte->state_changed()) {
604             rte->changed = false;
605             rte->sys_install();
606             if (!rte->is_range())
607                 sl_orig(rte);
608         }
611         else if (transit_changes &&
612                 rte->intra_area() &&
613                 rte->area() == BACKBONE &&
614                 !rte->is_range())
615             sl_orig(rte, true);
616     }
617 }
```

spfcalc.C

Figure 11.7 Postprocessing the results of the Dijkstra calculation: `OSPF::rt_scan()`.

611-615   Even when a backbone route hasn't changed, its summary-LSAs must be reorigi-
nated/flushed in the face of areas' transit status changes, which change the policy for
originating summary-LSAs.

11.2.6 Inter-area Routes

The full intra-AS calculation (Section 11.2) calculates all inter-area routes. When a modified summary-LSA is received by flooding, a single inter-area route is recalculated. In
both cases, the routine that ultimately calculates the inter-area route is `INrte::`
`run_inter_area()`, part of which is shown in Figure 11.8.

```
                                                                    ── summlsa.C
324      new_type = RT_NONE;
325      best_path = 0;
326      cost = LSInfinity;
327      summ_ap = ospf->SummaryArea();
329      for (lsap = summs; lsap; lsap = (summLSA *)lsap->link) {
330          RTRrte *rtr;
331          uns32 new_cost;
332          if (lsap->area() != summ_ap)
333              continue;
335          if (lsap->adv_rtr() == ospf->my_id()) {
336              new_type = RT_REJECT;
337              cost = LSInfinity;
338              best_path = 0;
339              break;
340          }
342          rtr = (RTRrte *) lsap->source;
343          if (!rtr || rtr->type() != RT_SPF)
344              continue;
346          if (lsap->adv_cost == LSInfinity)
347              continue;
349          new_cost = lsap->adv_cost + rtr->cost;
350          if (new_type != RT_NONE ) {
351              if (cost < new_cost)
352                  continue;
353              if (new_cost < cost)
354                  best_path = 0;
355          }
357          cost = new_cost;
358          new_type = RT_SPFIA;
359          best_path = MPath::merge(best_path, rtr->r_mpath);
360      }
                                                                    ── summlsa.C
```

Figure 11.8 Calculating a single inter-area route: `INrte::run_inter_area()`.

At the beginning of this function (not shown), the router checks to see that the current route is neither a direct route nor an intra-area route, both of which take precedence over inter-area routes. If the current route is an inter-area route, the router saves its state for later comparison purposes.

324-326   The best inter-area route found so far is reflected in **new_type**, **best_path**, and **cost**. In the beginning, they are set to indicate the lack of an inter-area route.

327   In OSPF, a router is allowed to look at the summary-LSAs only from a single area (lines **332-333**), here coded as **summ_ap**. If the router is attached to multiple areas, it can look only at area 0.0.0.0's summary-LSAs; in this case, if the router is not attached to area 0.0.0.0, **summ_ap** is set to **0**.

329   All the summary-LSAs for the prefix have been linked together in **INrte::summs** when the summary-LSAs are first installed in the link-state database and parsed by **summLSA::parse()**. The router will go through these LSAs, selecting the one providing the least cost.

335-340   If the router itself is advertising a summary-LSA for the prefix, the prefix is an aggregate (remember, we previously checked to make sure that the prefix didn't have an intra-area route). In this case, we are required to tell the kernel to discard datagrams matching the prefix, so as to avoid packet loops.

342-349   The cost of the inter-area route is the sum of the cost to the advertising area border router (**rtr->cost**) and the cost advertised in the body of the summary-LSA (**lsap->adv_cost**).

350-359   If this is a better cost than previously found inter-area routes, we install a new next hop (**rtr->r_mpath**). If instead the route is of equal cost, we add to the list of next hops in **best_path**.

360+   After all summary-LSAs have been examined, the router notes changes to a routing table entry's type and associated OSPF area by setting **INrte::changed**. Other changes will be detected by virtue of storing the routing table entry's state at the entry to the routine. In addition, if the routing table entry used to be an inter-area route but there are no longer any valid summary-LSAs for the prefix (**new_type == RT_NONE**), the routing table entry is marked as unreachable.

When a single changed summary-LSA has been received, the router recalculates the route for that prefix only, by calling **INrte::incremental_summary()**. In one case, the whole intra-AS routing calculation must be rerun, namely, when the received summary-LSA belongs to a transit area and the prefix's routing table entry is an intra-AS area 0.0.0.0 route. In this case, you would want to rerun the transit area adjustment algorithm (Section 11.2.7) from Section 16.3 of [75]. However, because that algorithm operates on the state created by the intra-AS routing calculation, which has not been saved, we need to run the intra-AS calculation again to retrieve the state.

Otherwise, **INrte::incremental_summary()** simply calls **INrte::run_inter_area()** to recalculate the inter-area route, if any, and then performs the postprocessing that was done by **OSPF::rt_scan()** for the whole intra-AS calculation.

This postprocessing includes adjustment for transit areas, (re)originating summary-LSAs if necessary, recalculating the paths to AS-external-LSAs' forwarding addresses, and clearing MOSPF entries listing the prefix as source.

11.2.7 Transit Area Adjustments: `RTE::run_transit_areas()`

After intra-area and inter-area paths have been calculated, the next hops of those routing table entries associated with area 0.0.0.0 may have to be changed to take into account any attached transit areas. This calculation is described in Section 16.3 of [75] and must be performed for both routes to networks (`class INrte`) and routes to routers (`class RTRrte`), both of which inherit from `class RTE`. The transit area adjustment is implemented by `RTE::run_transit_areas()` (Figure 11.9).

```
                                                            summlsa.C
399 void RTE::run_transit_areas(rteLSA *lsap)
401 {
403     for (; lsap; lsap = lsap->link) {
404         RTRrte *rtr;
405         uns32 new_cost;
406         if (!lsap->area()->is_transit())
407             continue;
408         if (lsap->adv_rtr() == ospf->my_id())
409             continue;
411         rtr = (RTRrte *) lsap->source;
412         if (!rtr || rtr->type() != RT_SPF)
413             continue;
414         new_cost = lsap->adv_cost + rtr->cost;
415         if (cost < new_cost)
416             continue;
417         else if (new_cost < cost)
418             r_mpath = 0;
421         r_mpath = MPath::merge(r_mpath, rtr->r_mpath);
422         cost = new_cost;
423     }
424 }
                                                            summlsa.C
```

Figure 11.9 Adjusting for transit areas: `RTE::run_transit_areas()`.

403   The router looks at the summary-LSAs in its link-state database for the network/router, looking for better or equal-cost paths that use the resources of the transit areas.

406-413   Only summary-LSAs belonging to transit areas are examined. The advertiser of the summary-LSA must be reachable by an intra-area path (lines **412-413**).

414   As in the inter-area calculation, the cost of the route is the sum of the distance to the advertising router (`rtr->cost`) and the cost advertised in the summary-LSA (`lsap->adv_cost`).

417-422   If the cost is better than the current routing table cost, the next hops through the transit area (`rtr->r_mpath`) replace the routing table entry's current next hops; if the cost is the same, the next hops through the transit area are added to those already present in the routing table entry.

11.3   Multipath Calculations

Equal-cost paths are calculated for all types of routing entries: intra-area, inter-area, and AS external. Rather than store the multiple next hops in the routing table entries themselves, a separate database of next hops has been created: `MPath::nhdb`. For example, if a router has two equal-cost paths, one through 10.1.1.1 and the other through 10.2.2.2, a corresponding entry in the next-hop database is created. If thousands of routing table entries have the same two equal-cost paths, they all point to the same entry in the next-hop database, `RTE::r_mpath`.

The methods for manipulating the next-hop database, `MPath::create()`, `MPath::merge()`, and `MPath::addgw()` are documented in Chapter 5, Building Blocks.

11.4   Preprocessing LSAs

The OSPF protocol requires that many consistency checks be performed on LSAs during the routing calculation. As some examples, links used in the Dijkstra calculation are required to be advertised by the routers on both ends (see Section 4.8 of [67] for an explanation of this requirement), and MaxAge LSAs cannot be used in routing calculations. In some OSPF routing calculations, you also want quick access to specific LSAs, such as all the summary-LSAs advertising a specific prefix.

To avoid performing these time-consuming checks and lookups during the routing calculation itself, the implementation preprocesses the LSAs when they are installed in the link-state database, saving the results of the consistency checks in a form that is easier for the routing calculations to use. For example, the in-memory copies of router-LSAs and network-LSAs have each (transit) link description stored in a `class TLink`. This data structure has a pointer to the neighboring LSA, `Tlink::tl_nbr`, which is installed (that is, nonzero) if and only if the neighboring LSA advertises a link back to the router/network-LSA. In this way, the routing calculation simply checks to make sure that pointers are nonnull.

LSA preprocessing is performed in the `LSA::parse()` routines. Preprocessing of a router-LSA is executed by calling `rtrLSA::parse()`. That function calls the function `TNode::tlp_link()` (Figure 11.10) for each link description in the router-LSA.

—— rtrlsa.C

```
490 void TNode::tlp_link(TLink *tlp)
492 {
493     TNode *nbr;
494     uns32 nbr_id;
495     Link *nlp;
497     nbr_id = tlp->l_id;
499     if (tlp->l_ltype == LT_TNET) {
500         nbr = (TNode *) lsa_ap->netLSAs.previous(nbr_id+1);
501         if (nbr == 0 || nbr->ls_id() != nbr_id)
502             return;
503     }
504     else if (!(nbr = (TNode *) lsa_ap->rtrLSAs.find(nbr_id, nbr_id)))
505         return;
508     if (!nbr->parsed)
509         return;
511     if (nbr->ls_type() == LST_RTR)
512         nbr->t_dest->changed = true;
514     for (nlp = nbr->t_links; nlp; nlp = nlp->l_next) {
515         TLink *ntlp;
516         if (nlp->l_ltype == LT_STUB)
517             continue;
518         if (nlp->l_id != ls_id())
519             continue;
520         if (nlp->l_ltype == LT_TNET && lsa_type != LST_NET)
521             continue;
522         if (nlp->l_ltype != LT_TNET && lsa_type == LST_NET)
523             continue;
525         ntlp = (TLink *) nlp;
526         tlp->tl_nbr = nbr;
527         ntlp->tl_nbr = this;
528         if (ntlp->l_fwdcst < tlp->tl_rvcst)
529             tlp->tl_rvcst = ntlp->l_fwdcst;
530         if (tlp->l_fwdcst < ntlp->tl_rvcst)
531             ntlp->tl_rvcst = tlp->l_fwdcst;
532     }
533 }
```

—— rtrlsa.C

Figure 11.10 Preprocessing router- and network-LSAs: `TNode::tlp_link()`.

490-497   This function is called for each transit link description in the router-LSA. The same function is also called when parsing network-LSAs. The link description is represented by `TLink *tlp`. The Link State ID of the neighboring LSA is given by `Tlink::l_id`.

499-503   The Link State ID may not uniquely identify a particular network-LSA. Here, the code picks any network-LSA having a matching Link State ID.

502,505   If the neighboring LSA cannot be found in the database, `Tlink::tl_nbr` remains `0`, and the link will not be used in the routing calculation.

508-509   If the neighboring LSA has not been preprocessed, it is not eligible to be used in the routing calculation, and so again the pointer to the neighboring LSA remains `0`. The most likely reason that the neighboring LSA cannot be used in the routing calculation is that its age is equal to MaxAge.

511-512   If the neighboring LSA is the endpoint of a virtual link, setting `RTRrte::changed` for the endpoint will cause recalculation of the virtual neighbor's IP address, even if the next-hop information for the virtual link endpoint doesn't change.

514-532   We go through the link descriptions in the neighboring LSA, looking for links back to the LSA that we are preprocessing. If we find a backlink (line `525` is reached), we install pointers in each LSA's link description. We also accumulate the best reverse cost (lines `528-531`) for use by the inter-area and inter-AS MOSPF routing calculations.

When an LSA is removed from the link-state database, its preprocessing must be undone. This function is performed by calling `LSA::unparse()`. In particular, when removing router-LSAs and network-LSAs from the link-state database, pointers to them are removed from their neighboring LSAs by calling `TNode::unlink()`. One complication when removing network-LSAs is that, if another network-LSA remains in the link-state database having the same Link State ID as the network-LSA being removed, that network-LSA must now be preprocessed so that it is now used by the routing calculations in place of the deleted network-LSA.

11.5   Routes to ASBRs

There may be multiple intra-area routes to an AS boundary router (ASBR), one for each area that the calculating router and the ASBR have in common, and an inter-area route as well. Each of these routes is stored in a `class RTRrte`. The router must decide which of these routes is the best, because only the best route will be used when processing AS-external-LSAs originated by the ASBR and advertised in ASBR-summary-LSAs. The best route is calculated by `ASBRrte::run_calculation()`, according to the rules in Sections 16.2 and 16.4.1 of [75]. The best route to the ASBR is then stored in the ASBR's `class ASBRrte`.

Everything except the prolog of `ASBRrte::run_calculation()` is given in Figure 11.11. This same routine is called both when the complete routing table is being recalculated and when only a single ASBR's path is being recalculated, due to the reception of a new ASBR-summary-LSA.

573-601   We are examining the intra-area paths to the ASBR. Each one is stored in a separate `class RTRrte`; all are linked together in `ASBRrte::parts`.

580-581   The ASBR should be setting the E bit in all its router-LSAs, informing the other routers that it is an ASBR. The OSPF specification does not explicitly state that you should

```
                                                       ─────── asexlsa.C
573     for (abr = parts; abr; abr = abr->asbr_link) {
574         SpfArea *ap;
576         if (abr->type() != RT_SPF)
577             continue;
580         if (!abr->e_bit())
581             continue;
582         if (!(ap = ospf->FindArea(abr->area())))
583             continue;
584         if (ap->is_stub())
585             continue;
587         if (preferred && abr->area() == BACKBONE)
588             continue;
589         else if (preferred) {
590             if (abr->cost > cost)
591                 continue;
592             if (abr->cost == cost && abr->area() < area())
593                 continue;
594         }
596         update(abr->r_mpath);
597         cost = abr->cost;
598         set_area(abr->area());
599         r_type = RT_SPF;
600         preferred = (abr->area() != BACKBONE);
601     }
604     if (r_type != RT_SPF)
605         run_inter_area();
607     if (intra_AS() && area() == BACKBONE)
608         run_transit_areas(summs);
610     if (intra_AS() && r_mpath == 0)
611         declare_unreachable();
613     if (state_changed() || otype != r_type || oa != area()) {
614         ospf->ase_sched = true;
615         ospf->asbr_orig(this);
616     }
617 }
                                                       ─────── asexlsa.C
```

Figure 11.11 Calculating the best route to an ASBR: `ASBRrte::run_calculation()`.

ignore paths in those areas where the ASBR is not declaring itself as such, but that is what we have chosen to implement.

584–585   This test is also not explicitly stated in the OSPF specification, but it definitely should be. You cannot safely forward packets addressed to specific external destinations through an OSPF stub area, because within the stub area, all external distinctions disappear, with the packet being forwarded instead on a possibly conflicting default path. As a result, routes to ASBRs through stub areas are discarded.

587-594   As stated in Section 16.4.1 of [75], paths through nonbackbone areas are `preferred` over paths through the backbone area 0.0.0.0. When multiple `preferred` paths are available, the one with the smallest cost is used. When equal-cost `preferred` paths are available, we take the one through the area with the largest OSPF Area ID, although this is not mandated by the OSPF specification (keeping the multiple paths would make the origination of ASBR-summary-LSAs more complicated).

The OSPF specification allows the router administrator to change the ASBR path preference based on an RFC1583Compatibility setting; if set to false, ASBR path preference follows the rules in 16.4.1 of [75], if set to true, the calculation from a previous revision of the OSPF specification [73] is used. Note that our implementation does not have an RFC1583Compatibility configuration variable but instead always acts as if this value were set to false. Why? Because setting the value to false in all routers is the only way to prohibit routing loops in all cases; in my opinion, a mix of settings of RFC1583Compatibility is no more likely to cause routing loops than having all routers set to true.

604-605   For a given ASBR, any intra-area path is preferred over an inter-area one. However, if no intra-area path has been found, we use `ASBRrte::run_inter_area()` to examine the ASBR-summary-LSAs in hopes of finding an inter-area path.

607-608   Just as with routes to IP network segments, we have to see whether the path to the ASBR needs to be adjusted in the presence of transit areas. The function `RTE:: run_transit_areas()` is used for both network segments (`class INrte`) and ASBRs.

613-616   If the best path to an ASBR has changed, the router schedules the AS-external route calculation, which recalculates all external routing entries and reoriginates any ASBR-summary-LSAs that need to be changed.

11.6   External Routes: `INrte::run_external()`

When the path to one or more ASBRs and/or forwarding addresses changes, the complete AS external routing calculation is scheduled by setting `OSPF::ase_sched`. Then, when the timer `DBageTimer` fires, all the external routing table entries are rebuilt by calling `OSPF::do_all_ases()`. That function in turn calls `INrte::run_external()` for every routing table that has either (1) one or more AS-external-LSAs advertising its prefix or (2) configured static routing information. The complete AS external routing calculation is also scheduled by `INrte::declare_unreachable()` when it detects that AS-external routing information is available for a formerly reachable intra-AS prefix. Alternatively, when an updated AS-external-LSA is received, its associated prefix's routing table entry is recalculated immediately by calling `INrte::run_external()` directly.

The routine `INrte::run_external()` performs a number of functions.

- It installs routes into the routing table for directly attached segments that are not running OSPF. These are passed to OSPF through the configuration interface as external routes with `cfgExRt::direct` set to 1 (see Section 13.9). They take precedence over any OSPF-learned routing information but are not advertised to other OSPF routers—in neither router-LSAs nor AS-external-LSAs.

- It installs static routes into the routing table, which are again configured by the mechanism in Section 13.9. Static routing information is stored in `INrte::exdata` and may be overridden by cheaper routes received in AS-external-LSAs.

- It compares the AS-external-LSAs advertising a route for the prefix, according to the preferences in Sections 16 and 16.4.1 of [75]. The AS-external-LSAs are linked in `INrte::ases`. If the most-preferred AS-external-LSA is better than any configured static route, the routing table entry is updated to point at that LSA's ASBR/forwarding address.

- If after examining the matching AS-external-LSAs, the routing table still reflects the configured static route and if `cfgExRt::noadv` is set to 0, the router itself originates an AS-external-LSA for the prefix.

Exercises

11.1   Change the intra-area calculation so that it does only one area at a time. Create a new routine that calls the intra-area calculation for each area in turn.

11.2   Extending the work done in exercise 11.1, change the routing calculation triggers so that you rerun the intra-area calculations only for those areas that change. Note that any area may cause the distance to an AS boundary router to change, requiring the rerunning of the external routing calculation. Also, if a transit area changes, you have to rerun the backbone area's Dijkstra calculation first in order to recover the state needed for a possible rerunning of the calculations in Section 11.2.7.

11.3   Modify `ASBRrte::run_calculation()` and `INrte::run_external()` to take into account an RFC1583Compatibility variable.

11.4   Allow multiple static routes to be configured for the same prefix.

12

MOSPF Implementation

The Multicast Extensions to OSPF, or MOSPF, enable a router to forward IP multicast datagrams. The MOSPF implementation calculates multicast routing table entries and installs them into the system's kernel through the system interface routine `OspfSysCalls::add_mcache()` (see Section 4.2). The system kernel installs multicast routing table entries on demand. When it receives a multicast datagram and has no matching multicast routing table entry, the kernel asks the MOSPF implementation to install the appropriate routing table entry, calling the OSPF entry point `OSPF::mclookup()` (see Section 4.3). For more information on MOSPF, consult Chapter 10 of [67] and the MOSPF protocol specification [66].

This chapter details how the MOSPF implementation creates and distributes the information necessary to calculate multicast routing table entries. The chapter also describes the multicast routing calculation itself.

A MOSPF router uses the Internet Group Management Protocol (IGMP, [19]) to discover multicast group members on its attached LANs. The MOSPF implementation contains an implementation of the router part of IGMP (Section 12.2). The system enables this IGMP implementation simply by passing received IGMP packets through the API routine `OSPF::rxigmp()`. Alternatively, if the system already has an IGMP implementation, it can pass changes in local group membership through the API routines `OSPF::join_indication()` and `OSPF::leave_indication()`. The OSPF API is described in detail in Section 4.3.

The MOSPF router then advertises the group membership of its local LANs to the rest of the MOSPF routing domain in group-membership-LSAs. The origination of group-membership-LSAs is described in Section 12.3. Together with the other types of LSAs in the link-state database (router-LSAs, network-LSAs, summary-LSAs, ASBR-summary-LSAs, and AS-external-LSAs), the group-membership-LSAs provide a view of the multicast topology, from which the path of multicast datagrams can be calculated.

Multicast routing table entries, also called multicast cache entries, are calculated by `OSPF::mclookup()`, which uses the pruned shortest-path trees calculated by `SpfArea::mospf_path_calc()` for each area to which the MOSPF router attaches. The MOSPF routing calculation is covered in Section 12.4.

When the multicast topology of the routing domain changes, some of the multicast routing table entries that have been installed in the system kernel may need to be altered. The MOSPF implementation forces recalculation of these entries by deleting them from the kernel, as described in Section 12.5.

The configuration of the MOSPF implementation to interact with other multicast routing protocols is the subject of Section 12.6.

12.1 MOSPF Data Structures

Several global configuration parameters affect the operation of MOSPF. These parameters are set by the API routine `OSPF::cfgOspf()`, which is described in Section 13.1. `OSPF::g_mospf_enabled`, which is read by `OSPF::mospf_enabled()`, indicates whether the MOSPF protocol is enabled. If MOSPF is disabled, the implementation will not store or flood group-membership-LSAs, and requests to calculate multicast routing table entries will return negative cache entries (see Section 4.2). `OSPF::inter_area_mc`, which is read by `OSPF::mc_abr()`, indicates whether the MOSPF router forwards multicast datagrams across area borders (that is, whether it is an inter-area multicast forwarder). The router will set the MC bit in the summary-LSAs that it originates if and only if it has been configured as an inter-area multicast forwarder.

Multicast forwarding can be enabled on an interface-by-interface basis, using the API routine `OSPF::cfgIfc()` (Section 13.2). `SpfIfc::if_mcfwd` can take three separate values. If equal to the default value of `IF_MCFWD_MC`, multicast datagrams will be forwarded over the interface in the normal fashion: as data-link multicasts. If equal to `IF_MCFWD_UNI`, multicast datagrams will instead be forwarded over the interface as data-link unicasts (see Section 6.4 of [66] for motivation). And if equal to `IF_MCFWD_BLOCKED`, multicast forwarding over the interface is blocked: The interface will not appear in multicast routing table entries: neither as an incoming nor as an outgoing interface.

Non-OSPF routing information for a prefix is passed to the router through `OSPF::cfgExRt()` (see Sections 10.3.2 and 13.9). If `ExRtData::mc` is set to `1`, the prefix is imported into the OSPF routing domain as a multicast source, causing the rest of the

MOSPF routers to calculate the appropriate multicast routing table entries (Section 12.6). Conversely, if `OSPF::inter_AS_mc` is set, the router will advertise itself as being on the forwarding path to group members in other routing domains.

The other data structures used extensively by the MOSPF implementation are as follows.

- The multicast routing table entry `struct MCache`, shown in Figure 4.5, dictates how to forward a particular multicast datagram. Every source and destination group combination has one of these data structures, as this is the way forwarding entries are commonly implemented in system kernels, although MOSPF calculates multicast routing tables by source prefix (note `MCache::mask`) and destination group. Each multicast routing table entry is stored in a `class MospfEntry`, which in turn is organized into the AVL tree `OSPF:: multicast_cache`.

- Multicast forwarding and IGMP work on physical interfaces instead of on IP subnets. A physical interface is represented in the code by a `class PhyInt` (Figure 12.1). There is one `PhyInt` for each physical interface number or `phyint` that has been declared through the configuration API `OSPF::cfgIfc()`. The collection of `PhyInt`s is organized into the AVLtree `OSPF::phyints`.

─── phyint.h
```
54 class PhyInt : public AVLitem {
56     bool operational;
57     InAddr my_addr;        // Associated IP address
58     SpfIfc *mospf_ifp;     // Associated MOSPF-enabled interface
59     // IGMP parameters
60     InAddr igmp_querier;// Current IGMP querier
61     IGMPQueryTimer qrytim;
62     StartupQueryTimer strqtim;
63     IGMPOtherQuerierTimer oqtim;
64     // IGMP configurable parameters
65     int robustness_variable;
66     int query_interval;
67     int query_response_interval;// Tenths of seconds
68     int group_membership_interval;
69     int other_querier_present_interval;
70     int startup_query_interval;
71     int startup_query_count;
72     int last_member_query_interval;// Tenths of seconds
73     int last_member_query_count;
91 };
```
─── phyint.h

Figure 12.1 The physical interface data structure: `class PhyInt`.

PhyInt::operational indicates the operational status of the physical interface, as can be determined through the system entry point **OspfSysCalls:: phy_operational()**. **PhyInt::my_addr** is the largest IP interface address that the router has attached to the physical network segment; this value will be used as the IP source address in all IGMP packets sent out the interface. **PhyInt::mospf_ifp** is one of the router's OSPF interfaces that both attaches to the physical subnet and is configured to forward multicast datagrams as data-link multicasts (set to **0** if there are none).

PhyInt::igmp_querier is the IP address of the physical network segment's current IGMP Querier. If the router itself is the Querier, **PhyInt:: igmp_querier == PhyInt::my_addr**, and the timer **PhyInt::qrytim** implements the periodic sending of IGMP Membership Queries.

PhyInt::strqtim implements the increased frequency of IGMP Membership Query transmissions when the physical interface first becomes operational. When another router is the Querier, the timer **PhyInt::oqtim** verifies that the Querier is still operational.

The rest of the elements in **class PhyInt** are the various IGMP parameters, as mandated by the IGMPv2 specification [27]. They are named according to that specification, and we shall not attempt to improve on the descriptions therein.

- An instance of **class GroupMembership** (Figure 12.2) keeps track of the membership in a particular group on a particular physical network segment. These data structures are organized into the AVL tree **OSPF::local_membership**, also called the *local group database*, indexed by group and **phyint**.

─── phyint.h
```
137 class GroupMembership : public AVLitem {
138     LeaveQueryTimer leave_tim;
139     GroupTimeoutTimer exp_tim;
140     V1MemberTimer v1_tim;
141     bool v1members;
142 public:
143     GroupMembership(InAddr group, int phyint);
148 };
```
─── phyint.h

Figure 12.2 Representing group membership on attached segments: **class GroupMembership**.

Suppose that **class GroupMembership** describes group membership in group G on the physical segment 6. When the timer **GroupMembership:: leave_tim** is running, the router has received an IGMPv2 Leave Group for G on segment 6 and is in the process of sending specific Queries to see whether any group members remain. If the timer `GroupMembership::exp_tim` fires, the router assumes that the lack of recent Group Membership Reports for G on segment 6 means that group members are no longer present. There are IGMPv1 [19] group G members on segment 6 if and only if `GroupMembership::v1members` is `true`. In that case, if IGMPv1 reports cease to be heard for G on segment 6, the timer `GroupMembership::v1_tim` will fire, and the router will assume that IGMPv1 members are no longer present.

- All operations on MOSPF's group-membership-LSAs are implemented in the file `ospfd/src/grplsa.C`. The only complicated operation is the origination of group-membership-LSAs, which is handled by the routine `SpfArea::grp_orig()` and is discussed in Section 12.3. In the router's link-state database, a group-membership-LSA is represented as a `class grpLSA` (inheriting from `class LSA`) and is a member of the AVL tree `SpfArea::grpLSAs`.

12.2 IGMPv2 Implementation

The MOSPF implementation includes an implementation of the router part of IGMPv2 [27]. This includes the following functionality, executing on all physical broadcast interfaces that are configured to forward IP multicast datagrams as data-link multicasts (that is, with `PhyInt::mospf_ifp != 0`).

- The router participates in the election of an IGMPv2 Querier.

- When the router itself is the Querier, it periodically sends Host Membership Queries out the physical interface.

- Even if it is not the Querier, the router keeps track of IGMPv2 group members on the attached broadcast segment. The segment's Designated Router will advertise the membership to all MOSPF routers in group-membership-LSAs, but we have all the MOSPF routers keep track of the group membership, just in case they become Designated Router in the future. The router monitors group membership through the reception of IGMPv2 Host Membership Reports and Leave Group Messages.

- The router also implements IGMPv1 [19] compatibility, keeping track of group members running IGMPv1 and disabling Leave Group procedures when any IGMPv1 members are present.

The IGMPv2 implementation does *not* originate IGMP Host Membership Reports. It is assumed that the system kernel will do this, as is the case for most UNIX variants and Microsoft Windows platforms. Use of the IGMP implementation, which is invoked simply by passing received IGMP packets to the API routine `OSPF::rxigmp()` (Section 4.3), is optional. If the system already has a full IGMP implementation, group membership changes can simply be passed to the MOSPF implementation through the API routines `OSPF::join_indication()` and `OSPF::leave_indication()`.

The IGMP implementation is contained in the file `ospfd/src/phyint.C`. A very brief description of the routines in that file follows.

`PhyInt::verify_igmp_capabilities()` determines whether the router should run IGMP on the interface and, if so, what IP address it should use as the source of the IGMP packets it transmits. In addition, if that address is smaller than the address of the current Querier or if there is no current Querier, the router begins Query duties on the interface. The assumption of Query duties, as implemented in `PhyInt::start_query_duties()`, involves sending `PhyInt::startup_query_count` Host Membership Queries separated by `PhyInt::startup_query_interval` seconds. `PhyInt::send_query(InAddr group)` formats and sends a Group Membership Query. The Query is a general query if `group` is equal to 0; otherwise, it is a specific query for membership in a single `group`.

The processing of received IGMP packets begins in `OSPF::rxigmp()`, which dispatches to other routines, based on the IGMP packet type `IgmpPkt::ig_type`. Received Host Membership Queries are handled by `PhyInt::received_igmp_query()`. If the source IP address in the received Query is smaller than the router's own IP address, the router resigns its Query duties by calling `PhyInt::stop_query_duties()`. If the router is not the Querier and if the received Query is for a specific group, the router vicariously participates in Leave Group processing by (re)setting `GroupMembership::exp_tim` appropriately. Received Host Membership Reports (v2 and v1) are processed by `PhyInt::received_igmp_report()`, which creates or updates the matching `GroupMembership` class. Received Leave Group messages are processed only if both the router is the Querier and no IGMPv1 members of the group are on the segment. In this case, `PhyInt::received_igmp_leave()` starts to aggressively time out membership in the group, while sending specific Queries to make sure that no other group members are present.

IGMP packet types other than those mentioned exist—for example, several are used by DVMRP [82]. Of these other IGMP types, only two are supported by the implementation: `IGMP_MTRACE_QUERY` and `IGMP_MTRACE_RESPONSE`, used by multicast traceroute [28]. However, multicast traceroute (or `mtrace`) has been implemented only for the OSPF simulator described in Chapter 15, An OSPF Simulator. The resulting `mtrace` code can be found in `ospfd/ospf_sim/mtrace.[Ch]`.

12.3   Propagating Group Membership: Group-membership-LSAs

Group-membership-LSAs are area-scoped LSAs and serve two purposes. First, they distribute local group membership—the group membership of the router's local LANs and of the router itself—throughout an OSPF area. Second, they are used to propagate group membership information from the nonbackbone OSPF areas to the backbone OSPF area 0.0.0.0.

The router (re)originates a group-membership-LSA for the group G when one of the following events occurs:

- When the first group G member appears on an attached LAN or when the router itself first joins G (`OSPF::join_indication()`).

- When group G members are no longer on an attached LAN or the router itself leaves the group G (`OSPF::leave_indication()`).

- When the router is an area border router and receives a new group-member-ship-LSA for group G in area A, where A is not the backbone (`OSPF::rtsched()`).

- When the router transitions into or out of the Designated Router role on a LAN that contains group G members. At this point, `SpfIfc::reorig_all_grplsas()` is called to reoriginate all necessary group-member-ship-LSAs.

- When the router acquires the first, or loses the last, full adjacency on an attached LAN having group G members. When there is at least one full adjacency, the group is associated with the LAN's network-LSA; otherwise, the group is associated with the router's router-LSA. Again, `SpfIfc::reorig_all_grplsas()` reoriginates the necessary group-membership-LSAs.

The function `SpfArea::grp_orig(InAddr group, int forced)`, part of which is seen in Figure 12.3, originates a group-membership-LSA for multicast group `group` into the OSPF area specified by `this`. As with all LSA origination methods, there is a `forced` argument, which when set to the value `true`, causes the reorigination to proceed even if the LSA contents are no different from before.

Before the code fragment in Figure 12.3, the router has verified that it has been configured to run MOSPF, has obtained the LS Sequence Number to use for the (re)origination, and has allocated a buffer in which to build the LSA and then formatted the standard link-state header in the beginning of the buffer, pointed to by `LShdr *hdr`.

134,136   The size of the group-membership-LSA, in bytes, is going to be `length`. At the moment, we have formatted only the standard link-state header, so `length` is set to `20`. The body of the group-membership-LSA will be a list of LSA references—those LSAs that should be labeled as having `group` members. The first LSA reference, `gmref`, will be added right after the link-state header.

135   The LSA references that can appear in the body of the group-membership-LSA are any of the network-LSAs that the router has originated and the router's own router-LSA. Whether a reference to the router's own router-LSA has already been added to the group-membership-LSA is indicated by `added_self`.

── grplsa.C

```
134        length = sizeof(LShdr);
135        added_self = false;
136        gmref = (GMref *) (hdr + 1);
137        iter.seek(group, 0);
138        while ((entry = iter.next()) && entry->index1() == group) {
139            PhyInt *phyp;
140            int phyint=(int)entry->index2();
141            if (phyint != -1) {
142                if (!(phyp = (PhyInt *)ospf->phyints.find((uns32) phyint,
                                                            0)))
143                    continue;
144                if (!phyp->mospf_ifp)
145                    continue;
146                if (phyp->mospf_ifp->area() == this &&
147                    phyp->mospf_ifp->if_nfull > 0) {
148                    if (phyp->mospf_ifp->if_state == IFS_DR) {
149                        gmref->ls_type = hton32(LST_NET);
150                        gmref->ls_id = hton32(phyp->mospf_ifp->if_addr);
151                        gmref++;
152                        length += sizeof(GMref);
153                    }
154                    continue;
155                }
156            }
157            // Add self instead
158            if (!added_self) {
159                added_self = true;
160                gmref->ls_type = hton32(LST_RTR);
161                gmref->ls_id = hton32(ospf->my_id());
162                gmref++;
163                length += sizeof(GMref);
164            }
165        }
169        if (!added_self && a_id == BACKBONE) {
170            AreaIterator a_iter(ospf);
171            SpfArea *a;
172            while ((a = a_iter.get_next()) && !added_self) {
173                AVLsearch g_iter(&a->grpLSAs);
174                LSA *glsa;
175                if (a == this)
176                    continue;
177                g_iter.seek(group, 0);
```

(Continued)

```
178                    while ((glsa = (LSA *)g_iter.next()) &&
                              glsa->index1() == group) {
179                        if (!glsa->parsed)
180                            continue;
181                        added_self = true;
182                        gmref->ls_type = hton32(LST_RTR);
183                        gmref->ls_id = hton32(ospf->my_id());
184                        gmref++;
185                        length += sizeof(GMref);
186                        break;
187                    }
188                }
189            }
```

─── grplsa.C

Figure 12.3 Originating group-membership-LSAs: SpfArea::grp_orig().

137-165   We are going to iterate through the group membership records for **group** in the local group database, using the iterator class **AVLsearch iter(&ospf->local_membership)**. Because **group** is the first index, all the records for **group** appear together (line **138**).

140-156   A group member is associated with the physical interface **phyp**. If this physical interface is running MOSPF (line **144**) and the router is originating a network-LSA for the attached network that itself belongs to the area into which we are originating (lines **146-148**), we add a reference to the network-LSA into the body of the group-membership-LSA (lines **149-152**).

158-164   If the router hasn't already referenced its own router-LSA in the group-membership-LSA, it does so now, because either **phyint == -1**, indicating that the router itself is a member of the group, or there is no network-LSA to label with the group.

169-189   If this is the backbone, the router must advertise the **group** membership from its nonbackbone areas into the backbone. The router looks for any nonbackbone group-membership-LSAs for **group** (lines **170-178**). If it finds such a group-membership-LSA and that LSA is not in the process of being flushed from the database (lines **179-180**), the router advertises **group** into the backbone by labeling itself with **group** membership (lines **181-185**).

After that code fragment, the router checks to make sure that at least one LSA reference has been added to the group-membership-LSA. If not, the group-membership-LSA is not originated; or, if it already exists in the database, the database copy is flushed. Otherwise, the group-membership-LSA origination is completed, using the standard call to **OSPF::lsa_reorig()**.

12.4   Routing Calculations

In MOSPF, multicast routing table entries are calculated in "on-demand" fashion. When it receives an IP multicast datagram, the system kernel looks up the matching routing multicast table entry, based on the datagram's source address and destination group. If no matching routing table entry is found, the system kernel calls the OSPF API routine `MCache *OSPF::mclookup(InAddr src, InAddr group)`, which calculates and returns a matching multicast routing table entry (also called a MOSPF routing cache entry). The format of the returned multicast routing table entry is shown in Figure 4.5.

We examine the multicast routing calculation later, but in a nutshell, the calculation works as follows. The router determines the path of the multicast datagram through each of its attached areas by calculating a pruned shortest-path tree for each area (`SpfArea::mospf_path_calc()`). This calculation is performed by using Dijkstra's SPF algorithm with special tiebreakers to ensure that all routers calculate the exact same trees. All branches without group members, namely, those that are not labeled by group-membership-LSAs for `group`, are pruned after the Dijkstra calculation. The root of the shortest-path trees is determined by finding the best-matching routing table entry for the multicast source, as implemented by `INrte *OSPF::mc_source(InAddr src)`. The last step is to merge all the pruned shortest-path trees from each attached area into a single multicast datagram delivery tree; this step is, of course, necessary only in area border routers. The router's position, or lack of position, on this delivery tree then yields the multicast routing table entry.

12.4.1   `OSPF::mclookup()`

A fragment of `MCache *OSPF::mclookup(InAddr src, InAddr group)` is given in Figure 12.4. Prior to this fragment, the routine has performed the following operations. It has checked to see whether the multicast group belongs to the set of nonroutable group addresses, namely, the space 224.0.0.0/24. If so, `0` is returned, indicating that the multicast datagram should not be forwarded. Then a check is made to see whether the multicast routing table entry has already been calculated, by performing a lookup in `OSPF::multicast_cache`. If found, the entry is simply returned. Finally, the best-matching prefix `INrte *rte` for `src` is found by calling `OSPF::mc_source()`. This prefix is then used to initialize the candidate list for Dijkstra's SPF algorithm (see Section 11.2). *Note:* `OSPF::mc_source()` differs from the algorithm specified in Section 11.2 of the MOSPF specification [66]. Since the writing of the MOSPF specification, the OSPF routing table lookup has been changed to always prefer the longest matching prefix, and we have changed the MOSPF lookup accordingly.

Viewing the pruned shortest path as a tree rooted at the multicast datagram's source, we term *upstream* (or *incoming*) those links in the pruned shortest path between

```
                                                                 ── mospf.C
178       // Calculate multicast path through each area
179       while ((ap = a_iter.get_next())) {
180           uns32 cost;
181           int path_case;
182           ap->mospf_path_calc(group, rte, path_case, cost, &ds_nodes);
184           if (ap->mospf_in_count == 0)
185               continue;
186           else if (!best_ap)
187               goto new_best_area;
188           else if (path_case < best_case)
189               goto new_best_area;
190           else if (path_case > best_case)
191               continue;
192           else if (ap->a_id == 0)
193               goto new_best_area;
194           else if (best_ap->a_id == 0)
195               continue;
196           else if (cost < best_cost)
197               goto new_best_area;
198           else if (cost > best_cost)
199               continue;
200           else if (ap->a_id < best_ap->a_id)
201               continue;
202         new_best_area:
203               best_ap = ap;
204               best_case = path_case;
205               best_cost = cost;
206       }
207
208       // If no incoming interface, add negative cache entry
209       if (!best_ap) {
210           add_negative_mcache_entry(src, rte, group);
211           return(0);
212       }
                                                                 ── mospf.C
```

Figure 12.4 Calculating multicast routing table entries: OSPF::mclookup().

the root and the calculating router and *downstream* (or *outgoing*) those links connecting the router with leaves containing group members.

179   The router iterates through all its attached areas. For each area, it will calculate a pruned shortest-path tree and will then merge that tree into a single delivery tree for the multicast datagram.

182   The router calculates the pruned shortest-path tree for the OSPF area ap by calling SpfArea::mospf_path_calc(). That routine will be examined in detail in Section 12.4.2. Values returned by that routine are as follows: path_case (call by reference) is a

general classification of the area's tree, listed by decreasing merge priority: `SourceIntraArea` means that the multicast source is contained inside OSPF area `ap`, `SourceInterArea1` means that the source is in an area that is not attached to the router, `SourceInterArea2` means that the source is in one of the router's attached areas but not in `ap`, `SourceExternal` means that the source is external to the OSPF routing domain, and `SourceStubExternal` means that `ap` is a stub area and that the best-matching prefix inside the stub area is the default route 0/0. The returned `cost` argument (again by reference) indicates the distance from the multicast source to the calculating router if the upstream portion of the shortest path through `ap` were used to forward the datagram. Those of the area's router-LSAs and network-LSAs that are immediately downstream from the calculating router are appended to `LsaList ds_nodes`. The number of upstream links directly attaching to the calculating router (they can be multiple, due to OSPF's representation of point-to-point links; see the discussion of "upstream node" in [66]) is recorded in `ap->mospf_in_count`, with the pointers to the corresponding incoming physical interfaces stored in `ap->mospf_in_phys`.

184-205   Here, the router is picking the attached OSPF area that will provide the incoming links in the merged datagram delivery tree. Only one area can supply the incoming links, whereas all the areas can contribute to the collection of downstream interfaces. Obviously, only those areas whose pruned trees have incoming links qualify (lines 184-185; virtual links and summary-links do *not* count). When multiple areas can provide incoming links (lines 188-201), we use the tiebreakers from Section 12.2.7 of [66]. In decreasing importance, these tiebreakers are best `path_type` (lines 188-191), backbone area is preferred (lines 192-195), area providing the cheaper cost *to* the source (lines 196-199), and the area with the highest OSPF Area ID (lines 200-201). Remember that all MOSPF routers have to use exactly the same tiebreakers in order to get consistent multicast datagram delivery trees.

209-212   If there is no incoming interface, the router should not forward the multicast datagram. `OSPF::add_negative_mcache_entry()` creates a discouraging multicast routing table entry and installs it in `OSPF::multicast_cache` and the system kernel. The routine then returns 0.

After the code fragment shown, the routing table entry is allocated and filled in. The routing table entry's incoming interfaces come from `best_ap->mospf_in_phys`. The list of immediately downstream router-LSAs and network-LSAs, accumulated over all attached areas and stored in `ds_nodes`, is converted into the routing table entry's downstream interfaces. Finally, any attached stub network interfaces having `group` members are added as downstream interfaces as well.

12.4.2 An Area's MOSPF SPF Calculation: `SpfArea::mospf_dijkstra()`

The pruned shortest-path calculation for an area is performed by the routine `SpfArea::mospf_path_calc()`. This routine (Figure 12.5) initializes the SPF candidate

list and then calls `SpfArea::mospf_dijkstra()` (Figure 12.6) for the Dijkstra SPF calculation, augmented with the appropriate MOSPF tiebreakers and pruning.

`SpfArea::mospf_path_calc()`

308   We are calculating the path for the datagram with source prefix `rte` and destination `group` through the area specified by `this`.

317-322   The router's upstream interfaces in the pruned shortest-path tree will be stored in `SpfArea::mospf_in_phys`. We make sure that this buffer is large enough by assuming that all interfaces to the area will be labeled as upstream.

325-327   The current number of upstream interfaces, `SpfArea::mospf_in_count`, is initial-ized to 0. The upstream and downstream interfaces this area will add to the multicast routing table entry are based on the location of the router's own router-LSA (`mylsa`) within the area's pruned shortest-path tree.

328-335   The MOSPF Dijkstra calculation is initialized similar to the unicast Dijkstra calcula-tion, as explained in Section 11.2.3.

337-350   Initialization of the Dijkstra candidate list depends on the location of the multicast datagram source relative to the area whose tree is being calculated. There are five distinct cases, as explained later. In each case, a number of router-LSAs or network-LSAs are initially added to the candidate list `cand`, by calling `SpfArea::mospf_possibly_add()`.

337-338   The source of the multicast datagram belongs to one of the router's attached areas. This breaks down into two separate cases. If the datagram's source belongs to the area whose tree is being calculated (case `SourceIntraArea`), the single router-LSA or net-work-LSA that advertises the source is added to the candidate list. This is the LSA with LS Type equal to `rte->r_ospf->lstype`, Link State ID equal to `rte->r_ospf->lsid`, and Advertising Router equal to `rte->r_ospf->rtid`. If the datagram's source belongs to a different area (case `SourceInterArea2`), the router-LSAs of those ABRs advertising summary-LSAs for the source prefix (perhaps after aggregation) are added to the candi-date list.

339-342   The source of the multicast datagram does not belong to one of the router's attached areas, but the area whose tree is being calculated is a stub area (case `SourceStubExternal`). The router-LSAs belonging to all the area's ABRs are added to the candidate list.

343-346   The source belongs to a remote area (case `SourceInterArea1`). The router-LSAs of those ABRs advertising summary-LSAs for the source prefix are added to the candidate list.

347-350   The source is external to the OSPF routing domain (case `SourceExternal`). The router-LSAs of all ASBRs belonging to the area and advertising AS-external-LSAs for the source prefix, the router-LSAs and network-LSAs yielding routes to those AS-external-LSAs' forwarding addresses, and the router-LSAs of ABRs advertising

```
———————————————————————————————————————————————— mospf.C
308 void SpfArea::mospf_path_calc(InAddr group, INrte *rte, int &mcase,
309                                 uns32 &cost, LsaList *downstream_nodes)
311 {
312     PriQ cand;
313     rtrLSA *rtr;
314     netLSA *net;
315     rtrLSA *mylsa;

317     // Initialize temporary area within area class
318     if (size_mospf_incoming < n_active_if) {
319         delete [] mospf_in_phys;
320         mospf_in_phys = new int[n_active_if];
321         size_mospf_incoming = n_active_if;
322     }

324     // Initialize Dijkstra state
325     mospf_in_count = 0;
326     cost = Infinity;
327     mylsa = (rtrLSA *) ospf->myLSA(this, LST_RTR, ospf->myid);
328     if (mylsa == 0 || !mylsa->parsed || ifmap == 0)
329         return;
330     rtr = (rtrLSA *) rtrLSAs.sllhead;
331     for (; rtr; rtr = (rtrLSA *) rtr->sll)
332         rtr->t_state = DS_UNINIT;
333     net = (netLSA *) netLSAs.sllhead;
334     for (; net; net = (netLSA *) net->sll)
335         net->t_state = DS_UNINIT;
336
337     if (rte->intra_area())
338         mcase = mospf_init_intra_area(cand, rte, 0, ILDirect);
339     else if (is_stub()) {
340         mcase = SourceStubExternal;
341         mospf_add_summlsas(cand, default_route, 0);
342     }
343     else if (rte->inter_area()) {
344         mcase = SourceInterArea1;
345         mospf_add_summlsas(cand, rte, 0);
346     }
347     else {
348         mcase = SourceExternal;
349         mospf_add_ases(cand, rte);
350     }

352     // Do the main Dijkstra calculation
353     mospf_dijkstra(group, cand, mcase == SourceIntraArea,
                        downstream_nodes);
354 }
———————————————————————————————————————————————— mospf.C
```

Figure 12.5 The path of a multicast datagram through an area: `SpfArea::mospf_path_calc()`.

summary-LSAs for those forwarding addresses and ASBRs are added to the candidate list by `SpfArea::mospf_add_ases()`.

353   The body of the pruned shortest-path tree calculation is performed by the routine `SpfArea::mospf_dijkstra()`, which sets the incoming interfaces in `SpfArea:: mospf_in_phys` and adds the downstream nodes to `downstream_nodes`.

`SpfArea::mospf_dijkstra()`

The multicast SPF calculation is performed in `SpfArea::mospf_dijkstra()`, which is shown in Figure 12.6.

366   In the area's shortest-path tree, oriented so that the root of the tree is at the top, nodes higher than the calculating router's router-LSA (`mylsa`) are termed *upstream*, whereas those lower are called *downstream*.

368-416   The main loop of the multicast calculation is similar to the unicast SPF calculation. The router-LSA or network-LSA on the candidate list (`cand`) that is closest to the root is removed from the candidate list (line `368`) and added to the shortest-path tree (line `371`). The neighbors of the just-added LSA are then examined and added to or repositioned on the candidate list (lines `387-415`).

375-385   The router determines whether the node just added to the shortest-path tree should add a downstream interface to the multicast routing table entry or cause an existing downstream interface to be modified. If the just-added node `v` is downstream, `nh` is the first node on the branch of the tree from `mylsa` to `v`. If `v` is labeled in the link-state database with group membership (determined by `TNode::has_members()`, which searches for a group-membership-LSA whose body references `v`), `nh` must appear as one of the multicast routing table entry's downstream interfaces. The closest group member through that interface (`nh->closest_member`) is at most the number of hops from `mylsa` to `v` (`v->t_ttl`). *Note: This logic performs the pruning of branches without group members.*

387-415   `v`'s neighboring nodes are examined for inclusion on the candidate list or in order to modify their positions on the candidate list. In the following, the current neighbor of `v` under consideration is referred to as `w`.

396-403   If `v` is the calculating router itself and if the link under consideration (`tlp`) points upstream, set the incoming interface(s) in the multicast routing table entry appropriately. If the node immediately upstream is a router, add as incoming interfaces all point-to-point links connecting the two routers (line `400`).

405-409   Only bidirectional links and MOSPF-enabled routers and network segments are used in the multicast tree calculation.

413   When the multicast source belongs to the area whose tree is being calculated, the path cost is the sum of forward link costs. In all other cases, reverse link cost is used. See Chapter 8 in [67] for an explanation of reverse link costs in MOSPF.

414   `SpfArea::mospf_possibly_add()` is used to add `w` to the candidate list. If `w` is already on the candidate list, its position may be modified according to the MOSPF tie-breakers, listed here in decreasing order: (1) lesser-cost paths are preferred

—— mospf.C

```
359 void SpfArea::mospf_dijkstra(InAddr group, PriQ &cand, bool
                                  use_forward,
360                               LsaList *ds_nodes)
362 {
363     TNode *V;
364     TNode *nh=0;
365
366     mylsa = (rtrLSA *) ospf->myLSA(this, LST_RTR, ospf->my_id());
367
368     while ((V = (TNode *) cand.priq_rmhead())) {
369         int i, j;
370         Link *lp;
371         V->t_state = DS_ONTREE;
372         /* If downstream, determine whether or not this
373          * branch of the delivery tree should be pruned.
374          */
375         if ((V->t_downstream) && (nh = V->t_mospf_dsnode) != 0) {
376             byte mbr_ttl=255;
377             if (V->has_members(group))
378                 mbr_ttl = V->t_ttl;
379             if (!nh->in_mospf_cache || nh->closest_member > mbr_ttl)
380                 nh->closest_member = mbr_ttl;
381             if (!nh->in_mospf_cache) {
382                 nh->in_mospf_cache = true;
383                 ds_nodes->addEntry(nh);
384             }
385         }
387         for (lp = V->t_links, i=0, j=0; lp != 0; lp = lp->l_next, i++) {
388             TLink *tlp;
389             TNode *W;
390             int il_type;
391             uns32 cost;
392             if (lp->l_ltype == LT_STUB)
393                 continue;
394             tlp = (TLink *) lp;
396             if ((V == mylsa) &&
397                 (mylsa->t_parent != 0) &&
398                 (tlp->tl_nbr == mylsa->t_parent) &&
399                 (lp->l_ltype != LT_VL) &&
400                 (mylsa->t_parent->lsa_type != LST_NET || j == 0)) {
401                 mospf_in_phys[j++] = ifmap[i]->if_phyint;
402                 mospf_in_count = j;
403             }
```

(Continued)

```
404                 // Only use bidirectional links
405                 if (!(W = tlp->tl_nbr))
406                     continue;
407                 // Prune non-MOSPF nodes
408                 if (!(W->lsa_opts & SPO_MC))
409                     continue;
410                 // Possibly add to candidate list
411                 il_type = ((lp->l_ltype == LT_VL) ? ILVirtual : ILNormal);
412                 cost = V->cost0;
413                 cost += (use_forward ? tlp->l_fwdcst : tlp->tl_rvcst);
414                 mospf_possibly_add(cand, W, cost, V, il_type, i);
415             }
416         }
417 }
```
—— mospf.C

Figure 12.6 The MOSPF SPF calculation: `SpfArea::mospf_dijkstra()`.

(`TNode::cost0`), (2) paths with incoming virtual links are preferred over incoming router-to-router or network-to-router links (`TNode::cost1`), (3) parent network-LSAs are preferred over parent router-LSAs (`TNode::tie0`), and (4) parents with higher Link State IDs are preferred (`TNode::tie1`). See the documentation of `class PriQElt` in Chapter 5, Building Blocks.

12.5   Cache Maintenance and MOSPF–IGMP Interaction

Changes in the link-state database indicate changes in network topology, which in turn may modify the paths of multicast datagrams. As the paths of multicast datagrams change, so must the contents of multicast routing table entries. However, because MOSPF calculates multicast routing table entries in an on-demand fashion, a MOSPF router need not recalculate all its routing table entries at once. Instead, it can just delete all entries that may be affected by a particular topology change and let the system kernel ask for new routing table entries when they are necessary. That is the strategy taken by this MOSPF implementation. A list of topology changes and the multicast routing table entries that are deleted as a result are listed in Table 12.1.

Table 12.1 MOSPF Routing Table Maintenance

Events	Multicast Routing Table Entries Deleted
The full unicast routing table calculation is rerun, or all the unicast external routing table entries are recalculated, or the multicast forwarding configuration of an interface changes.	All multicast routing table entries (`OSPF::mospf_clear_cache()`).
A new/updated summary-LSA is received.	All multicast entries whose source falls under the prefix advertised by the summary-LSA are deleted (`OSPF::mospf_clear_inter_source()`).
A new/updated AS-external-LSA is received.	All multicast entries matching the external source advertised in the AS-external-LSA are deleted (`OSPF::mospf_clear_external_source()`).
A new/updated group-membership-LSA for group G is received.	All multicast routing table entries referencing G are deleted (`OSPF::mospf_clear_group()`).

Deleting a multicast routing table entry involves removing it from `OSPF::multicast_cache` and removing it from the system kernel by using `OspfSysCalls::del_mcache()`.

Note that for internal topology changes (router-LSAs and network-LSAs), we must wait for the unicast routing table calculation to run (`OSPF::full_calculation()`) before deleting the multicast routing table entries. The reason is the root of the multicast tree in those cases is based on an output of the unicast routing calculation.

12.6   Interaction with Other Routing Protocols

The MOSPF implementation in this book does not contain an implementation of the interaction between MOSPF and DVMRP, as described in Section 10.6 of [67]. If you were to run DVMRP and this MOSPF implementation in a router to connect a MOSPF domain to the MBONE (Multicast Backbone), you would

1. Import a default multicast route into the MOSPF domain, as long as you had learned one or more DVMRP routes. This is implemented by calling `OSPF::cfgExRt()` for the 0/0 prefix, setting `CfgExRt::mc` to 1. If the router does not want to advertise a default route for unicast routing, `CfgExRt::cost` should be set to `LSInfinity`. Multicast traffic sourced external to the MOSPF domain will now be forwarded to group members in the MOSPF domain.

2. Advertise the router to the rest of the MOSPF domain as a wildcard multicast receiver by setting `OSPF::inter_AS_mc`. Multicast traffic sourced internally to the MOSPF domain can now reach the DVMRP domain.

3. Advertise the intra-area and inter-area OSPF prefixes, stored in `inrttbl`, into DVMRP as multicast sources. Multicast traffic sourced internally to the MOSPF domain will now be forwarded to group members in the DVMRP domain.

In order for multicast datagrams with external sources to reach the MOSPF domain, DVMRP must not send prunes for any groups present in the MOSPF domain. A group's presence can be inferred by the presence of group-membership-LSAs for the group, contained within `SpfArea::grpLSAs`. (*Note:* Only MOSPF area 0.0.0.0 has a full view of the MOSPF domain's group membership.)

There are additional complications when you want to dual home the MOSPF domain into the MBONE or when you want to run the MOSPF domain as an MBONE transit network. However, these situations are described in Section 10.6 of [67] and use the same implementation building blocks that have been described previously.

Exercises

12.1   A prefix external to the OSPF domain can be imported as a multicast-only source by setting its AS-external-LSA's MC bit but setting the cost of the LSA to `LSInfinity`. Add support for this to the implementation by checking `ExRtData::mc` before returning the `ExRtData` to the heap in `OSPF::ase_orig()`.

12.2   Modify `OSPF::cfgOspf()` so that `OSPF::inter_AS_mc` can be set through the configuration API.

12.3   Calculate the `cost` argument in `SpfArea::mospf_path_calc()`. Come up with an example area configuration for which the tiebreaker on `cost` is necessary.

12.4   Fix the following bug. In lines `339-342` of `SpfArea::mospf_path_calc()`, you should check to see whether the multicast source matches any more specific summary-LSA belonging to the stub area. If so, instead of the `default_route`, the prefix advertised in this summary-LSA should be handed to `SpfArea::mospf_add_summlsas()`.

12.5   When group membership on a stub network changes, modify the code to call `OSPF::mospf_clear_group()`. Why isn't it necessary to call `OSPF::mospf_clear_cache()` when MOSPF becomes disabled?

12.6   Split the configuration of `CfgExRt::mc` into a call separate from `OSPF::cfgExRt()` so that no single external process need coordinate the importing of unicast and multicast routes.

13

Configuration and Monitoring

In this chapter, we discuss the configuration of the OSPF software. Configuration is accomplished through the `OSPF::cfgXXX()` entry points. A separate entry point is provided for each of the major configurable data structures in the implementation, which roughly correspond to tables in the standard OSPF MIB [5]: global OSPF parameters, OSPF areas, area aggregates, interfaces, advertised host addresses, virtual links, cryptographic authentication keys, neighbors, and imported external routing information.

Every `OSPF::cfgXXX()` entry point has two arguments. The first is a data structure that both identifies the data instance being configured and contains the complete list of configurable parameters for the instance. The second argument identifies whether the action is an add (`ADD_ITEM`) or a request to delete the instance (`DELETE_ITEM`). A request to add an already existing data instance dynamically changes the instance's configured parameters. A request to delete a nonexistent instance is simply ignored.

A separate section in this chapter is devoted to each of the configuration entry points. Configurable parameters specified in the first argument are organized into a table showing member name, MIB equivalent (if any), and value ranges. In some cases, there is a related MIB value, but the encoding of our configuration parameter may not match the MIB values exactly; in this case, the MIB equivalent is asterisked.

Each of these data structures can be dynamically reconfigured without restarting the OSPF implementation. However, reconfiguration does sometimes have consequences, which are detailed at the end of each relevant section.

A mechanism is also provided to download an entire new configuration into OSPF, checkpointing the previous configuration so that items no longer mentioned can be automatically deleted. This mechanism, described in Section 13.11, is used by the Linux port of OSPF (see Chapter 14, A Routing Daemon for Linux), which rereads its configuration from a disk file on the receipt of the appropriate signal.

Also included in this chapter are several other control features available from the implementation: the ability to gracefully shut down the OSPF routing process (Section 13.10), the ability to configure the OSPF code to act as a host instead of as a router (Section 13.12), and a monitoring interface enabling access to runtime statistics and internal data, such as the link-state database and the IP routing table (Section 13.13).

13.1 Global Parameters

The entry point for configuring global parameters is **OSPF::cfgOspf(struct CfgGen *msg)**. Unlike all other configuration entry points, this one has no second argument specifying add/modify/delete, as global variables have only a single instance. Parameters contained in the **CfgGen** argument are displayed in Table 13.1.

Table 13.1 Global Configuration Variables: **struct CfgGen**

CfgGen Member (MIB Equivalent)	Description
lsdb_limit (ospfExtLsdbLimit)	Maximum number of nondefault AS-external-LSAs that will be held in link-state database ([68]). If 0, there is no maximum.
mospf_enabled (ospfMulticastExtensions*)	If nonzero, MOSPF is enabled.
inter_area_mc (ospfMulticastExtensions*)	If nonzero and MOSPF is enabled, router will forward multicast datagrams across area borders.
ovfl_int (ospfExitOverflowInterval)	Time in seconds before attempting to exit Overflow State (Section 10.3.4).
new_flood_rate	Maximum number of locally originated LSAs that will be introduced per second.
max_rxmt_window	Maximum number of back-to-back retransmitted Link State Update packets that will be sent to any neighbor.
max_dds	Number of neighbors with which the router will simultaneously undergo Database Exchange (see Section 8.3). Default = 2.
host_mode	If nonzero, OSPF implementation will act as a host and not as a router (see Section 13.12).

(Continued)

`log_priority`	Integer between 0 and 5, inclusive, controlling log message display. Only messages with level greater than or equal to `log_priority` are printed.
`refresh_rate`	If larger than 1,800, router will increase the rate of refreshing each AS-external-LSA to this many seconds, using DoNotAge (Section 6.5). If set to a value greater than `2**16` hours, AS-external-LSAs will never be refreshed.

Because the router's OSPF Router ID cannot be changed and must be known at the very start, it is not included as one of the global parameters. Instead, Router ID is the argument to the constructor for the global OSPF class (see Section 4.3).

Also unlike all configuration entry points, `OSPF::cfgOspf()` need not be called. In this case, the global parameters are assigned default values, as shown in Figure 13.1.

```
—————————————————————————————————————————————————— ospf.C
199  void CfgGen::set_defaults()
200
201  {
202      lsdb_limit = 0;       // Maximum number of AS-external-LSAs
203      mospf_enabled = 0;    // Running MOSPF?
204      inter_area_mc = 1;    // Inter-area multicast forwarder?
205      ovfl_int = 300;       // Time to exit overflow state
206      new_flood_rate = 1000;     // # self-orig LSAs per second
207      max_rxmt_window = 8;       // # back-to-back retransmissions
208      max_dds = 2;               // # simultaneous DB exchanges
209      host_mode = 0;        // act as router
210      log_priority = 4;     // Base logging priority
211      refresh_rate = 0;     // Don't originate DoNotAge LSAs
212      sys->ip_forward(true);
213  }
—————————————————————————————————————————————————— ospf.C
```

Figure 13.1 Setting default values for global parameters: `CfgGen::set_defaults()`.

Changing global parameters dynamically can have the following consequences. Some parameter changes affect the global makeup of the router's link-state database, namely, whether the router is running MOSPF and whether it is running as a router or as a host. Changes to these parameters cause the router to drop and to reestablish all its adjacencies.

Other possible consequences when reconfiguring global parameters follow.

- When the router's ability to forward multicasts across area borders changes, it notifies other OSPF routers of the change by reoriginating its summary-LSAs.

- If the maximum number of nondefault AS-external-LSAs decreases and if the router is suddenly over the limit, it will immediately go into Database Overflow State ([68]).

- If the time interval to exit Database Overflow changes and if the router is already in Database Overflow State, the router will ignore the length of time it has already been in Overflow State and will exit that state in the configured number of seconds from now.

13.2 Interface Parameters

An OSPF interface is added, modified, or deleted through the entry point `OSPF::cfgIfc(struct CfgIfc *msg, int status)`. An interface is identified by its IP address `CfgIfc::address`, analogous to the MIB variable ospfIfIpAddress. Unnumbered interfaces are identified by their physical interface number `CfgIfc::phyint`, similar to the MIB's ospfAddressLessIf. The configurable items for each interface are listed in Table 13.2.

Table 13.2 Configurable Interface Parameters: `struct CfgIfc`

CfgIfc Member (MIB Equivalent)	Description
`mask`	The IP address mask associated with the attached network segment.
`mtu`	Maximum transmission unit for the interface. The largest IP datagram, in bytes, that can be sent out the interface without fragmentation.
`IfIndex`	The interface's MIB-II IfIndex. Advertised in router-LSAs for unnumbered interfaces.
`area_id` (ospfIfAreaId)	The OSPF area to which the interface attaches. Equivalently, the OSPF area to which the attached network segment belongs.
`IfType` (ospfIfType*)	The OSPF interface type. One of `IFT_BROADCAST` (broadcast), `IFT_PP` (point to point), `IFT_NBMA` (nonbroadcast but still multiaccess), or `IFT_P2MP` (Point-to-MultiPoint).
`dr_pri` (ospfIfRtrPriority)	The Designated Router Priority of the interface. An integer between 0 and 255, inclusive; 0 means ineligible to become Designated Router. Otherwise, in the case of simultaneous claims to be Designated Router, the one with the highest Designated Priority wins.
`xmt_dly` (ospfIfTransitDelay)	Transmission delay for LSAs flooded out the interface, in seconds. Must be at least 1.
`rxmt_int` (ospfIfRetransInterval)	Number of seconds before unacknowledged LSAs will be retransmitted to attached neighbors.

(Continued)

hello_int (ospfIfHelloInterval)	Interval between OSPF Hellos sent out the interface, in seconds.
if_cost (ospfIfMetricValue*)	The cost that will be advertised for the interface in router-LSAs. An integer between 1 and 65,535, inclusive.
dead_int (ospfIfRtrDeadInterval)	Number of seconds to detect an inoperational neighbor, due to lack of Hellos from said neighbor.
poll_int (ospfIfPollInterval)	On NBMA networks, the rate in seconds at which Hellos are sent to inoperational neighbors, in order to detect their reappearance.
auth_type (ospfIfAuthType)	The authentication mechanism used for packets sent and received on the interface. One of **AUT_NONE** (no authentication), **AUT_PASSWD** (simple cleartext password), or **AUT_CRYPT** (OSPF cryptographic authentication).
auth_key (ospfIfAuthKey)	When using simple cleartext authentication, the 8-octet password used in packets. Keys for OSPF cryptographic authentication are configured separately, as discussed in Section 13.3.
mc_fwd (ospfIfMulticastForwarding*)	The method for forwarding multicast datagrams on the interface. One of **IF_MCFWD_BLOCKED** (multicast forwarding disabled), **IF_MCFWD_MC** (forward as data-link multicasts), or **IF_MCFWD_UNI** (forward as data-link unicasts). **IF_MCFWD_MC** is normal.
demand (ospfIfDemand*)	If nonzero, the interface should be treated as a demand circuit, reducing flooding and Hello traffic as specified in [64].
passive	If nonzero, interface is advertised in LSA, but OSPF control traffic is neither sent nor received on the interface.

It is not possible to disable an interface (MIB variable ospfIfAdminStat); the interface must instead be deleted from the configuration by setting **status = DELETE_ITEM**. Virtual links are configured through a separate entry point, as discussed in Section 13.6.

When an interface is deleted, its state is set to Down, and all associated neighbors are deleted. If this interface was the last active interface attaching to the area, the router may no longer be an area border router. If so, it will reoriginate its router-LSA for the other actively attached area, deleting its area border router status indication (bit B in the router-LSA).

For many of the interface parameters (**hello_int**, **dead_int**, **auth_type**, and **auth_key**), we simply let changes take their natural course rather than taking immediate action. For example, when the HelloInterval changes, the router will start rejecting Hellos from its previous neighbors, eventually leading to adjacencies being destroyed (unless the neighbors' HelloIntervals also change).

Changes to a number of interface parameters (**mask**, **IfIndex**, **if_cost**) may change the contents of the router's router-LSA, causing the router to attempt an immediate reorigination of the LSA. Changes to **mask** and **mc_fwd** will similarly cause immediate reorigination of the associated network segment's network-LSA, if the router is currently Designated Router.

If the interface's Designated Router Priority (**dr_pri**) changes, the router immediately reruns its Designated Router calculation, assuming that the interface is already past the **IFS_WAIT** (Waiting) state. This logic handles the cases when the router is newly eligible (or ineligible) to become Designated Router.

Major changes cause the router to restart the interface, setting its state to Down, deleting any associated neighbors, and starting the interface state machine again with the up event. These major changes have to do with either which LSAs are flooded over the interface (changes to **area_id**, **demand**, and **passive**) or how the interface is represented internal to the implementation (**IfType**). Changes to the way multicast datagrams are forwarded over the interface (**mc_fwd**) cause the deletion of the MOSPF routing cache, as the path of multicast datagrams may change accordingly.

13.3 Cryptographic Authentication Keys

Cryptographic authentication keys are added and deleted from an OSPF interface by using the entry point **OSPF::cfgAuKey(struct CfgAuKey *key, int status)**. The interface to which the key is to be associated is identified by the IP address **CfgAuKey::address** or, for unnumbered interfaces, the physical interface number **CfgAuKey::phyint**. Multiple keys can be present simultaneously on an interface, with each key identified by its **CfgAuKey::key_id**. For example, when smoothly transitioning a network segment from one key to another, both the old and the new keys would overlap for some time. The authentication algorithm used for all keys is the MD5 message digest algorithm in [91]. The configurable parameters for each cryptographic authentication key are described in Table 13.3.

Table 13.3 Configuration of an Authentication Key: **struct CfgAuKey**

CfgAuKey Member	Description
auth_key	The 16-octet secret used to generate and to verify the MD5 message digests, or signatures, that are appended to each OSPF packet when using OSPF cryptographic authentication.
start_accept	The number of seconds from now when the router will start accepting packets signed with this key.
start_generate	The number of seconds from now when the router is allowed to sign transmitted packets with this key. When the router could possibly use two or more keys, the one with the later **start_generate** is chosen.
stop_generate	The number of seconds before the router will stop signing transmitted packets with this key. When equal to **0**, the key will always be legal for signing packets.
stop_accept	The number of seconds before the router will stop accepting packets signed with this key. If set to **0**, the router will always accept packets signed with the key.

Cryptographic keys cannot be configured via the OSPF MIB, as SNMP is not considered a secure enough mechanism for configuring secret keys. Therefore, the parameters cited have no MIB equivalents. In our OSPF implementation, cryptographic keys cannot be configured for virtual links. There are no immediate consequences on addition or deletion of a cryptographic authentication key, although the rules governing packet reception change accordingly.

13.4 Area Parameters

Areas are added and deleted from the OSPF router's configuration by using the entry point `OSPF::cfgArea(struct CfgArea *msg, int status)`. The area is identified by its OSPF Area ID `CfgArea::area_id`. The parameters that can be configured for an area are listed in Table 13.4.

Table 13.4 Configurable Area Parameters: `struct CfgArea`

`cfgArea` Member (MIB Equivalent)	Description
`stub` (ospfImportAsExtern*)	If nonzero, the area is an OSPF stub area and will not originate or flood AS-external-LSAs. Default value = `0`.
`dflt_cost` (ospfStubMetric*)	If the area is a stub area and if the router is an area border router, the type-3 default summary-LSA originated into the stub area by the router will advertise this value as cost. Default value = `1`.
`import_summs` (ospfAreaSummary*)	If equal to `0` and if the area is a stub area, the router will refuse to originate summary-LSAs into the stub area. Default value = `1`.

An OSPF area can be added implicitly to the router's configuration by adding other configuration items referencing an undefined area. An example would be adding an interface to area 0.0.0.2 when it had not been previously referenced in an `OSPF::cfgArea()` call. In these cases, the area is created with the default values shown in Table 13.4.

Deleting an area forces the router to delete all the attached interfaces and the area's link-state database. The routing calculation will be rerun, any routes associated with the area will be removed from the routing table, and summary-LSAs for the deleted area's network segments will be flushed from the other areas.

A change in an active area's stub status changes the set of LSAs that the router can keep in its database and flood throughout the area, adding or deleting AS-external-LSAs. To accomplish this and to maintain synchronization with its neighbors, the router forces all its interfaces to the area into a Down state, deletes its link-state database for the area, and then brings the interfaces back up. Neighbor relationships are then reestablished, and the database for the area is relearned.

If you change the `dflt_cost` parameter for a stub area, the router reoriginates the default summary-LSA into the area. If you change the `import_summs` parameter for the stub area, the router reevaluates which summary-LSAs should be originated into the area, originating or flushing LSAs as necessary.

13.5   Area Route Aggregation

Route aggregation can be configured in an area border router by using the `OSPF::cfgRnge(struct CfgRnge *msg, int status)` entry point. Each aggregation directive is identified by the area whose routes are being aggregated (`CfgRnge::area_id`) and the aggregated prefix that will be advertised to other areas, expressed in network (`CfgRnge::net`) and mask (`CfgRnge::mask`) format.

When one or more of the area's reachable network segments fall under a configured aggregated prefix, the component network segments will not be advertised to other areas in separate summary-LSAs. Instead, a single summary-LSA for the aggregate prefix will be advertised, with cost equal to the distance to the farthest component. However, if `CfgRnge::no_adv` is nonzero, the summary-LSA for the aggregate will also be suppressed, hiding all the component segments from the other areas.

We allow the configuration of overlapping aggregates. For example, the aggregates 10/8 and 10.1/16 could be configured for area 0.0.0.2. By suppressing the advertisement of the less specific aggregate 10/8, we could hide all the net-10 subnets in area 0.0.0.2 except those matching 10.1/16.

Deleting, adding, or modifying an area aggregate causes the router to reevaluate all summary-LSAs falling under the aggregate, originating and/or flushing summary-LSAs as appropriate. Changes to these LSAs will cause the router to rerun its routing calculations, adding or deleting discard entries from the routing table in the process.

13.6   Virtual Link Parameters

Virtual links are configured to establish or to enhance connectivity of the single backbone area 0.0.0.0. Virtual links are added, modified, or deleted through the `OSPF::cfgVL(struct CfgVL *msg, int status)` entry point. Each virtual link is identified by the combination of the nonzero area providing the virtual link's transit services (`CfgVL::transit_area`) and the Router ID of the OSPF router at the other end of the virtual link (`CfgVL::nbr_id`). The rest of the configurable parameters for a virtual link, a subset of those configurable for physical interfaces (Table 13.2), are summarized in Table 13.5.

Table 13.5 Configurable Virtual Link Parameters: `struct CfgVL`

CfgVL Member (MIB Equivalent)	Description
`xmt_dly` (ospfVirtIfTransitDelay)	Transmission delay for LSAs flooded over the virtual link, in seconds. Must be at least `1`.
`rxmt_int` (ospfVirtIfRetransInterval)	Number of seconds before unacknowledged LSAs will be retransmitted to the virtual neighbor.
`hello_int` (ospfVirtIfHelloInterval)	Interval between OSPF Hellos sent over the virtual link, in seconds.
`dead_int` (ospfVirtIfRtrDeadInterval)	Number of seconds to detect an inoperational virtual neighbor, due to lack of Hellos from said neighbor.
`auth_type` (ospfVirtIfAuthType)	The authentication mechanism used for packets sent and received over the virtual link. One of `AUT_NONE` (no authentication) or `AUT_PASSWD` (simple cleartext password).
`auth_key` (ospfVirtIfAuthKey)	When using simple cleartext authentication, the 8-octet password used in OSPF packets.

Deleting a virtual link will destroy the adjacency with the virtual neighbor, causing the router to reoriginate its backbone router-LSA. If this was the only virtual link using `CfgVL::transit_area` as its transit area, the router will reoriginate the router-LSA for the transit area as well, this time with bit V turned off.

Adding a virtual link does not have an immediate effect. However, if the configured endpoint is reachable through the configured transit area, the router will begin bringing up the adjacency by sending Hellos to the newly configured virtual neighbor.

13.7 Nonbroadcast Neighbors

It may be necessary to statically configure neighbors on nonbroadcast network segments—either NBMA or Point-to-MultiPoint—as neighbor relationships cannot be discovered on these segments through broadcast/multicast services. A neighbor is configured through the `cfgNbr(struct CfgNbr *msg, int status)` entry point.

Each neighbor is identified by its IP interface address on the nonbroadcast network segment: `CfgNbr::nbr_addr`. On NBMA networks, the router must know which neighbors are eligible to become Designated Router, so it can send Hellos to the eligible routers in an effort to maintain a consistent view of the segment's Designated Router. To that end, a neighbor's Designated Router Priority is configured (`CfgNbr::dr_eligible`), although the only important data point is whether the neighbor's Priority is nonzero.

When a static neighbor is deleted, the neighbor relationship is destroyed. However, the relationship may reappear if Hellos are received from the neighbor, which would be the case if the router were still configured as a neighbor in the neighboring router. Conversely, if an existing dynamic neighbor is converted to a statically configured one, the neighbor relationship is torn down and reestablished, due to the incompatibilities in the internal storage of dynamic versus static neighbors.

13.8 Loopback Addresses and Attached Hosts

You can configure prefixes that will be advertised as stub networks in one of the router's router-LSAs. These prefixes may be addresses belonging to the router itself, perhaps assigned to the router's loopback interface. Or they may be addresses assigned to directly attached hosts that themselves do not run OSPF, and so the router is advertising their addresses by proxy. In either case, we call these prefixes *host routes*. Host routes are added/deleted through the `OSPF::cfgHost(struct CfgHost *msg, int status)` entry point.

The host route is identified by its prefix (`CfgHost::net` and `CfgHost::mask`) and the area that you want to advertise it in (`CfgHost::area_id`). You are allowed to add the same host prefix to multiple areas, by configuring multiple host routes. However, when a host route's configured area is currently unattached, it will be advertised in one of the attached areas' router-LSAs instead. This makes configuring a host prefix in multiple areas unnecessary and ensures that host routes always remain reachable in the OSPF domain, which is the usually desired property for addresses assigned to a router's loopback interface.

The host route will be advertised in the appropriate router-LSA with a cost of `CfgHost::cost`. The range of allowable values is between 0 and 65,535, inclusive.

Addition or deletion of a host route will cause the router to reoriginate the appropriate router-LSA.

13.9 External Routes

A prefix that you wish to be imported into the OSPF domain as an external route, and therefore advertised by the router in an AS-external-LSA, is configured through the `OSPF::cfgExRt(struct CfgExRt *msg, int status)` entry point. These routes may be configured by a human operator, in which case they are called static routes, or imported from another TCP/IP routing protocol, generally based on human-specified pattern-matching rules. The prefix that you wish imported is specified by `CfgExRt::net` and `CfgExRt::mask`. The rest of the parameters that can be configured for an imported external route are shown in Table 13.6. Configuration of imported routes is covered by the IP Forwarding Table MIB [4], and we reference the related elements in that MIB in Table 13.6. Only a single external route (next hop, cost, and so on) can be configured for any prefix.

Table 13.6 Configuration of Imported External Routes: `struct CfgExRt`

`CfgExRt` Member (Forwarding MIB Equivalent)	Description
`type2` (ipCidrRouteMetric2*)	If equal to `1`, the prefix will be advertised using an OSPF external type-2 metric. If `0`, it will be advertised using an external type-1 metric.
`mc`	If equal to `1`, the prefix will be advertised as a source of multicast datagrams. Used only when running MOSPF.
`direct`	If equal to `1`, the prefix belongs to a locally attached subnet that is not running OSPF. These prefixes are installed in the local routing table as direct routes but are *not* imported into the OSPF routing domain.
`noadv`	If equal to `1`, the prefix will be installed in the routing table but will *not* be imported into the OSPF routing domain.
`cost` (ipCidrRouteMetric1)	The cost of the route, translated into the OSPF metric (external type 1 or type 2, as defined by `CfgExRt::type2`). Range between `0` and `2**24-1`, inclusive.
`phyint` (ipCidrRouteIfIndex)	The physical interface out which packets destined for the prefix will be forwarded. Ignored if `CfgExRt::gw` is reachable through an intradomain OSPF path.
`gw` (ipCidrRouteNextHop)	The next-hop address to be used for packets forwarded to the destination prefix. If reachable via intradomain OSPF routing, will also be used as the forwarding address in OSPF AS-external-LSAs.
`tag`	The 32-bit external route tag to be advertised in the prefix's AS-external-LSA. Recommended tag settings in [106] are not enforced.

Processing of a configured external route is a two-step process.

1. The next hop and the outgoing interface specified for the external route are validated. If the next hop is not reachable via intradomain OSPF routing *and* the outgoing physical interface is not operational, the configured external route is not used. It is kept in the router's configuration, however, and will be used when changing conditions warrant.

2. The configured cost of the route is compared to any other routes learned for the prefix through OSPF. If the configured cost is better, the route is added to the router's routing table as a static route and is advertised in an AS-external-LSA. If the configured cost is the same as that advertised by another router, the tie-breakers in Section 12.4.4.1 of [75] are observed if appropriate; otherwise, the configured route takes preference.

13.10 Graceful Exit

When you are intentionally removing an OSPF router from service for, say, periodic maintenance, you would like to do so with as little disruption as possible. You would like for the other routers to immediately route around the router you are removing and for its LSAs to be deleted immediately from the other routers' databases rather than having them continue to consume resources in those routers for up to an hour. The OSPF implementation has such a procedure, which we have called *orderly shutdown*, or *graceful exit*. Graceful exit is invoked by calling the API routine `OSPF::shutdown()`, (Figure 13.2).

```
                                                                      — ospf.C
644 void OSPF::shutdown(int seconds)
646 {
647     AreaIterator aiter(this);
648     SpfArea *a;
649
650     if (shutdown_phase)
651         return;
653     shutdown_phase++;
654     // Set timer
655     countdown = seconds;
656     // Flush self-originated LSAs
657     flush_self_orig(FindLSdb(0, LST_ASL));
658     while ((a = aiter.get_next())) {
659         flush_self_orig(FindLSdb(a, LST_RTR));
660         flush_self_orig(FindLSdb(a, LST_SUMM));
661         flush_self_orig(FindLSdb(a, LST_ASBR));
662         flush_self_orig(FindLSdb(a, LST_GM));
663     }
664 }
                                                                      — ospf.C
```

Figure 13.2 Invoking OSPF's graceful exit: `OSPF::shutdown()`.

13.10.1 `OSPF::shutdown()`

This procedure implements the first phase of graceful exit.

644   The graceful-exit procedure requires cooperation of the neighboring routers, which flood flush requests for the router's self-originated LSAs to the rest of the network. If the neighboring routers do not acknowledge these flush requests, the graceful-exit procedure can last indefinitely. To limit the procedure's extent, the maximum length of the procedure is passed to this routine as the argument **seconds**. When the maximum

length is set to `0`, the router will exit on the next 1-second timer tick, regardless of whether the graceful-exit procedure has completed.

650-653   The graceful-exit procedure is executed in phases. The current phase is indicated by `shutdown_phase`. If on entry to `OSPF::shutdown()` the router is already in the process of shutting down (`shutdown_phase != 0`), the router ignores the redundant shutdown request. It should also be noted that as long as the router is undergoing shutdown, it will refuse to (re)originate any LSAs (see Section 7.1.1).

657-663   In this first phase of graceful exit, all the router's self-originated LSAs are flushed from the routing domain, except any network-LSAs that the router may have originated. This action will cause all routers to immediately route packets around the exiting router, as its router-LSA will be removed from their network map. We don't want to flush network-LSAs yet, however; the router cannot relinquish any Designated Router duties because of the need to maintain flooding during the flush, and hence flushing network-LSAs would prevent forwarding between other routers attached to the associated network segment.

The next phase of graceful exit is entered when either (1) the LSAs that are trying to be flushed have been acknowledged and therefore deleted from the database, indicated by the list `OSPF::MaxAge_list` becoming empty, or (2) the time `seconds` elapses. The next phase, and in fact all further phases, are invoked by calling `OSPF::shutdown_continue()` (Figure 13.3).

13.10.2 `OSPF::shutdown_continue()`

This procedure implements the follow-on to the first phase.

680-686   In the second phase of graceful exit, any network-LSAs that have been originated are flushed. This potentially disrupts traffic, so only 1 second elapses before the next stage.

689-690   In the third and last stage, the router sends out empty Hellos. This will immediately relinquish Designated Router and Backup Designated Router duties, forcing new routers to originate network-LSAs and to take up responsibility for reliable flooding over the segment. Also, any adjacencies with neighboring routers will be dropped immediately, guaranteeing that neighbors won't waste time retransmitting Link State Update packets to the exiting router after it has departed.

692-704   In the last stage, the OSPF implementation also withdraws any routes that it has installed in the system's kernel routing table. This handles the case of shutting down routing but wanting the node to stay up and to act like a host.

706   `OspfSysCalls::halt()` is used to terminate the OSPF program, additionally informing the system of the fact.

```
                                                                   ospf.C
669 void OSPF::shutdown_continue()
671 {
672     AreaIterator aiter(this);
673     IfcIterator iiter(this);
674     SpfArea *a;
675     SpfIfc *ip;
676     INrte *rte;
677     INiterator iter(inrttbl);
678
679     switch(shutdown_phase++) {
680       case 1:
681         // Reset timer
682         countdown = 1;
683         // Flush network-LSAs
684         while ((a = aiter.get_next()))
685             flush_self_orig(FindLSdb(a, LST_NET));
686         break;
687       case 2:
688         // Send empty Hellos
689         while((ip = iiter.get_next()))
690             ip->send_hello(true);
691         // Withdraw routing entries
692         while ((rte = iter.nextrte())) {
693             switch(rte->type()) {
694               case RT_SPF:
695               case RT_SPFIA:
696               case RT_EXTT1:
697               case RT_EXTT2:
698               case RT_STATIC:
699                 sys->rtdel(rte->net(), rte->mask(), rte->last_mpath);
700                 break;
701               default:
702                 break;
703             }
704         }
705         // Exit program
706         sys->halt(0, "Shutdown complete");
707         break;
708       default:
709         sys->halt(0, "Shutdown complete");
710         break;
711     }
712 }
                                                                   ospf.C
```

Figure 13.3 The other phases of graceful exit: `OSPF::shutdown_continue()`.

13.11 Rereading Entire Configuration

We provide the option of downloading a completely new configuration into the OSPF router, with minimal disruption, and deleting those configuration items that are no longer mentioned. The mechanism that performs this rereading consists of the **class ConfigItem** and the entry points **OSPF::cfgStart()** and **OSPF::cfgDone()**. The Linux **ospfd** routing daemon described in Chapter 14, A Routing Daemon for Linux, uses this mechanism to reread its configuration from the disk file **/etc/ospfd.conf** each time it receives a **SIGHUP** signal.

The **class ConfigItem** (Figure 13.4) is inherited by all OSPF classes that contain configuration data. These classes are **class OSPF** (global configuration data), **class SpfArea** (OSPF area configuration), **class Range** (configured area aggregates), **class HostAddr** (configured host or loopback addresses), **class SpfIfc** (interface configuration data), **class CryptK** (configured cryptographic authentication keys), **class StaticNbr** (statically configured neighbors), and **class ExRtData** (external routing data to be imported into OSPF). When constructed, all these classes containing configuration data are enqueued on the global doubly linked list **ConfigItem *cfglist** implemented by the class members **ConfigItem::next** and **ConfigItem::prev**.

── config.h

```
25 class ConfigItem {
26     ConfigItem *prev;
27     ConfigItem *next;
28 protected:
29     int updated;
30 public:
31     ConfigItem();
32     virtual ~ConfigItem();
33     virtual void clear_config() = 0;
34     friend class OSPF;
35 };
```

── config.h

Figure 13.4 Base class inherited by all configurable OSPF classes: **class ConfigItem**.

To download a new configuration, one calls **OSPF::cfgStart()** to checkpoint the current configuration; provides a new set of configuration data, using the **OSPF::cfgXXX()** routines; and then calls **OSPF::cfgDone()** to tell the OSPF implementation that the reconfiguration has completed. The entry point **OSPF::cfgStart()** runs through global list **cfglist**, setting **ConfigItem::updated** to **false** in each configurable class to indicate that the class has not yet been mentioned in the new configuration.

When a class's configuration is updated, its configuration routine then sets **ConfigItem::updated** to **true**; for example, the interface configuration routine

`OSPF::cfgIfc()` sets the referenced interface class's `SpfIfc::updated` member to
`true`. After the reconfiguration, `OSPF::cfgDone()` goes back through the global list
`cfglist`, calling the virtual function `ConfigItem::clear_config()` for all those configurable classes that have not been mentioned by the reconfiguration; these are simply
the classes with `ConfigItem::updated` still set to `false`. Usually, the `clear_config()`
function simply deletes the class, but sometimes it reinstates the configuration of an
OSPF component to a default state. An example of the latter can be seen in
`OSPF::clear_config()`.

13.12 Host Wiretapping

One of the weakest parts of the IP stack is the determination by hosts of the correct
router (also in this context called gateway, for historical reasons) to send data packets
having off-net destinations. Architecturally, the host has a list of routers, either configured statically or learned dynamically through ICMP Router Discovery [20]. Off-net
data packets are initially sent to one of the routers, although possibly not the optimal
router. If a suboptimal router is chosen, an ICMP redirect [78] is sent back to the host,
informing it of the better router to use for future packets. The host is then in charge of
maintaining a cache of redirects, deleting them when they are no longer valid.

What is the problem with this approach? First, when the routing topology changes,
especially when one of the locally attached routers becomes unavailable, the ICMP redirect cache is slow to react. Second, the redirect mechanism does not help multihomed
hosts (those hosts with multiple network interfaces) choose which interface to use when
sending off-net packets.

For this reason, hosts commonly run routing protocols to determine the next-hop
router to use for off-net packets. Typically, RIP is used, embodied, for example, in the
`routed` program used by hosts running a variant of UNIX. The hosts need only *listen* to
the routing updates generated by the routers, leading to the terms "wiretapping" or
"listen-only" for the hosts' limited participation in the routing.

In fact, RIP is so commonly used to download the routing information into hosts
that even if the routers are running OSPF as their routing protocol, they are often configured to additionally send RIP updates solely for the benefit of their local hosts. To avoid
the necessity of running a second routing protocol just for the hosts' benefit, we have
included a "listen-only" implementation of OSPF that hosts can run. We also call this
running OSPF in *host mode*.

13.12.1 Requirements

When a host is participating in a routing protocol, you would like to make the following
three functional requirements in order to ensure that your routing system continues to
function smoothly.

1. You don't want the host to appear as a router in the routing system. In particu-
    lar, you don't want your real routers to forward any traffic to the hosts except
    the traffic destined for the host itself.

2. You don't want the host to increase the resource demands on the routers and/or
    network as a result of the host's participating in the routing protocol.

3. You don't want the hosts to play any crucial part in the routing algorithm. In
    particular, hosts may be administered separately from the routers, and you
    don't want a host going up and down (which the router administrator may be
    helpless to prevent) to disrupt the routing system in any way.

13.12.2 Mechanisms

The host mode of OSPF is implemented in the following pieces.

-   Host mode is configured by setting the global parameter `CfgGen::host_mode`
    to a nonzero value; you can tell whether the OSPF software is currently in host
    mode by examining `OSPF::host_mode`. See Section 13.1 for the configuration of
    global parameters.

-   If you change the OSPF implementation to host mode while it is running (that
    is, perform a dynamic reconfiguration), you essentially restart OSPF processing,
    freeing the current link-state database and resynchronizing with the neighbor-
    ing routers (`OSPF::cfgOspf()`).

-   In host mode, we disable IP forwarding within the system's operating system
    kernel by calling `OspfSysCalls::ip_forward(false)`.

-   When in host mode, the router refuses to originate any LSAs. If the change to
    host mode has just been made, the host will receive its previously originated
    LSAs when it resynchronizes with its neighbors. It will flush these LSAs. Refus-
    ing to originate LSAs while in host mode is a simple operation: We simply
    ensure that, while in host mode, `OSPF::ospf_get_seqno()`, the first operation
    in (re)originating any LSA, returns a failure indication. See Section 7.1 for all the
    details concerning LSA origination.

-   When in host mode, the host must never be elected Designated Router on its
    attached network segments. This is accomplished by forcing an advertisement
    of a DR Priority of 0 in the host's Hello packets (`SpfIfc::build_hello()`) and
    by making sure that the host disqualifies itself in its own Designated Router cal-
    culation (`SpfIfc::ifa_elect()`).

-   When in host mode, the host initializes the intra-area routing calculation
    (implemented with Dijkstra's algorithm) differently. Normally, it starts the cal-
    culation by putting its router-LSA on the Dijkstra candidate list. In host mode,

however, it has no router-LSA and so puts the LSAs associated with attached network segments or, if the network segment is a point-to-point link, the LSA associated with the adjacent router, on the candidate list. See Section 11.2.4 for details.

How does this implementation of OSPF host mode meet the requirements for host wiretapping set forth in the previous section? Requirement 1 is met, as a host that does not originate any LSAs will not be included in the routers' routing calculation and so will not be installed as a next hop for any addresses. Requirement 2 is partially met. Because we want to be sure that the host has an accurate routing table, we have it synchronize link-state databases with the local OSPF routers. This adds flooding traffic to the local network segment but not beyond. Also, on broadcast and NBMA segments, the host's Router ID will be added to the local segment's network-LSA, increasing the size of the link-state database by 4 bytes for all routers. Requirement 3 is met by preventing the host from becoming the segment's Designated Router. At worst, a host going up and down will cause one or two LSAs to be modified, but the temporary unreachability that can occur as the result of a Designated Router change will not occur.

Running host-mode OSPF in the hosts does increase the configuration load on the network administrator. The administrator will have to configure the hosts' OSPF interface parameters to match the routers' and to assign each participating host an OSPF Router ID.

13.13 Monitor Interface

Various state information about the OSPF implementation can be obtained dynamically through the entry point `OSPF::monitor(struct MonMsg *msg, byte type, int size, int conn_id)`. In the two sample ports provided with the OSPF implementation, the `ospfd` routing daemon for Linux (Chapter 14, A Routing Daemon for Linux) and the OSPF routing simulator (Chapter 15, An OSPF Simulator), this monitoring interface has been combined with the packetized TCP support (`class TcpPkt` in Chapter 5, Building Blocks) to provide monitoring through a command line interface or a Web browser. For more information, see the `ospfd_mon` and `ospfd_browser` man pages in Appendix A, Manual Pages.

Every call to the monitoring entry point elicits a call to the monitoring response routine `OspfSysCalls::monitor_response(struct MonMsg *rsp, uns16 type, int size, int conn_id)`, reporting the query results. The first argument to the monitoring entry point, `struct MonMsg`, carries most of the information specifying the request or response and is shown in Figure 13.5. If `MonMsg::hdr.exact` is nonzero, the query is equivalent to SNMP's "get"; if `0`, the query is a "get-next." The caller indicates the indices for the get or get-next operation in `MonMsg::body`. The second argument to the monitoring entry point, **type**, indicates the type of structure being queried, as indicated in Table 13.7.

Table 13.7 Monitoring Queries and Responses

Statistics	Query		Response	
	Argument **type**	Indices **MonMsg::body** Member	Argument **type**	Returned Data **MonMsg::body** Member
General	`MonReq_Stat`	n/a	`Stat_Response`	`StatRsp`
Area	`MonReq_Area`	`MonRqArea`	`Area_Response`	`AreaRsp`
Interface	`MonReq_Ifc`	`MonRqIfc`	`Ifc_Response`	`IfcRsp`
Virtual link	`MonReq_VL`	`MonRqVL`	`Ifc_Response`	`IfcRsp`
Neighbor	`MonReq_Nbr`	`MonRqNbr`	`Nbr_Response`	`NbrRsp`
Virtual neighbor	`MonReq_VLNbr`	`MonRqVL`	`Nbr_Response`	`NbrRsp`
LSA	`MonReq_LSA`	`MonRqLsa`	`LSA_Response`	`MonRqLsa`
Routing table entry	`MonReq_Rte`	`MonRqRte`	`Rte_Response`	`RteRsp`

In the monitoring response, **MonMsg::hdr.retcode** indicates success (**0**) or failure (**1**), and the returned statistics are contained in **MonMsg::body**. The **type** argument indicates the kind of information returned (Table 13.7). The **conn_id** argument echoes that in the original request, enabling multiple monitoring sessions to be active at once, each with a separate **conn_id**. Responses can be matched to queries by comparing **MonMsg::hdr.id**.

All statistics are returned in network byte order. Brief descriptions of the statistics returned are contained in the following sections.

13.13.1 General Statistics

StatRsp::n_ase_import is the number of AS-external-LSAs that the router itself is currently importing into the OSPF router domain. The router is an ASBR if and only if this number is nonzero. The router runs the Dijkstra calculation on all areas at once, with **StatRsp::n_dijkstra** counting the number of times this calculation is performed; equivalently, this is the number of times the complete routing table calculation has been performed. The number of areas to which the router is currently attached is given by **StatRsp::n_area**; the router is an area border router if and only if this number is greater than **1**. **StatRsp::n_dbx_nbrs** is the number of neighbors with which the router is currently undergoing Database Exchange; while nonzero, the router will hold on to

—————————————————————————————————— config.h

```
179  struct MonHdr {
180      byte version;
181      byte retcode;
182      byte exact;
183      byte id;
184  };
185
186  struct MonMsg {
187      MonHdr hdr;
188      union {
189          MonRqArea arearq;// Requests
190          MonRqIfc ifcrq;
191          MonRqVL vlrq;
192          MonRqNbr nbrrq;
193          MonRqLsa lsarq;
194          MonRqRte rtrq;
195
196          StatRsp statrsp;// Responses
197          AreaRsp arearsp;
198          IfcRsp ifcrsp;
199          NbrRsp nbrsp;
200          RteRsp rtersp;
201      } body;
202  };
```

—————————————————————————————————— config.h

Figure 13.5 Information carried in monitoring requests and responses: `struct MonMsg`.

any MaxAge LSAs in its database. If the router is running MOSPF, `StatRsp::mospf` is set to `1`; otherwise, it is set to `0`. Likewise, `StatRsp::inter_area_mc` indicates whether the router is forwarding multicast datagrams across area borders; `StatRsp::inter_AS_mc`, whether the router is forwarding multicast datagrams to/from other routing domains; and `StatRsp::overflow_state`, whether the router is currently in Database Overflow state. The major and minor release numbers of the OSPF implementation are given by `StatRsp::vmajor` and `StatRsp::vminor`, respectively; the software on the CD-ROM is labeled with version 0.1.

The rest of the general statistics come right out of the ospfGeneralGroup of the OSPF MIB [5]: ospfRouterId (`StatRsp::router_id`), ospfExternLsaCount (`StatRsp::n_aselsas`), and ospfExternLsaCksumSum (`StatRsp::asexsum`). `StatRsp::extdb_limit` is analogous to ospfExtLsdbLimit, the only difference being that the reserved value indicating no limit on the number of AS-external-LSAs in the database is `0` for the former and `-1` for the latter.

13.13.2 Area Statistics

The area whose statistics you wish to see is specified by its OSPF Area ID **MonRqArea::area_id**. Returned area statistics are contained in **struct AreaRsp**. The number of router interfaces that have been configured to attach to the area is given by **AreaRsp::n_cfgifcs**, with **AreaRsp::n_ifcs** counting the currently operational subset. The number of routers currently reachable inside the area is given by **AreaRsp::n_routers**, with the router counting itself as one. The LSAs in the area's link-state database are enumerated by LS Type: **AreaRsp::n_rtrlsas** for router-LSAs, **AreaRsp::n_netlsas** for network-LSAs, **AreaRsp::n_summlsas** for summary-LSAs, **AreaRsp::n_asbrlsas** for ASBR-summary-LSAs, and **AreaRsp::n_grplsas** for group-membership-LSAs. If nonzero, **AreaRsp::transit** indicates that the area is supporting one or more virtual links, **AreaRsp::demand** indicates that all the routers in the area support the Demand Circuit Extensions to OSPF [64], **AreaRsp::stub** indicates that the area is an OSPF stub area, and **AreaRsp::import_summ** indicates that summary-LSAs will be originated into the area (the latter can be turned off only for stub areas). **AreaRsp::n_ranges** indicates the number of area aggregates (ospfAreaAggregateEntry in the OSPF MIB) that have been configured for the area. **AreaRsp::area_id** and **AreaRsp::dbxsum** are the equivalents of the OSPF MIB variables ospfAreaId and ospfAreaLsaCksumSum, respectively.

13.13.3 Interface Statistics

An interface is specified by its IP address **MonRqIfc::if_addr** or, if the interface is unnumbered, by its physical interface number **MonRqIfc::phyint**. Requests for numbered interfaces should set **MonRqIfc::phyint** to **-1**.

Returned interface statistics are contained in **struct IfcRsp**. Most of the interface statistics are right out of the OSPF MIB, namely, ospfIfIpAddress (**IfcRsp::if_addr**), ospfAddressLessIf (**IfcRsp::if_IfIndex**), ospfIfAreaId (**IfcRsp::area_id**), ospfIfRtrPriority (**IfcRsp::if_drpri**), ospfIfTransitDelay (**IfcRsp::if_xdelay**), ospfIfRetransInterval (**IfcRsp::if_rxmt**), ospfIfHelloInterval (**IfcRsp::if_hint**), ospfIfRtrDeadInterval (**IfcRsp::if_dint**), ospfIfPollInterval (**IfcRsp::if_pint**), ospfIfDesignatedRouter (**IfcRsp::if_dr**), ospfIfBackupDesignatedRouter (**IfcRsp::if_bdr**), ospfIfAuthType (**IfcRsp::if_autype**), and ospfIfMetricValue (**IfcRsp::if_cost**).

IfcRsp::if_phyint gives the interface's physical interface number (Section 4.2). For numbered interfaces, the IP subnet mask is given by **IfcRsp::if_mask**. The maximum-sized IP packet that can be forwarded out the interface without fragmentation is listed in **IfcRsp::mtu**; this value is advertised in Database Description packets sent out the interface. The interface is a demand-based circuit if and only if **IfcRsp::if_demand** is nonzero; flooding of LSA refreshes, and possibly Hellos, will be suppressed on these interfaces. The method for forwarding multicast datagrams out the interface is given by `IfcRsp::if_mcfwd`, with a value of 0 indicating that multicast forwarding out the interface is prohibited, 1 indicating that they use the standard data-link multicast encapsulation, and 2 that they are forwarded as data-link unicasts. `IfcRsp::if_nnbrs` is the number of active neighbors associated with the interface, with `IfcRsp::if_nfull` counting the fully adjacent subset. An ASCII string describing the interface's state, in terms of the standard OSPF interface FSM, is given by `IfcRsp::if_state`, with strings describing the OSPF interface type and the name of the underlying physical interface given by `IfcRsp::type` and `IfcRsp::phyname`, respectively.

13.13.4 Virtual Link Statistics

A virtual link is requested by its transit area (`MonRqVL::transit_area`) and the OSPF Router ID of its other endpoint(`MonRqVL::endpoint_id`). The returned statistics use the same data structure, `struct IfcRsp`, as used for regular OSPF interfaces. In this data structure, the two items that are specific to virtual links, `IfcRsp::transit_id` and `IfcRsp::endpt_id`, correspond to the variables ospfVirtIfAreaId and ospfVirtIfNeighbor in the standard OSPF MIB.

13.13.5 Neighbor Statistics

A neighbor is requested by its associated interface's physical interface number (`MonRqNbr::phyint`) and the neighbor's IP address (`MonRqNbr::nbr_addr`). Both indexes must be set correctly; the get-next function can always be used to discover the values if they are not known.

Several of the reported statistics are variables from the OSPF MIB: ospfNbrIpAddr (`NbrRsp::n_addr`), ospfNbrRtrId (`NbrRsp::n_id`), ospfNbrOptions (`NbrRsp::n_opts`), ospfNbrPriority (`NbrRsp::n_pri`), and ospfNbrLsRetransQLen (`NbrRsp::rxmt_count`).

`NbrRsp::phyint` is the physical interface number of the neighbor's associated interface. The number of LSAs remaining to be sent to the neighbor in Database Description packets is given by `NbrRsp::n_ddlst`, with `NbrRsp::n_rqlst` the number of updated LSAs that the router is requesting from the neighbor; both these statistics are nonzero only when the router is undergoing Database Exchange with the neighbor. `NbrRsp::n_rxmt_window` is the current maximum number of back-to-back Link State Update packets that the router would be willing to send to the neighbor. The neighbor's current opinion of the attached segment's Designated Router and Backup Designated Router is given by `NbrRsp::n_dr` and `NbrRsp::n_bdr`, respectively. The byte specifying master/slave status—Init and More bits in the last Database Description packet received from the neighbor—can be found in `NbrRsp::n_imms`. If `NbrRsp::n_adj_pend` is nonzero, the router intends to become fully adjacent to the neighbor but because of the rate-limit on simultaneous exchanges (Section 8.3) has not started the Database Exchange process. The ASCII string `NbrRsp::n_state` reports the state of the neighbor, according to the OSPF neighbor state machine. The name of the physical interface associated with the neighbor is indicated by `NbrRsp::phyname`.

13.13.6 Virtual Neighbor Statistics

A virtual neighbor is requested by its virtual link's transit area (`MonRqVL::transit_area`) and the OSPF Router ID of the link's other endpoint (`MonRqVL::endpoint_id`). Virtual neighbor statistics are returned in a `struct NbrRsp`, the same data structure that was used for regular neighbors. The two items that are specific to virtual neighbors are `NbrRsp::transit_id` and `NbrRsp::endpt_id`, which have OSPF MIB analogs ospfVirtNbrArea and ospfVirtNbrRtrId, respectively.

13.13.7 LSAs

A Link State Advertisement is identified by its containing OSPF Area ID (`MonRqLsa::area_id`) and its LS Type (`MonRqLsa::ls_type`), Link State ID (`MonRqLsa::ls_id`), and Advertising Router (`MonRqLsa::adv_rtr`). For AS-external-LSAs, the Area ID is ignored in requests and is set to 0.0.0.0 in replies. In a successful reply, the LSA's Area, LS Type, Link State ID, and Advertising Router are copied into the `MonMsg::body.lsarq` structure, followed immediately by the entire LSA, as it would appear when flooded onto a network segment.

13.13.8 Routing Table Entries

Routing table entries are requested by their prefixes, represented as a network number (`MonRqRte::net`) and mask (`MonRqRte::mask`). When the routing table entry for a prefix (`RteRsp::net` and `RteRsp::mask`) is returned, the following information is provided. An ASCII string `RteRsp::type` reports the type of route: *Direct* for directly attached subnets; *SPF* for intra-area routes; *SPFIA* for inter-area routes; *SPFE1* and *SPFE2* for routes learned from AS-external-LSAs with external type-1 and type-2 metrics, respectively; *Reject* for discard routes installed because of configured aggregates; and *Static* for configured routes that the router is itself importing in AS-external-LSAs. `RteRsp::cost` is the route's cost; for external type-2 routes, this is the type-2 metric component of the cost, with the internal cost to the advertising ASBR/forwarding address reported in `RteRsp::o_cost`. The tag advertised with the route is given by `RteRsp::tag`. `RteRsp::n_paths` equal-cost paths for the prefix are then appended, with each path represented by the name of the physical outgoing interface (`RteRsp::hops[].phyname`) and the IP address of the next hop (`RteRsp::hops[].gw`).

Exercises

13.1   Add to the configuration the ability to disable or to enable the logging of specific messages, based on their message number (see Chapter 5, Building Blocks).

13.2   How are `CfgExRt::type2` and ipCidrRouteMetric2 in the *IP Forwarding Table MIB* [4] related?

13.3   Implement the monitoring of the remaining variables in the OSPF MIB [5].

13.4   When implementing dynamic reconfiguration, care must be taken to make sure that deleted data structures are no longer referenced. Along these lines, fix the following bug. When an interface is deleted, its `class SpfIfc` should no longer be referenced in `SpfArea::ifmap`; nor should it be referenced in the next-hop database, which consists of a collection of `MPath` classes. (*Hint:* Make sure that `SpfArea::delete_from_ifmap()` is called to remove the interface from the area's interface map, and store the IP address of the interface in `struct NH` *instead* of a pointer to an `SpfIfc` class).

14

A Routing Daemon for Linux

This chapter discusses the port of the `ospfd` software to the Linux operating system, running on x86-based PCs. Installation of the software was discussed in Section 2.1. Configuration of the software is covered in Section 14.1. Section 14.2 discusses how to customize the configuration command syntax. Dynamic reconfiguration and the graceful shutdown of the `ospfd` software are covered in Sections 14.3 and 14.4, respectively. Monitoring the operation of `ospfd` software is the subject of Section 14.5. Limitations of the Linux port are itemized in Section 14.6. The chapter ends with a discussion of the porting details (Section 14.7).

14.1 The `ospfd` Configuration

The `ospfd` configuration is in the file `/etc/ospfd.conf`. The configuration file is organized into a three-level hierarchy, as indicated in Figure 14.1. At the top level are the global OSPF parameters, configuration of each OSPF area to which the router is attached, and external routes that the router should import into the OSPF routing domain. Within each area is the definition of any attached hosts belonging to the area, any virtual links using the area as transit area, the interfaces belonging to the area, and any address aggregation to be performed at the area's border. Within each interface appear any statically configured neighbors and the interface's authentication keys.

A simple example of an `ospfd` configuration file is shown in Figure 14.2. The router's OSPF Router ID has been set to 10.1.3.6, and the router has two interfaces. The

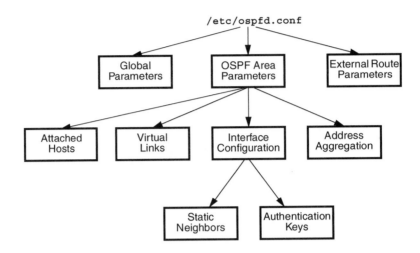

Figure 14.1 Hierarchical arrangement of the `ospfd` configuration file `/etc/ospfd.conf`.

first interface, with address 10.1.3.6 and cost 1, attaches to area 0.0.0.0. The second inter-face, having address 128.22.156.6 and cost 2, attaches to area 0.0.0.1. OSPF has a large number of possible configuration parameters. When parameters are not specified, such as the interface HelloInterval in this example, they are automatically set to the default values specified in the OSPF MIB [5].

```
routerid 10.1.3.6
area 0.0.0.0
interface 10.1.3.6 1
area 0.0.0.1
interface 128.22.156.6 2
```

Figure 14.2 Sample `ospfd` configuration file.

Most configuration commands are optional. To get the default behavior, you simply omit the associated command from the `ospfd` configuration file. However, the syntax of individual commands is quite unforgiving: When you do give a command, you must specify the command name exactly and include all arguments in their correct order.

14.1.1 Global Configuration

A list of the global configuration commands is shown in Figure 14.3. The **routerid** *id* command—the only command that *must* be present in the `ospfd` configuration file—sets the OSPF Router ID to *id* in IP address dotted decimal format. By convention, the

OSPF Router ID should be set to one of the IP addresses belonging to the Linux workstation.

```
routerid id
host_mode
ospfExtLsdbLimit count
mospf
no_inter_area_mc
ospfExitOverflowInterval seconds
ase_orig_rate count
lsu_rxmt_window count
dd_sessions count
log_level level
refresh_rate seconds
```

Figure 14.3 Global configuration commands.

If present, the `host_mode` command indicates that the `ospfd` software should run as a host instead of as a router (see Section 13.12). The `ospfExtLsdbLimit` and `ospfExit-OverflowInterval` commands are used to control the behavior of the OSPF Database Overflow extensions [68]; `ospfExtLsdbLimit` *count* sets the maximum number of non-default AS-external-LSAs that the router will keep in its link-state database to the value *count*. Setting the value to 0 means that the router sets no limit on the number of AS-external-LSAs, which is the default. The configuration command `ospfExitOverflow-Interval` *seconds* sets the number of seconds after entering the Overflow State before the router will attempt to reoriginate its self-originated nondefault AS-external-LSAs. Setting the value to 0 means that the router will never try to reoriginate its AS-external-LSAs; 300 seconds is the default.

The Multicast Extensions to OSPF (MOSPF, [66]) are enabled using the `mospf` command. This will turn the Linux machine into a multicast router, running MOSPF as its multicast routing protocol. If you do not want the multicast router to forward multicast datagrams across area boundaries, use the `no_inter_area_mc` command. The router determines whether it will be forwarding multicast datagrams across Autonomous System boundaries by the presence of imported external routes with the MC bit set (see Section 14.1.9).

When `ospfd` first starts up or when it is reconfigured to import more external routes, it will not import all of the routes at once. The `ase_orig_rate` *count* command sets the number of AS-external-LSAs that the router will originate per second. The default value is 1,000. See Section 10.3.2 for more details.

The `lsu_rxmt_window` *count* command sets the maximum number of back-to-back Link State Update packets that will be sent to the neighbor when retransmitting LSAs that the neighbor has failed to acknowledge. Its default value is 8. See Section 9.5 for more details.

The number of simultaneous Database Exchange sessions that the router will partic-ipate in is controlled by the **dd_sessions** *count* command. When set to *count*, the router will simultaneously perform *count* sessions that the router initiated and *count* sessions initiated by its neighbors. See Section 13.1 for details.

The **log_level** *level* command controls which logging messages will be printed in the file **/var/log/ospfd.log** (see Section 14.5). The refresh rate of the AS-external-LSAs originated by the router can be changed from the default of 30 minutes by the command **refresh_rate** *seconds*. This feature is implemented by using DoNotAge LSAs, as explained in Section 6.5.

14.1.2 Area Configuration

A list of the area configuration commands appears in Figure 14.4. Configuration of an area begins with the **area** *area_id* command, where *area_id* is the area's OSPF Area ID, formatted as an IP address. If the area is an OSPF stub area and if the router is an area border router, the **stub** *default_cost* command is used, where *default_cost* is the cost of the default summary-LSA that the router will import into the stub area. In a stub area, you can also turn off the origination of summary-LSAs into the area by using the **no_summaries** command.

Within the context of a given area, one must define all interfaces attaching to the area, hosts belonging to the area, virtual links using the area as transit area, and address aggregation for the area. After the area command for a given area, the configuration file remains in that area's context until the next area command appears in the file.

```
area area_id
stub default_cost
no_summaries
```

Figure 14.4 Area configuration commands.

14.1.3 Interface Configuration

An OSPF interface is configured by using the **interface** *identifier cost* command (Figure 14.5). The *identifier* can be either the interface's IP address or the Linux name of the interface, such as **wan0**. The *cost* argument is the metric that OSPF will advertise for the interface; it should be a number between 1 and 65,535, inclusive. The interface command must be given within the context of the area to which the interface attaches.

The **ospfd** software reads interface information out of the Linux kernel when it ini-tializes and when it is reconfigured. Configured OSPF interfaces are checked against those present in the kernel; those present in **/etc/ospfd.conf** but not in the kernel are ignored.

```
interface identifier cost
mtu size
IfIndex value
nbma
ptmp
ospfIfRtrPriority priority
ospfIfTransitDelay seconds
ospfIfRetransInterval seconds
ospfIfHelloInterval seconds
ospfIfRtrDeadInterval seconds
ospfIfPollInterval seconds
ospfIfAuthType type
ospfIfAuthKey string
ospfIfMulticastForwarding type
on-demand
passive
```

Figure 14.5 Interface configuration commands.

The OSPF interface type (ospfIfType in the OSPF MIB) is automatically set, depending on the interface information found in the Linux kernel. If the **POINTTOPOINT** flag is set in the kernel (look at the output of `ifconfig -a`), the interface defaults to a point-to-point interface; otherwise, if the **BROADCAST** flag is set in the kernel, the interface defaults to a broadcast interface, and all other interfaces default to NBMA interfaces. The **nbma** command can be used to change the type of any interface to NBMA. Similarly, the **ptmp** command changes the OSPF interface type to Point-to-MultiPoint.

The maximum transmission unit (MTU) for the interface is also read out of the Linux kernel but can be overridden by using the `mtu size` command, in which case the MTU should be specified as the maximum size, in bytes, of an IP packet that can be transmitted without fragmentation out the interface. The MTUs of the data links commonly in use in the Internet can be found in [61].

The MIB-II IfIndex value for the interface can be configured by using the `IfIndex value` command. The IfIndex is used for informational purposes only and then only when advertising unnumbered interfaces in the router-LSA.

The Designated Router Priority of an interface is specified by using the `ospfIf-RtrPriority priority` command. The default value of priority is `1`.

The various interface timers are configured by using commands whose names are the same as the associated OSPF MIB variables: `ospfIfTransitDelay, ospfIfRetransInterval, ospfIfHelloInterval, ospfIfRtrDeadInterval`, and `ospfIfPollInterval`. Their values are specified in seconds and default to the defaults in the OSPF MIB.

Null or simple password authentication is configured by using the `ospfIfAuthType type` and `ospfIfAuthKey string` commands. For null authentication, `type` is set to `0` (the default); for simple password, `type` is set to `1`. For simple password authentication, the password is given by an 8-octet or shorter value in *string*. Values less than 8 octets are padded with zeroes. Stronger authentication is configured separately by using the **md5key** command (Section 14.1.8).

When MOSPF is running to make the Linux box into a multicast router, the **ospfIfMulticastForwarding** *type* command is used to specify whether and, if so, how multicast data traffic is to be forwarded out the interface. Using the same values for *type* that are specified in the OSPF MIB, **1** (blocked) indicates that the interface should not be used for multicast forwarding, **2** (multicast, and the default) indicates that IP multicast datagrams should be forwarded as data-link multicasts, and **3** (unicast) indicates that IP multicast datagrams should be forwarded as data-link unicasts.

The **on-demand** command tells **ospfd** to treat the interface as connecting to a demand circuit [64]; as a result, it will attempt to suppress redundant flooding and Hellos sent over the interface. Links appropriate to treat as demand circuits include dial-up links, ISDN, and low-speed permanent circuits.

The **passive** command tells **ospfd** to advertise the interface in its router-LSA but not to send or to receive OSPF control traffic on the interface. Similar functionality can be achieved with the **host** command (Section 14.1.6).

Virtual links are configured separately. The use the **vlink** command (Section 14.1.5).

14.1.4 Area Aggregate Configuration

The **aggregate** *prefix* command (Figure 14.6) specifies that, instead of advertising each route separately, a collection of an area's network segments should be aggregated, advertising a single aggregated *prefix* to other areas. The prefix is specified in CIDR notation, such as 10.0.0.0/8. Optionally, you can use the **suppress** command to specify that the advertisement of the matching intra-area routes be suppressed. This enables addresses to remain private to a given area. This command is given within the context of the area whose network segments are to be aggregated.

```
aggregate prefix
suppress
```

Figure 14.6 Area aggregate configuration.

14.1.5 Virtual Link Configuration

OSPF virtual links are configured by using the **vlink** *endpoint* command (Figure 14.7). The *endpoint* argument is the OSPF Router ID of the area border router at the other end of the virtual link, expressed in dotted decimal notation. The virtual link's transit area is inferred from the current area context.

```
vlink endpoint
ospfVirtIfTransitDelay seconds
ospfVirtIfRetransInterval seconds
ospfVirtIfHelloInterval seconds
ospfVirtIfRtrDeadInterval seconds
ospfVirtIfAuthType type
ospfVirtIfAuthKey
```

Figure 14.7 Virtual link configuration.

The various virtual link timers are configured by using commands whose names are the same as those of the associated OSPF MIB variables: `ospfVirtIfTransitDelay`, `ospfVirtIfRetransInterval`, `ospfVirtIfHelloInterval`, and `ospfVirtIfRtrDead-Interval`. Their values are specified in seconds and default to the defaults in the OSPF MIB.

Null or simple password authentication for the virtual link is configured by using the `ospfVirtIfAuthType` *type* and `ospfVirtIfAuthKey` *string* commands. For null authentication, *type* is set to `0` (the default); for simple password, *type* is set to `1`. For simple password authentication, the password is given by an 8-octet or shorter value in *string*. Values less than 8 octets are padded with zeroes.

14.1.6 Host Configuration

The **host** *prefix cost* command is used to specify prefixes you want advertised in the router-LSA so that they will appear in routing tables as internal OSPF routes. If the Linux machine is being used for Internet access, the *prefix* could be a pool of addresses assigned to dial-up customers. Or, the *prefix* could be a loopback address assigned to the Linux machine itself. The *prefix* is formatted as a CIDR prefix (for example, 128.186.0.0/16), and *cost* is the metric that will be advertised for the prefix in the router's OSPF router-LSA. The prefix is assigned to an area according to the current area context.

14.1.7 Static Neighbors

Over nonbroadcast network segments that will connect more than two routers, it may be impossible to discover neighboring routers, forcing configuration of the identity of the other OSPF routers attaching to the nonbroadcast segment. (These networks can be run in either OSPF NBMA or Point-to-MultiPoint mode, depending on the interface configuration in Section 14.1.3.) This is accomplished with the **neighbor** *address priority* command: *address* is the neighbor's IP address on the nonbroadcast network and *priority* is the neighbor's Designated Router priority. Priority need not be exact, but it must reflect whether the neighbor is eligible to become Designated Router on the nonbroadcast segment; restricting *priority* to **0** (ineligible) or **1** (eligible) is sufficient. Also, *priority* must still be specified if the interface is in Point-to-MultiPoint mode, even though it will be ignored. The **neighbor** command should be given within its associated interface's context.

14.1.8 Authentication Keys

Nontrivial authentication on a network segment is achieved by specifying OSPF cryptographic authentication (Figure 14.8) on the interface to the segment, via the **md5key** *keyid secret* command. All OSPF routers on the segment must be configured with a *keyid* and *secret* combination in common (see Section 11.7 of [67]). The *keyid* identifies the key and is a number between 1 and 255, inclusive. The *secret* is a string of up to 16 octets long (if less, the remaining octets will be set to **0**). To maintain security, the *secret* must be known only to the OSPF routers attached to the network segment and to no one else.

```
md5key keyid key
startaccept date
startgenerate date
stopgenerate date
stopaccept date
```

Figure 14.8 Cryptographic authentication configuration commands.

Multiple keys may be specified for an interface, each distinguished by *keyid*. Multiple keys are used during the smooth transition from one key to another. Each key must be specified within the appropriate interface's context.

The **startaccept, startgenerate, stopgenerate**, and **stopaccept** commands are used to limit the lifetime of a given key. Each of these commands takes a date and time, in the form MM:DD:YY@hh:mm:ss, where MM is the month (1–12), DD the day of the month, YY the year, and hh, mm, and ss the hour, minute, and second in local time. The time that the router is willing to accept packets signed with a given key is bounded below by **startaccept** and above by **stopaccept**. The time that a router uses a given key to sign its own packets is bounded below by **startgenerate** and above by **stopgenerate**. When unspecified, the key is used for both receiving and transmitting packets, with no expiration time.

Simple password configuration is part of the top-level interface configuration. (See Section 14.1.3.)

14.1.9 Importing External Routes

Each prefix to be imported into the OSPF routing domain is specified in a **route** *prefix nexthop type cost* command (Figure 14.9). The IP destination of the external route is given by *prefix*, expressed in CIDR notation. Also given with the route is *nexthop*, the next hop expressed either as an IP address of the next hop or, for unnumbered point-to-point links, as the name of the outgoing interface; *type*, indicating an OSPF external type-1 or type-2 metric (see Section 6.2 of [67]); and the *cost* to be advertised with the route. If an intra-AS path is available to *nexthop*, the next hop will be advertised as the route's forwarding address in the AS-external-LSA.

```
route prefix nexthop type cost
mcsource
tag tag_value
```

Figure 14.9 Importing external routes.

Each configured external route is also added to the Linux kernel's routing table unless a better-cost AS-external-LSA is received from another router. In other words, the **route** command in the **ospfd** configuration file is a way of adding static routes to the kernel, just like the Linux **/sbin/route** command.

The **mcsource** command is used to label the destination as a multicast source when it is imported in an AS-external-LSA. This is useful when running a MOSPF domain as part of a larger multicast system (see Section 10.6 of [67]).

The **tag** *tag_value* command is used to tag the imported external route with the 32-bit integer value *tag_value*. The default external route tag is 0.

14.2 Changing Configuration Syntax

You can change the syntax used in the **ospfd** configuration file **/etc/ospfd.conf**. For example, you could make the syntax match the Cisco router's OSPF configuration syntax, or GATED's configuration syntax. New Tcl code must be written defining the new configuration commands, replacing the current commands defined in **/usr/sbin/ospfd.tcl**.

To further understand what must be done to change the **ospfd** configuration syntax, we examine the **ospfd** configuration process in more detail. Configuration is performed at initialization and reconfiguration when the Linux signal **SIGUSR1** is received (see Section 14.3). In either case, the **LinuxOspfd::read_config()** routine is called (Figure 14.10). Assuming that you have defined a new configuration syntax, the program flows as follows.

351-362 **LinuxOspfd::read_config()** creates a new Tcl interpreter and then registers a base set of Tcl commands that have been implemented in C++. Of these commands,

—— `ospfd_linux.C`

```
342  void LinuxOspfd::read_config()
344  {
345      Tcl_Interp *interp; // Interpretation of config commands
346      char sendcfg[] = "sendcfg";
347      int namlen;
348      char *filename;
349
350      new_router_id = 0;
351      interp = Tcl_CreateInterp();
353      Tcl_CreateCommand(interp, "routerid", SetRouterID, 0, 0);
354      Tcl_CreateCommand(interp, "sendgen", SendGeneral, 0, 0);
355      Tcl_CreateCommand(interp, "sendarea", SendArea, 0, 0);
356      Tcl_CreateCommand(interp, "sendagg", SendAggregate, 0, 0);
357      Tcl_CreateCommand(interp, "sendhost", SendHost, 0, 0);
358      Tcl_CreateCommand(interp, "sendifc", SendInterface, 0, 0);
359      Tcl_CreateCommand(interp, "sendvl", SendVL, 0, 0);
360      Tcl_CreateCommand(interp, "sendnbr", SendNeighbor, 0, 0);
361      Tcl_CreateCommand(interp, "sendextrt", SendExtRt, 0, 0);
362      Tcl_CreateCommand(interp, "sendmd5", SendMD5Key, 0, 0);
364      namlen = strlen(INSTALL_DIR) + strlen(ospfd_tcl_src);
365      filename = new char[namlen+1];
366      strcpy(filename, INSTALL_DIR);
367      strcat(filename, ospfd_tcl_src);
368      if (Tcl_EvalFile(interp, filename) != TCL_OK)
369          syslog(LOG_INFO, "No additional TCL commands");
370      delete [] filename;
372      read_kernel_interfaces();
374      if (Tcl_EvalFile(interp, ospfd_config_file) != TCL_OK) {
375          syslog(LOG_ERR, "Error in config file, line %d",
                     interp->errorLine);
376          return;
377      }
379      if (!ospf || ospf->my_id() != new_router_id) {
380          syslog(LOG_ERR, "Failed to set Router ID");
381          return;
382      }
384      ospf->cfgStart();
386      Tcl_Eval(interp, sendcfg);
387      Tcl_DeleteInterp(interp);
389      ospf->cfgDone();
390  }
```

—— `ospfd_linux.C`

Figure 14.10 Reading `ospfd` configuration.

routerid tells the **ospfd** software of its OSPF Router ID, causing the global **class OSPF *ospf** to be allocated. The **routerid** command must be called directly (or indirectly if you are changing the syntax of OSPF Router ID configuration) when reading the **ospfd** configuration file. The other commands—**sendgen** through **sendmd5**—are helper commands that are used by the Tcl code to download the configuration information into the **ospfd** application.

368-377   The file **ospfd_tcl_src** (set to **/usr/sbin/ospfd.tcl**) is then read, which defines your new configuration command syntax. Then the interface information is read out of the Linux kernel to supplement and double-check the OSPF configuration, which is subsequently read out of **ospfd_config_file** (set to **/etc/ospfd.conf**).

379-386   After verifying that the OSPF Router ID has been correctly set, the OSPF application is told via **OSPF::cfgStart()** that it is about to be (re)configured. The Tcl **sendcfg** routine, which you must have written as part of your new configuration (or reused the existing one) is then called, which downloads all the configuration information from your Tcl into the **ospfd** application, using the built-in commands **sendgen** through **sendmd5**.

389   Finally, **OSPF::cfgDone()** is called to complete the (re)configuration.

14.3 Dynamic Reconfiguration

The **ospfd** software can be reconfigured dynamically, without having to restart the program. Simply edit the **ospfd** configuration file **/etc/ospfd.conf** to reflect the new configuration, and then send the **USR1** signal to the **ospfd** program to tell it to reread its configuration file. The **USR1** signal can be sent by using the Linux command **kill -s USR1** *pid*, where *pid* is the Linux process ID of the **ospfd** program.

All configuration parameters can be changed dynamically, with the exception of the OSPF Router ID. In order to change the OSPF Router ID, the **ospfd** program should be shut down (see Section 14.4) and restarted after the configuration file has been edited.

When certain configuration parameters are changed, some disruption in routing is unavoidable. For example, when an interface's Designated Router Priority is changed, it forces the rerunning of the Designated Router calculation for the interface. A complete list of the actions that **ospfd** takes on the various configuration changes can be found in Chapter 13, Configuration and Monitoring.

14.4 Graceful Shutdown

If the **ospfd** program exits without being able to properly clean up, the OSPF routing domain suffers in several ways. First, it may take as long as **RouterDeadInterval** seconds before the other OSPF routers route around the failed **ospfd**. Second, the kernel routing table will continue to be full of the routing information the **ospfd** had discovered right before its exit, which may now be stale. Third, LSAs originated by the failed `ospfd` may persist in other routers' databases for up to an hour.

However, a graceful shutdown procedure (Section 13.10) has been provided for `ospfd`. Graceful shutdown can be invoked by sending the `ospfd` program the `HUP` signal: `kill -s HUP` *pid*, where *pid* is the Linux process ID of the `ospfd` program.

When graceful shutdown is invoked, the `ospfd` program flushes all its locally originated LSAs and forces its neighbors to immediately reroute by sending out empty Hellos, thereby dropping its adjacencies. At the end of the graceful shutdown procedure, `ospfd` withdraws from the kernel routing table all the routes that it has inserted.

The graceful-shutdown procedure can take some time, especially the flushing of locally originated LSAs, which waits on acknowledgments from `ospfd`'s OSPF neighbors. For this reason, a 10-second limit is put on the flushing of LSAs, after which the rest of the graceful-shutdown procedure is performed even if all locally originated LSAs have yet to be flushed.

14.5   Monitoring `ospfd` Operation

The `ospfd` program logs significant events to the file `/var/log/ospfd.log`. Each line of the file is a separate log message, consisting of a timestamp, a message number, and an ASCII description of an event. For a complete description of the logging messages `ospfd` produces, see Chapter 5, Building Blocks, and Appendix B, OSPFD Logging Messages.

The `log_level` *level* command can control which messages are logged. A logging level is specified each time a message is printed, with levels ranging from 1 to 5; the more serious messages are printed with greater levels. Setting the logging level to *level* means that only messages of greater than or equal *level* will be printed. Setting the logging level to 1 prints all messages, and a logging level of 6 prints none. The default logging level is 4.

Errors `ospfd` encounters when invoking Linux system calls are logged by using the Linux `syslog` facility. In a standard Linux installation, these messages can then be found in the file `/var/log/messages`.

Two separate monitoring programs—`ospfd_mon` and `ospfd_browser`—are also supplied with `ospfd`. These monitoring programs can display in human-readable format all the information found in the OSPF MIB, such as the list of active neighbors, the link-state database, and so on. See Appendix A, Manual Pages, for details.

14.6   Caveats

Although `ospfd` turns a Linux box into an OSPF router, you should keep in mind some restrictions. First and foremost, a wide variety of network interface cards are available for PCs, but not all of them work well under Linux. You should try to restrict yourself to using cards that have been proved to work well; see, for example, the recommended hardware list for the Red Hat Linux distribution [86].

Following are other issues to keep in mind when using `ospfd` on Linux.

- The `ospfd` code does not read the contents of the Linux kernel routing table when starting up; nor does it monitor changes to the routing table from other sources (the Linux `route` command or other routing daemons, such as `routed` or `gated`) during `ospfd` operation. These other route sources may interfere with the Linux box's ability to forward routes according to the OSPF protocol.

- If the `ospfd` code exits abnormally—if, for example, it crashes or receives an unexpected signal—its routes remain in the kernel routing table, and IP forwarding remains turned on.

- The Linux kernel does not check interfaces for liveness. For example, if your Ethernet transceiver becomes unplugged, you may get some messages on your console, but Linux will not declare the interface down. The `ospfd` software checks to see only whether the interface has been `ifconfig`ed up. It would be better to periodically check that packets—any kind of packets, not necessarily OSPF protocol packets—are being transmitted and received on an interface.

- Although the OSPF specification allows you to send OSPF protocol packets on point-to-point and nonbroadcast interfaces to the multicast destinations 224.0.0.5 and 224.0.0.6, Linux does not. Routers attempting to talk to `ospfd` over these types of interfaces must accept unicast addresses instead and convert multicast destinations to appropriate unicast destinations when sending (see Section 14.7.4).

- Under Linux, OSPF cannot discover neighbors on NBMA or Point-to-Multi-Point interfaces. Neighbors on these interface types must be configured as described in Section 14.1.7.

- If you want to use the full capabilities of the `ospfd` demand circuit support, namely, dropping the data-link connection during periods of inactivity, you'll need support for this in the appropriate Linux network drivers.

- Linux does not support unnumbered serial lines.

- The MOSPF support in `ospfd` uses the kernel support developed for `mrouted` and DVMRP. However, `mrouted` supports only broadcast interfaces and tunnels; because tunnels are not supported by MOSPF, this leaves the MOSPF support within `ospfd` restricted to broadcast interfaces only.

14.7   Implementation Details

Data specific to the Linux port of `ospfd` is kept in the **class LinuxOspfd** (Figure 14.11),
which derives indirectly from the base **class OspfSysCalls**. The **class Linux**, itself a
derived class of `OspfSysCalls`, encapsulates Linux-specific behavior that is used by
both the Linux `ospfd` port and the Linux OSPF simulator (see Chapter 15, An OSPF
Simulator). A pointer to the single global **LinuxOspfd** class is kept in the variable
`ospfd_sys` (and also copied into `OspfSysCalls *sys`).

```
──────────────────────────────────────────────────────────── ospfd_linux.h
22 class LinuxOspfd : public Linux {
23     enum {
24         MAXIFs=255, // Maximum number of interfaces
25     };
26     int netfd;  // File descriptor used to send and receive
27     int igmpfd; // File descriptor for multicast routing
28     int udpfd;  // UDP file descriptor for ioctl's
29     timeval last_time; // Last return from gettimeofday
30     int next_phyint; // Next phyint value
31     PatTree phyints; // Physical interfaces
32     AVLtree interface_map; // IP addresses to phyint
33     AVLtree directs; // Directly attached prefixes
34     class BSDPhyInt *phys[MAXIFs];
35     rtentry m;
36     FILE *logstr;
37 public:
38     LinuxOspfd();
39     ~LinuxOspfd();
40     void time_update();
41
60     void read_config();
61     void read_kernel_interfaces();
62     void one_second_timer();
63     void rtentry_prepare(InAddr, InMask, MPath *mpp);
64     void add_direct(InAddr, InMask);
65     int get_phyint(InAddr);
66     bool parse_interface(char *, in_addr &, BSDPhyInt * &);
67     void raw_receive(int fd);
70 };
──────────────────────────────────────────────────────────── ospfd_linux.h
```

Figure 14.11 Linux-specific `ospfd` data: the **LinuxOspfd** class.

The raw socket used to send and to receive OSPF protocol packets is `netfd`. The
HDRINCL socket option is invoked on this socket, so complete IP packet headers are built

by the `ospfd` application when transmitting OSPF packets. A separate datagram socket, `udpfd`, is required because various Linux `ioctls`—for example, those used to obtain kernel interface information—cannot be performed on raw sockets.

We assign Linux interfaces consecutive integer values called `phyints`; the next value to be assigned appears in `next_phyint`. Those Linux interfaces that we have read out of the kernel in `LinuxOspfd::read_kernel_interface()` are stored in `phyints`, where they can be looked up, based on their Linux names (for example, "eth1"). Each interface is represented by a `BSDPhyInt` class.

Interfaces are also cross-indexed, based on their IP interface addresses in `interface_map`, where they can be looked up by `get_phyint()`. Each element of `interface_map` is a `BSDIfMap` class. Interfaces are also cross-indexed based on their assigned small-integer `phyint` in `phys[]`. Directly attached IP subnets are stored in `directs`, enabling `ospfd` to leave the maintenance of these subnets' kernel routing table entries to the kernel itself (see Section 14.7.4); adding a subnet to `directs` is done by calling `add_direct()`.

The `LinuxOspfd` class also provides methods for each of the system interface functions in the base `OspfSysCalls class` (see Section 14.7.4). These have been omitted from Figure 14.11 for space reasons.

14.7.1 Initialization

Initialization starts in the constructor for the `LinuxOspfd` class. The constructor opens the `syslog` interface, the `ospfd` logging file `/var/log/ospfd.log`, the raw socket `netfd`, and the datagram socket `udpfd`. The constructor then starts a random-number generator.

The `ospfd` configuration is then read (see Section 14.2). As a part of reading the configuration, the interface information is read out of the Linux kernel, using the Linux `SIOCGIFCONF ioctls` and associated `ioctls`, such as `SIOCGIFNETMASK`. The loopback interface and interfaces not having IP addresses are ignored. When the OSPF Router ID is read from the configuration, the OSPF class constructor is called, initializing the OSPF application code.

Signal handlers are then established for the Linux signals `SIGALRM` (handling a 1-second timer), `SIGUSR1` (to indicate reconfiguration requests), and `SIGHUP` (for requesting graceful shutdown). The main loop then executes until a graceful shutdown request is received.

14.7.2 Main Loop

The main loop is illustrated in Figure 14.12. The function of the main loop is simply to receive OSPF protocol packets from the network, to hand them to the OSPF application code for processing, and to keep the OSPF application code informed of elapsed time (in seconds and milliseconds).

124   We call the OSPF timer routine `OSPF::tick()` to execute any pending OSPF application timers.

126   The call to `OSPF::timeout()` tells us how many milliseconds into the future until the next OSPF application will fire. We hand this value to `select()` as the maximum amount of time to wait for the reception of an OSPF protocol packet.

140   Signal processing is turned on, so it is possible that the Linux `select()` call was interrupted by `SIGALRM`, `SIGHUP`, or `SIGUSR1`. Any other error returned by `select()` is unexpected and is considered fatal.

145   We update the elapsed time, stored in `sys_etime`. See Section 14.7.3 for details.

147   The OSPF application code is not reentrant, so we need to block the signal processing before calling into the OSPF application.

151-155   Any received OSPF and IGMP packets are passed to `LinuxOspfd::raw_receive()` for processing. The kernel passes `ospfd` the complete packet, including the IP header. When running Linux v2.2 or higher, the Linux socket interface also tells `ospfd` which interface the packet was received on; otherwise, we ultimately pass `OSPF::rxpkt()` (or `OSPF::rxigmp()`) a first argument of `-1`, which tells the application to try to figure out the receiving interface, based on the packet's IP source address.

14.7.3 Timekeeping

It is up to the system to keep the OSPF application informed of the elapsed time since program start. Elapsed time is stored in the variable `sys_etime`. The elapsed time is updated in two functions: `LinuxOspfd::time_update()` and `LinuxOspfd::one_second_timer()`, as shown in Figure 14.13.

LinuxOspfd::time_update() is called every time through the main loop. The Linux `gettimeofday()` routine is called, and the difference between the current call and the last call (stored in `LinuxOspfd::last_time`) is added to the elapsed time, as long as a second boundary is not crossed.

LinuxOspfd::one_second_timer() is called once a second and sets the elapsed time to the next whole second. This function is used so that the program notion of time does not depend solely on `gettimeofday()`, which may vary wildly when someone resets the Linux system's time and date.

14.7.4 Linux System Call Interface

Most of the system interface calls in the `LinuxOspfd` class are self-explanatory. We provide only the highlights.

```
                                                              ospfd_linux.C
111    while (1) {
112        int msec_tmo;
113        int err;
114        FD_ZERO(&fdset);
115        FD_ZERO(&wrset);
116        n_fd = ospfd_sys->netfd;
117        FD_SET(ospfd_sys->netfd, &fdset);
118        ospfd_sys->mon_fd_set(n_fd, &fdset, &wrset);
119        if (ospfd_sys->igmpfd != -1) {
120            FD_SET(ospfd_sys->igmpfd, &fdset);
121            n_fd = MAX(n_fd, ospfd_sys->igmpfd);
122        }
124        ospf->tick();
126        msec_tmo = ospf->timeout();
128        ospf->logflush();
129        // Allow signals during select
130        sigprocmask(SIG_SETMASK, &osigset, NULL);
131        if (msec_tmo != -1) {
132            timeval timeout;
133            timeout.tv_sec = msec_tmo/1000;
134            timeout.tv_usec = (msec_tmo % 1000) * 1000;
135            err = select(n_fd+1, &fdset, &wrset, 0, &timeout);
136        }
137        else
138            err = select(n_fd+1, &fdset, &wrset, 0, 0);
139        // Handle errors in select
140        if (err == -1 && errno != EINTR) {
141            syslog(LOG_ERR, "select failed %m");
142            exit(1);
143        }
145        ospfd_sys->time_update();
146        // Block signals in OSPF code
147        sigprocmask(SIG_BLOCK, &sigset, &osigset);
148        // Process received data packet, if any
149        if (err <= 0)
150            continue;
151        if (FD_ISSET(ospfd_sys->netfd, &fdset))
152            ospfd_sys->raw_receive(ospfd_sys->netfd);
153        if (ospfd_sys->igmpfd != -1 &&
154            FD_ISSET(ospfd_sys->igmpfd, &fdset))
155            ospfd_sys->raw_receive(ospfd_sys->igmpfd);
156        // Process monitor queries and responses
157        ospfd_sys->process_mon_io(&fdset, &wrset);
158    }
                                                              ospfd_linux.C
```

Figure 14.12 The main processing loop in `ospfd`.

```
                                                              ─── ospfd_linux.C
231 void LinuxOspfd::time_update()
232
233 {
234     timeval now;          // Current idea of time
235     int timediff;
236
237     (void) gettimeofday(&now, NULL);
238     timediff = 1000*(now.tv_sec - last_time.tv_sec);
239     timediff += (now.tv_usec - last_time.tv_usec)/1000;
240     if ((timediff + sys_etime.msec) < 1000)
241         sys_etime.msec += timediff;
242     last_time = now;
243 }
244
249 void LinuxOspfd::one_second_timer()
250
251 {
252     timeval now;          // Current idea of time
253
254     (void) gettimeofday(&now, NULL);
255     sys_etime.sec++;
256     sys_etime.msec = 0;
257     last_time = now;
258 }
                                                              ─── ospfd_linux.C
```

Figure 14.13 Functions keeping track of elapsed time.

LinuxOspfd:sendpkt(InPkt *pkt, int phyint, InAddr gw)

The code for **LinuxOspfd::sendpkt()** is shown in Figure 14.14. The interface the packet is to be sent out is indicated by **phyint**.

66-69   Because Linux does not allow you to send multicast packets out point-to-point interfaces or nonbroadcast interfaces, we change the destination address to a unicast address before sending. When sending packets on an NBMA or Point-to-MultiPoint interface, the OSPF application will always call **sendpkt()** separately for each neighbor, with **gw** set to the neighbor's IP address.

72-81   If the destination is still a multicast address, the **setsockopt IP_MULTICAST_IF** must be used to tell the kernel which interface to send the packet on.

96-109   In Linux kernel versions 2.2 and higher, we can use the **IP_PKTINFO** facility to force the packet to be sent out the desired interface. This same facility also tells **Linux-Ospfd::raw_receive()** the receiving interface for incoming OSPF packets, so that we can correctly implement the reception sanity checks specified in Section 8.2 of [75]. In

```
                                                              ─ system.C
56 void LinuxOspfd::sendpkt(InPkt *pkt, int phyint, InAddr gw)
57
58 {
59     BSDPhyInt *phyp;
60     msghdr msg;
61     iovec iov;
62     size_t len;
63     sockaddr_in to;
64
65     phyp = phys[phyint];
66     if (phyp->flags & IFF_POINTOPOINT)
67         pkt->i_dest = hton32(phyp->dstaddr);
68     else if (gw != 0)
69         pkt->i_dest = hton32(gw);
70     pkt->i_chksum = ~incksum((uns16 *)pkt, sizeof(pkt));
71
72     if (IN_CLASSD(ntoh32(pkt->i_dest))) {
73         in_addr mcaddr;
74         mcaddr.s_addr = hton32(phyp->addr);
75         if (setsockopt(netfd, IPPROTO_IP, IP_MULTICAST_IF,
76                        (char *)&mcaddr, sizeof(mcaddr)) < 0) {
77             syslog(LOG_ERR, "IP_MULTICAST_IF %s: %m",
78                    inet_ntoa(mcaddr));
79             return;
80         }
81     }
82
83     len = ntoh16(pkt->i_len);
84     to.sin_family = AF_INET;
85     to.sin_addr.s_addr = pkt->i_dest;
86     msg.msg_name = (caddr_t) &to;
87     msg.msg_namelen = sizeof(to);
88     iov.iov_len = len;
89     iov.iov_base = pkt;
90     msg.msg_iov = &iov;
91     msg.msg_iovlen = 1;
92     msg.msg_flags = MSG_DONTROUTE;
93 #if LINUX_VERSION_CODE < LINUX22
94     msg.msg_control = 0;
95     msg.msg_controllen = 0;
96 #else
97     byte cmsgbuf[128];
98     cmsghdr *cmsg;
99     in_pktinfo *pktinfo;
```

(Continued)

```
100        msg.msg_control = cmsgbuf;
101        msg.msg_controllen = CMSG_SPACE(sizeof(in_pktinfo));
102        cmsg = CMSG_FIRSTHDR(&msg);
103        cmsg->cmsg_len = CMSG_LEN(sizeof(in_pktinfo));
104        cmsg->cmsg_level = SOL_IP;
105        cmsg->cmsg_type = IP_PKTINFO;
106        pktinfo = (in_pktinfo *) CMSG_DATA(cmsg);
107        pktinfo->ipi_ifindex = phyint;
108        pktinfo->ipi_spec_dst.s_addr = 0;
109 #endif
110
111        if (sendmsg(netfd, &msg, MSG_DONTROUTE) == -1)
112            syslog(LOG_ERR, "sendmsg failed: %m");
113 }
```
── system.C

Figure 14.14 `LinuxOspfd::sendpkt()`.

Linux versions prior to 2.2, we simply have to assume that the receiving interface is the correct one.

111   Setting the flags in **sendmsg()** to **MSG_DONTROUTE** tells the kernel that the destination must be on one of the router's directly connected interfaces. OSPF protocol packets that must be forwarded multiple hops—namely, those maintaining virtual links—are instead sent by using **LinuxOspfd::sendpkt(InPkt *pkt)**.

LinuxOspfd::rtadd()

This function adds or modifies a routing entry in the Linux kernel. It is shown in Figure 14.15.

345   Routing table entries for directly attached subnets are not modified by **ospfd** but instead are the responsibility of the Linux kernel.

351-352   The previous set of next hops for the routing table entry is **ompp**. If we are modifying an existing route, we must delete it first; otherwise, the previous next hops will still remain in the kernel.

353   **LinuxOspfd::rtentry_prepare()** formats the **rtentry** structure that will be handed to the kernel in the **SIOCADDRT ioctl**. This structure is statically allocated in the **LinuxOspfd** class as **LinuxOspfd::m**.

355-356   Reject routes tell the kernel to discard matching IP packets instead of forwarding them. They are installed in OSPF area border routers that perform aggregation; see Section 11.2 of [75] for details.

357-368   Even though the Linux kernel supports multipath and **ospfd** calculates up to **Mpath::MAXPATH** equal-cost paths for each routing table entry, we currently install only the first path into the Linux kernel.

```
                                                          —————— system.C
341 void LinuxOspfd::rtadd(InAddr net, InMask mask, MPath *mpp,
342                    MPath *ompp, bool reject)
344 {
345     if (directs.find(net, mask))
346         return;
347     if (!mpp) {
348         rtdel(net, mask, ompp);
349         return;
350     }
351     if (ompp)
352         rtdel(net, mask, ompp);
353     rtentry_prepare(net, mask, mpp);
354     // Reject route?
355     if (reject)
356         m.rt_flags |=  RTF_REJECT;
357     else
358         m.rt_flags |= (RTF_UP | RTF_GATEWAY);
359
360     // Add through ioctl
361     if (-1 == ioctl(udpfd, SIOCADDRT, (char *)&m)) {
362         if (errno == EEXIST) {
363             ioctl(udpfd, SIOCDELRT, (char *)&m);
364             if (-1 != ioctl(udpfd, SIOCADDRT, (char *)&m))
365                 return;
366         }
367         syslog(LOG_ERR, "SIOCADDRT: %m");
368     }
369 }
                                                          —————— system.C
```

Figure 14.15 `LinuxOspfd::rtadd()`.

Other System Functions

`LinuxOspfd::phy_operational()` merely checks whether the `ifconfig` status of the interface is up and does not try to verify that the interface is working.

The single raw socket `LinuxOspfd::netfd` is used to receive and to transmit OSPF packets out all interfaces. For that reason, the `LinuxOspfd::open()` and `Linux-Ospfd::close()` functions are no-ops.

In Linux, you can join multicast groups only on broadcast interfaces. Hence, `LinuxOspfd::join()` and `LinuxOspfd::leave()` check the interface's `IFF_BROADCAST` flag before invoking the `IP_ADD_MEMBERSHIP` and `IP_DROP_MEMBERSHIP` setsockopts, respectively.

Exercises

14.1   Write your own `/usr/sbin/ospfd.tcl` file, implementing the Cisco OSPF configuration syntax instead of that documented in this chapter.

14.2   `LinuxOspfd::read_kernel_interfaces()` adds interfaces found in the Linux kernel to `LinuxOspfd::phyints`. Modify `read_kernel_interfaces()` so that interfaces no longer in the kernel are removed from `phyints`.

14.3   Create a global `ospfd` configuration option whereby routes added by `ospfd` to the Linux kernel will be kept, instead of deleted, on graceful exit.

14.4   The `neighbor` configuration command has been made subordinate to the `interface` configuration command. However, if you are building the configuration file through SNMP, this organization is somewhat awkward, as you then need to obtain interface address masks *while* you build the configuration file in order to figure out where in the file to place the neighbor. Change `ospfd.tcl` so that the `neighbor` commands are no longer subordinate to the `interface` commands and can instead be grouped together at the bottom of the configuration file.

14.5   Port the `ospfd` routing daemon to another UNIX-like operating system.

14.6   `LinuxOspfd::rtadd()` is implemented by using the SIOCADDRT ioctl. This is the best-known way of modifying the routing table in BSD networking stacks, although not the most flexible of interfaces. In particular, note that in order to change the next hop in a routing table entry, you first have to delete the previous next hop. In an environment in which `ospfd` is the only routing protocol modifying the kernel routing table, a more robust mechanism would be simply to replace any existing next hops in the routing table entry, if any, making the `ompp` argument in Figure 14.15 unnecessary. Change the implementation of `LinuxOspfd::rtadd()` along these lines, using the Linux `rtnetlink` interface. (On other UNIX derivatives, you can use the BSD routing socket.)

14.7   Modify the `LinuxOspfd::rtadd()` function to install multiple paths into the Linux kernel.

15

An OSPF Simulator

The OSPF simulator `ospfd_sim` allows you to simulate an entire OSPF network on a single workstation, running either Linux or Windows 95. Because the simulated routers are running copies of the `ospfd` software, the simulator is a very useful tool for debugging `ospfd` software problems and for testing extensions to the `ospfd` software when you don't have enough real OSPF routers to test with. The simulator can also be used to validate OSPF configurations: After inputting your network design into the simulator, you can verify that all routers have complete routing tables, examine their databases for synchronization and size, evaluate failure scenarios, and so on. The OSPF simulator is also a good teaching tool for people wanting to see the OSPF protocol in action, on a network of their own choosing.

The simulator has a Tk/Tcl graphical user interface (GUI), which displays a map of the OSPF network that you are simulating. Colors on the map indicate the state of database synchronization between simulated routers, along with an indication of simulated time down to the tenth of a second. From the GUI, you can modify the map, adding/deleting routers, network segments, interfaces, virtual links, area aggregates, and so on. Between simulation runs, the configuration is stored in an ASCII file consisting of Tk/Tcl commands. If desired, this file can be modified in a text editor to produce large network configurations more quickly than through the GUI.

Logging messages from the simulated routers are written to standard output, with simulated time and OSPF Router ID of the logging router prepended. The same monitoring programs used to monitor the Linux **ospf** routing daemon can also be used to collect OSPF statistics from the simulated routers.

Detailed information on how to run the OSPF simulator, including the format of the configuration file, can be found in the **ospf_sim** manual page in Appendix A. In this chapter, we will concentrate on describing the implementation of the simulator.

15.1   Software Architecture

The simulator is implemented as a collection of processes, communicating via TCP and UDP (User Datagram Protocol) sockets. In the following sections, we will detail the simulator's process organization and its interprocess communication. We will use the simple simulated network in Figure 15.1 as an illustration. This simulated network was invoked by the command **ospf_sim simple.cfg**.

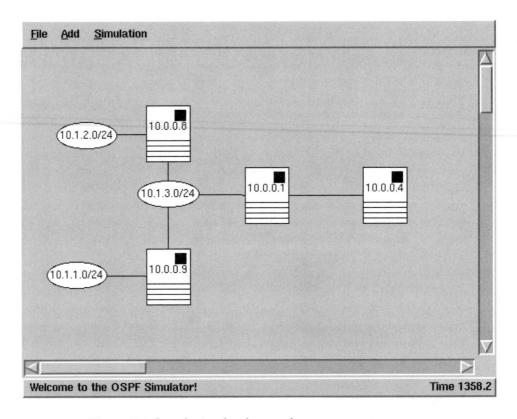

Figure 15.1 Sample simulated network: **ospf_sim simple.cfg**.

The configuration file (`simple.cfg`) used to generate this simulation is shown in Figure 15.2. The file consists of four routers, three broadcast network segments, and a point-to-point link between routers 10.0.0.1 and 10.0.0.4. The interface commands create interfaces from the routers to network segments by specifying the IP interface address of the router on the segment; for example, the command `interface 10.0.0.1 10.1.3.1 3 0 1` specifies that router 10.0.0.1 has an interface on network segment 10.1.3.0/24, with IP address of 10.1.3.1 and OSPF cost of 3. The `pplink` command specifies both halves of the point-to-point link at once, with the IP interface address 126.1.0.1 assigned to the Router 10.0.0.1 end and address 126.4.0.1 assigned to the other (remember, OSPF does not require that addresses assigned to a point-to-point link lie on a common subnet). For more detail on the syntax of the configuration file, see the `ospf_sim` man page in Appendix A.

```
router 10.0.0.1 282 167 1
router 10.0.0.4 417 167 1
router 10.0.0.8 169.0 96.0 1
router 10.0.0.9 169.0 260.0 1
broadcast 10.1.3.0/24 0.0.0.0 169.0 165.0 0
broadcast 10.1.2.0/24 0.0.0.0 75.0 98.0 0
broadcast 10.1.1.0/24 0.0.0.0 63.0 258.0 0
pplink 10.0.0.1 126.1.0.1 1 10.0.0.4 126.4.0.1 1 0.0.0.0 0
interface 10.0.0.1 10.1.3.1 3 0 1
interface 10.0.0.8 10.1.3.8 3 0 1
interface 10.0.0.8 10.1.2.8 1 0 1
interface 10.0.0.9 10.1.3.9 3 0 1
interface 10.0.0.9 10.1.1.9 1 0 1
```

Figure 15.2 The simulator configuration file `simple.cfg`.

15.1.1 Process Architecture

The simulator has a single controlling process that executes the `ospf_sim` program. This process first opens a server socket, where it listens for incoming control connections from the simulated routers. The process then reads the configuration file specified on the command line (a default configuration, representing the network depicted in Figure 6.6 of [67], is used if no configuration file is specified), displays the network map and spawns a separate `ospfd_sim` process for each simulated router.

Each simulated router opens a UDP socket to receive simulated IP data packets (OSPF protocol packets and any other kind of IP packet, such as ICMP echoes, that are simulated), listens on a port for incoming monitoring connections, and then opens up a TCP control connection to the simulation controller's server socket. The simulation controller then downloads the router's OSPF configuration over the controller connection. The identities of the simulated routers' UDP ports are also exchanged over the control connections so that each simulated router knows how to send data to the others. The control connections between the simulation controller and the simulated routers remain open throughout the simulation, to maintain time synchronization (Section 15.1.3) and to download any dynamic configuration changes from controller to simulated router.

The spawning of `ospfd_sim` processes is logged to standard output, together with the usual logging messages produced by the `ospfd` software. The first few logging messages produced by the simulation in Figure 15.1 are shown in Figure 15.3. In particular, the first line indicates that the simulated router 10.0.0.1 is running as process 20231 and is listening on TCP port 1387 for monitoring connections. The third line indicates that it was spawned by executing the command `ospfd_sim 10.0.0.1 1385` (1385 is the server port that the simulation controller is listening on for incoming control connections). As configuration information is downloaded into the simulated routers, they issue logging messages, such as OSPF.002 and OSPF.004, to announce the new configurations taking effect.

```
0:000 (10.0.0.1) OSPF.113: PID 20231 ospfd_mon port 1387
0:000 (10.0.0.4) OSPF.113: PID 20232 ospfd_mon port 1389
0:000 (10.0.0.1) OSPF.113: invoked: ospfd_sim 10.0.0.1 1385
0:000 (10.0.0.8) OSPF.113: PID 20233 ospfd_mon port 1391
0:000 (10.0.0.4) OSPF.113: invoked: ospfd_sim 10.0.0.4 1385
0:000 (10.0.0.1) OSPF.001: ospfd Starting
0:000 (10.0.0.8) OSPF.113: invoked: ospfd_sim 10.0.0.8 1385
0:000 (10.0.0.4) OSPF.001: ospfd Starting
0:000 (10.0.0.8) OSPF.001: ospfd Starting
0:050 (10.0.0.1) OSPF.002: Adding  Area 0.0.0.0
0:050 (10.0.0.4) OSPF.002: Adding  Area 0.0.0.0
0:050 (10.0.0.8) OSPF.002: Adding  Area 0.0.0.0
0:050 (10.0.0.1) OSPF.004: Adding  Ifc 126.1.0.1
0:050 (10.0.0.4) OSPF.004: Adding  Ifc 126.4.0.1
0:050 (10.0.0.8) OSPF.004: Adding  Ifc 10.1.3.8
0:050 (10.0.0.9) OSPF.113: PID 20234 ospfd_mon port 1393
```

Figure 15.3 Initial logging messages indicating spawned simulated routers.

The monitoring programs `ospfd_mon` and `ospfd_browser` (see man pages in Appendix A) can be attached to any of the simulated routers' monitoring ports in order to display operational statistics. These include IP routing tables, OSPF link-state databases, and so on.

Figure 15.4 displays the communication occurring between the processes involved in the simulation of Figure 15.1. Simulated data packets are forwarded in the simulation analogous to IP data packet forwarding in a real network: They go hop by hop through simulated routers. In particular, if a data packet is to be forwarded from router 10.0.0.8 to router 10.0.0.4 (this could be an ICMP echo or OSPF packets flowing over a virtual link configured between the two routers), it would go through the simulated router 10.0.0.1 (legend lists control connections, simulated data packets, and ports).

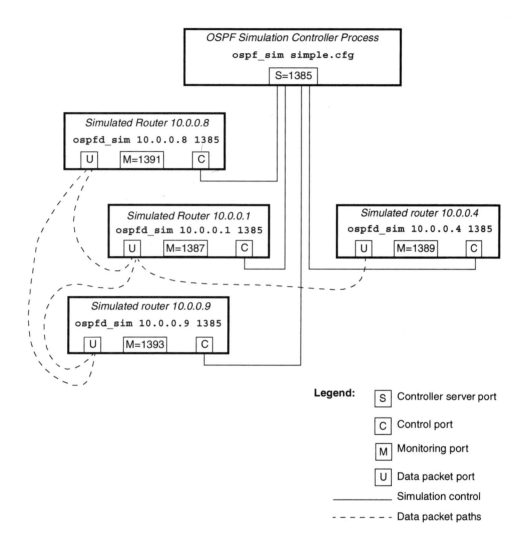

Figure 15.4 Process architecture of the OSPF simulator.

15.1.2 Simulation Control

The control connections between the simulation controller process and each simulated router are packetized TCP connections, using the **TcpPkt** class documented in Chapter 5, Building Blocks. Each control message or packet has a type and a subtype field.

Messages from the controller to each simulated router include the following:

- *Configuration messages*. These have type SIM_CONFIG and subtype indicating the object being configured. For example, if the subtype is equal to CfgType_Ifc, an OSPF interface is being (re)configured on the simulated router, and the body of the message is struct CfgIfc carrying the interface's new parameters. See Chapter 13, Configuration and Monitoring for more information about configuration of the ospfd software.

- *Configuration deletion requests*. The message type is SIM_CONFIG_DEL, and the subtype indicates the object to delete (coded in the same way as configuration requests).

- *Time ticks*. The controller maintains the simulation clock and downloads simulated clock ticks into each simulated router as message type SIM_TICK (Section 15.1.3).

- *IP address to data port mappings*. The simulator keeps track of each simulated router's IP addresses and UDP data port and downloads these mappings to the other simulated routers (message type SIM_ADDRMAP) so that they can send each other data packets (Section 15.1.4).

- *Terminating a simulated router*. The graceful shutdown of a simulated router is invoked by sending the router a message of type SIM_SHUTDOWN.

Messages from each simulated router to the simulation controller include the following:

- *Data port notification*. When each simulated router first comes up, it sends the controller a message of type SIM_HELLO to identify the simulated router's UDP data port.

- *Tick responses*. A simulated router acknowledges each time tick (message type SIM_TICK_RESPONSE) so that the controller can keep the simulated router's time synchronized. Each response to a time tick also contains the link-state database checksum so that the controller can display graphically the state of link-state database synchronization.

- *Logging messages*. OSPF logging messages (Chapter 5, Building Blocks) generated by the simulated router are sent to the controller as message type SIM_LOGMSG, where they are displayed on the controller's standard output.

15.1.3 Simulated Time

The simulation controller maintains time synchronization among the simulated routers. The controller sends timer ticks to each simulated router at the rate of TICKS_PER_SECOND (currently 20) ticks per simulated second. However, after sending a tick to each simulated router, the controller requires that before the next round of ticks is sent, each simulated router acknowledge the tick—thereby keeping all the routers on the same tick. The controller also ensures that simulated time runs no faster than real time, delaying between ticks if necessary.

You can pause the simulation from the graphical user interface. This pause is implemented simply by preventing the controller from sending new ticks. During the pause, the simulated routers are still running and can be examined with the `ospfd_mon` and `ospfd_browser` applications.

If a simulated router crashes or is terminated with a signal, the controller will notice the control connection closing and will delete the router from the list of nodes from which tick responses are expected (`SimCtl::simnodes`). As a result, the simulation will continue. However, if instead the simulated router itself is paused, perhaps by attaching a debugger and stopping the router at a breakpoint, the simulation pauses until the router's execution continues or is terminated. This behavior is very useful for debugging and is something I always wanted to do with a real router—that is, freeze the network state during a problem so that I could examine it at my leisure.

15.1.4 Data Packet Flow

Every simulated network segment is assigned a unique integer value, starting at 1. In our example, 10.1.3.0/24 will be assigned 1, 10.1.2.0/24 the value 2, 10.1.1.0/24 the value 3, and the point-to-point link the value 4. In logging messages and monitoring commands, you will sometimes see 10.1.3.0/24 referred to as N1. Also, when interfaces attaching to 10.1.3.0/24 are downloaded into their simulated routers, the interface's `CfgIfc::phyint` will be set to 1.

OSPF packets and other simulated IP packets are sent hop by hop from the source simulated router to the next-hop simulated router and finally to the destination simulated router, simulating the path of a real IP packet. These packets do not go through the simulation controller. Instead, the controller has downloaded the next-hop IP address to UDP port mappings so that each hop knows the UDP port of the next-hop simulated router.

In order to prevent a data packet from being forwarded across the entire network in a single tick, we have made the simplifying assumption that each packet hop takes `LINK_DELAY` (currently set to 10) milliseconds. This is enforced by stamping all packet transmissions with the time they are sent and then delaying receive processing until the appropriate timer tick. (This means that it takes 200 simulated milliseconds to flood an LSA across a network of diameter 20.) The function that receives simulated data packets, delaying their processing, if necessary, is `SimSys::process_uni_fd()` (Figure 15.5).

165-173   A simulated data packet is received on the simulated router's data port `SimSys::uni_fd`. Simulated data packets consist of an entire IP packet, with a `struct SimPktHdr`

── ospfd_sim.C

```
154 void SimSys::process_uni_fd()
155
156 {
157     int plen;
158     sockaddr_in addr;
159     socklen fromlen=sizeof(addr);
160     SimPktHdr *pkthdr;
161     InPkt *pkt;
162     SPFtime rcvd;
163     SPFtime limit;
164
165     plen = recvfrom(uni_fd, buffer, sizeof(buffer),
166                     0, (sockaddr *)&addr, &fromlen);
167     pkthdr = (SimPktHdr *) buffer;
168     pkt = (InPkt *) (pkthdr+1);
169     if (plen < (int) sizeof(SimPktHdr) ||
170         plen < (int) (sizeof(SimPktHdr) + ntoh16(pkt->i_len))) {
171         perror("recvfrom");
172         return;
173     }
174
175     rcvd = pkthdr->ts;
176     time_add(rcvd, LINK_DELAY, &pkthdr->ts);
177     time_add(sys_etime, 1000/TICKS_PER_SECOND, &limit);
178     if (time_less(pkthdr->ts, limit))
179         rxpkt(pkthdr);
180     else
181         queue_rcv(pkthdr, plen);
182 }
```

── ospfd_sim.C

Figure 15.5 Receiving simulated OSPF packets: `SimSys::process_uni_fd()`.

prepended to indicate the time that the packet was sent (`SimPktHdr::ts`) and the physical network that the packet was transmitted onto (`SimPktHdr::phyint`).

175-176   We're going to delay receive processing of the packet `LINK_DELAY` (currently set to 10) milliseconds from the time that it was transmitted.

177   The upper edge of the current timer tick is calculated as `limit`.

178-179   If the packet can be processed immediately, `SimSys::rxpkt()` is called to process the received packet. That routine determines whether the packet should be forwarded or whether it is an OSPF, IGMP, or ICMP packet that is addressed to the simulated router itself.

180-181   If the packet processing must be delayed, the call to `SimSys::queue_rcv()` appends the packet onto the pending receive queue, whose head is `SimSys::rcv_head` and whose tail is `SimSys::rcv_tail`. The call to `SimSys::process_rcvqueue()` from the main loop will then process the received packet when enough time has transpired.

We send the data packets over the loopback interface so that we won't interfere with other workstations. Originally, the sending of multicast packets was coded as sending a multicast UDP packet over the loopback interface. However, this was not supported over all platforms that I was trying to get the simulator to run on. I also experimented with sending to the broadcast address, to the same effect. I settled on the behavior of replicating the simulated multicast datagram in the sender because it was the most portable, although not the most efficient, solution.

15.2 The Simulation Controller Process: `ospf_sim`

In this section, we explore the operation of the simulation controller in more detail, focusing on its initialization, main loop, and major data structures.

15.2.1 Initialization

The controller is a Tk/Tcl application. It begins by creating a Tcl interpreter and then reading the Tcl file `ospf_sim.tcl`, which defines various Tcl commands and creates the map window. These commands can be classified as follows:

- Configuration commands, which are used in the simulation configuration file. Examples of these commands are the `router` command, which creates a simulated router, and the `interface` command, which creates an interface between a simulated router and a simulated network segment.

- Display commands, such as `draw_router`, which displays a router on the network map; `draw_network`, a network segment; and so on.

- Commands implementing the graphical user interface, including the Tk/Tcl code to manage the menus appearing at the top of the network map and to deal with various mouse movements.

The simulation configuration data is held internally in Tcl variables, all having the `_att` suffix. For example, `router_att` is a two-dimensional Tcl array holding the configuration of all the simulated routers. The Tcl command `sendcfg` downloads all the configuration data into a specified simulated router.

After reading `ospf_sim.tcl`, the controller registers the Tcl commands that have been written in C++. These commands include `startrtr`, which spawns a simulated router process, and the commands that download individual portions of a simulated router's OSPF configuration, such as `sendifc`, which is used to download a single OSPF interface.

The controller then opens a server port, on which it listens for incoming control connections from the simulated routers. Finally, the controller reads the simulation's configuration file, spawning a simulated router each time the `router` command is encountered, and asks Tcl to call the routine `tick()` at a frequency of `TICKS_PER_SECOND` times each second. The controller's main loop then takes over.

15.2.2 Main Loop

Tcl implements the main loop of the simulation controller itself. At the end of initialization, the controller simply makes a call to the Tcl library routine `Tk_MainLoop()`, which never returns. Tcl handles keyboard input and mouse movements by the human running the simulation, calling the appropriate Tk/Tcl handling routines.

The only additional processing we have added is the periodic execution of the `tick()` routine, which performs the following operations.

- All incoming control messages from the simulated routers are processed by repeatedly calling `SimCtl::process_replies()`. These messages include tick responses and logging messages.

- The controller recolors the nodes, based on the current states of their link-state databases.

- If all simulated routers have replied to the last `SIM_TICK` message, the simulation time is incremented, and a new tick message is sent to all simulated routers.

- All pending control messages are sent to the simulated routers by using `SimCtl::send_data()`, until either they are all sent or the controller would block when sending.

15.2.3 The `class SimCtl`

A single `class SimCtl` contains all the global data for the simulation controller. The class is shown in Figure 15.6. Throughout the code implementing the controller (`ospfd/ospf_sim/sim.C`), the class is pointed to by the global `class SimCtl *sim`.

8   Information from each of the simulated routers is stored in a `class SimNode`. These classes are organized in the `AVLtree SimCtl::simnodes`, indexed by simulated router's OSPF Router ID. Data stored for each router includes the control connection for the node, pending control transmissions, whether the node has acknowledged the last tick, the last database statistics received from the node, and so on.

9-10   The simulated routers are also organized by control connection, to simplify control I/O. The maximum control file number, needed by `select()`, is stored in `SimCtl::max_fd`.

```
                                                          ———————— simctl.h
 6 class SimCtl {
 7     Tcl_Interp *interp;
 8     AVLtree simnodes;
 9     class SimNode *nodes[NOFILE];
10     int maxfd;
11     int server_fd;
12     int n_ticks;
13     bool running;
14     bool frozen;
15     // Port assignments
16     int assigned_port;
17     AVLtree ifmaps;
18     // Database statistics
19     PatTree stats;
20 public:
21     inline SimCtl(Tcl_Interp *ti);
22     inline int elapsed_seconds();
23     inline int elapsed_milliseconds();
24     void delete_router(class SimNode *node);
25     bool process_replies();
26     bool send_data();
27     void incoming_call();
28     void simnode_handler_read(int fd);
29     void store_mapping(uns32 net_or_addr, uns32 rtr);
30     void send_addrmap(class SimNode *);
31     void send_addrmap_increment(class IfMap *, class SimNode *);
57 };
                                                          ———————— simctl.h
```

Figure 15.6 The controller's main data structure: class `SimCtl`.

11,16   `SimCtl::server_fd` is the socket on which the controller listens for incoming control connections, which is connected to TCP port `SimCtl::assigned_port`.

12,22-23   `SimCtl::n_ticks` is the current simulation time in ticks, where **TICKS_PER_SECOND** ticks make a simulated second. This can be converted to seconds and milliseconds by using `SimCtl::elapsed_seconds()` and `SimCtl::elapsed_milliseconds()`.

13   `SimCtl::running` is set when the controller has read its entire configuration file. Until the entire configuration file is read, configuration updates are not downloaded into the simulated routers.

14   `SimCtl::frozen` is set when you want to prevent the controller from advancing the simulated time, which essentially freezes the state of the simulated network.

17   The **class IfMap** is used to map an IP interface address to its simulated router. These classes are organized in the **AVLtree SimCtl::ifmaps**, indexed by IP interface address.

19   Link-state database statistics—the number of LSAs in the database and the sum of the LSAs' checksums—are stored in **class NodeStats**. If two simulated routers have synchronized databases, they point to the same **NodeStats** class. To make it easy to keep track of how many different database states are currently in the network, **NodeStats** classes are stored in the Patricia tree **SimCtl::stats**, where the key is the raw database statistics themselves. This works only if the compiler packs the raw database statistics in the **struct DBStats**.

24   When the control connection to a simulated router is closed, the simulated router is declared inoperational by **SimCtl::delete_router()**. The simulated router is removed from **SimCtl::simnodes**, and its addresses are removed from **SimCtl::ifmaps**, notifying the other simulated routers accordingly.

27   Requests to open an incoming control connection are processed by **SimCtl::incoming_call()**. A new control connection is created, and a temporary **SimNode** class is allocated until a received **SIM_HELLO** message indicates the Router ID of the simulated router on the other end of the connection. Temporary **SimNode** structures have **SimNode::id()** equal to 0.

28   **SimCtl::simnode_handler_read()** handles control messages from a given simulated router, processing them according to their type and subtype.

29-31   **SimCtl::store_mapping()** saves a mapping between an IP address and its simulated router. For unnumbered point-to-point links, mappings between the segment's **phyint** and the routers at either end of the link are stored. When a simulated router first identifies itself to the controller, **SimCtl::send_addrmap()** is used to download all current mappings into the router. Dynamic changes in address mappings are downloaded into all simulated routers by **SimCtl::send_addrmap_increment()**; deletion of an address mapping is accomplished by setting its associated UDP port (**AddrMap::port**) to 0.

15.3   A Simulated OSPF Router: The **ospfd_sim** Process

Each simulated router is a separate process running the **ospfd_sim** application, which is itself a port of the **ospfd** software to the simulation environment. As described in detail in Chapter 4, Porting Guide, porting the **ospfd** software consists of writing three pieces of code: initialization, a main loop to process received OSPF packets and timing, and a system interface to provide the **ospfd** software with such services as packet transmission. This section will address in detail how these pieces were implemented for the simulated routers running **ospfd_sim**.

15.3.1 Initialization

The simulation controller spawns a simulated router process, giving the simulated router's OSPF Router ID and the controller's server port as arguments to the `ospfd_sim` application. The `ospfd_sim` application then initializes in the following steps.

1. A control connection to the controller's server port is established. It is over this connection that the router will receive configuration and timing information.

2. The system interface is created as `class SimSys *simsys`, which inherits from the base `class OspfSysCalls`. Besides containing the implementation of the system interface for the `ospfd` code, the `SimSys` class contains simulation-specific information, such as the control connection socket (`SimSys::ctl_fd`).

3. The simulated router opens a UDP port (`SimSys::uni_fd`), where it will send and receive simulated OSPF packets.

4. A `SIM_HELLO` message is sent over the control connection, identifying the router and its UDP port to the controller.

5. A server port (`SimSys::ospfd_mon_port`) is opened, where the simulated router listens for monitoring connections. The processing of monitoring requests is exactly the same in the simulated router as in the Linux port of the `ospfd` routing daemon.

6. The `ospfd` software is initialized by creating the `class OSPF *ospf`, using the OSPF Router ID as argument.

The main loop then begins executing, and continues until the simulated router is terminated.

15.3.2 Main Loop

The main loop of the simulated router consists of a call to `select()` to detect I/O activity on a number of sockets. These sockets are the control connection to the simulation controller, possibly multiple monitoring connections, and the UDP port that sends and receives simulated OSPF packets.

The control connection uses the packetized TCP support provided by the `class TcpPkt` documented in Chapter 5, Building Blocks. All reads and writes over the control connection use the nonblocking support provided by the `TcpPkt` class. In particular, if `select()` indicates that bytes can be written to the control connection, a call to the control connection's `TcpPkt::sendpkt()` routine is issued in the main loop. The control message types have already been documented in Section 15.1.2. Implementation details about their reception by the simulated router follow.

- Message types **SIM_CONFIG** and **SIM_CONFIG_DEL** are converted to the appropriate **OSPF::cfgXXX** API routines by **SimSys::config()**.

- When a tick (message type **SIM_TICK**) is received, the simulated router increments its elapsed time, invokes the **ospfd** timer processing by calling the **OSPF::tick()** API routine, processes queued OSPF packets (**SimSys::process_rcvqueue()** in Section 15.1.4), and then acknowledges the tick to the controller (message type **SIM_TICK_RESPONSE**). However, because the control connection is not read until all data packets have been received, tick acknowledgments are not received by the simulation controller until all OSPF packets scheduled for that tick have been processed.

- Each mapping among an IP address and simulated router and UDP port (message type **SIM_ADDRMAP**) is stored in a **class AddressMap**, which is organized into an **AVLtree SimSys::address_map**, where they are indexed by both IP address and the owning simulated router's OSPF Router ID.

- Shutdown requests (message type **SIM_SHUTDOWN**) are mapped into the **ospfd** API routine **OSPF::shutdown()**.

Monitoring connections also use the nonblocking, packetized TCP support provided by **class TcpPkt**. The message types used on these connections are documented in Section 13.13. The list of active monitoring connections is kept in **AVLtree SimSys::monfds**, indexed by file descriptor.

15.3.3 Receiving Simulated OSPF Packets

The reception of simulated OSPF packets is handled by the function **SimSys::rxpkt(SimPktHdr *pkthdr)**, which is displayed in Figure 15.7.

195-197   Simulated packets always have a complete IP header, prepended with the identifier of the network segment where they are to be transmitted and received (**SimPktHdr::phyint**) and the time that the packet was transmitted (**SimPktHdr::ts**).

200-219   The function **SimSys::get_port_addr()** indicates which simulated router owns the destination address specified by this packet. If the destination belongs to another simulated router, we look up the destination in our IP routing table (line **202**) and then forward the packet to its next hop (line **217**). Note that the simulated router uses the IP routing table kept in the **ospfd** software itself, by accessing the API routine **OSPF::ip_lookup()**.

224   Multicast packets may be forwarded, depending on the receiving interface (**pkthdr->phyint**).

221,225   If the destination is one of our own unicast addresses or a multicast address, we call **SimSys::local_demux()**. The packet is then demultiplexed, based on IP protocol number, with OSPF packets handed to the API routine **OSPF::rxpkt()**, which takes both the receiving interface and the packet (including IP header) as arguments.

```
                                                          ─── ospfd_sim.C
189 void SimSys::rxpkt(SimPktHdr *pkthdr)
190
191 {
192     InPkt *pkt;
193     InAddr daddr;
194
195     pkt = (InPkt *) (pkthdr+1);
196     daddr = ntoh32(pkt->i_dest);
197     xmt_stamp = pkthdr->ts;
198     if (!IN_CLASSD(daddr)) {
199         InAddr home;
200         if ((!get_port_addr(daddr, home)) || (home != ospf->my_id())) {
201             MPath *mpp;
202             if ((mpp = ospf->ip_lookup(daddr)) == 0) {
203                 sendicmp(ICMP_TYPE_UNREACH, ICMP_CODE_UNREACH_HOST,
204                          0, 0, pkt, 0, 0, 0);
205             }
206             // Decrement TTL. We don't use checksums in the
207             // IP header of simulated packets
208             else if (pkt->i_ttl == 0 || pkt->i_ttl-- == 1) {
209                 sendicmp(ICMP_TYPE_TTL_EXCEED, 0, 0, 0, pkt, 0, 0, 0);
210             }
211             else {
212                 InAddr gw;
213                 SpfIfc *ip;
214                 gw = mpp->NHs[0].gw;
215                 if (gw != 0 && (ip = mpp->NHs[0].o_ifp) &&
                        ip->unnumbered())
216                     gw = (InAddr) -1;
217                 sendpkt(pkt, mpp->NHs[0].phyint, gw);
218             }
219         }
220         else
221             local_demux(pkthdr);
222     }
223     else {
224         mc_fwd(ntoh32(pkthdr->phyint), pkt);
225         local_demux(pkthdr);
226     }
227 }
                                                          ─── ospfd_sim.C
```

Figure 15.7 Receiving simulated OSPF packets: **SimSys::rxpkt()**.

15.3.4 Simulated System Interface

The `ospfd` software uses the system interface (`class OspfSysCalls`) to perform platform-specific functions, such as sending packets, updating the platform's IP forwarding table, and so on. In the simulated OSPF routers, the system interface is implemented in a superclass of `OspfSysCalls`, `class SimSys`. Some interesting details about the implementation of the simulated system interface follow.

- The send routine which lets the system pick the outgoing interface, `SimSys::sendpkt(InPkt *pkt)`, determines the next-hop IP address and outgoing interface by consulting the IP routing table kept by the `ospfd` software itself, through the API routine `OSPF::ip_lookup()`. The simulation environment does not keep the equivalent of a "kernel routing table," and the system interfaces to add and to delete entries from the kernel routing table (`SimSys::rtadd()` and `SimSys::rtdel()`) are both no-ops.

- The simulated router's own group membership, manipulated through `SimSys::join()` and `SimSys::leave()`, is kept in an `AVLtree SimSys::membership`, indexed by group and network segment number (`phyint`).

- Each of the simulated router's physical interfaces is represented by a `class PhyintMap`. These are stored in the `AVLtree SimSys::port_map`, indexed by `phyint`. Enabling multicast datagram forwarding on an interface puts the interface into promiscuous mode by setting `PhyintMap::promiscuous`.

- The `SimSys::halt()` routine simply calls `exit()` to terminate the `ospfd_sim` process after attempting to log the reason over the control connection.

15.4 Monitoring and Debugging

The graphical interface of the simulator tells you whether the individual simulated routers are running and indicates the network synchronization state of the link-state database. For more detailed OSPF information, you have to look at the logging information printed on the simulator standard output or use the monitoring applications `ospfd_mon` and `ospfd_browser`, which can connect to individual simulated routers through their monitoring port. The monitoring port number can be determined by examining the initial logging messages printed by the simulator, as described in Section 15.1.1.

The `ospfd_mon` application is a command line application that can dump statistics about OSPF neighbors, the link-state database, the routing table, and so on. This application takes the monitoring port of the simulated router as one of its arguments, as described in the `ospfd_mon` manual page in Appendix A.

The `ospfd_browser` application provides similar functionality but in the form of a Web-browser CGI application. The initial page displayed by this application allows you to select the simulated router to be monitored, again by specifying its monitoring port. Appendix A also contains a manual page for `ospfd_browser`.

Debuggers, such as `gdb`, can be used to analyze crash dumps produced by the simulation controller or any of the simulated routers and can be attached to any of the running processes, whose process ID can be determined either from the initial set of logging messages or from system commands, such as `ps` on Linux. As mentioned in Section 15.1.3, breakpointing one of the simulated routers effectively freezes the network state, where it can be examined through the monitoring applications.

Exercises

15.1   Try running the same simulation on both Linux and Windows. Which platform runs the simulation faster? Why do you think that is? Try removing hardware differences from the equation by performing the experiment on a PC that can dual-boot both Linux and Windows.

Appendix A

Manual Pages

This appendix contains UNIX-style manual (man) pages for the programs whose sources are included with this book. These man pages provide brief descriptions of the programs and their usage, suitable for browsing online.

The man pages included in the appendix are:

- `ospfd(8)`. This is the Linux port of the OSPF routing software, implementing an OSPF routing daemon under Linux. This program turns a Linux workstation into an OSPF router, just as the `routed` program allows the workstation to participate in a RIP routing domain.

- `ospfd_browser(1)`. This CGI application [16] allows you to monitor the `ospfd` routing daemon—or any of the simulated OSPF routers running in the OSPF routing simulator `ospf_sim`—through a Web browser.

- `ospfd_mon(1)`. This program can be used to monitor the operation of the OSPF routing software. By specifying command line switches, you can monitor either the OSPF routing daemon or one of the simulated routers running in the OSPF simulator.

- `ospfd_sim(1)`. This application implements a simulated router in the OSPF simulator. Normally started automatically by the routing simulator, `ospfd_sim` can be started by hand for debugging purposes.

- `ospf_sim(1)`. This OSPF routing simulator allows you to simulate a network of OSPF routers on a workstation running either Linux or Windows.

NAME

ospfd—the OSPF routing daemon

SYNOPSIS

/usr/sbin/ospfd

DESCRIPTION

The ospfd program implements the OSPF routing protocol, turning the workstation into an OSPF router. This program is a port of the OSPFD software to UNIX-like operating systems. Appropriate OSPF exchanges are invoked with neighboring OSPF routers, and routing table entries are calculated according to the OSPF protocol specification and installed into the kernel, where they will be used to forward data traffic. The ospfd program is usually invoked in a system boot script.

At program initialization, IP interface information is read from the kernel. The configuration file /etc/ospfd.conf is then read to obtain the router's OSPF configuration: the router's OSPF Router ID, the cost and the area assignment of each interface, and so on.

Errors encountered by the program when attempting to use various system calls are logged to the syslog daemon. Events encountered while running the OSPF protocol are written to the logging file /var/log/ospfd.log. The required severity of an event before it is logged can be adjusted in the configuration file.

Program behavior can be modified dynamically, sending the program signals by using kill(1). To dynamically reconfigure the OSPF routing daemon, edit the configuration file /etc/ospfd.conf and then send the program the USR1 signal. To shut down the OSPF routing daemon, send the HUP or the TERM signal. Before shutting down, the routing daemon will attempt to remove its self-originated LSAs from the other OSPF routers' link-state databases and will notify its OSPF neighbors of its impending demise by sending empty OSPF Hello packets.

Operational statistics can be read out of the ospfd routing daemon by using the ospfd_mon program or via a Web browser through the CGI application ospfd_browser. Available statistics include the state of all OSPF interfaces and neighbors, the contents of the OSPF link-state database, and the routing table that OSPF has calculated.

The workstation can be configured to be in "host mode." In this case, OSPF will be used to calculate the workstation's routing table, but the workstation will not originate any OSPF LSAs. As a result, other OSPF routers will not forward transit traffic to the workstation, and it will be able to operate as an IP host instead of as an IP router.

When the Multicast Extensions to OSPF (MOSPF) are enabled in the configuration file, the workstation is also turned into a multicast router. The resulting functionality is similar to the **mrouted** routing daemon, except that MOSPF is used to calculate the path of multicast datagrams instead of **mrouted**'s DVMRP.

Configuration File Syntax

The following describes the syntax of the **ospfd** configuration file **/etc/ospfd.conf**, an ASCII file that can be written with any text editor. Each line of the configuration file is a command. The meanings of some commands depend on the order in which they appear in the configuration file. For example, an interface defined with the **interface** command is assigned to the area that has most recently been defined in an **area** command.

The following are the global configuration commands.

- **routerid** *id* sets the OSPF Router ID to *id*, which is specified in dotted decimal format. This is the only required configuration command and must appear in the first line of the file.

- **host_mode** tells the workstation to act only as a host; it uses OSPF to calculate its routing table but doesn't advertise any routing capability, by refusing to originate any LSAs.

- **ase_orig_rate** *n_ases* tells the router to rate-limit the number of AS-external-LSAs that it imports into the routing domain to *n_ases* per second; the default rate is 1,000/second.

- **lsu_rxmt_window** *window* sets the maximum number of back-to-back Link State Update packets that will be sent to a neighbor when retransmitting LSAs to *window*; the default value is 8.

- **log_level** *level* controls the number of events that will be logged to the file **/var/log/ospfd.log**. The argument *level* is a number between 0 and 5, inclusive; the larger the number, the fewer the number of messages logged—only the more significant ones.

- **dd_sessions** *n_sessions* sets the maximum number of concurrent Database Exchange sessions that the router will participate in to *n_sessions* initiated by neighbors and an equal number initiated by the router itself (default value is 2).

- **ospfExtLsdbLimit** *ase_limit* sets the maximum number of nondefault AS-external-LSAs that can be held in the router's link-state database to *ase_limit*. When set, *ase_limit* should be the same in all OSPF routers, as described in RFC 1765 [68].

- **ospfExitOverflowInterval** *exit_interval* specifies that a router that hits the limit of nondefault AS-external-LSAs should exit Overflow State in *exit_interval* seconds.

- **mospf** enables the multicast extensions to OSPF (MOSPF; RFC 1584 [66]).

- **no_inter_area_mc** prevents the router from forwarding multicast datagrams across OSPF area boundaries; this takes effect only when MOSPF has been enabled.

The following commands specify an OSPF area's configuration.

- **area** *area_id* adds the area with Area ID of *area_id* (specified in dotted decimal notation) to the router's configuration so that it can be referenced in later commands. Subsequent commands modify the previously specified area.

- **stub** *default_cost* specifies that the area is a stub area and that if the router becomes an area border router, it should originate a default summary-LSA with cost of *default_cost* into the stub area.

- **no_summaries** tells the router not to summarize routing information into the area in summary-LSAs; this command applies only to stub areas.

The **interface** *address cost* command configures an OSPF interface, enabling OSPF on an IP interface whose address is *address*; this interface must already be known to the kernel. The interface will be advertised as having a cost of *cost*, and the interface will be assigned to the area most previously specified in an **area** command. The following commands modify the previously specified interface.

- **mtu** *size* specifies the interface's maximum transmission unit (MTU), the largest IP datagram in bytes that can be sent out the interface without fragmentation; it defaults to the MTU read out of the kernel.

- **IfIndex** *index* sets the interface's MIB-II IfIndex value, which will be advertised for unnumbered links.

- **nbma** sets the interface type to NBMA, and **ptmp** sets the interface type to Point-to-MultiPoint; if the interface type is not set, it defaults according to the interface flags set in the kernel.

- **ospfIfRtrPriority** *pri* sets the interface's Designated Router Priority to *pri*, a value between 0 and 255, inclusive.

The next set of commands sets the various OSPF timer constants associated with the interface.

- **ospfIfTransitDelay** *tdly* sets the interface's transit delay to *tdly* seconds.

- **ospfIfRetransInterval** *rxint* sets the retransmission interval to *rxint* seconds.

- **ospfIfHelloInterval** *hint* specifies that Hello packets are to be sent every *hint* seconds.

- **ospfIfRtrDeadInterval** *dint* specifies that neighbors are declared unreachable if they are not heard from for *dint* seconds.

- **ospfIfPollInterval** *pint* indicates that Hellos are sent to dead neighbors at the reduced rate of one Hello every *pint* seconds (NBMA networks only).

The rest of the interface commands follow.

- **ospfIfAuthType** *autype* sets the type authentication to be used on the interface— an *autype* of 0 indicates none (the default), 1 simple password, and 2 crypto-graphic authentication. If simple password authentication is used, the password is set by using **ospfIfAuthKey** *aukey*, where *aukey* is an ASCII string of eight characters or less.

- **ospfIfMulticastForwarding** *mc_fwd* sets the type of multicast forwarding per-formed on the interface if MOSPF is enabled; *mc_fwd* set to 0 indicates that multi-cast forwarding is disabled, 1 that multicast forwarding uses data-link multicast multicast (the default), and 2 that multicast datagrams are forwarded as data-link unicasts.

- **on-demand** specifies that the interface should be treated as a demand circuit as defined in RFC 1793 [64].

- **passive** indicates that the interface should be advertised in OSPF LSAs but that OSPF protocol packets should not be sent or received over the interface.

The following commands configure address aggregation at area borders.

- **aggregate** *prefix* tells the router to aggregate all the intra-area routes associated with the previously specified area and that fall within *prefix* into a single sum-mary-LSA, to be advertised to all other areas. Prefixes are specified using CIDR notation, for example, 10.1.0.0/16.

- **suppress** tells the router to advertise neither the previously specified aggregate nor any of its contributors, essentially making a range of IP addresses private to a given area.

The **host** *prefix cost* command is used to advertise loopback addresses. An entire range of loopback addresses can be specified in *prefix*, using CIDR notation. The addresses are assigned to the previously specified area and are advertised in the router-LSA associated with that area, with a cost of *cost*.

The command **vlink** *endpoint* adds a virtual link, with Router ID of the other end-point specified in *endpoint*. The virtual link's transit area is the area given in the previous area command. The following commands modify the timers and authentication parame-ters associated with the virtual link, analogous to the similar commands used for regular OSPF interfaces.

- **ospfVirtIfTransitDelay** *tdly*

- **ospfVirtIfRetransInterval** *rxint*

- **ospfVirtIfHelloInterval** *hint*

- `ospfVirtIfRtrDeadInterval` *dint*

- `ospfVirtIfAuthType` *autype*

- `ospfVirtIfAuthKey` *aukey*

To add a neighbor on an NBMA or a Point-to-MultiPoint network segment, use `neighbor` *addr pri*. The neighbor's IP interface address on the NBMA or Point-to-Multi-Point segment is given by *addr*. The neighbor's eligibility to become an NBMA segment's Designated Router is specified by whether the *pri* argument is nonzero.

The following commands add or modify an external prefix that should be imported into the OSPF routing domain in an AS-external-LSA.

- `route` *prefix nexth type metric* indicates that *prefix* (CIDR notation) should be imported by using an external metric type of *type* (1 or 2) and a cost of *metric* (between 0 and 2*24-2, inclusive). The IP address of the next hop toward the prefix is given by *nexth*; this will be used as the AS-external-LSA's forwarding address if it is reachable within the OSPF routing domain.

- `mcsource` indicates that the previously specified external route should be advertised as a multicast source.

- `tag` *tagval* indicates that the previously specified external route should have its external route tag set to *tagval* (a 32-bit integer).

The `md5key` *keyid key* command adds an MD5 key to an interface that is using cryptographic authentication as its authentication mechanism. The added key has Key ID equal to *keyid* (a value between 1 and 255, inclusive) and key equal to the 16-byte (or less) ASCII string *key*. The following commands indicate the activation interval for the previously specified MD5 key. Each of these commands takes a time constant *datestr*, formatted as *date@time*, where *date* and *time* can take any of the formats supported by `strptime()`.

- `startaccept` *datestr*

- `startgenerate` *datestr*

- `stopgenerate` *datestr*

- `stopaccept` *datestr*

Example Configuration File

As an example, the configuration file for a router with OSPF Router ID of 10.1.1.1 and two interfaces with addresses 10.1.3.6 and 10.2.4.5, both attaching to area 0.0.0.2, could be as simple as follows:

```
routerid 10.1.1.1
area 0.0.0.2
```

```
interface 10.1.3.6 1
interface 10.2.4.5 1
```

IP masks for the interfaces and the interfaces' types would be read out of the kernel. To use interface timers other than the default or to use cryptographic authentication on the interfaces, and so on, additional lines would have to be added to the configuration file.

FILES

- `/etc/ospfd.conf`. The `ospfd` configuration file.

- `/usr/sbin/ospfd.tcl`. The Tcl script that reads the `ospfd` configuration file.

- `/var/log/ospfd.log`. The `ospfd` log file.

SEE ALSO

`ifconfig(8)`, `kill(1)`, `ospfd_browser(1)`, `ospfd_mon(1)`, `routed (8)`, `signal()`, `strptime(3C)`, `syslog(8)`

NAME

`ospfd_browser`— the CGI application to monitor `ospfd` routing daemons

SYNOPSIS

`http://localhost/cgi-bin/ospfd_browser`

DESCRIPTION

This CGI application allows the operational statistics of the OSPF routing daemon `ospfd` to be accessed via a Web browser. At the bottom of each page are links allowing you to display

- Global OSPF statistics
- The state of all the router's OSPF interfaces
- The state of all the router's OSPF neighbors
- The router's attached OSPF areas
- The link-state database of any of the router's attached areas
- The database of AS-external-LSAs
- A detailed listing of any of the router's link-state advertisements (LSAs)
- The routing table calculated by OSPF

The CGI application communicates with the OSPF routing daemon via a packetized TCP connection that carries nonstandard queries and responses. The first page displays queries for the host and the port to which the TCP connection should be directed. The default values displayed are those for an `ospfd` routing daemon running on the HTTP server's workstation. By specifying a different host for the TCP connection endpoint, `ospfd` routing daemons on other workstations can be monitored.

In addition, the CGI application can monitor the simulated routers running under the OSPF simulator `ospf_sim`. In that case, a different port number must be specified on the initial page. See the `ospf_sim` manual page for details.

The same information can be obtained through a command line interface by using the program `ospfd_mon`. See that man page for more detail on the meanings of displayed statistics.

BUGS

Because the CGI application communicates with the monitored **ospfd** program by using nonstandard packet formats, the program cannot monitor all OSPF routers, as it could if it were SNMP-based.

SEE ALSO

`ospfd(8), ospfd_mon(1), ospf_sim(1)`

NAME

`ospfd_mon`—an `ospfd` monitoring tool

SYNOPSIS

`/usr/sbin/ospfd_mon` [*host*] [`-p` *port*]

DESCRIPTION

This program presents a command line interface from which you can gather operational statistics of the OSPF routing daemon `ospfd`. The program communicates with the OSPF routing daemon via a packetized TCP connection that carries nonstandard queries and responses. The endpoints of the TCP connection can be specified in the *host* and *port* arguments. By default, the program will attempt to connect to the local `ospfd` daemon, whose monitoring port is 12767. By specifying a different host for the TCP connection endpoint, `ospfd` routing daemons on other workstations can be monitored. By specifying a different port number, simulated OSPF routers running under the OSPF simulator `ospf_sim` can be monitored; see the `ospf_sim` manual page for details.

When started, the program displays the OSPF statistics of the router to which it connects and a command line prompt. At this prompt, you can enter any of the following monitoring commands:

- `statistics`. Displays the global OSPF statistics.

- `interfaces`. Displays the state of all the router's OSPF interfaces. `#Nbr` indicates the number of active neighbors associated with the interface. `#Adj` enumerates the number of neighbors in Full state. For virtual links, the virtual link's transit area is displayed in the column used ordinarily for the corresponding physical interface's name, and the interface address column contains the OSPF Router ID of the virtual link's other endpoint.

- `neighbors`. Displays the state of all the router's OSPF neighbors. `#DD` indicates the number of Database Description packets that still must be sent to the neighbor. `#Req` indicates the number of LSAs currently being requested from the neighbor. `#Rxmt` indicates the number of LSAs that have been flooded to the neighbor but have yet to be acknowledged.

- `areas`. Displays the router's attached OSPF areas.

- `database` *area_id*. Displays the link-state database of the OSPF area having Area ID equal to *area_id*.

- **as-externals**. Displays the database of AS-external-LSAs.

- **adv** *type ls_id adv_rtr area_id*. Displays in gory detail the LSA belonging to the *area_id* database and having LS Type equal to *type*, Link State ID equal to *ls_id*, and Advertising Router equal to *adv_rtr*. The *area_id* argument need not be specified when displaying AS-external-LSAs.

- **routes**. Displays the routing table calculated by OSPF. If the outgoing interface is an unnumbered point-to-point link, the displayed next hop is the IfIndex advertised by the neighboring router.

- **exit**. Terminates the application.

The same information can be obtained via a Web browser through the CGI application **ospfd_browser**.

BUGS

Because **ospfd_mon** communicates with the monitored **ospfd** program by using nonstandard packet formats, the program cannot monitor all OSPF routers, as it could if it were SNMP-based.

The **ospfd_mon** program does a poor job at validating input, so typing the wrong number of arguments, or arguments with the wrong type, can cause the application to crash. This, however, will not adversely affect the monitored **ospfd** routing daemon, and **ospfd_mon** can safely be restarted. The names of the commands can always be abbreviated safely, however.

This program should not be confused with **ospf_monitor**. The latter is a program written by Rob Coltun to monitor his OSPF implementation, which has been a standard part of the **gated** distribution. The **ospf_monitor** program also used a nonstandard query and response mechanism—one that is, unfortunately, totally different from the one used by **ospfd_mon**.

SEE ALSO

ospfd(8), ospfd_browser(1), ospf_sim(1)

NAME

`ospfd_sim`—a simulation of a single OSPF router

SYNOPSIS

`ospfd_sim` *router_id controller_port*

DESCRIPTION

This program, which simulates an OSPF router whose OSPF router ID is *router_id*, is a port of the OSPFD software to the simulation environment provided by the `ospf_sim` program. The program is normally spawned automatically by the `ospf_sim` process that is controlling the simulation. The second argument, *controller_port*, is the port where the controlling `ospf_sim` process is waiting for connections. The simulated router must connect to the controlling process in order to access configuration and timing information and to discover how to send packets to the other simulated OSPF routers involved in the simulation.

   The database synchronization state of the simulated router and logging messages produced by the simulated router are reported to the controlling `ospf_sim` process. The operational statistics of the simulated router may be obtained with the CGI application `ospfd_browser` or the program `ospfd_mon`.

   You may want to start a simulated router by hand if one of a simulation's routers terminates. In this case, the *controller_port* argument can be determined by examining the logging messages that the controlling `ospf_sim` process has printed on its standard output.

BUGS

Unfortunately, the name of this program is very similar to that of the OSPF routing simulator `ospf_sim`. Mistakenly typing the name of this program when trying to start the simulator will produce just a syntax reminder.

SEE ALSO

`ospfd_browser(1)`, `ospfd_mon(1)`, `ospf_sim(1)`

NAME

`ospf_sim`—an OSPF routing simulator

SYNOPSIS

`ospf_sim` [*config_file*]

DESCRIPTION

The `ospf_sim` program allows you to simulate a network of OSPF routers. This simulation can be used to debug the `ospfd` routing software and is also useful for analyzing OSPF configurations for validity. For example, a proposed division of an OSPF routing domain into areas can be simulated to verify that the OSPF area rules are met, even under failure conditions. The simulator can also be used as an OSPF teaching tool.

The simulator is a graphical application built with the Tk/Tcl toolkit. A map of the simulated network is displayed: its routers, network segments, and their interconnections. The routers on the map are color coded to indicate their current state. White means that the router is operational but has not synchronized its link-state database with its neighbors; orange, that the router has synchronized with one or more neighbors; and red, that the router is not functioning. The largest group of synchronized routers is colored green. As a result, the end state of an area configuration has the routers belonging to the largest area colored green and all others colored orange.

The simulator spawns each of the simulated routers as a separate process. Each simulated router executes the `ospfd_sim` application, which is a port of the `ospfd` software to the simulation environment. A control connection is established between `ospf_sim` and each simulated router for the purpose of downloading configuration information, timekeeping, and collecting database synchronization statistics and logging messages.

A file *config_file* containing a network configuration can be given as an optional argument. The configuration file syntax is described later. If no configuration file is specified, the simulator begins with a default configuration that implements the network diagram on the flyleaf. You can modify this configuration by using the graphical user interface. At any point, you can save the network configuration to a file: either the one originally specified on the command line (**Save**) or a new file name (**Save As**).

The simulation can be modified from the graphical user interface in the following ways. The status of each operation performed by the GUI, as well as instructions for operations requiring map navigation, are displayed in the bar at the bottom of the map.

- *Addition of elements to the network map.* Using the **Add** menu, you can add routers, network segments, interfaces between them, and point-to-point connections between routers to the map.

- *Other reconfiguration of simulated routers.* Much of a simulated router's configuration is not displayed graphically but can be modified in the **Add** menu nonetheless. These configuration items include virtual links, imported external routing information, and nonbroadcast neighbors.

- *Disabling network components.* The operational status of simulated routers and interfaces can be toggled by using the **Toggle** menu.

- *Starting and stopping the simulation.* The simulation can be suspended and restarted by using the **Simulation** menu.

- *Executing network diagnostics.* From the **Diagnostics** menu, you can run the commonly used routing diagnostic tools **ping**, **traceroute**, and **mtrace**. From this menu, you can also add and delete group members on the simulated network segments.

Logging messages from the simulated routers are accumulated by the OSPF routing simulator and are displayed on the simulator's standard output stream. Each logging message is prefixed by the current simulation time, expressed in simulated seconds and milliseconds since the simulation was begun, and the OSPF Router ID of the router logging the message.

Operational statistics of each simulated router can be accessed through the CGI application **ospfd_browser** or the command line application **ospfd_mon**. These applications must connect to the simulated router's monitoring port, the determination of which is described in the discussion on ports.

The simulator assigns each network segment a number, starting with 1, and these numbers appear in all logging messages and monitoring responses about the network, prefixed by the capital letter **N**. For example, the first **network** or **pplink** directive appearing in the configuration file will be assigned the name **N1**, and so on.

Simulated Time

The OSPF simulator distributes timer ticks to each of the simulated routers, with **TICKS_PER_SECOND=20** timer ticks per simulated second. The simulator keeps the time in each of the simulated routers synchronized by requiring all simulated routers to acknowledge the current tick before a new tick is generated. The simulation is suspended by simply suspending the sending of ticks to the simulated routers.

Simulated time is displayed in the bottom-right corner of the map, in seconds and milliseconds since the simulation was begun.

Configuration File Syntax

The following describes the format of the simulator's configuration file, which can be created either with a text editor or automatically, using the graphical user interface's **Save** and **Save As** commands. Each of the lines in the configuration file consists of one of the following commands. Some of the commands take (**x**, **y**) coordinates, specifying where to display the object in the screen. The upper-left corner of the map has coordinates (0,0); the lower-right corner is (2000,2000), with the **x** coordinate increasing as you go right and the **y** coordinate increasing as you go down. By default, the lower-right corner of the displayed portion of the map has coordinates (600, 350); to see the rest of the map, you have to use the scroll bars.

> **router** *rtr_id x y mospf*

Add a router with OSPF Router ID *rtr_id* (dotted decimal format) at the map coordinates (*x, y*). The router runs MOSPF if and only if *mospf* is nonzero.

> **host** *rtr_id x y*

Add a host at the map coordinates (*x, y*). This host will run the OSPF protocol to calculate its routing tables but will not advertise LSAs. Nor will it forward transit traffic; that is, it's not a router. However, because it is still running the OSPF protocol, it needs to be assigned an OSPF Router ID *rtr_id*.

> **interface** *rtr_id addr cost passive ospf*

Add an interface to the router with OSPF Router ID *rtr_id*. The IP address of the interface is *addr*, and OSPF will advertise the interface with a metric of *cost* (1-65,534, inclusive). This command connects routers to network segments. Connections between routers are established with the **pplink** command. If *passive* is nonzero, the interface will be advertised in router-LSAs but will not send and receive OSPF protocol packets. If *ospf* is set to zero, the interface will be added to the simulated router's routing table but will not run OSPF; nor will it be advertised by OSPF.

> **broadcast** *prefix area x y demand*
> **nbma** *prefix area x y demand*
> **ptmp** *prefix area x y demand*

Add a broadcast, NBMA, or Point-to-MultiPoint network segment at the map coordinates (*x, y*). It will be assigned the set of addresses designated by *prefix*, which is input in CIDR notation (for example, 10.1.0.0/16) and will also be assigned to Area ID *area* (dotted decimal notation). If *demand* is nonzero, the segment will be a demand circuit as defined in RFC 1793 [64].

> **pplink** *rtr_id1 addr1 cost1 rtr_id2 addr2 cost2 area demand*

Add a point-to-point link between two routers. Router *rtr_id1* will be one end of the link, its IP interface address on the link will be *addr1,* and it will advertise the link with metric *cost1.* Likewise, the other end, *rtr_id2,* will assign the IP interface address of *addr2* and will advertise a metric of *cost2.* If you want the link to be unnumbered, assign both *addr1* and *addr2* to be 0.0.0.0. The link will be assigned to Area ID *area.* If *demand* is nonzero, the link will be a demand circuit as defined in RFC 1793 [64].

> **vlink** *rtr_id1 rtr_id2 area*

Create a virtual link between routers *rtr_id1* and *rtr_id2.* The Area ID of the virtual link's transit area will be *area.*

> **aggr** *rtr_id area prefix noadv*

Add an area aggregate to router *rtr_id.* The router will aggregate all intra-area routes belong to Area ID *area* and falling under *prefix* (CIDR notation) into a single summary-LSA to be advertised into other areas. If *noadv* is nonzero, the aggregate and all its contributors will be suppressed.

> **stub** *rtr_id area default_cost import*

Tell router *rtr_id* that Area ID *area* is to be treated as a stub area. If the router is an area border router, it should originate a default summary-LSA of cost *default_cost* into the stub area. If *import* is set to 0, the router will be inhibited from advertising other summary-LSAs into the stub area.

> **extrt** *rtr_id prefix nh etype cost noadv*

Router *rtr_id* will import the external route *prefix* (CIDR notation) into the OSPF routing domain in an AS-external-LSA. The AS-external-LSA will specify an external metric type of *etype* (1 or 2), and a metric of *cost.* If the next hop *nh* for the external route is set to something other than 0.0.0.0, the route will be imported only if the next hop is reachable via an intradomain path; in that case, the AS-external-LSA's forwarding address will be set to *nh.* If *noadv* is nonzero, the external route will be added to the router's routing table but will *not* be advertised in an AS-external-LSA.

> **loopback** *rtr_id prefix area*

The router *rtr_id* will advertise the address *prefix* (CIDR notation) in its router-LSA for Area ID *area*. The address *prefix* will be treated as a set of addresses belonging to the router but not attached to any particular OSPF interface. Instead, one can think of the address as belonging to an internal loopback interface.

```
neighbor rtr_id addr drpri
```

Add the neighbor whose IP address is *addr* to the configuration of router *rtr_id*; *addr* should be an address on the network segment shared by the router and its neighbor. If *drpri* is 0, the neighbor is ineligible to become Designated Router on the shared network segment; otherwise, the neighbor is assumed capable of becoming Designated Router.

Configuration File Example

The following configuration file is used as the default configuration in the absence of any configuration file specified on the command line. This default configuration implements the network diagram on the flyleaf.

```
router 10.0.0.1 210 209 1
router 10.0.0.2 248 122 1
router 10.0.0.3 313 120 1
router 10.0.0.4 349 209 1
router 10.1.1.8 124.0 116.0 1
router 10.0.0.9 125.0 267.0 1
router 10.0.0.10 246.0 40.0 1
router 10.0.0.11 313.0 40.0 1
router 10.0.0.12 399.0 96.0 1
router 10.0.0.13 519.0 94.0 1
router 10.0.0.5 453.0 166.0 1
router 10.0.0.6 453.0 246.0 1
router 10.0.0.7 387.0 290.0 1
router 10.0.0.14 528.0 297.0 1
broadcast 10.1.3.0/24 0.0.0.2 125.0 191.0 0
broadcast 10.1.2.0/24 0.0.0.2 45.0 119.0 0
broadcast 10.1.1.0/24 0.0.0.2 43.0 266.0 0
broadcast 10.2.2.0/24 0.0.0.1 380.0 20.0 0
broadcast 10.2.1.0/24 0.0.0.1 178.0 21.0 0
broadcast 10.4.1.0/24 0.0.0.4 460.0 42.0 0
broadcast 10.4.2.0/24 0.0.0.5 459.0 330.0 0
broadcast 10.3.7.0/24 0.0.0.3 537.0 165.0 0
broadcast 10.8.2.0/24 0.0.0.3 529.0 244.0 0
pplink 10.0.0.1 0.0.0.0 1 10.0.0.2 0.0.0.0 1 0.0.0.0 0
pplink 10.0.0.1 0.0.0.0 2 10.0.0.3 0.0.0.0 2 0.0.0.0 0
pplink 10.0.0.1 0.0.0.0 1 10.0.0.4 0.0.0.0 1 0.0.0.0 0
interface 10.0.0.1 10.1.3.1 3 0 1
```

```
loopback 10.0.0.1 1.0.0.1/32 0.0.0.0
pplink 10.0.0.2 0.0.0.0 2 10.0.0.4 0.0.0.0 2 0.0.0.0 0
loopback 10.0.0.2 1.0.0.2/32 0.0.0.0
pplink 10.0.0.3 0.0.0.0 1 10.0.0.4 0.0.0.0 1 0.0.0.0 0
loopback 10.0.0.3 1.0.0.3/32 0.0.0.0
pplink 10.0.0.4 192.168.4.1 3 10.0.0.5 192.168.5.1 3 0.0.0.3 0
pplink 10.0.0.4 192.168.4.2 3 10.0.0.6 192.168.6.1 3 0.0.0.3 0
loopback 10.0.0.4 1.0.0.4/32 0.0.0.0
interface 10.1.1.8 10.1.3.8 3 0 1
interface 10.1.1.8 10.1.2.8 1 0 1
interface 10.0.0.9 10.1.3.9 3 0 1
interface 10.0.0.9 10.1.1.9 1 0 1
interface 10.0.0.10 10.2.1.10 1 0 1
pplink 10.0.0.10 0.0.0.0 3 10.0.0.2 0.0.0.0 3 0.0.0.1 0
pplink 10.0.0.10 0.0.0.0 3 10.0.0.11 0.0.0.0 3 0.0.0.1 1
interface 10.0.0.11 10.2.2.11 1 0 1
pplink 10.0.0.11 0.0.0.0 3 10.0.0.3 0.0.0.0 3 0.0.0.1 1
interface 10.0.0.12 10.4.1.12 1 0 1
pplink 10.0.0.12 0.0.0.0 3 10.0.0.5 0.0.0.0 3 0.0.0.4 0
interface 10.0.0.13 10.4.1.13 1 0 1
pplink 10.0.0.13 0.0.0.0 3 10.0.0.5 0.0.0.0 3 0.0.0.4 0
interface 10.0.0.5 10.3.7.5 1 0 1
pplink 10.0.0.5 0.0.0.0 3 10.0.0.6 0.0.0.0 3 0.0.0.3 0
pplink 10.0.0.6 0.0.0.0 3 10.0.0.7 0.0.0.0 3 0.0.0.5 0
pplink 10.0.0.6 0.0.0.0 3 10.0.0.14 0.0.0.0 3 0.0.0.5 0
interface 10.0.0.6 10.8.2.6 1 0 1
interface 10.0.0.7 10.4.2.7 1 0 1
interface 10.0.0.14 10.4.2.6 1 0 1
extrt 10.0.0.2 1.0.0.0/8 0.0.0.0 2 1 0
extrt 10.0.0.2 2.0.0.0/8 0.0.0.0 2 1 0
extrt 10.0.0.2 4.0.0.0/8 11.0.0.254 2 1 0
extrt 10.0.0.2 3.0.0.0/8 0.0.0.0 1 10 0
extrt 10.0.0.12 5.0.0.0/8 0.0.0.0 1 10 0
extrt 10.0.0.12 6.0.0.0/8 0.0.0.0 1 10 0
extrt 10.1.1.8 0.0.0.0/0 10.1.2.254 1 1 0
extrt 10.1.1.8 3.0.0.0/8 0.0.0.0 2 1 0
vlink 10.0.0.4 10.0.0.5 0.0.0.3
vlink 10.0.0.4 10.0.0.6 0.0.0.3
aggr 10.0.0.1 0.0.0.2 10.1.0.0/16 0
aggr 10.0.0.2 0.0.0.1 10.2.0.0/16 0
aggr 10.0.0.3 0.0.0.1 10.2.0.0/16 0
```

Ports

Under certain circumstances, it becomes necessary to discover the identity of certain TCP ports that are used by the simulation. If you want to monitor a simulated router by using the CGI application `ospfd_browser` or the command line monitoring program `ospfd_mon`, you need to know the port that a given simulated router is listening on for monitoring connections. If you want to restart a particular simulated router, you must execute the `ospfd_sim` program by hand, giving as arguments the simulated router's OSPF Router ID and the port on which `ospf_sim` is accepting control connections.

When the OSPF simulator starts, two lines are printed on standard output for each simulated router, as in the following example:

```
0:300 (10.0.0.2) OSPF.113: PID 1012 ospfd_mon port 1032
0:300 (10.0.0.2) OSPF.113: invoked: ospfd_sim 10.0.0.2 1025
```

These messages mean that the simulated router 10.0.0.2 is running as process 1012 and is listening on TCP port 1032 for monitoring connections. The process ID can be used if you want to halt the simulated router—`kill -s SEGV 1012` would stop the simulated router, producing a core dump in the process, whereas `kill -s HUP 1012` would cause the simulated router to gracefully exit. The process ID is also needed if you are trying to attach `gdb` to a simulated router for debugging purposes. The command `ospfd_mon -p 1032` will connect you to the simulated router 10.0.0.2 for the purpose of dumping various OSPF statistics.

The second line indicates that `ospf_sim` is accepting control connections on TCP port 1025. To restart the simulated router 10.0.0.2, the command `ospfd_sim 10.0.0.2 1025` is executed, which is precisely how `ospf_sim` spawned the simulated router 10.0.0.2 in the first place.

BUGS

Certain failures cannot be simulated. For example, two routers having the same OSPF Router ID cannot be simulated.

As implemented, two routers are considered to be synchronized when (1) they have the same set of AS-external-LSAs, (2) the lowest Area ID that each router sees is the same, and (3) the two routers agree on that area's link-state database. Consequently, the largest area will not necessarily be colored green. However, if area 0 is the largest area, all routers belonging to area 0 will be colored green as long as the OSPF area configuration rules have been satisfied.

If you want to simulate a physical network segment that has multiple assigned IP prefixes, you have to add multiple separate network segments in the simulator. The prefixes cannot be tied together, which you would want to do to accurately simulate MOSPF behavior in the multiple prefix case.

SEE ALSO

`kill(1), ospfd(8), ospfd_browser(1), ospfd_mon(1), ospfd_sim(1), signal()`

Appendix B

OSPFD Logging Messages

This appendix lists the various logging messages that can be produced by the OSPF implementation. The format of each message is given, together with its logging level and a brief description of the message's meaning. A general discussion of the implementation's message logging can be found in Chapter 5, Building Blocks.

Messages have been divided into three broad categories. Messages about the configuration and administration of the OSPF router are numbered starting at 1. Error messages are numbered starting at 100. Informational messages start at 200.

When describing message formats, the following shorthand is used:

- *%string*. A text string, such as an error description.

- *%integer*. An integer value, such as the length of a packet in bytes.

- *%spfpkt*. An OSPF packet description, which consists of the OSPF packet type and the IP source and destinations of the packet. An example packet description would be **Hello 10.2.2.11->224.0.0.5**.

- *%ippkt*. An IP packet, identified by its source and destination addresses, such as **10.2.2.2->10.2.2.254**.

- *%lsa*. An OSPF link-state advertisement or LSA, expressed as the 3-tuple of the LSA's LS type, Link State ID, and Advertising Router fields. For example, the router-LSA originated by router 10.0.0.11 would be denoted by **LSA(1,10.0.0.11,10.0.0.11)**.

- *%area.* An OSPF area, identified by its Area ID, such as **Area 0.0.0.1**.

- *%interface.* An OSPF interface. Virtual links are identified by their transit area and the OSPF Router ID of the virtual link's remote endpoint (**VL Area 0.0.0.3 Endpt 10.0.0.4**). Unnumbered interfaces are identified by the name of the underlying physical interface (**Ifc s10**). Numbered interfaces are identified by their IP interface address (**Ifc 192.168.5.1**).

- *%neighbor.* An OSPF neighbor. Neighbors on multiaccess network segments are identified by their IP addresses (**Nbr 10.1.3.1**). Otherwise, neighbors are identified by their OSPF Router ID and associated interface (**Nbr 10.0.0.4 Ifc s10**).

- *%rte.* An IP routing table entry, which is printed as a prefix, the routing table entry type, and cost. One example is: **10.2.0.0/16 inter-area cost 16**.

- *%ipaddr.* An IPv4 address, printed in dotted decimal notation.

B.1 Configuration and Management Messages

Message: **OSPF.001: ospfd Starting**
Level: 5
Discussion: The OSPF routing daemon has started.

Message: **OSPF.002: Adding** *%area*
Level: 5
Discussion: A new OSPF area has been added to the OSPF configuration. This operation is necessary only for those areas to which the router will connect to directly. See Section 13.4 for further details.

Message: **OSPF.003: Deleting** *%area*
Level: 5
Discussion: An OSPF area has been deleted from the router's configuration.

Message: **OSPF.004: Adding** *%interface*
Level: 5
Discussion: A new OSPF interface has been configured in the router. See Section 13.2 for information about interface configurations.

Message: **OSPF.005: Deleting** *%interface*
Level: 5
Discussion: One of the router's OSPF interfaces has been deleted. The router will stop sending and receiving OSPF packets on the interface and will stop advertising the interface in LSAs.

B.2   Error Messages

Message: `OSPF.100: Received packet too short` *%spfpkt*
Level: 3
Discussion: An OSPF packet that is too short to be processed has been received. The packet is physically smaller than the length indicated by the IP header, physically smaller than the length indicated by the OSPF header, or smaller than the minimum-sized OSPF packet. The packet is discarded.

Message: `OSPF.101: Received bad OSPF version number` *%spfpkt*
Level: 3
Discussion: An OSPF packet has been received with an OSPF version number other than 2. The packet is discarded.

Message: `OSPF.102: No matching receive interface` *%spfpkt*
Level: 3
Discussion: The router has no interface that can match the received OSPF packet. This could indicate that (1) multiple IP subnets have been configured on the physical wire and that the router does not participate in all of them, (2) there is a disagreement on the subnet's OSPF area assignment, (3) there is a disagreement on the subnet's mask, or (4) there is a half-configured virtual link. In any case, the packet is discarded.

Message: `OSPF.103: No matching neighbor` *%spfpkt*
Level: 3
Discussion: An OSPF packet has been received from a router with which no neighbor relationship has yet been established. Such packets are ignored until the neighbor relationship is established with the receipt of an OSPF Hello packet from the neighbor. This message is common when the router restarts, because its former neighbors may still be trying to flood LSAs over a now defunct adjacency.

Message: `OSPF.104: Authentication failure` *%spfpkt*
Level: 5
Discussion: A received packet has failed OSPF's authentication procedures. This could mean that there is a misconfiguration; there is an intruder; there are multiple OSPF instances on a single wire, distinguished by their OSPF authentication keys; or a packet has been corrupted. For null and trivial password protection, this message also covers packet checksum failures.

Message: `OSPF.105: Not DR/Backup, but rcvd` *%spfpkt*
Level: 3
Discussion: A router that is neither the Designated Router nor the Backup Designated Router on the subnet has received a packet from the subnet addressed to AllDRouters.

This could mean that the router's multicast filters are not working correctly or that there are multiple subnets on a single wire, with the router Designated Router (or Backup DR) on some but not all of them.

Message: `OSPF.106: Bad LSA checksum` *%lsa %neighbor*
Level: 5
Discussion: An LSA has been received from a neighbor via flooding, and the LSA fails the checksum calculation. The LSA is discarded. Most likely, the LSA has been damaged during transmission, and retransmission of the LSA by the neighbor will be successful. However, if checksum failures persist, an improperly coded checksum algorithm is implicated. One possible confusing situation is the following. The LSA checksum uses the Fletcher checksum, whose one's complement arithmetic would seem to make the four checksum values 0x0000, 0xffff, 0x00ff, and 0xff00 equivalent. However, many implementations accept only 0xffff. We take the position "conservative in what you send and liberal in what you accept" and generate only 0xffff while accepting all three.

Message: `OSPF.107: AS-external-LSAs in stub area` *%lsa %neighbor*
Level: 5
Discussion: A neighbor is trying to flood an AS-external-LSA over an interface belonging to a stub area. This violates the OSPF spec, and the AS-external-LSA is discarded. Unfortunately, if you see this message once, you'll probably see it repeatedly, as the neighbor keeps trying.

Message: `OSPF.108: Unrecognized LS type` *%lsa %neighbor*
Level: 5
Discussion: An LSA that is not supported has been received in an LS Update packet from a neighbor. The LSA is discarded. Currently, this implementation supports only the standard LS Types 1–5 and the optional group-membership-LSA (LS Type 6). It is not an error to see this message for multicasted Link State Updates, which contain LSAs if any of the routers on the local segment support them.

Message: `OSPF.109: Old ack` *%lsa %neighbor*
Level: 4
Discussion: An acknowledgment has been received from a neighbor for an LSA that is less recent than the database copy of the LSA. The acknowledgment is ignored. Perhaps the neighbor has refused the latest copy of the LSA due to the MinLSArrival logic in Step 5a of RFC 2328's Section 13 [75].

Message: `OSPF.110: Bad ack` *%lsa %neighbor*
Level: 5

Discussion: Because it references a more recent instance of the LSA than is in the database, an LSA acknowledgment received from a neighbor is being ignored. Perhaps the latest LSA instance has been rejected due to MinLSArrival processing.

Message: `OSPF.111`: `Unhandled case` *%string1* `state` *%string2* *%interface*
Level: 5
Discussion: An event *%string1* has occurred on an interface in state *%string2*. This event was not anticipated by the interface FSM and so is being ignored, which is probably the correct action.

Message: `OSPF.112`: `Unhandled case` *%string1* `state` *%string2* *%neighbor*
Level: 5
Discussion: An event *%string1* has occurred on a neighbor in state *%string2*. This event was not anticipated by the neighbor FSM and so is being ignored, which is probably the correct action.

Message: `OSPF.113`: *%string*
Level: can't be turned off
Discussion: The OSPF implementation has encountered an error, described by *%string*, while trying to invoke a system interface call (see Chapter 4, Porting Guide).

Message: `OSPF.114`: `non-DoNotAge routers present` *%lsa* *%neighbor*
Level: 5
Discussion: An LSA has been received from a neighbor during flooding. The LSA has DoNotAge set, but some OSPF routers are not capable of DoNotAge processing. We accept the LSA but turn off its DoNotAge bit. This is nonstandard practice but avoids stalling the Database Exchange process when the DoNotAge capability of the network is changing.

Message: `OSPF.115`: `send fails, no valid source` *%spfpkt* *%interface*
Message: `OSPF.115`: `send fails, no valid source` *%spfpkt* *%neighbor*
Level: 5
Discussion: We are trying to send an OSPF packet out an unnumbered interface or to a neighbor over an unnumbered interface but don't have another address to use in the IP source address field of the packet. The packet is discarded instead of being sent.

Message: `OSPF.116`: `Received IGMP packet too short` *%ippkt*
Level: 5
Discussion: The physical length of a received IGMP packet is less than the length indicated by the IP header. The packet is discarded.

Message: `OSPF.117: Received IGMP packet bad xsum` *%ippkt*
Level: 5
Discussion: A received IGMP packet fails to checksum correctly, indicating packet corruption. The packet is discarded.

Message: `OSPF.118: No matching interface for received IGMP` *%ippkt*
Level: 5
Discussion: An IGMP packet has been received, and its IP source address does not belong to any of the router's directly connected interfaces. The IGMP packet is discarded. *Note:* There are legitimate reasons for the IP source address of some IGMP packets to belong to a remote subnet, such as multicast traceroute. These packets should be handled by the system kernel instead of being given to the OSPF/MOSPF routing process.

B.3   Informational Messages

Message: `OSPF.200: DR Election` *%interface* `DR` *%ipaddr1* `Back` *%ipaddr2*
Level: 4
Discussion: The Designated Router election has been rerun for an attached network segment (the one the *interface* attaches to), and the identity of the segment's Designated Router and/or Backup Designated Router has changed. The identities of the new Designated Router and Backup Designated Router are printed, as their IP addresses (*ipaddr1* and *ipaddr2*, respectively) on the segment. Normally, this message is a result of the router recently attaching to the segment or of the previous Designated Router and/or Backup Designated Router failing.

Message: `OSPF.201: Received` *%spfpkt*
Level: 1
Discussion: A received OSPF protocol packet has passed incoming validation checks and will now be processed according to its OSPF packet type.

Message: `OSPF.202: Sent` *%spfpkt %interface*
Message: `OSPF.202: Sent` *%spfpkt %neighbor*
Level: 1
Discussion: An OSPF protocol packet is being transmitted—either multicast out an interface or directly to a specified neighbor.

Message: `OSPF.203: New` *%lsa*
Level: 1
Discussion: A new instance of the specified LSA has been received from a neighbor by the flooding process and is being installed into the link-state database.

Message: `OSPF.204: Originating` *%lsa*
Level: 3
Discussion: The router is originating a new instance of one of its own (self-originated) LSAs. The LSA will be installed in the link-state database and flooded throughout the rest of the OSPF routing domain.

Message: `OSPF.205: Received self-orig` *%lsa*
Level: 4
Discussion: The router has received an LSA instance that is newer than the database copy (if any) but that indicates that it was originated by the router itself. This is probably an LSA that the router originated before it was last restarted. The router originates a new instance of the LSA with the next highest LS Sequence Number, or flushes the LSA if the router no longer wants it advertised.

Message: `OSPF.206: Failed MinArrival` *%lsa %neighbor*
Level: 4
Discussion: The router has received an update for an LSA that has just recently (within the last MinLSArrival seconds) been installed into the link-state database. The router discards the LSA, forcing the neighbor to retransmit. This mechanism rate-limits the origination of LSAs, even if the ultimate originator is not obeying the restriction to update each LSA at most once every MinLSInterval seconds. Unfortunately, the MinLS-Arrival check sometimes misbehaves during Database Exchange, causing needless LSA retransmissions.

Message: `OSPF.207: Duplicate ack` *%lsa %neighbor*
Level: 1
Discussion: The neighbor is acknowledging the correct instance of an LSA, but for some reason, the router already knows that the neighbor has the LSA. The acknowledgment is simply ignored.

Message: `OSPF.208: Rxmt` *%lsa %neighbor*
Level: 4
Discussion: An LSA is being retransmitted to a neighbor because the neighbor has not acknowledged the LSA. Possibly either the update or the acknowledgment was discarded or corrupted by the network. Also, the neighbor could have intentionally discarded the update, due to the MinLSArrival check. Continual retransmissions of the same LSA instance are usually an indication of an interoperability problem or, sometimes, of a router with an extremely congested output queue.

Message: `OSPF.209: Rxmt DD` *%neighbor*
Level: 4
Discussion: The router is performing the Database Exchange process with a neighbor and is playing the role of master. Because the neighbor has not acknowledged the router's

last Database Description packet by sending one that echoes the DD Sequence Number, the router is forced to retransmit the last Database Description packet. If the neighbor does not acknowledge within the RouterDeadInterval, the router will restart the Database Exchange process.

Message: `OSPF.210:` `Rxmt LsReq` *%lsa %neighbor*
Level: 4
Discussion: A request for a given LSA is being retransmitted to a neighbor. Repeated unsatisfied requests indicate an interoperability problem and will eventually force the Database Exchange process to be restarted.

Message: `OSPF.211:` `Flushing` *%lsa*
Level: 3
Discussion: To delete an LSA from the OSPF routing domain, its age is being set to MaxAge, and it is being reflooded. After the flood is acknowledged, the LSA will be removed from the router's link-state database and its associated memory freed.

Message: `OSPF.212:` `Freeing` *%lsa*
Level: 3
Discussion: The LSA is being removed from the router's link-state database, and its associated memory will be freed.

Message: `OSPF.213:` `Refreshing` *%lsa*
Level: 1
Discussion: An LSA is being refreshed by increasing its LS Sequence Number by 1, rebuilding its contents, and reflooding it. Unless you have configured the OSPF implementation to set the DoNotAge bit in the LSAs it originates, this happens whenever the age of a self-originated LSA hits LSRefreshTime (30 minutes). When DoNotAge is configured, the refresh interval becomes configurable.

Message: `OSPF.214:` `Reflooding MaxAge` *%lsa*
Level: 3
Discussion: One of the LSAs in the router's link-state database has hit the LS Age of MaxAge. This LSA is then reflooded so that all other routers will remove the LSA from their databases at more or less the same time. This LSA was probably originated by an OSPF router that has been removed from service or that has been for some other reason unreachable for a long time.

Message: `OSPF.215:` `Deferring` *%lsa*
Level: 3
Discussion: Reorigination of a particular LSA is being deferred until MinLSInterval seconds have elapsed since its last origination. Note that after MinLSInterval seconds, the

LSA may or may not be reoriginated, depending on whether its contents have changed since the last origination.

Message: OSPF.216: **Seqno wrap** %*lsa*
Level: 5
Discussion: The sequence number of a self-originated LSA has hit the maximum allowable value of MaxSequenceNumber. In order to reoriginate the LSA, the LSA must first be flushed from the routing domain and then reoriginated, using the initial LS Sequence Number of 0x80000001. Because sequence number wrap should happen at most only once in every 300 years, this message indicates either an error condition in some router or an attack on the network ([107]).

Message: OSPF.217: **Adding** %*rte*
Level: 3
Discussion: The OSPF implementation is adding or modifying a particular entry with the kernel's IP routing table.

Message: OSPF.218: **Adding** %*rte*
Level: 3
Discussion: The OSPF implementation is adding a reject or discard entry to the kernel routing table. Matching IP datagrams should be discarded instead of forwarded. These entries are added when aggregating routing information at area borders, in order to prevent possible routing loops.

Message: OSPF.219: **Deleting** %*rte*
Level: 3
Discussion: A prefix is now unreachable and so is being deleted from the kernel routing table.

Message: OSPF.220: **Join** %*ipaddr* %*interface*
Level: 4
Discussion: The OSPF implementation has joined the multicast group *ipaddr* on the physical *interface*, because it wishes to receive OSPF packets sent to that group address. This function is performed when an interface first comes up (AllSPFRouters) and when a router is elected Designated Router or Backup Designated Router (AllDRouters).

Message: OSPF.221: **Leave** %*ipaddr* %*interface*
Level: 4
Discussion: The OSPF implementation no longer wants to receive packets multicast to *ipaddr* on *interface*, so it leaves the multicast group. This behavior is invoked when the router relinquishes Designated Router and Backup Designated Router duties.

Message: `OSPF.222: Ifc FSM` *%string1* `<-` *%string2* `event` *%string3* *%interface*
Level: 1, 4, or 5
Discussion: The interface state has changed. The interface FSM has processed the event described by *string3* and has transitioned from the state named by *string2* into the new state *string1*. If this is a state regression—that is, the event is some kind of failure—the message is logged with level 5. Otherwise, if the new interface state is one of the terminal states (P-P, DROther, Backup, or DR) the level is 4, with all other state changes logged at level 1.

Message: `OSPF.223: Nbr FSM` *%string1* `<-` *%string2* `event` *%string3* *%neighbor*
Level: 1, 4, or 5
Discussion: The neighbor state has changed. The neighbor FSM has processed the event described by *string3* and has transitioned from the state named by *string2* into the new state *string1*. If this is a state regression—that is, the neighbor is now further away from being fully adjacent—the message is logged with level 5. Otherwise, if the new neighbor state is one of the terminal states (2-Way or Full), the level is 4, with all other state changes logged at level 1.

Message: `OSPF.224: MTU mismatch` *%neighbor* `mtu` *%integer*
Level: 5
Discussion: A received Database Description packet has notified the router that the neighbor's maximum transmission unit (MTU) for the interface, listed as *integer*, does not match the router's MTU for the interface. Because this mismatch could lead to black holes for large data packets and could also inhibit link-state database synchronization, the router prevents an adjacency from forming with the neighbor.

Message: `OSPF.225: Importing` *%lsa*
Level: 4
Discussion: A newly configured external route is being imported into the OSPF routing domain as an AS-external-LSA. The external route is imported only if it is better than any other routes that are currently being advertised by OSPF routers to the destination.

Message: `OSPF.226: Refreshing DoNotAge` *%lsa*
Level: 1
Discussion: The router has been configured to originate AS-external-LSAs with the DoNotAge bit set. The time has come to refresh one of these LSAs, according to the configured refresh interval.

Message: `OSPF.229: New IGMP Querier` *%ipaddr* *%interface*
Level: 4

Discussion: The identity of the IGMP Querier has changed on the printed interface. The IP address of the new Querier is *ipaddr*. Because IGMPv2 is running, the Querier is the IGMPv2 router with the smallest IP address on the attached network segment.

Message: `OSPF.230: Multicast cache request` *%ipaddr1 -> %ipaddr2*
Level: 5
Discussion: MOSPF has been asked to calculate the multicast path for a datagram with source *ipaddr1* and destination group *ipaddr2*. The level of this message has been set high for MOSPF testing but should be set back to 1 in an operational MOSPF router to limit the number of messages produced.

Message: `OSPF.231: New group` *%ipaddr* on *%interface*
Level: 4
Discussion: The system has indicated that a new group *ipaddr* has just appeared on the attached network segment. This is usually an indication from IGMP that the first Membership Report has been heard for a given group. However, the message can also indicate that an internal application has joined a multicast group independent of interface, in which case the interface is omitted from the message. New groups can cause MOSPF to generate group-membership-LSAs and adjust the path of multicast datagrams accordingly.

Message: `OSPF.232: Group expired` *%ipaddr* on *%interface*
Level: 4
Discussion: The system has indicated that members of group *ipaddr* are no longer on the attached network segment. This is usually an indication from IGMP that the Membership Reports are no longer being heard for a given group. However, the message can also indicate that an internal application has left a multicast group independent of interface, in which case the interface is omitted from the message. Group expiration can cause MOSPF to reoriginate or to flush group-membership-LSAs and to adjust the path of multicast datagrams accordingly.

Message: `OSPF.233: Received IGMP packet, type` *%integer %ippkt*
Level: 1
Discussion: A seemingly valid IGMP packet has been received, with the first byte (IGMP type) equal to *integer*. We will demultiplex on this value and do the appropriate processing. The IGMP types supported are IGMP Membership Query (17), V1 Membership Report (18), V2 Membership Report (22), and the IGMP Leave Message (23). The OSPF simulator also supports the IGMP multicast traceroute messages, but they are handled in a code path separate from the one generating `OSPF.233`.

B.4   Halt Messages

In certain places in the OSPF code, internal consistency checks are executed to check that the code logic is correct. When one of these checks fails, it means that an implementation error has been uncovered. In these cases, we call `OspfSysCalls::halt()`, which prints an error message and causes the program to exit with a given error code, dumping core for possible failure analysis. Further explanation of the halt codes follows.

Code: 1
Message: `Corrupted LS database`
Explanation: The LS Checksums of all of the LSAs in the link-state database are periodically verified. If the checksum of an LSA does not validate, the LSA has somehow been corrupted in program memory.

Code: 2
Message: `Bad LS type`
Explanation: An attempt is being made to add an unknown type of LSA to the link-state database. This should have been caught earlier, by `OSPF::FindLSdb()`.

Code: 3
Message: `Remove operational interface`
Explanation: An attempt has been made to remove an interface from an area, and the interface is still operational. Interfaces should always be brought into Down state before being removed.

Code: 5
Message: `Bad authtype on transmit`
Explanation: An attempt is being made to use an unknown authentication type to generate authentication data for an outgoing OSPF packet. This should have been caught by `OSPF::cfgIfc()`.

Exercises

1. Implement the unimplemented message `OSPF.210: Rxmt LsReq` in the OSPF code. Besides printing the neighbor that you are retransmitting to, also print the first LSA that you are requesting, as this helps in debugging problems.

2. Implement the message `OSPF.216: Seqno wrap` at the appropriate place in the OSPF implementation.

3. Modify `OSPF::cfgIfc()` so that unsupported authentication types are automatically changed to use Null authentication.

Appendix C

Projects

This appendix lists development tasks for extending the OSPF software that has been included with this book. These tasks are more ambitious than the exercises appearing at the end of each chapter. Each project is briefly described herein.

The OSPF code in this book is covered by the GNU General Public License, which has been reproduced in Appendix D. According to the terms of this license, any derivative works must also be made available under the same license. Readers wishing to contribute the results of their project implementations, or any other enhancement of their own devising, to the general `ospfd` distribution should send e-mail to `ospfd-contributions@ospf.org`.

Project name: Link liveness

Project description: Figure out a way to detect that the operational status of a Linux IP interface has changed. At that point, call `OSPF::phy_up()` or `OSPF::phy_down()` so that OSPF will take the correct actions.

Project name: Packet monitor for simulator

Project description: Add a network analyzer option to the `Add` and `Delete` pull-down menus. The user clicks on the network or point-to-point link they want to monitor. The user should also be prompted for the file name. Multiple networks/links can use the same file, in which case their packets will be intertwined. In the file, packets are displayed in ASCII, with the time and network where they were received from prepended.

Project name: OSPF MIB

Project description: The OSPF implementation in this book provides access to all the information in the OSPF MIB [5] but through a proprietary mechanism described in Section 13.13. The goal of this project is to provide a get/get-next interface that allows data to be requested in MIB syntax and that can be connected to an SNMP agent, perhaps using a protocol like AgentX.

Project name: Multiple interfaces to a single IP subnet

Project description: Implement the algorithm in Appendix F of RFC 2328 [75], allowing multiple OSPF interfaces to attach to the same IP subnet.

Project name: OSPF for IPv6

Project description: When OSPF was modified to function as an IPv6 routing protocol [14], the basic protocol mechanisms were preserved, but the formats of LSAs were changed significantly. This requires rewriting a number of the source files in the book's OSPFv2 implementation.

Project name: Opaque-LSAs

Project description: Opaque-LSAs [12] are the standard way of extending the OSPF protocol, enabling the addition of new information to the OSPF link-state database. For example, Opaque-LSAs have been proposed to add shortcut, multicast pruning, and traffic engineering information to the OSPF link-state database.

Project name: NSSA areas.

Project description: NSSA areas [13], an enhancement to OSPF stub area support, allow a small number of external routes to be imported into the area, while at the same time relying mostly on default routing in order to keep the size of the area's link-state database to a minimum. For more information, see Section 7.4 of [67].

Appendix D

GNU General Public License

GNU GENERAL PUBLIC LICENSE, Version 2, June 1991

Copyright (C) 1989, 1991 Free Software Foundation, Inc. 675 Mass Ave, Cambridge, MA 02139, USA. Everyone is permitted to copy and distribute verbatim copies of this license document, but changing it is not allowed.

Preamble

The licenses for most software are designed to take away your freedom to share and change it. By contrast, the GNU General Public License is intended to guarantee your freedom to share and change free software--to make sure the software is free for all its users. This General Public License applies to most of the Free Software Foundation's software and to any other program whose authors commit to using it. (Some other Free Software Foundation software is covered by the GNU Library General Public License instead.) You can apply it to your programs, too.

When we speak of free software, we are referring to freedom, not price. Our General Public Licenses are designed to make sure that you have the freedom to distribute copies of free software (and charge for this service if you wish), that you receive source code or can get it if you want it, that you can change the software or use pieces of it in new free programs; and that you know you can do these things.

To protect your rights, we need to make restrictions that forbid anyone to deny you these rights or to ask you to surrender the rights. These restrictions translate to certain responsibilities for you if you distribute copies of the software, or if you modify it.

For example, if you distribute copies of such a program, whether gratis or for a fee, you must give the recipients all the rights that you have. You must make sure that they, too, receive or can get the source code. And you must show them these terms so they know their rights.

We protect your rights with two steps: (1) copyright the software, and (2) offer you this license which gives you legal permission to copy, distribute and/or modify the software.

Also, for each author's protection and ours, we want to make certain that everyone understands that there is no warranty for this free software. If the software is modified by someone else and passed on, we want its recipients to know that what they have is not the original, so that any problems introduced by others will not reflect on the original authors' reputations.

Finally, any free program is threatened constantly by software patents. We wish to avoid the danger that redistributors of a free program will individually obtain patent licenses, in effect making the program proprietary. To prevent this, we have made it clear that any patent must be licensed for everyone's free use or not licensed at all.

The precise terms and conditions for copying, distribution and modification follow.

GNU GENERAL PUBLIC LICENSE TERMS AND CONDITIONS FOR COPYING, DISTRIBUTION AND MODIFICATION

0. This License applies to any program or other work which contains a notice placed by the copyright holder saying it may be distributed under the terms of this General Public License. The "Program", below, refers to any such program or work, and a "work based on the Program" means either the Program or any derivative work under copyright law: that is to say, a work containing the Program or a portion of it, either verbatim or with modifications and/or translated into another language. (Hereinafter, translation is included without limitation in the term "modification".) Each licensee is addressed as "you".

Activities other than copying, distribution and modification are not covered by this License; they are outside its scope. The act of running the Program is not restricted, and the output from the Program is covered only if its contents constitute a work based on the Program (independent of having been made by running the Program). Whether that is true depends on what the Program does.

1. You may copy and distribute verbatim copies of the Program's source code as you receive it, in any medium, provided that you conspicuously and appropriately publish on each copy an appropriate copyright notice and disclaimer of warranty; keep intact all the notices that refer to this License and to the absence of any warranty; and give any other recipients of the Program a copy of this License along with the Program.

You may charge a fee for the physical act of transferring a copy, and you may at your option offer warranty protection in exchange for a fee.

2. You may modify your copy or copies of the Program or any portion of it, thus forming a work based on the Program, and copy and distribute such modifications or work under the terms of Section 1 above, provided that you also meet all of these conditions:

a) You must cause the modified files to carry prominent notices stating that you changed the files and the date of any change.

b) You must cause any work that you distribute or publish, that in whole or in part contains or is derived from the Program or any part thereof, to be licensed as a whole at no charge to all third parties under the terms of this License.

c) If the modified program normally reads commands interactively when run, you must cause it, when started running for such interactive use in the most ordinary way, to print or display an announcement including an appropriate copyright notice and a notice that there is no warranty (or else, saying that you provide a warranty) and that users may redistribute the program under these conditions, and telling the user how to view a copy of this License. (Exception: if the Program itself is interactive but does not normally print such an announcement, your work based on the Program is not required to print an announcement.)

These requirements apply to the modified work as a whole. If identifiable sections of that work are not derived from the Program, and can be reasonably considered independent and separate works in themselves, then this License, and its terms, do not apply to those sections when you distribute them as separate works. But when you distribute the same sections as part of a whole which is a work based on the Program, the distribution of the whole must be on the terms of this License, whose permissions for other licensees extend to the entire whole, and thus to each and every part regardless of who wrote it.

Thus, it is not the intent of this section to claim rights or contest your rights to work written entirely by you; rather, the intent is to exercise the right to control the distribution of derivative or collective works based on the Program.

In addition, mere aggregation of another work not based on the Program with the Program (or with a work based on the Program) on a volume of a storage or distribution medium does not bring the other work under the scope of this License.

3. You may copy and distribute the Program (or a work based on it, under Section 2) in object code or executable form under the terms of Sections 1 and 2 above provided that you also do one of the following:

a) Accompany it with the complete corresponding machine-readable source code, which must be distributed under the terms of Sections 1 and 2 above on a medium customarily used for software interchange; or,

b) Accompany it with a written offer, valid for at least three years, to give any third party, for a charge no more than your cost of physically performing source distribution, a complete machine-readable copy of the corresponding source code, to be distributed under the terms of Sections 1 and 2 above on a medium customarily used for software interchange; or,

c) Accompany it with the information you received as to the offer to distribute corresponding source code. (This alternative is allowed only for noncommercial distribution and only if you received the program in object code or executable form with such an offer, in accord with Subsection b above.)

The source code for a work means the preferred form of the work for making modifications to it. For an executable work, complete source code means all the source code for all modules it contains, plus any associated interface definition files, plus the scripts used to control compilation and installation of the executable. However, as a special exception, the source code distributed need not include anything that is normally distributed (in either source or binary form) with the major components (compiler, kernel, and so on) of the operating system on which the executable runs, unless that component itself accompanies the executable.

If distribution of executable or object code is made by offering access to copy from a designated place, then offering equivalent access to copy the source code from the same place counts as distribution of the source code, even though third parties are not compelled to copy the source along with the object code.

4. You may not copy, modify, sublicense, or distribute the Program except as expressly provided under this License. Any attempt otherwise to copy, modify, sublicense or distribute the Program is void, and will automatically terminate your rights under this License. However, parties who have received copies, or rights, from you under this License will not have their licenses terminated so long as such parties remain in full compliance.

5. You are not required to accept this License, since you have not signed it. However, nothing else grants you permission to modify or distribute the Program or its derivative works. These actions are prohibited by law if you do not accept this License. Therefore, by modifying or distributing the Program (or any work based on the Program), you indicate your acceptance of this License to do so, and all its terms and conditions for copying, distributing or modifying the Program or works based on it.

6. Each time you redistribute the Program (or any work based on the Program), the recipient automatically receives a license from the original licensor to copy, distribute or modify the Program subject to these terms and conditions. You may not impose any further restrictions on the recipients' exercise of the rights granted herein. You are not responsible for enforcing compliance by third parties to this License.

7. If, as a consequence of a court judgment or allegation of patent infringement or for any other reason (not limited to patent issues), conditions are imposed on you (whether by court order, agreement or otherwise) that contradict the conditions of this License, they do not excuse you from the conditions of this License. If you cannot distribute so as to satisfy simultaneously your obligations under this License and any other pertinent obligations, then as a consequence you may not distribute the Program at all. For example, if a patent license would not permit royalty-free redistribution of the Program by all those who receive copies directly or indirectly through you, then the only way you could satisfy both it and this License would be to refrain entirely from distribution of the Program.

If any portion of this section is held invalid or unenforceable under any particular circumstance, the balance of the section is intended to apply and the section as a whole is intended to apply in other circumstances.

It is not the purpose of this section to induce you to infringe any patents or other property right claims or to contest validity of any such claims; this section has the sole purpose of protecting the integrity of the free software distribution system, which is implemented by public license practices. Many people have made generous contributions to the wide range of software distributed through that system in reliance on consistent application of that system; it is up to the author/donor to decide if he or she is willing to distribute software through any other system and a licensee cannot impose that choice.

This section is intended to make thoroughly clear what is believed to be a consequence of the rest of this License.

8. If the distribution and/or use of the Program is restricted in certain countries either by patents or by copyrighted interfaces, the original copyright holder who places the Program under this License may add an explicit geographical distribution limitation excluding those countries, so that distribution is permitted only in or among countries not thus excluded. In such case, this License incorporates the limitation as if written in the body of this License.

9. The Free Software Foundation may publish revised and/or new versions of the General Public License from time to time. Such new versions will be similar in spirit to the present version, but may differ in detail to address new problems or concerns.

Each version is given a distinguishing version number. If the Program specifies a version number of this License which applies to it and "any later version", you have the option of following the terms and conditions either of that version or of any later version published by the Free Software Foundation. If the Program does not specify a version number of this License, you may choose any version ever published by the Free Software Foundation.

10. If you wish to incorporate parts of the Program into other free programs whose distribution conditions are different, write to the author to ask for permission. For software which is copyrighted by the Free Software Foundation, write to the Free Software Foundation; we sometimes make exceptions for this. Our decision will be guided by the two goals of preserving the free status of all derivatives of our free software and of promoting the sharing and reuse of software generally.

NO WARRANTY

11. BECAUSE THE PROGRAM IS LICENSED FREE OF CHARGE, THERE IS NO WARRANTY FOR THE PROGRAM, TO THE EXTENT PERMITTED BY APPLICABLE LAW. EXCEPT WHEN OTHERWISE STATED IN WRITING THE COPYRIGHT HOLDERS AND/OR OTHER PARTIES PROVIDE THE PROGRAM "AS IS" WITHOUT WARRANTY OF ANY KIND, EITHER EXPRESSED OR IMPLIED, INCLUDING, BUT NOT LIMITED TO, THE IMPLIED WARRANTIES OF MERCHANTABILITY AND FITNESS FOR A PARTICULAR PURPOSE. THE ENTIRE RISK AS TO THE QUALITY AND PERFORMANCE OF THE PROGRAM IS WITH YOU. SHOULD THE PROGRAM PROVE DEFECTIVE, YOU ASSUME THE COST OF ALL NECESSARY SERVICING, REPAIR OR CORRECTION.

12. IN NO EVENT UNLESS REQUIRED BY APPLICABLE LAW OR AGREED TO IN WRITING WILL ANY COPYRIGHT HOLDER, OR ANY OTHER PARTY WHO MAY MODIFY AND/OR REDISTRIBUTE THE PROGRAM AS PERMITTED ABOVE, BE LIABLE TO YOU FOR DAMAGES, INCLUDING ANY GENERAL, SPECIAL, INCIDENTAL OR CONSEQUENTIAL DAMAGES ARISING OUT OF THE USE OR INABILITY TO USE

THE PROGRAM (INCLUDING BUT NOT LIMITED TO LOSS OF DATA OR DATA BEING RENDERED INACCURATE OR LOSSES SUSTAINED BY YOU OR THIRD PARTIES OR A FAILURE OF THE PROGRAM TO OPERATE WITH ANY OTHER PROGRAMS), EVEN IF SUCH HOLDER OR OTHER PARTY HAS BEEN ADVISED OF THE POSSIBILITY OF SUCH DAMAGES.

END OF TERMS AND CONDITIONS

How to Apply These Terms to Your New Programs

If you develop a new program, and you want it to be of the greatest possible use to the public, the best way to achieve this is to make it free software which everyone can redistribute and change under these terms.

To do so, attach the following notices to the program. It is safest to attach them to the start of each source file to most effectively convey the exclusion of warranty; and each file should have at least the "copyright" line and a pointer to where the full notice is found.

<one line to give the program's name and a brief idea of what it does.> Copyright (C) 19yy <name of author>

This program is free software; you can redistribute it and/or modify it under the terms of the GNU General Public License as published by the Free Software Foundation; either version 2 of the License, or (at your option) any later version.

This program is distributed in the hope that it will be useful, but WITHOUT ANY WARRANTY; without even the implied warranty of MERCHANTABILITY or FITNESS FOR A PARTICULAR PURPOSE. See the GNU General Public License for more details.

You should have received a copy of the GNU General Public License along with this program; if not, write to the Free Software Foundation, Inc., 675 Mass Ave, Cambridge, MA 02139, USA.

Also add information on how to contact you by electronic and paper mail.

If the program is interactive, make it output a short notice like this when it starts in an interactive mode:

Gnomovision version 69, Copyright (C) 19yy name of author Gnomovision comes with ABSOLUTELY NO WARRANTY; for details type 'show w'. This is free software, and you are welcome to redistribute it under certain conditions; type 'show c' for details.

The hypothetical commands 'show w' and 'show c' should show the appropriate parts of the General Public License. Of course, the commands you use may be called something other than 'show w' and 'show c'; they could even be mouse-clicks or menu items--whatever suits your program.

You should also get your employer (if you work as a programmer) or your school, if any, to sign a "copyright disclaimer" for the program, if necessary. Here is a sample; alter the names:

Yoyodyne, Inc., hereby disclaims all copyright interest in the program 'Gnomovision' (which makes passes at compilers) written by James Hacker.

<signature of Ty Coon>, 1 April 1989 Ty Coon, President of Vice

This General Public License does not permit incorporating your program into proprietary programs. If your program is a subroutine library, you may consider it more useful to permit linking proprietary applications with the library. If this is what you want to do, use the GNU Library General Public License instead of this License.

Bibliography

1. Alaettinoglu, C., T. Bates, E. Gerich, D. Karrenberg, D. Meyer, M. Terpstra, and C. Villamizer. *Routing Policy Specification Language (RPSL)*, April 1997.

2. Almquist, P. *Type of Service in the Internet Protocol Suite*. RFC 1349, July 1992.

3. Apostolopoulos, G., D. Williams, S. Kamat, R. Guerin, A. Orda, and T. Przygienda. *QoS Routing Mechanisms and OSPF Extensions*. RFC 2676, August 1999.

4. Baker, F. *IP Forwarding Table MIB*. RFC 2096, January 1997.

5. Baker, F., and R. Coltun. *OSPF Version 2 Management Information Base*. RFC 1850, November 1995.

6. Bradley, T., and C. Brown. *Inverse Address Resolution Protocol*. RFC 1293, January 1992.

7. Brodnik, A., S. Carlsson, M. Degermark, and S. Pink. *Small Forwarding Tables for Fast Routing Lookups*. ACM SIGCOMM '97, September 1997.

8. Casner, S. *Frequently Asked Questions (FAQ) on the Multicast Backbone (MBONE)*. `<ftp://ftp.isi.edu/mbone/faq.txt>`, 1993.

9. Casner, S. `mtrace` *UNIX manual page*. mtrace(8).

10. Cisco Systems. *Cisco IOS Software Configuration*. `<http://cio.cisco.com/univercd/data/doc/software.htm>`.

11. Cisco Systems. *Introduction to Enhanced IGRP*. Cisco Technical Report #3.

12. Coltun, R. *The OSPF Opaque LSA Option.* RFC 2370, July 1998.

13. Coltun, R., and V. Fuller. *The OSPF NSSA Option.* RFC 1587, March 1994.

14. Coltun, R., D. Ferguson, and J. Moy. *OSPF for IPv6.* RFC 2740, December 1999.

15. Comer, D. *Internetworking with TCP/IP, Vol. 1: Principles, Protocols, and Architecture.* Prentice-Hall, 1995.

16. *Common Gateway Interface.* `http://hoohoo.ncsa.uiuc.edu/cgi`.

17. Conta, A., and S. Deering. *Internet Control Message Protocol (ICMPv6) for the Internet Protocol Version 6 (IPv6).* RFC 1885, December 1995.

18. Cornell GateDaemon project. `ospf_monitor` *UNIX manual page.* ospf_monitor(8).

19. Deering, S. *Host Extensions for IP Multicasting.* RFC 1112, May 1988.

20. Deering, S. *ICMP Router Discovery Messages.* RFC 1256, September 1991.

21. Deering, S. *Multicast Routing in a Datagram Internetwork.* Stanford Technical Report STAN-CS-92-1415. Department of Computer Science, Stanford University. `<ftp://gregorio.stanford.edu/vmtp/sd-thesis.ps>`, December 1991.

22. Deering, S. "Multicast Routing in Internetworks and Extended LANs." ACM SIGCOMM Summer 1988 Proceedings, August 1988.

23. Deering, S., and R. Hinden. *Internet Protocol, Version 6 (IPv6) Specification.* RFC 1883, December 1995.

24. Deering, S., A. Thyagarajan, and W. Fenner. `mrouted` *UNIX manual page.* mrouted(8).

25. deSouza, O., and M. Rodrigues. *Guidelines for Running OSPF over Frame Relay Networks.* RFC 1586, March 1994.

26. Eriksson, H. "MBONE: The Multicast Backbone." *Communications of the ACM* 37, no. 8, August 1994.

27. Fenner, W. *Internet Group Management Protocol, Version 2.* October 1996.

28. Fenner, W., and S. Casner. *A "traceroute" Facility for IP Multicast.* Work in progress.

29. Ferguson, D. *The OSPF External Attributes LSA.* Work in progress.

30. Floyd, S., and V. Jacobson. "The Synchronization of Periodic Routing Messages." ACM SIGCOMM '93 Conference Proceedings, September 1993.

31. Fuller, V., T. Li, J. Yu, and K. Varadhan. *Classless Inter-Domain Routing (CIDR): An Address Assignment and Aggregation Strategy.* RFC 1519, September 1993.

32. GATED project Web pages. `<http://www.gated.org>`.

33. Gross, P. *Choosing a Common IGP for the IP Internet (The IESG's Recommendation to the IAB).* RFC 1371, October 1992.

34. Halabi, B. *Internet Routing Architectures.* Cisco Press. New Riders Publishing, 1997.

35. Hinden, R. *Internet Routing Protocol Standardization Criteria.* RFC 1264, October 1991.

36. Hinden, R., and S. Deering. *IP Version 6 Addressing Architecture.* RFC 1884, December 1995.

37. Huitema, C. *IPv6: The New Internet Protocol.* Prentice-Hall, 1997.

38. Huitema, C. *Routing in the Internet.* Prentice-Hall, 1996.

39. Internet Architecture Board. *Applicability Statement for OSPF.* RFC 1370, October 1992.

40. Internet Architecture Board, J. Postel, ed. *Internet Official Protocol Standards.* RFC 2200, June 1997.

41. Jacobson, V. "Congestion Avoidance and Control." *Computer Communication Review* 18, no. 4, August 1988.

42. Kaliski, B., and M. Robshaw. "Message Authentication with MD5." *CryptoBytes* (RSA Labs Technical Newsletter) 1, no. 1. `<http://www.rsa.com/PUBS/crypto1.pdf>`, Spring 1995.

43. Katz, D. *Transmission of IP and ARP over FDDI Networks.* RFC 1390, January 1993.

44. Khanna, A., and J. Zinky. "The Revised ARPANET Routing Metric." Proceedings, *ACM SIGCOMM 1989*, Austin. September 1989.

45. Kleinrock, L., and F. Kamoun. "Hierarchical Routing for Large Networks: Performance Evaluation and Optimization." *Computer Networks* 1. 1977.

46. Knuth, D. *The Art of Computer Programming, Vol. 3, Second Edition, Sorting and Searching.* Addison-Wesley, 1998.

47. Kumar, V. *MBONE: Multicast Multimedia for the Internet.* New Riders Publishing, 1997.

48. Laubach, M. *Classical IP and ARP over ATM.* RFC 1577, January 1994.

49. Lawrence, J., and D. Piscitello. *The Transmission of IP Datagrams over the SMDS Service.* RFC 1209, March 1991.

50. McCanne, S., and V. Jacobson. `sd` *distribution.* `<ftp://ftp.ee.lbl.gov/conferencing/sd>`.

51. McCanne, S., and V. Jacobson. `vat` *distribution.* `<ftp://ftp.ee.lbl.gov/conferencing/vat>`.

52. McCanne, S., and V. Jacobson. `wb` *distribution.* `<ftp://ftp.ee.lbl.gov/conferencing/wb>`.

53. McCoy, W. *Implementation Guide for the ISO Transport Protocol.* RFC 1008, June 1987.

54. McCloghrie, K., and M. Rose. *Management Information Base for Network Management of TCP/IP-Based Internets: MIB-II.* RFC 1213, March 1991.

55. McCloghrie, K., and M. Rose. *Structure and Identification of Management Information for TCP/IP-Based Internets.* RFC 1155, May 1990.

56. McKenzie, A. *ISO Transport Protocol Specification. ISO DP 8073.* RFC 905, April 1984.

57. McQuillan, J., I. Richer, and E. Rosen. *ARPANET Routing Algorithm Improvements.* BBN Report 3803. Bolt Beranek and Newman, April 1978.

58. McQuillan, J., I. Richer, and E. Rosen. "The New Routing Algorithm for the ARPANET." *IEEE Transactions on Communications* COM-28, no. 5, May 1980.

59. Maufer, T., and C. Semeria. *Introduction to IP Multicast Routing.* Work in progress.

60. Meyer, D. *Administratively Scoped IP Multicast.* RFC 2365, July 1998.

61. Mogul, J., and S. Deering. *Path MTU Discovery.* RFC 1191, April 1990.

62. Mogul, J., and J. Postel. *Internet Standard Subnetting Procedure.* RFC 950, August 1985.

63. Moy, J. *Experience with OSPF.* RFC 1246, July 1991.

64. Moy, J. *Extending OSPF to Support Demand Circuits.* RFC 1793, April 1995.

65. Moy, J. *MOSPF: Analysis and Experience.* RFC 1585, March 1994.

66. Moy, J. *Multicast Extensions to OSPF.* RFC 1584, March 1994.

67. Moy, J. *OSPF: Anatomy of an Internet Routing Protocol.* Addison-Wesley, 1998.

68. Moy, J. *OSPF Database Overflow.* RFC 1765, March 1995.

69. Moy, J. *OSPF Protocol Analysis.* RFC 1245, July 1991.

70. Moy, J. *OSPF Specification.* RFC 1131 (obsoleted by RFC 1247), October 1989.

71. Moy, J. *OSPF Standardization Report.* RFC 2329, April 1998.

72. Moy, J. *OSPF Version 2.* RFC 1247 (obsoleted by RFC 1583), August 1991.

73. Moy, J. *OSPF Version 2.* RFC 1583 (obsoleted by RFC 2178), March 1994.

74. Moy, J. *OSPF Version 2.* RFC 2178 (obsoleted by RFC 2328), July 1997.

75. Moy, J. *OSPF Version 2.* RFC 2328, April 1998.

76. Murphy, S., M. Badger, and B. Wellington. *OSPF with Digital Signatures.* RFC 2154, June 1997.

77. Ousterhout, J. *Tcl and the Tk Toolkit.* Addison-Wesley, 1994.

78. Postel, J. *Internet Control Message Protocol.* RFC 792, September 1981.

79. Postel, J. *Internet Protocol.* RFC 791, September 1981.

80. Postel, J. *User Datagram Protocol.* RFC 768, August 1980.

81. Pummill, T., and B. Manning. *Variable Length Subnet Table for IPv4.* RFC 1878, December 1995.

82. Pusateri, T. *Distance Vector Multicast Routing Protocol.* Work in progress.

83. Pusateri, T. *IP Multicast over Token-Ring Local Area Networks.* RFC 1469, June 1993.

84. Pusateri, T. `ospfquery` *UNIX manual page.*
    `<http://www.jnx.com/~pusateri/ospfquery.html>`.

85. RAToolSet. `<http://www.isi.edu/ra/RAToolSet>`.

86. Red Hat Software, *Red Hat Hardware Compatibility Lists.* `<http://www.redhat.com/support/docs/hardware.html>`

87. Reynolds, J., and J. Postel. *Assigned Numbers.* RFC 1700, October 1994.

88. RFC Index. `<ftp://ds.internic.net/rfc/rfc-index.txt>`.

89. Rigney, C., A. Rubens, W. Simpson, and S. Willens. *Remote Authentication Dial-In User Service (RADIUS).* RFC 2138, April 1997.

90. Rijsinghani, A. *Computation of the Internet Checksum via Incremental Update.* RFC 1624, May 1994.

91. Rivest, R. *The MD5 Message-Digest Algorithm.* RFC 1321, April 1992.

92. Rose, M. *The Simple Book, An Introduction to Management of TCP/IP-Based Internets.* Prentice-Hall, 1991.

93. Rosen, E. "The Updating Protocol of ARPANET's New Routing Algorithm." *Computer Networks* 4, 1980.

94. Rosen, E. "Vulnerabilities of Network Control Protocols: An Example." *Computer Communication Review,* July 1981.

95. `routed` *UNIX manual page.* routed(8).

96. Schneier, B. *Applied Cryptography.* Wiley, 1994.

97. Schoffstall, M., M. Fedor, J. Davin, and J. Case. *A Simple Network Management Protocol (SNMP).* RFC 1157, May 1990.

98. Sedgewick, R. *Algorithms in C++.* Addison-Wesley, 1992.

99. Steenstrup, M. *Routing in Communications Networks.* Prentice-Hall, 1995.

100. Stevens, R. *TCP/IP Illustrated, Volume 1: The Protocols.* Addison-Wesley, 1994.

101. Thaler, D. *Interoperability Rules for Multicast Routing Protocols.* RFC 2715, October 1999.

102. Thurletti, T. `ivs` *distribution.* `<ftp://zenon.inria.fr/rodeo/ivs/version3.6>`.

103. `traceroute` UNIX manual page. `<http://ack.berkeley.edu/cgi-bin/traceroute.8>`.

104. Trusted Information Systems. *OSPF with Digital Signatures, Implementation Information.* `<http://www.tis.com/docs/research/network/ospf.html>`.

105. UNH InterOperability Lab. `<http://www.iol.unh.edu>`.

106. Varadhan, K., S. Hares, and Y. Rekhter. *BGP4/IDRP for IP-OSPF Interaction.* RFC 1745, December 1991.

107. Vetter, B., F. Wang, and F. Wu. "An Experimental Study of Insider Attacks for the OSPF Routing Protocol." `<http://shang.csc.ncsu.edu/papers/Wu-AESoIAftORP.ps.gz>`.

108. Waitzman, D., C. Partridge, and S. Deering. *Distance Vector Multicast Routing Protocol.* RFC 1075, November 1988.

109. Waldvogel, M., G. Varghese, J. Turner, and B. Plattner. *"Scalable High Speed IP Routing Lookups."* ACM SIGCOMM '97, September 1997.

110. Wang, F., B. Vetter, and F. Wu. "Secure Routing Protocols: Theory and Practice." `<http://shang.csc.ncsu.edu/papers/CCR-SecureRP2.ps.gz>`.

111. Wright, G., and R. Stevens. *TCP/IP Illustrated, Volume 2: The Implementation.* Addison-Wesley, 1995.

112. Zhang, Z. *Fixing Backbone Partition with Dynamic Virtual Links.* Work in progress.

Index

Register
Your Book

at www.aw.com/cseng/register

You may be eligible to receive:

- Advance notice of forthcoming editions of the book
- Related book recommendations
- Chapter excerpts and supplements of forthcoming titles
- Information about special contests and promotions throughout the year
- Notices and reminders about author appearances, tradeshows, and online chats with special guests

Contact us

If you are interested in writing a book or reviewing manuscripts prior to publication, please write to us at:

Editorial Department
Addison-Wesley Professional
75 Arlington Street, Suite 300
Boston, MA 02116 USA
Email: AWPro@aw.com

Addison-Wesley

Visit us on the Web: http://www.aw.com/cseng